ZATCH BELL!™

1

STORY AND ART BY

MAKOTO RAIKU

ZATCH BELL!

1

CONTENTS

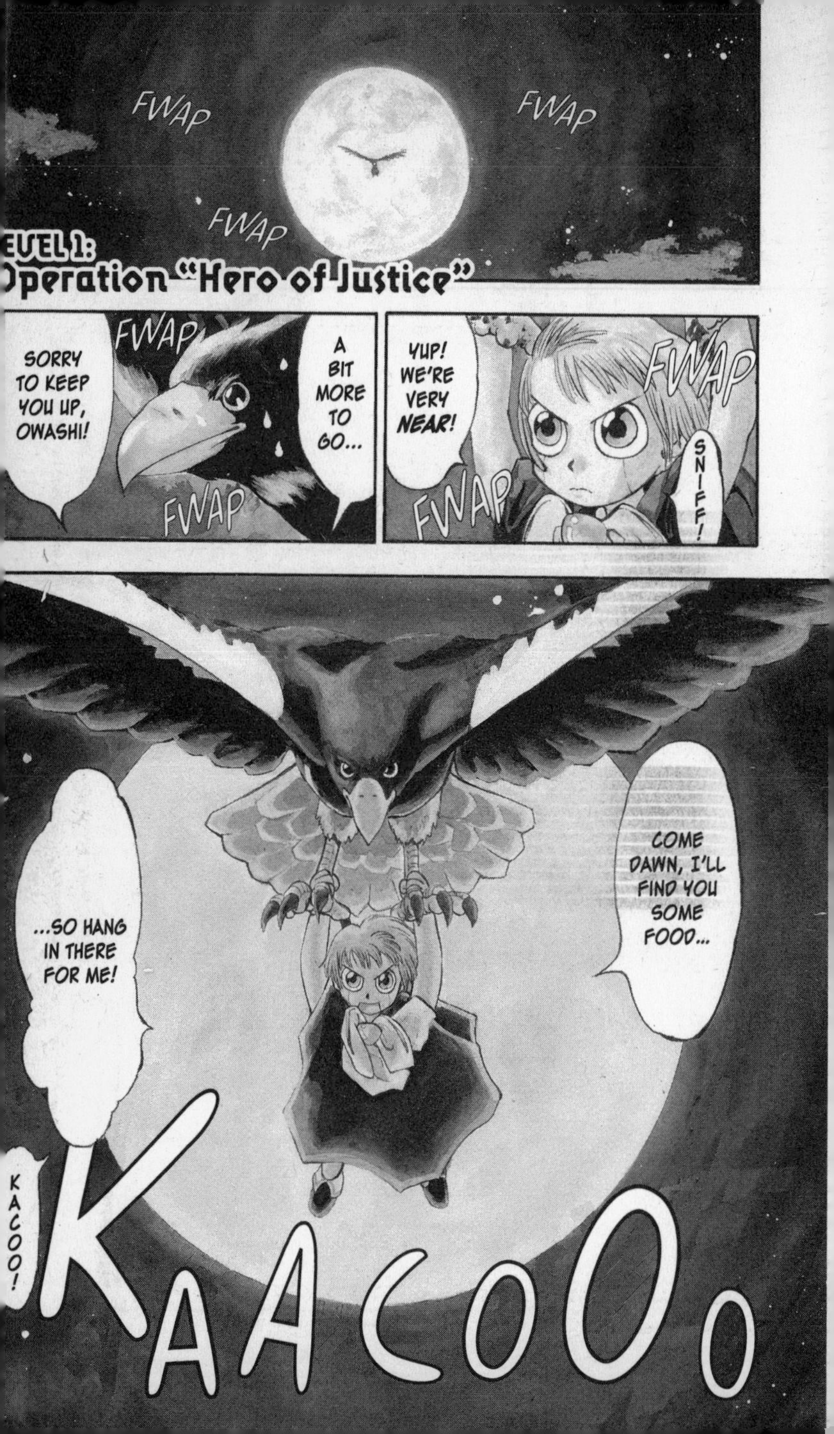
FWAP
FWAP
FWAP
EVEL 1:
peration “Hero of Justice”
FWAP
YUP! WE'RE VERY NEAR!
SNIFF!
FWAP
A BIT MORE TO GO...
FWAP
SORRY TO KEEP YOU UP, OWASHI!
FWAP
COME DAWN, I'LL FIND YOU SOME FOOD...
...SO HANG IN THERE FOR ME!
KACOO!
KAACOOo

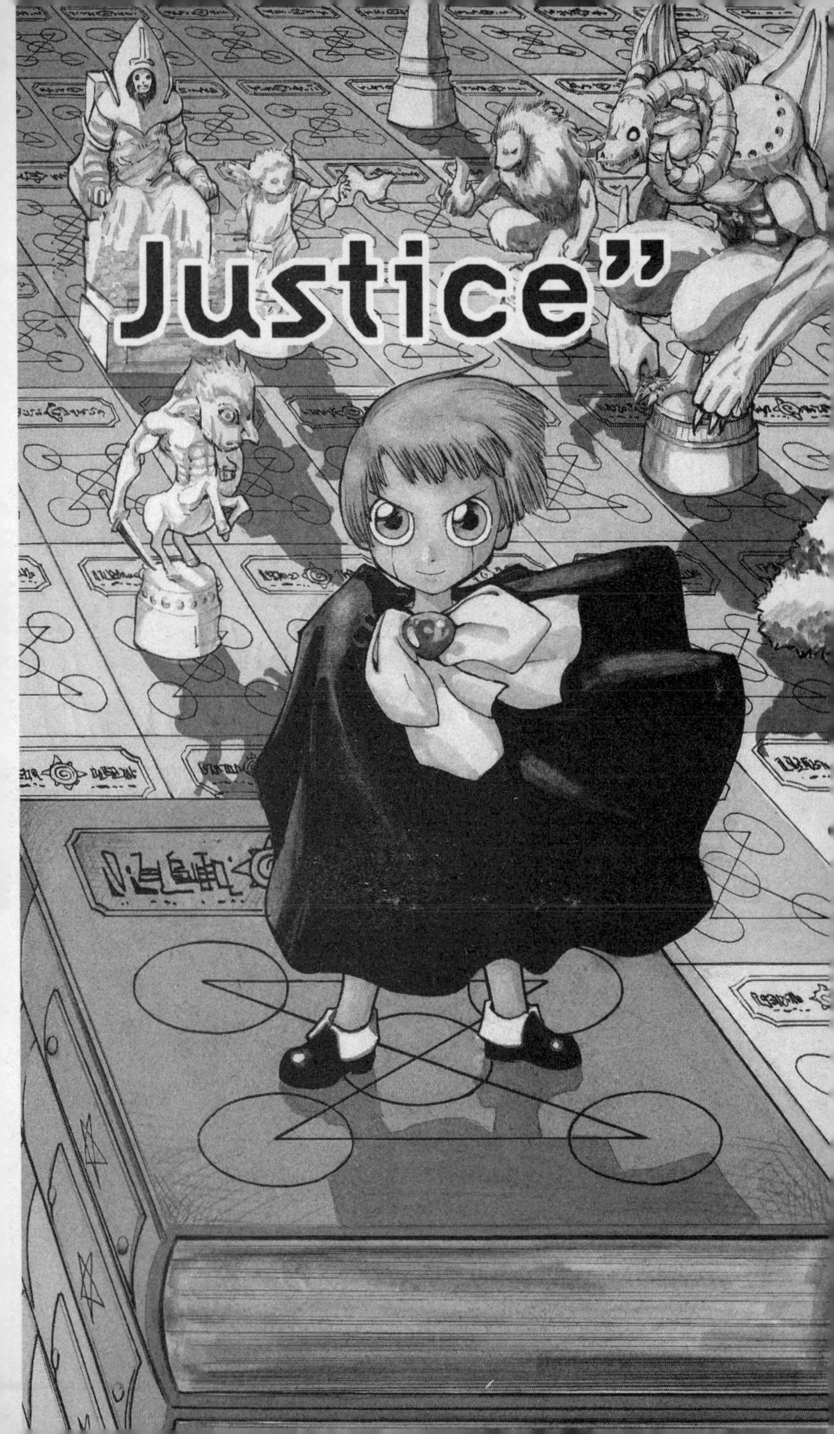
Justice”

ZATCH BELL!™

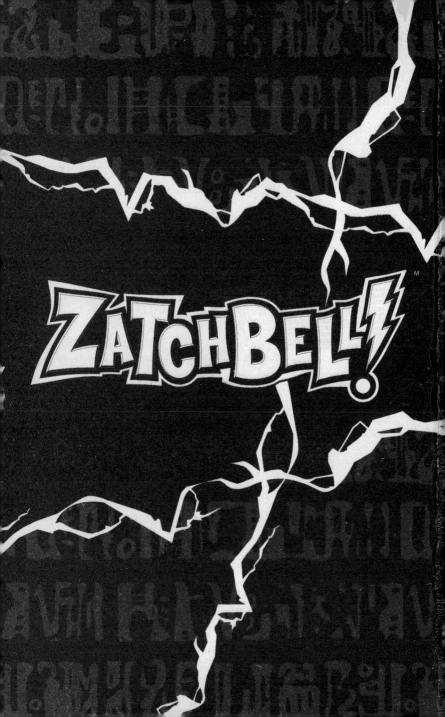

ZATCH BELL!
Vol. 1

STORY AND ART BY
MAKOTO RAIKU

English Adaptation/Fred Burke
Translation/David Ury
Touch-up Art & Lettering/Melanie Lewis
Design/Izumi Hirayama
Special Thanks/Jessica Villat, Miki Macaluso, and Mitsuko Kitajima
Editor/Frances E. Wall

Managing Editor/Annette Roman
Director of Production/Noboru Watanabe
Vice President of Publishing/Alvin Lu
Sr. Director of Acquisitions/Rika Inouye
Vice President of Sales & Marketing/Liza Coppola
Publisher/Hyoe Narita

Printed in the U.S.A.

Published by VIZ Media, LLC
P.O. Box 77010
San Francisco, CA 94107

10 9 8 7 6 5 4 3 2 1
First printing, July 2005

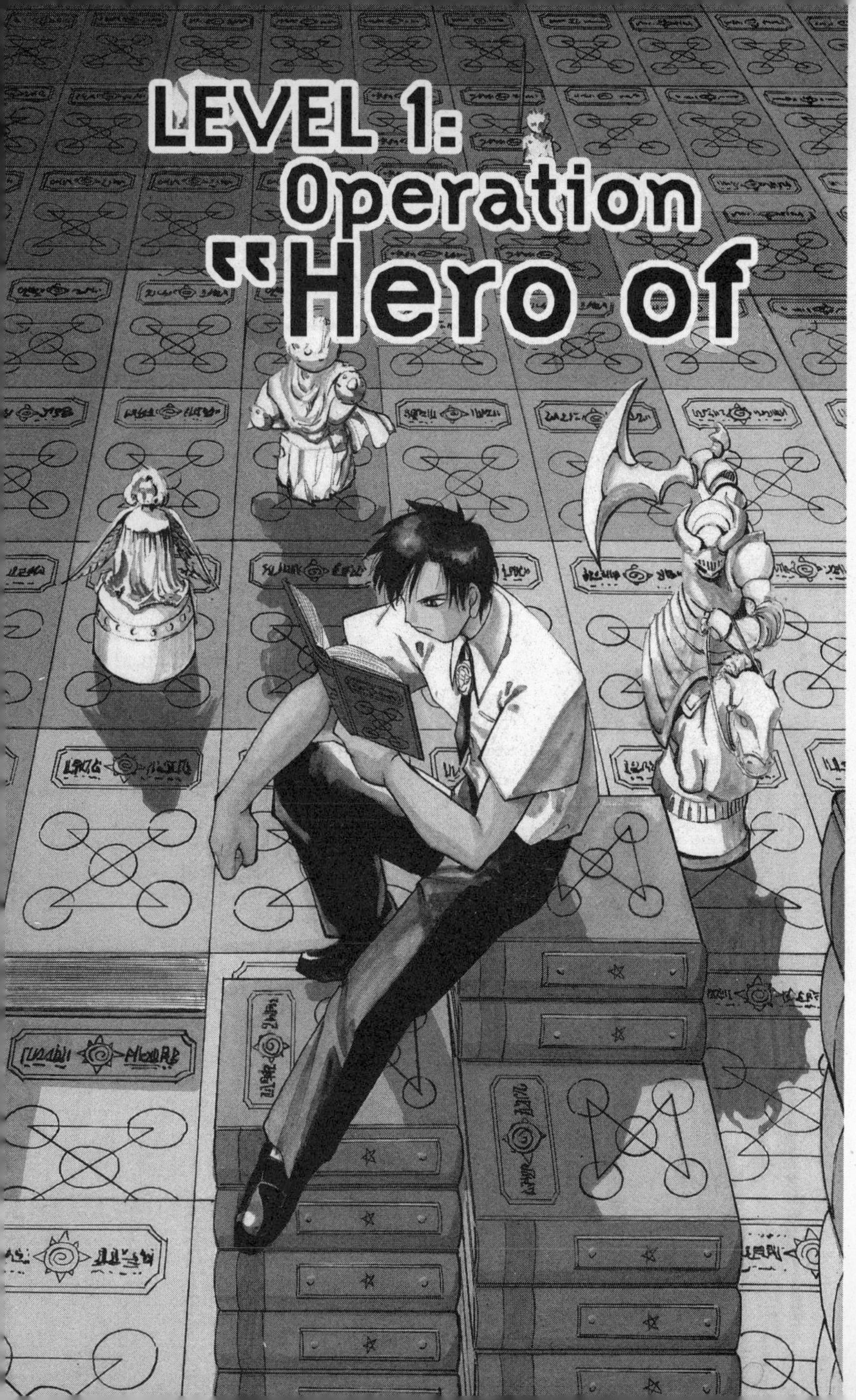
LEVEL 1:
Operation
"Hero of

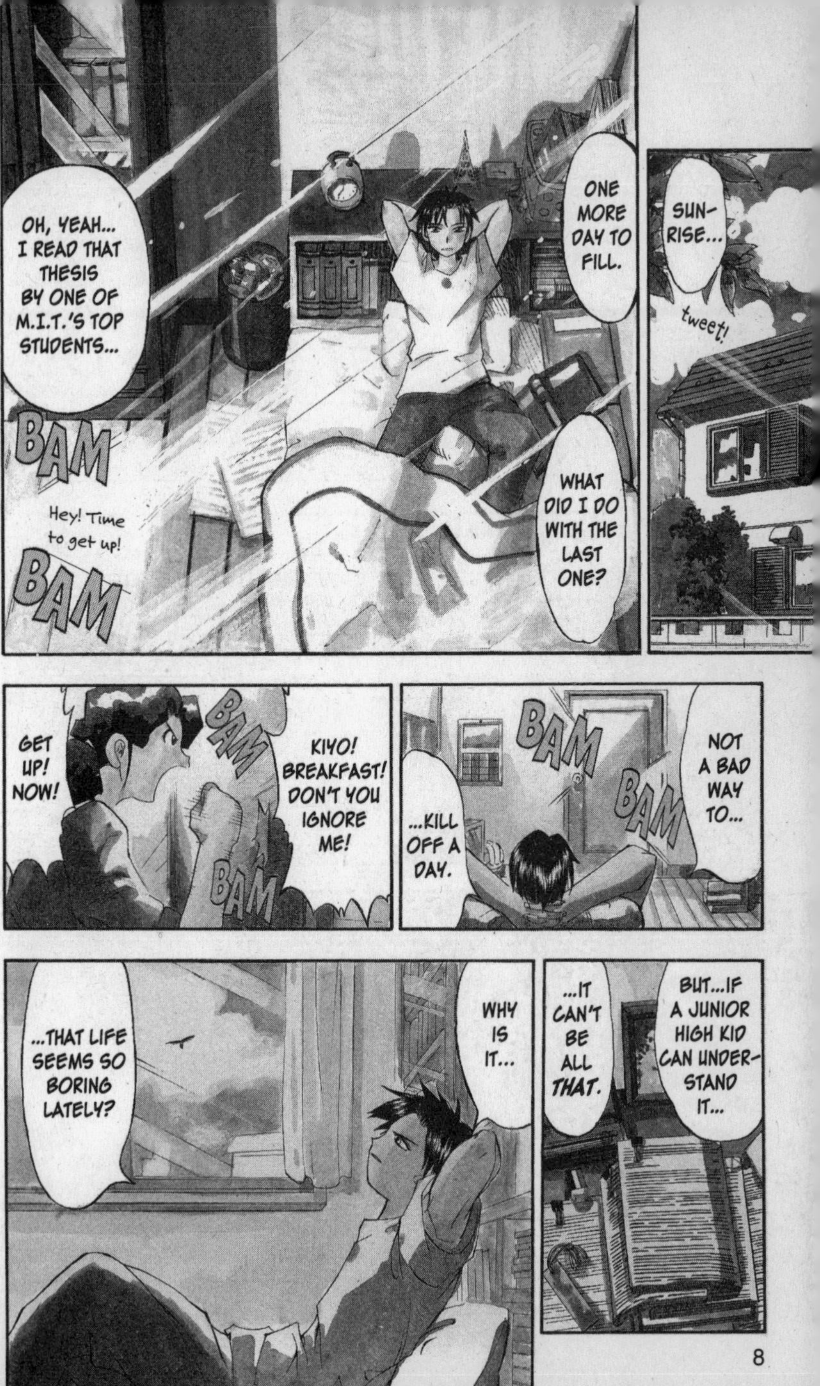
SUN-RISE...
tweet!
ONE MORE DAY TO FILL.
WHAT DID I DO WITH THE LAST ONE?
OH, YEAH... I READ THAT THESIS BY ONE OF M.I.T.'S TOP STUDENTS...
BAM
Hey! Time to get up!
BAM
NOT A BAD WAY TO...
BAM
BAM
...KILL OFF A DAY.
BAM
KIYO! BREAKFAST! DON'T YOU IGNORE ME!
GET UP! NOW!
BAM
BUT...IF A JUNIOR HIGH KID CAN UNDER-STAND IT...
...IT CAN'T BE ALL *THAT*.
WHY IS IT...
...THAT LIFE SEEMS SO BORING LATELY?

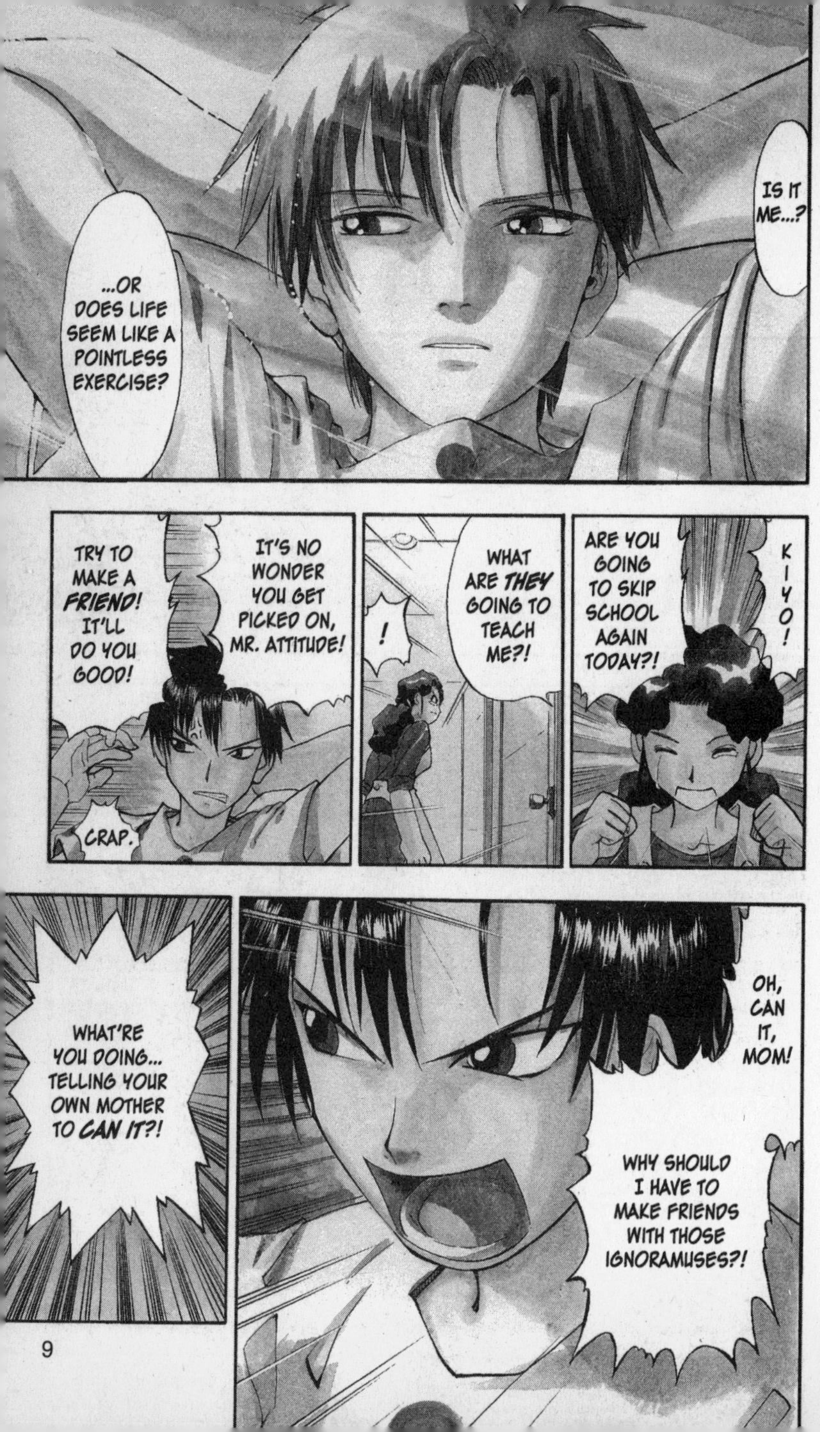
IS IT ME...?
...OR DOES LIFE SEEM LIKE A POINTLESS EXERCISE?
KIYO!
ARE YOU GOING TO SKIP SCHOOL AGAIN TODAY?!
!
WHAT ARE *THEY* GOING TO TEACH ME?!
IT'S NO WONDER YOU GET PICKED ON, MR. ATTITUDE!
TRY TO MAKE A *FRIEND*! IT'LL DO YOU GOOD!
CRAP.
OH, CAN IT, MOM!
WHY SHOULD I HAVE TO MAKE FRIENDS WITH THOSE IGNORAMUSES?!
WHAT'RE YOU DOING... TELLING YOUR OWN MOTHER TO *CAN IT*?!

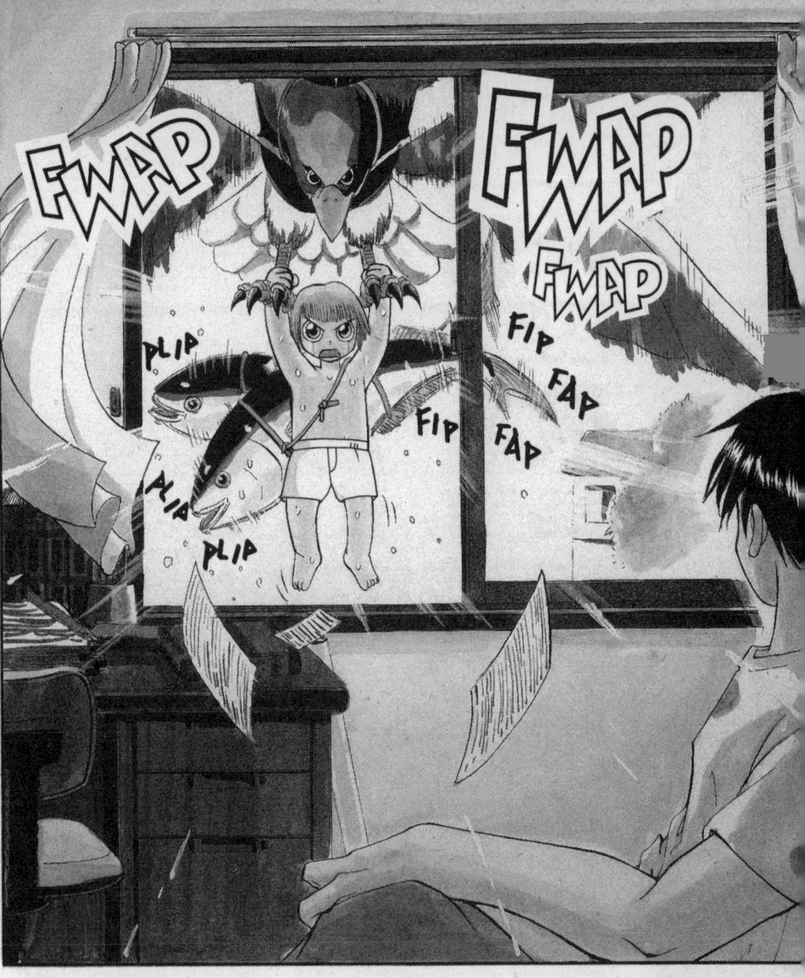
FWAP
FWAP
FIP
FAP
FIP
FAP
FWAP
PLIP
PLIP
PLIP

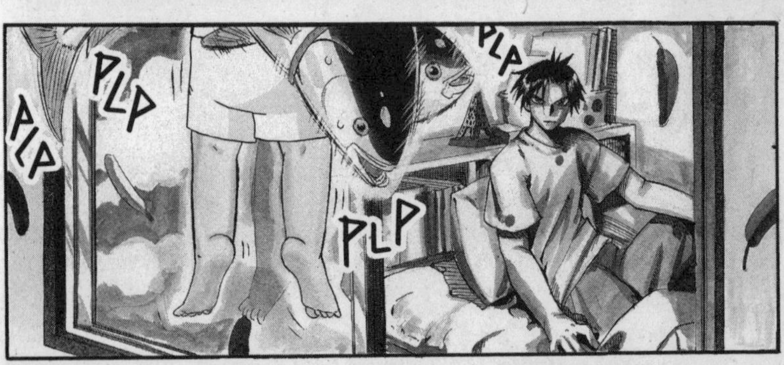
PLP
PLP
PLP
PLP

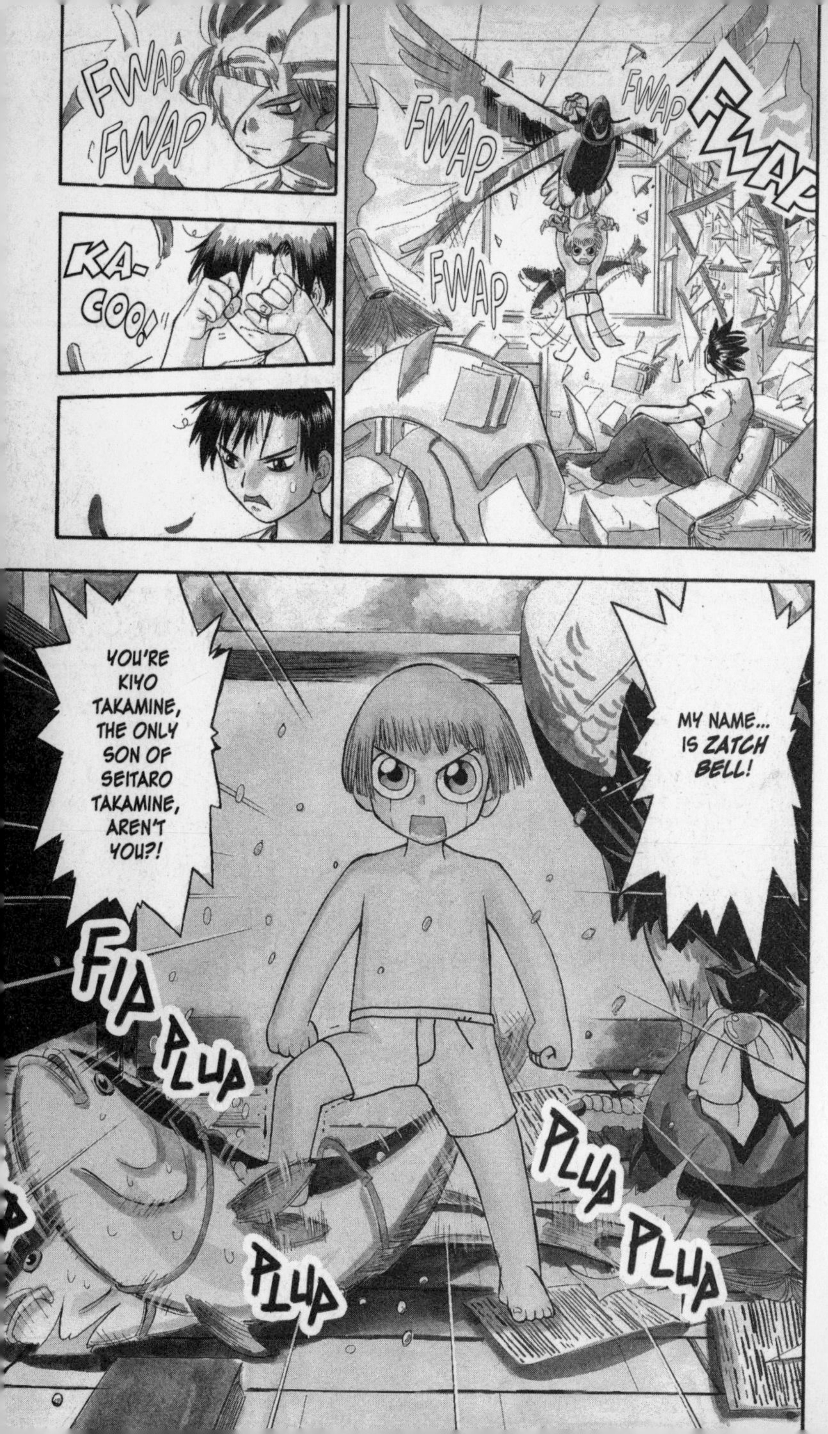

FWAP
FWAP
FWAP
FWAP
FWAP
FWAP
KA-COO!
MY NAME... IS ZATCH BELL!
YOU'RE KIYO TAKAMINE, THE ONLY SON OF SEITARO TAKAMINE, AREN'T YOU?!
PLUP PLUP
FLIP PLUP
PLUP

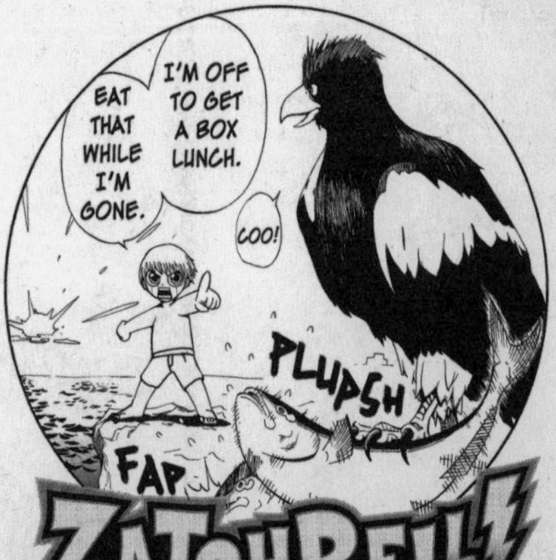
I'M OFF TO GET A BOX LUNCH.
EAT THAT WHILE I'M GONE.
COO!
PLUPSH
FAP

ZATCHBELL!

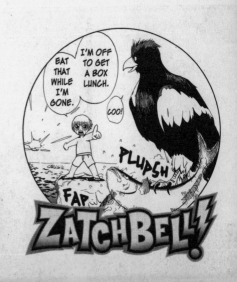

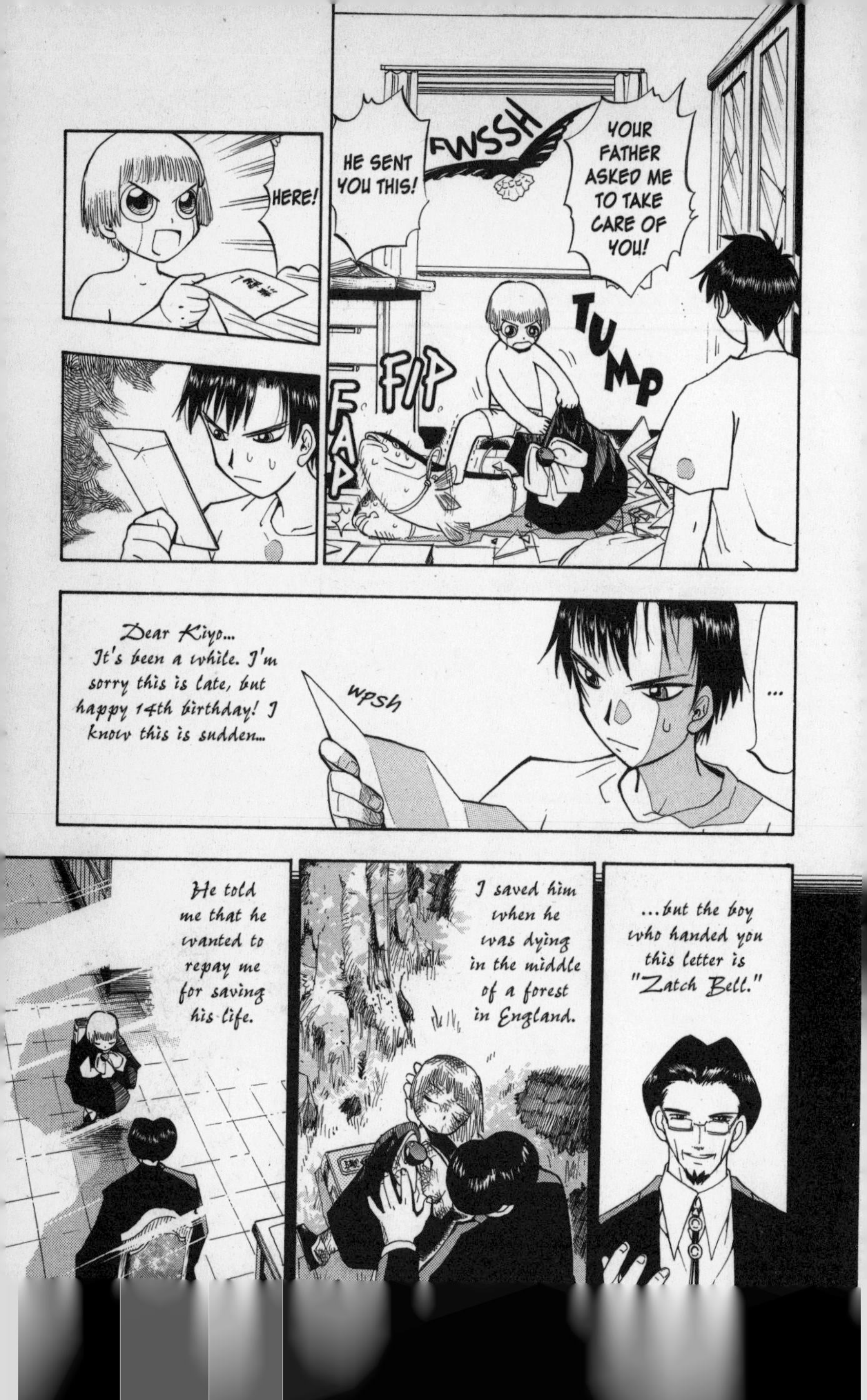
YOUR FATHER ASKED ME TO TAKE CARE OF YOU!
FWSSH
HE SENT YOU THIS!
TUMP
FIP
FAP
HERE!
...
wpsh
Dear Kiyo... It's been a while. I'm sorry this is late, but happy 14th birthday! I know this is sudden...
...but the boy who handed you this letter is "Zatch Bell."
I saved him when he was dying in the middle of a forest in England.
He told me that he wanted to repay me for saving his life.

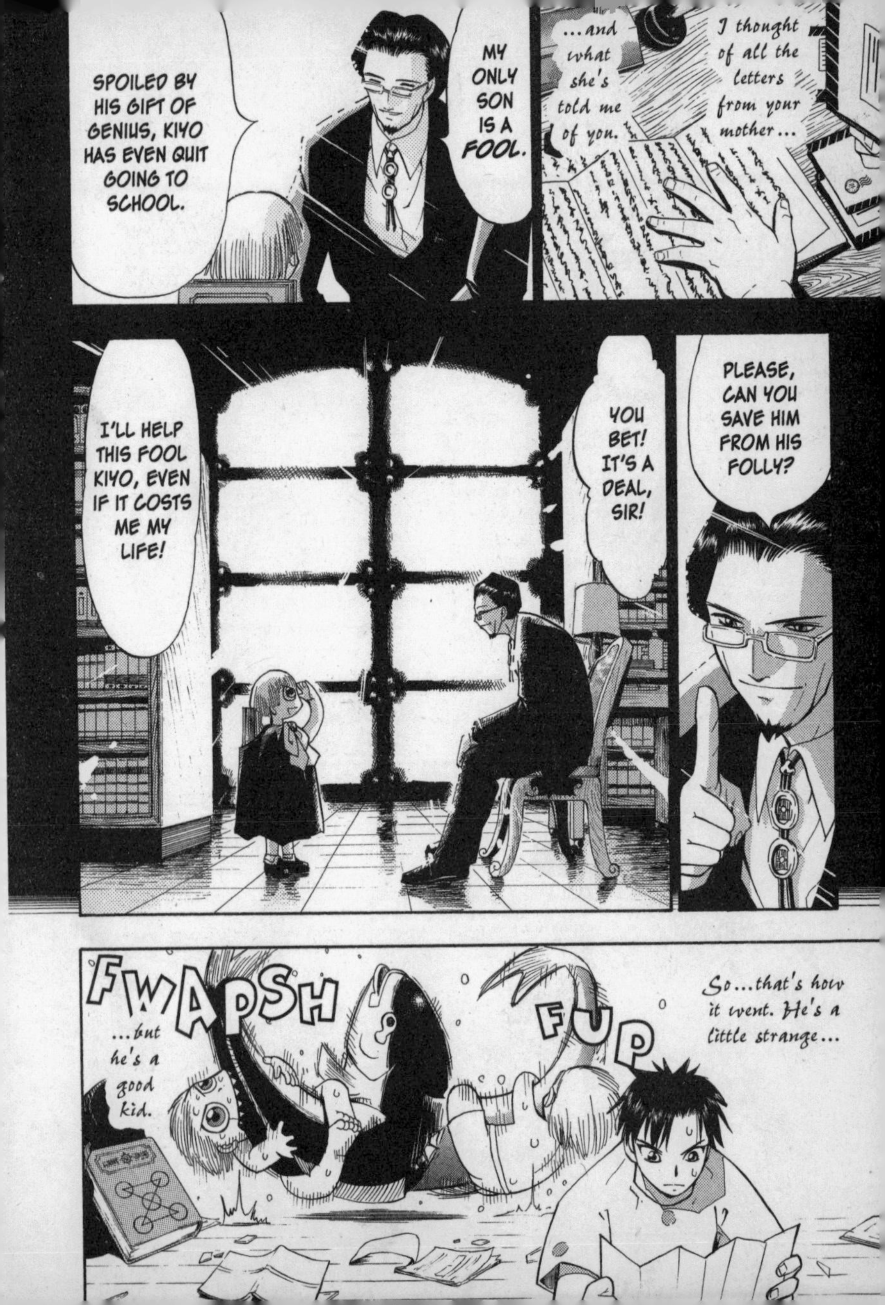
I thought of all the letters from your mother...
...and what she's told me of you.
MY ONLY SON IS A FOOL.
SPOILED BY HIS GIFT OF GENIUS, KIYO HAS EVEN QUIT GOING TO SCHOOL.
PLEASE, CAN YOU SAVE HIM FROM HIS FOLLY?
YOU BET! IT'S A DEAL, SIR!
I'LL HELP THIS FOOL KIYO, EVEN IF IT COSTS ME MY LIFE!
So...that's how it went. He's a little strange...
FUP
FWAPSH
...but he's a good kid.

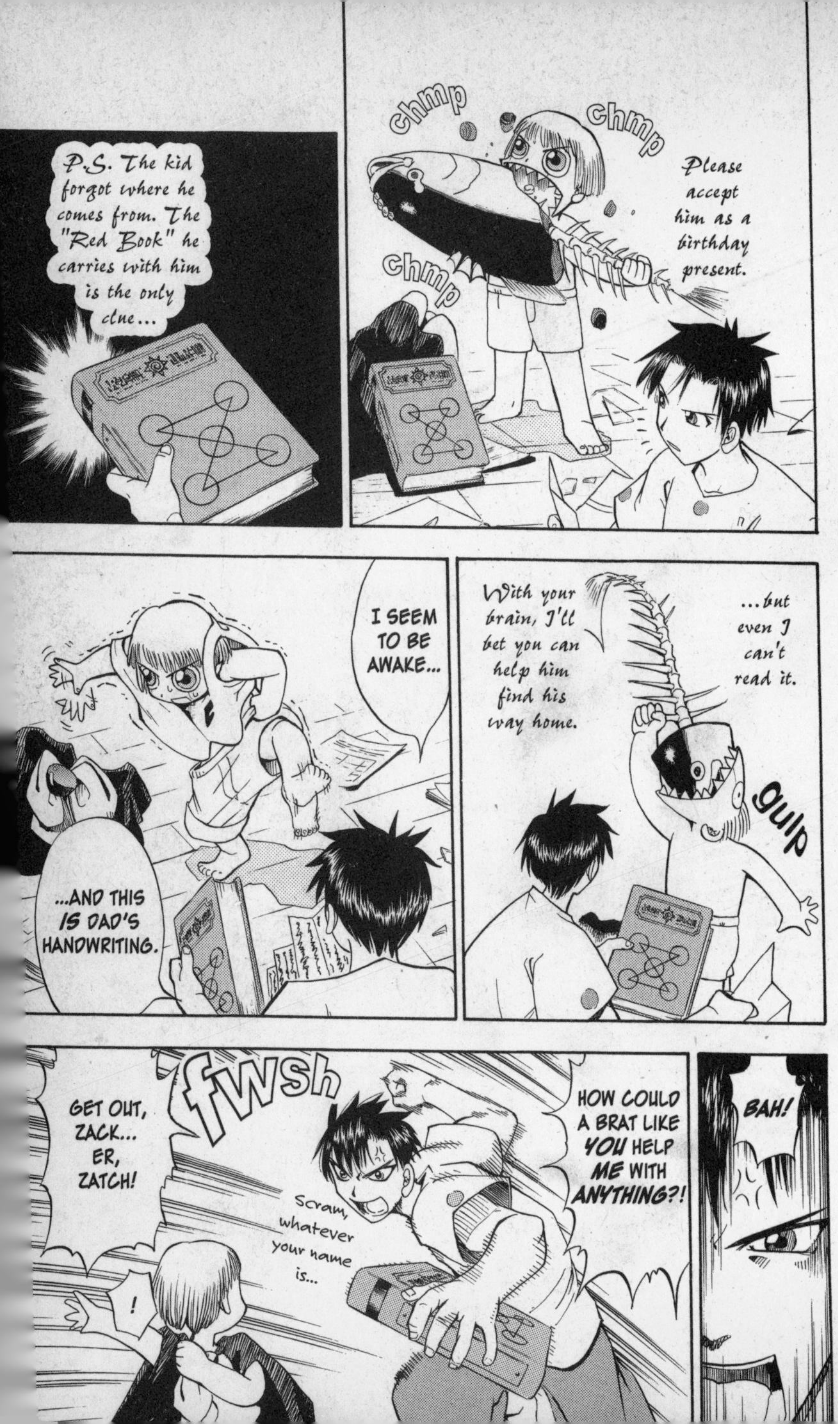
chmp
Please accept him as a birthday present.
chmp
chmp
P.S. The kid forgot where he comes from. The "Red Book" he carries with him is the only clue...
...but even I can't read it.
With your brain, I'll bet you can help him find his way home.
gulp
I SEEM TO BE AWAKE...
...AND THIS IS DAD'S HANDWRITING.
BAH!
HOW COULD A BRAT LIKE YOU HELP ME WITH ANYTHING?!
fwsh
GET OUT, ZACK... ER, ZATCH!
Scram, whatever your name is...
!

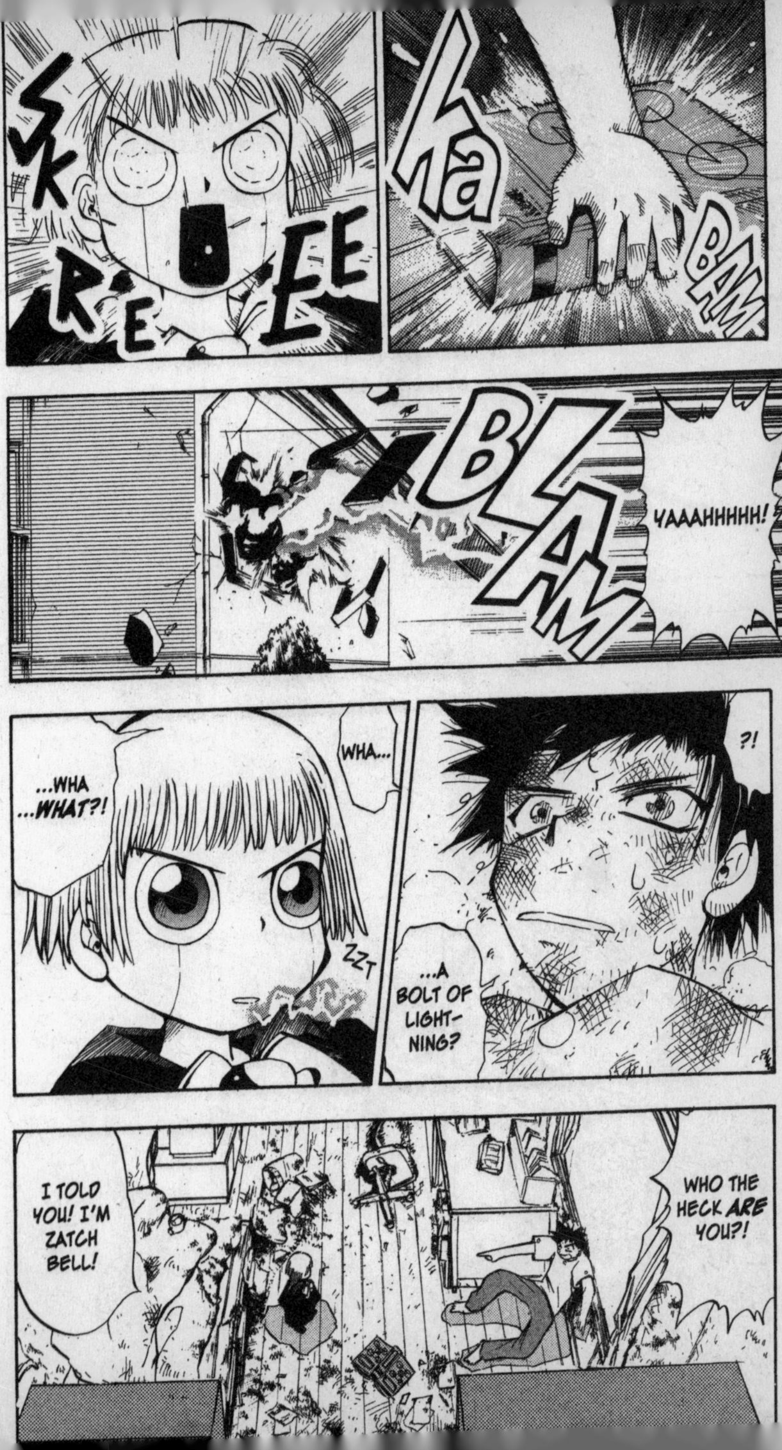
ka
BAM
SKREEEE
YAAAHHHHH!
BLAM
?!
...A BOLT OF LIGHT-NING?
WHA...
...WHA ...WHAT?!
ZZT
WHO THE HECK ARE YOU?!
I TOLD YOU! I'M ZATCH BELL!

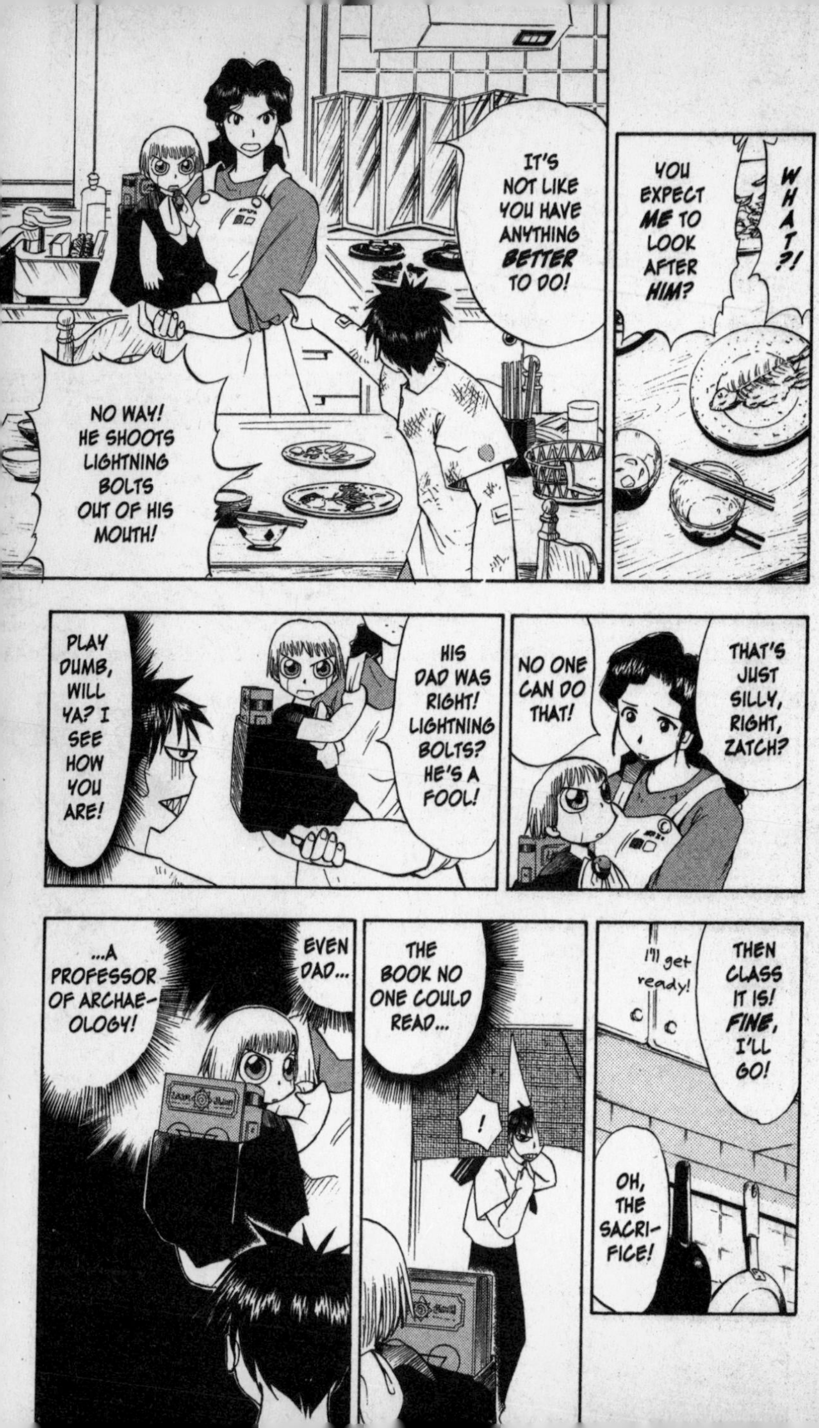
WHAT?!
YOU EXPECT ME TO LOOK AFTER HIM?
IT'S NOT LIKE YOU HAVE ANYTHING BETTER TO DO!
NO WAY! HE SHOOTS LIGHTNING BOLTS OUT OF HIS MOUTH!
THAT'S JUST SILLY, RIGHT, ZATCH?
NO ONE CAN DO THAT!
HIS DAD WAS RIGHT! LIGHTNING BOLTS? HE'S A FOOL!
PLAY DUMB, WILL YA? I SEE HOW YOU ARE!
THEN CLASS IT IS! FINE, I'LL GO!
I'll get ready!
OH, THE SACRIFICE!
THE BOOK NO ONE COULD READ...
!
EVEN DAD...
...A PROFESSOR OF ARCHAEOLOGY!

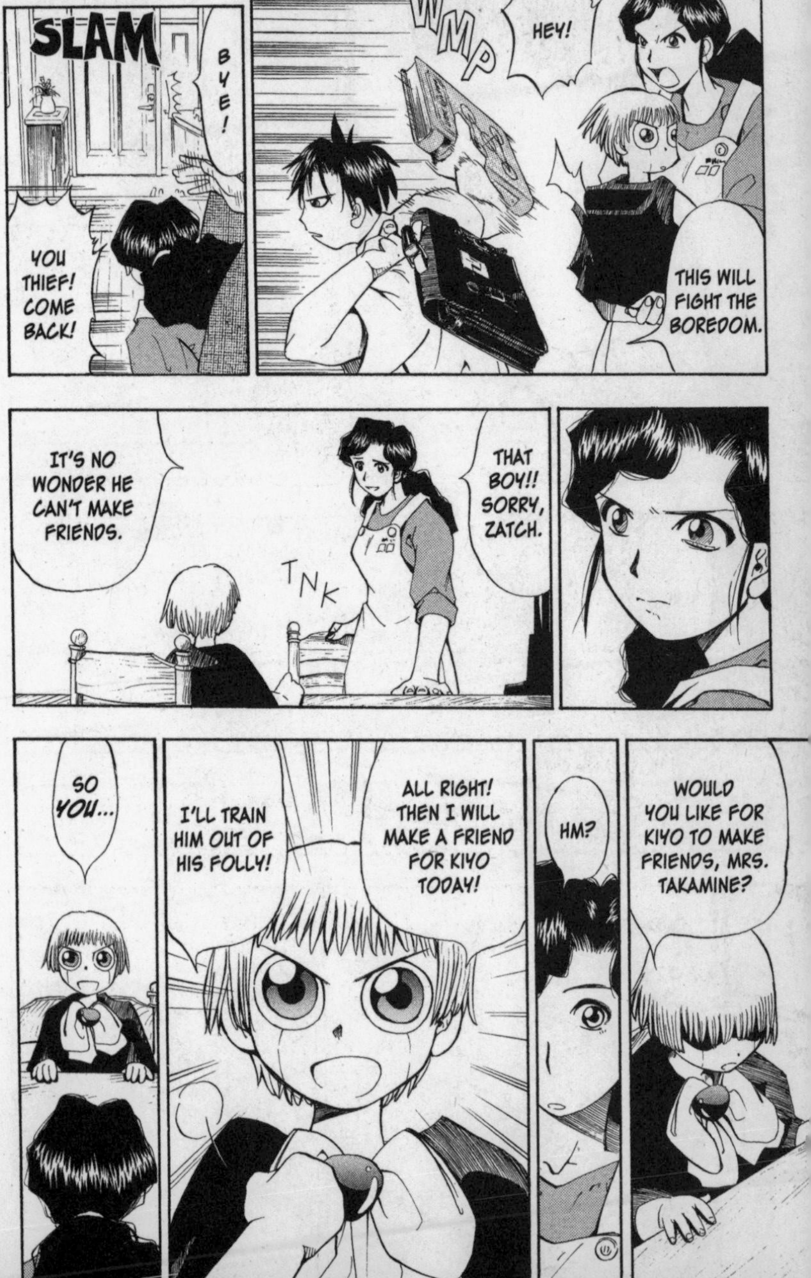
HEY!
WMP
THIS WILL FIGHT THE BOREDOM.
BYE!
SLAM
YOU THIEF! COME BACK!
THAT BOY!! SORRY, ZATCH.
TNK
IT'S NO WONDER HE CAN'T MAKE FRIENDS.
WOULD YOU LIKE FOR KIYO TO MAKE FRIENDS, MRS. TAKAMINE?
HM?
ALL RIGHT! THEN I WILL MAKE A FRIEND FOR KIYO TODAY!
I'LL TRAIN HIM OUT OF HIS FOLLY!
SO *YOU*...

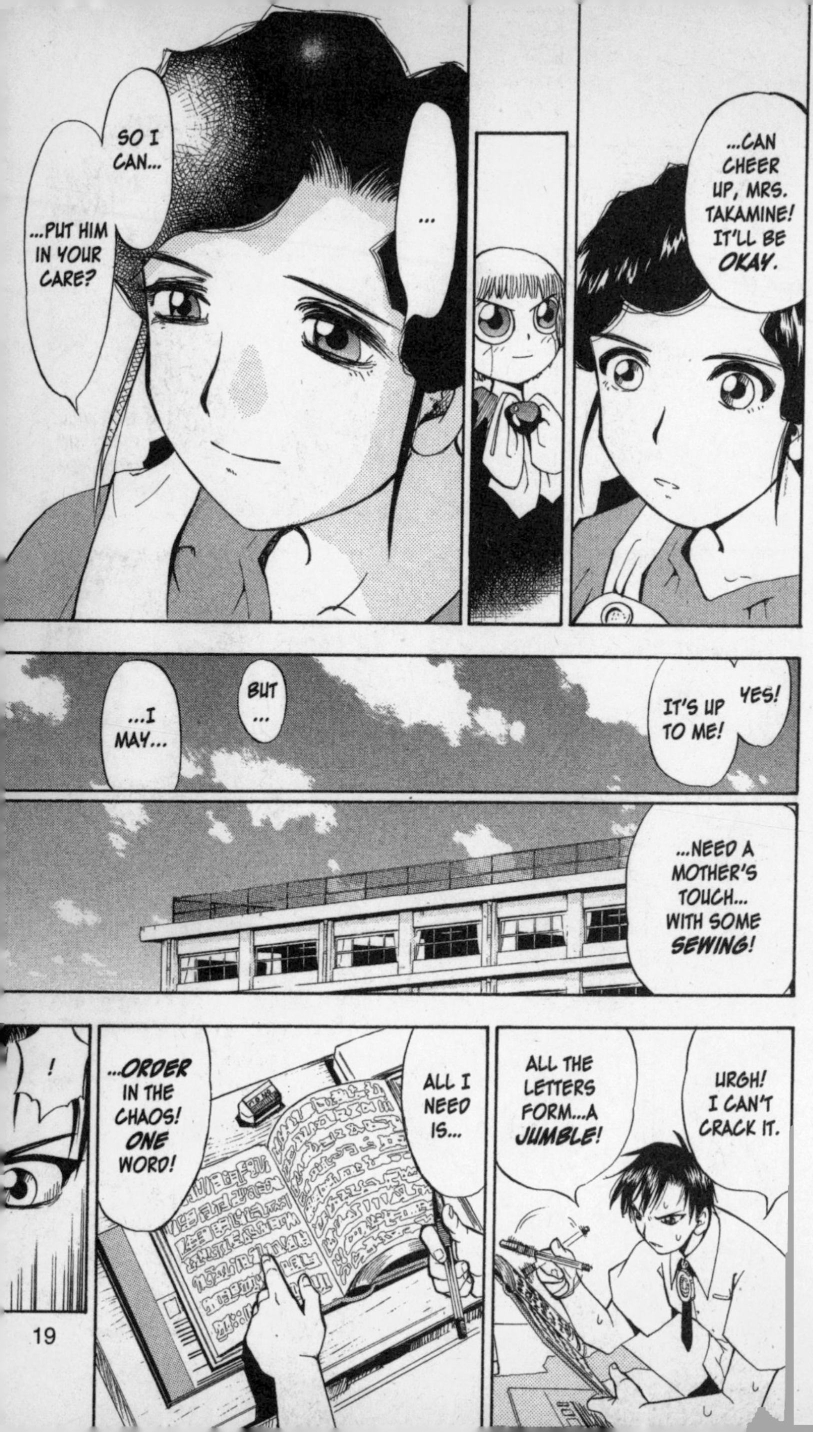
...CAN CHEER UP, MRS. TAKAMINE! IT'LL BE OKAY.
...
SO I CAN...
...PUT HIM IN YOUR CARE?
YES!
IT'S UP TO ME!
BUT ...
...I MAY...
...NEED A MOTHER'S TOUCH... WITH SOME SEWING!
URGH! I CAN'T CRACK IT.
ALL THE LETTERS FORM...A JUMBLE!
ALL I NEED IS...
...ORDER IN THE CHAOS! ONE WORD!
!

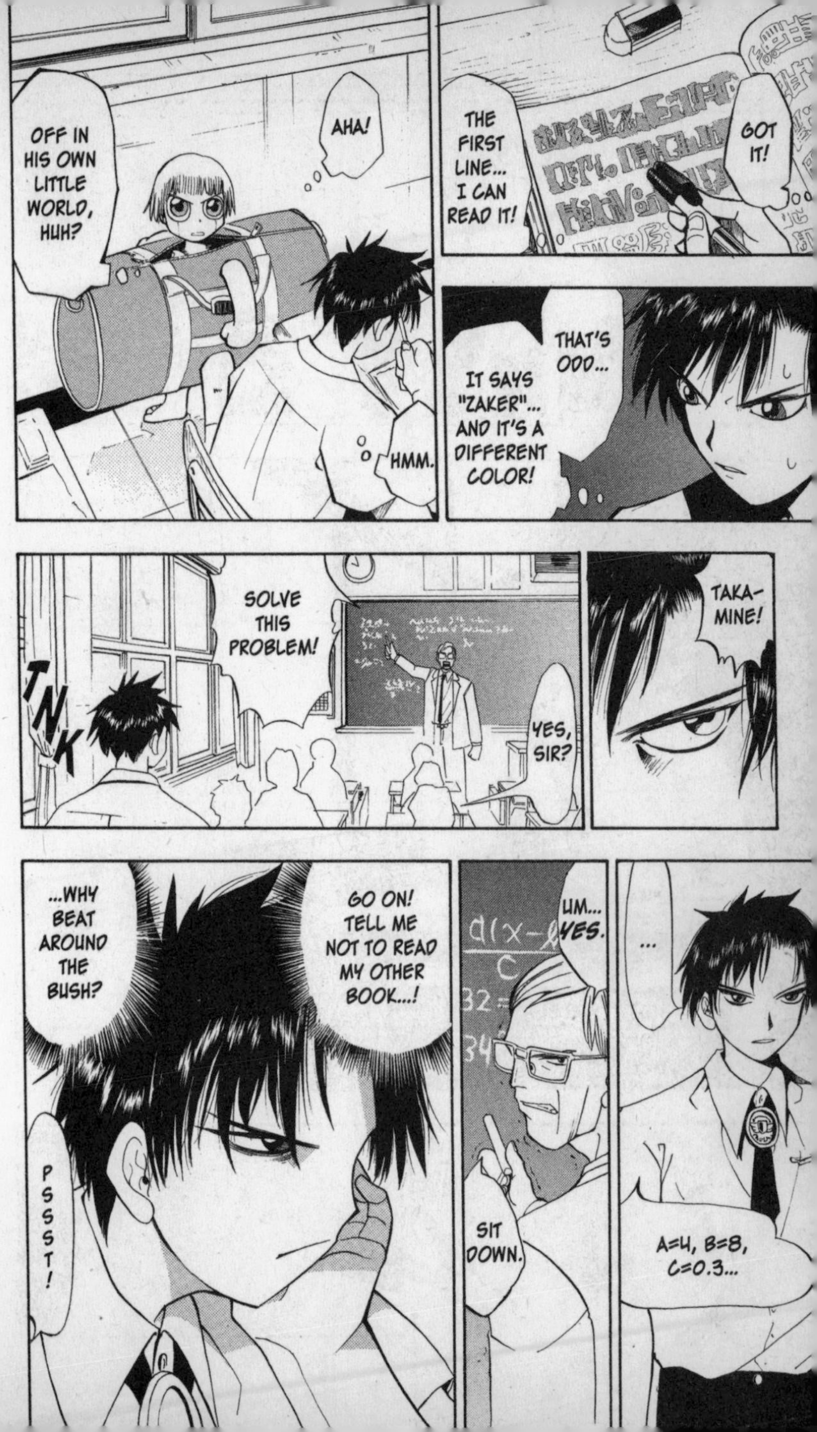
GOT IT!
THE FIRST LINE... I CAN READ IT!
THAT'S ODD...
IT SAYS "ZAKER"... AND IT'S A DIFFERENT COLOR!
AHA!
OFF IN HIS OWN LITTLE WORLD, HUH?
HMM.
TAKA-MINE!
SOLVE THIS PROBLEM!
YES, SIR?
TNK
...
A=4, B=8, C=0.3...
UM... YES.
SIT DOWN.
GO ON! TELL ME NOT TO READ MY OTHER BOOK...!
...WHY BEAT AROUND THE BUSH?
PSSST!

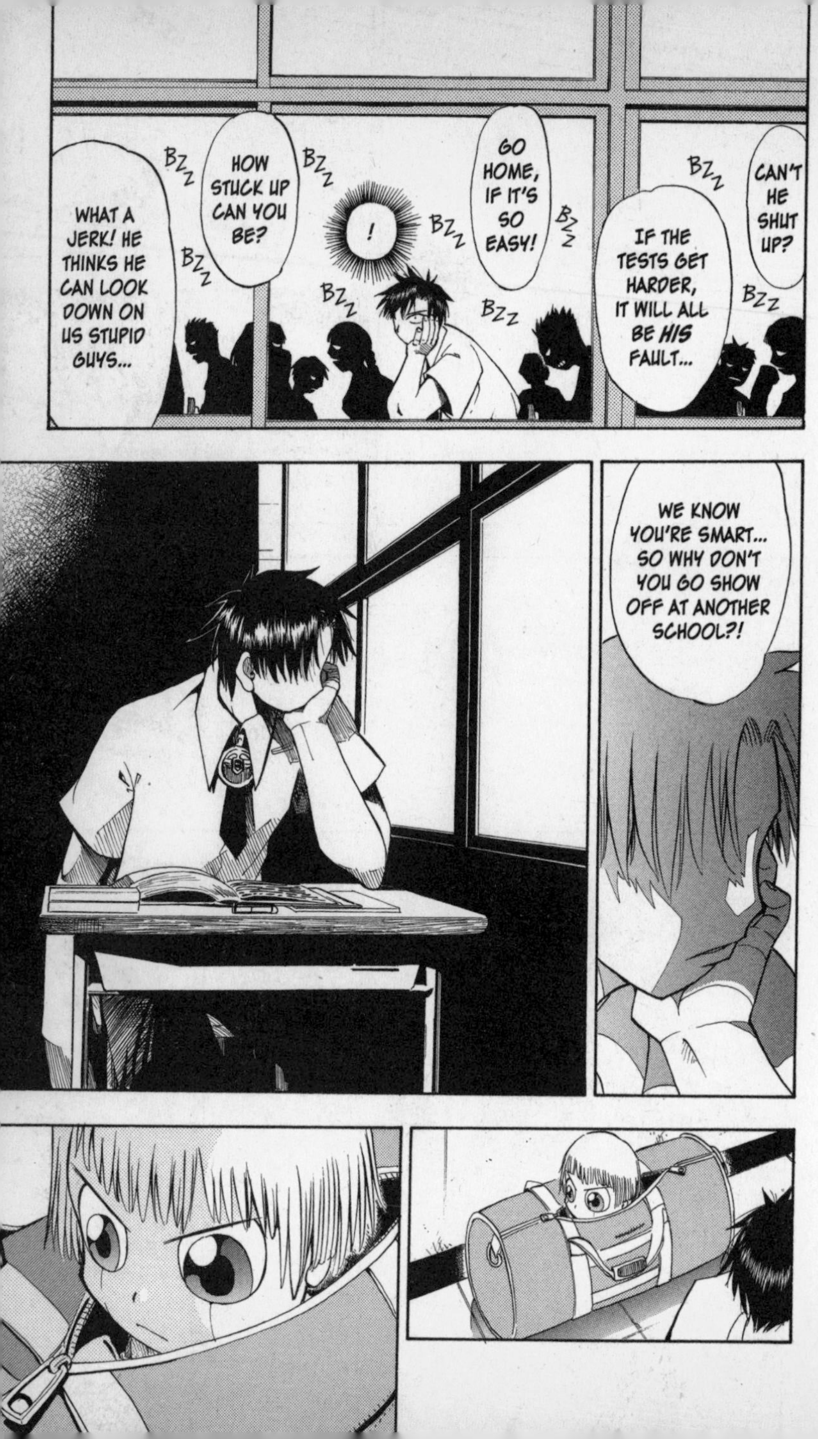

CAN'T HE SHUT UP?
BZZ
BZZ
IF THE TESTS GET HARDER, IT WILL ALL BE HIS FAULT...
BZZ
BZZ
GO HOME, IF IT'S SO EASY!
BZZ
!
BZZ
HOW STUCK UP CAN YOU BE?
BZZ
BZZ
BZZ
WHAT A JERK! HE THINKS HE CAN LOOK DOWN ON US STUPID GUYS...
WE KNOW YOU'RE SMART... SO WHY DON'T YOU GO SHOW OFF AT ANOTHER SCHOOL?!

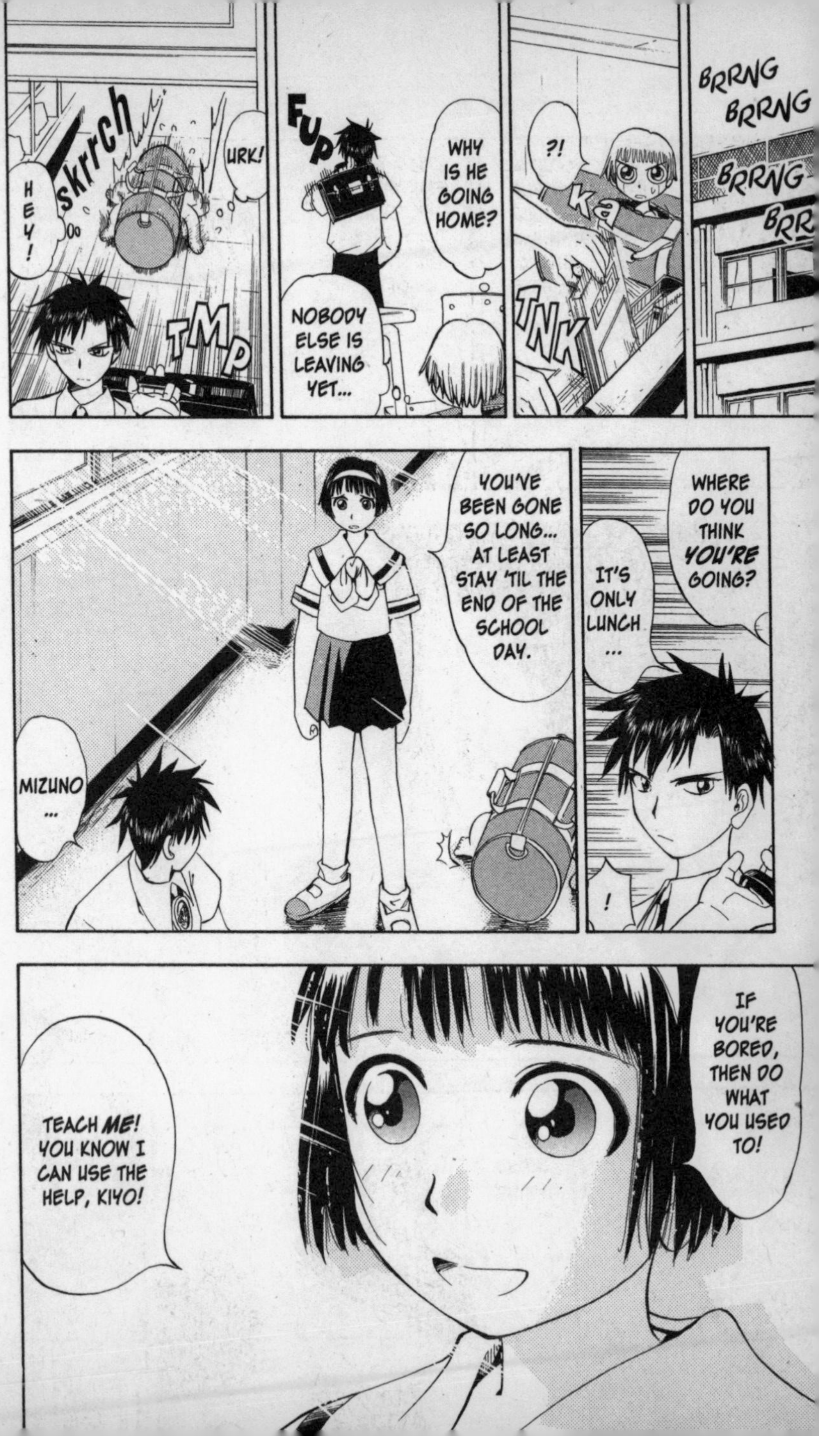
BRRNG
BRRNG
BRRNG
BRR
?!
ka
TNK
WHY IS HE GOING HOME?
FUP
NOBODY ELSE IS LEAVING YET...
URK!
skrrch
HEY!
TMP
WHERE DO YOU THINK *YOU'RE* GOING?
IT'S ONLY LUNCH...
!
YOU'VE BEEN GONE SO LONG... AT LEAST STAY 'TIL THE END OF THE SCHOOL DAY.
MIZUNO...
IF YOU'RE BORED, THEN DO WHAT YOU USED TO!
TEACH *ME*! YOU KNOW I CAN USE THE HELP, KIYO!

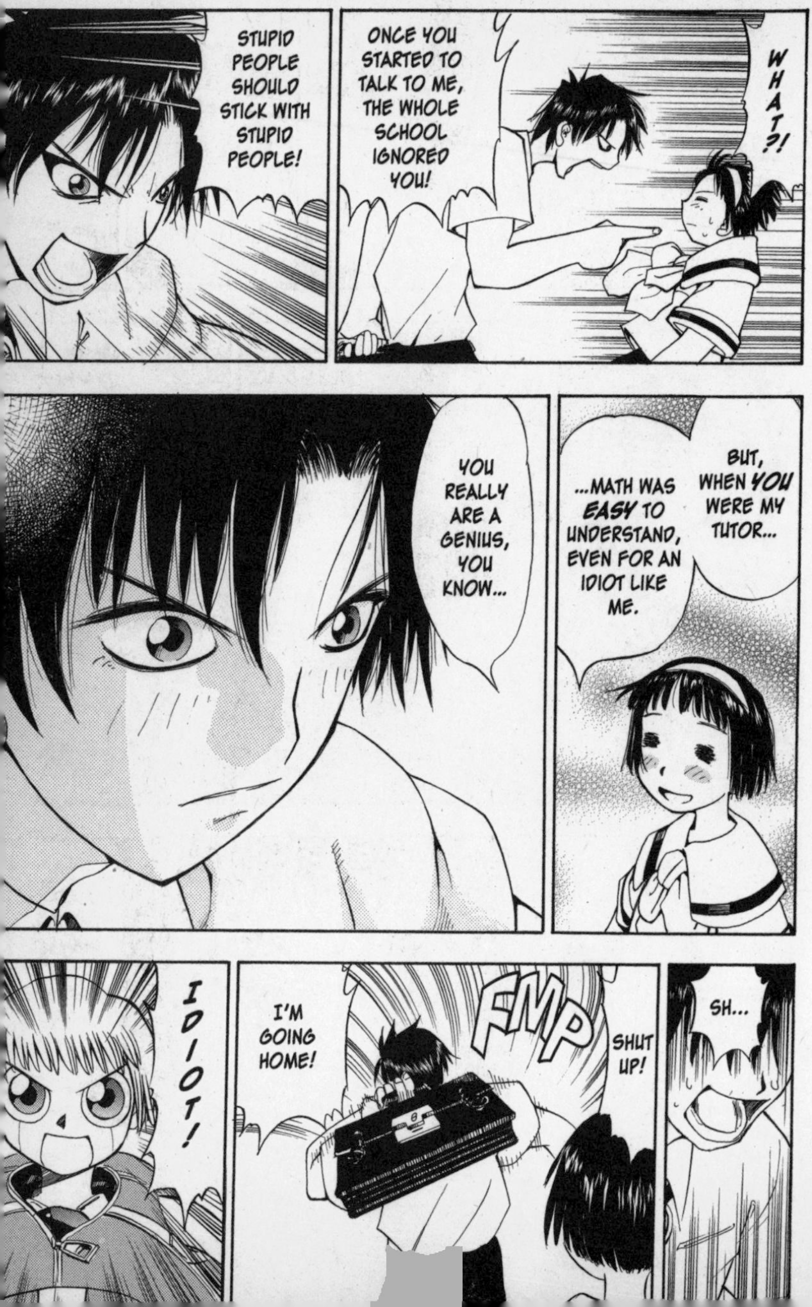
WHAT?!
ONCE YOU STARTED TO TALK TO ME, THE WHOLE SCHOOL IGNORED YOU!
STUPID PEOPLE SHOULD STICK WITH STUPID PEOPLE!
BUT, WHEN YOU WERE MY TUTOR...
...MATH WAS EASY TO UNDERSTAND, EVEN FOR AN IDIOT LIKE ME.
YOU REALLY ARE A GENIUS, YOU KNOW...
SH...
SHUT UP!
FMP
I'M GOING HOME!
IDIOT!

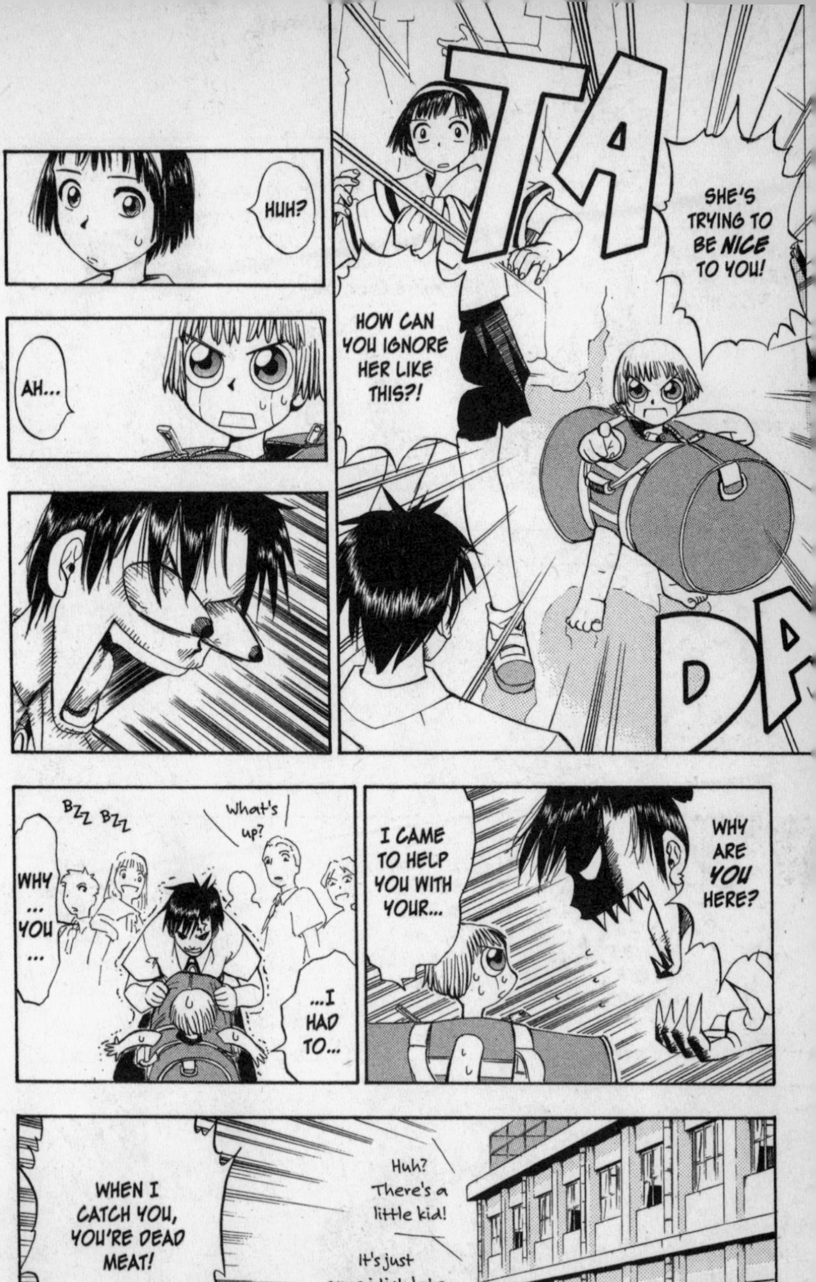
TA
SHE'S TRYING TO BE NICE TO YOU!
HOW CAN YOU IGNORE HER LIKE THIS?!
DA
HUH?
AH...
WHY ARE YOU HERE?
I CAME TO HELP YOU WITH YOUR...
What's up?
BZZ BZZ
WHY ... YOU ...
...I HAD TO...
Huh? There's a little kid!
It's just some idiot, late to school...
WHEN I CATCH YOU, YOU'RE DEAD MEAT!

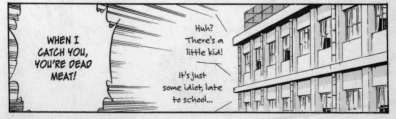

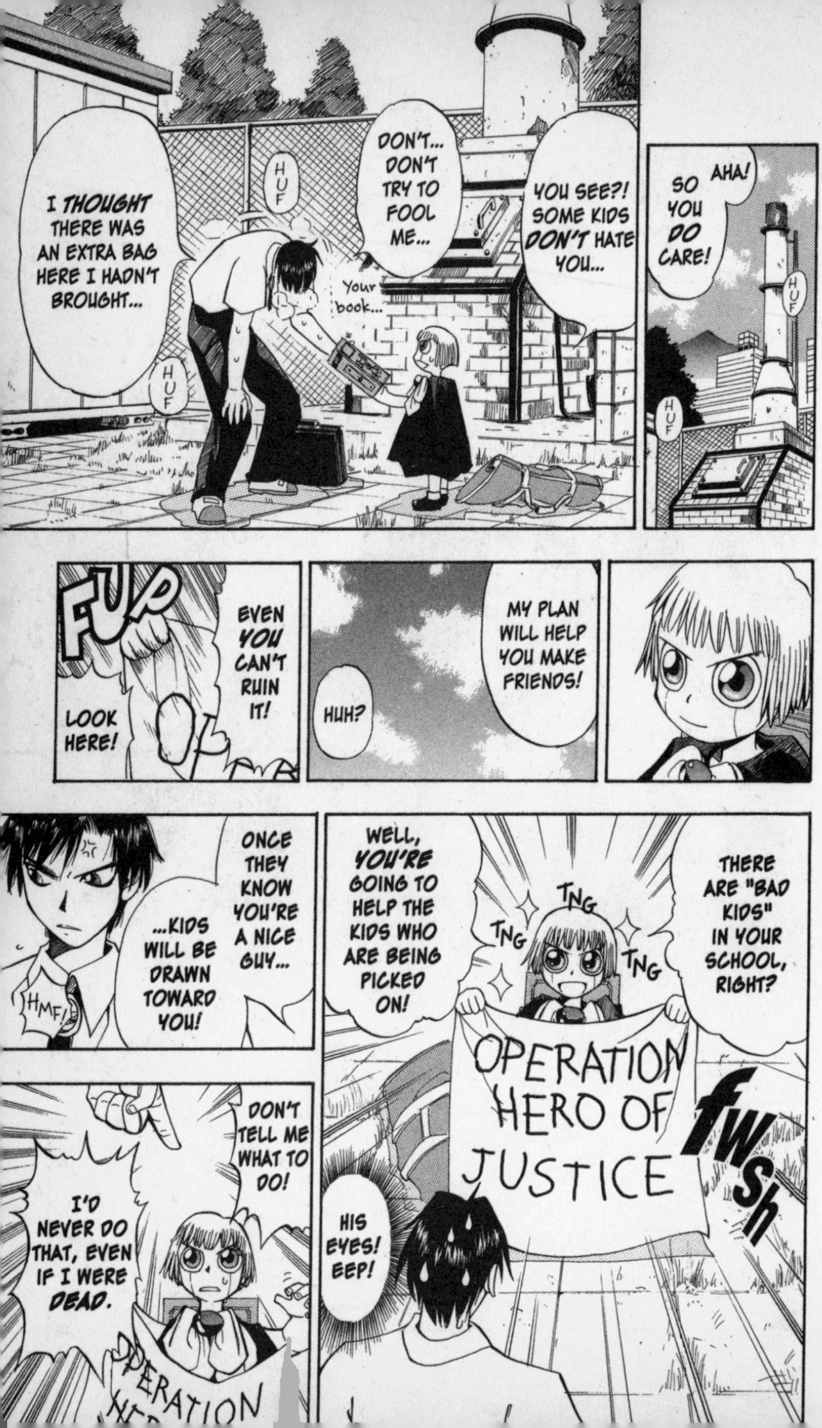
AHA!
SO YOU DO CARE!
HUF
HUF
YOU SEE?! SOME KIDS DON'T HATE YOU...
DON'T... DON'T TRY TO FOOL ME...
HUF
Your book...
I THOUGHT THERE WAS AN EXTRA BAG HERE I HADN'T BROUGHT...
HUF
MY PLAN WILL HELP YOU MAKE FRIENDS!
HUH?
EVEN YOU CAN'T RUIN IT!
FUP
LOOK HERE!
THERE ARE "BAD KIDS" IN YOUR SCHOOL, RIGHT?
TNG
TNG
TNG
WELL, YOU'RE GOING TO HELP THE KIDS WHO ARE BEING PICKED ON!
OPERATION HERO OF JUSTICE
fwsh
HIS EYES! EEP!
ONCE THEY KNOW YOU'RE A NICE GUY...
...KIDS WILL BE DRAWN TOWARD YOU!
HMF!
DON'T TELL ME WHAT TO DO!
I'D NEVER DO THAT, EVEN IF I WERE DEAD.
OPERATION

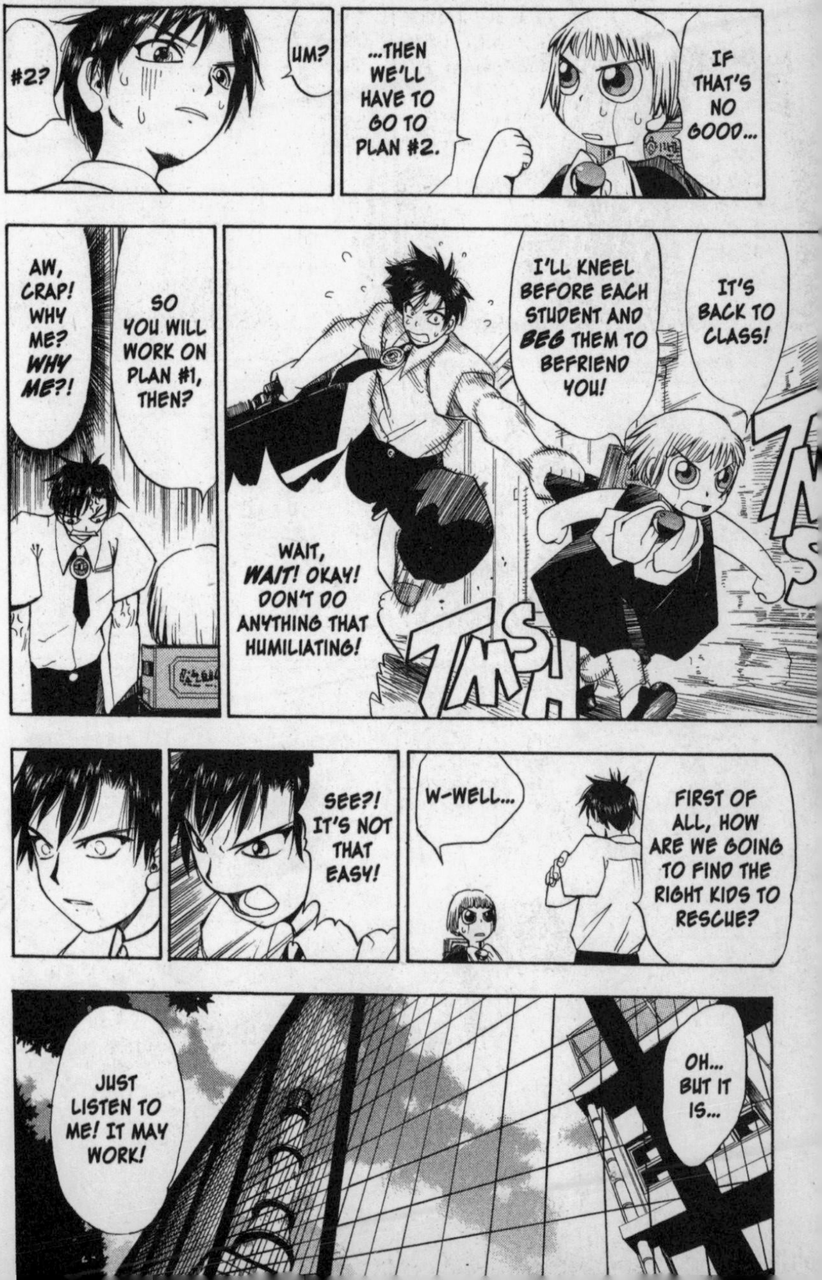
IF THAT'S NO GOOD...
...THEN WE'LL HAVE TO GO TO PLAN #2.
UM?
#2?
IT'S BACK TO CLASS!
I'LL KNEEL BEFORE EACH STUDENT AND BEG THEM TO BEFRIEND YOU!
WAIT, WAIT! OKAY! DON'T DO ANYTHING THAT HUMILIATING!
TMSH
SO YOU WILL WORK ON PLAN #1, THEN?
AW, CRAP! WHY ME? WHY ME?!
FIRST OF ALL, HOW ARE WE GOING TO FIND THE RIGHT KIDS TO RESCUE?
W-WELL...
SEE?! IT'S NOT THAT EASY!
OH... BUT IT IS...
JUST LISTEN TO ME! IT MAY WORK!

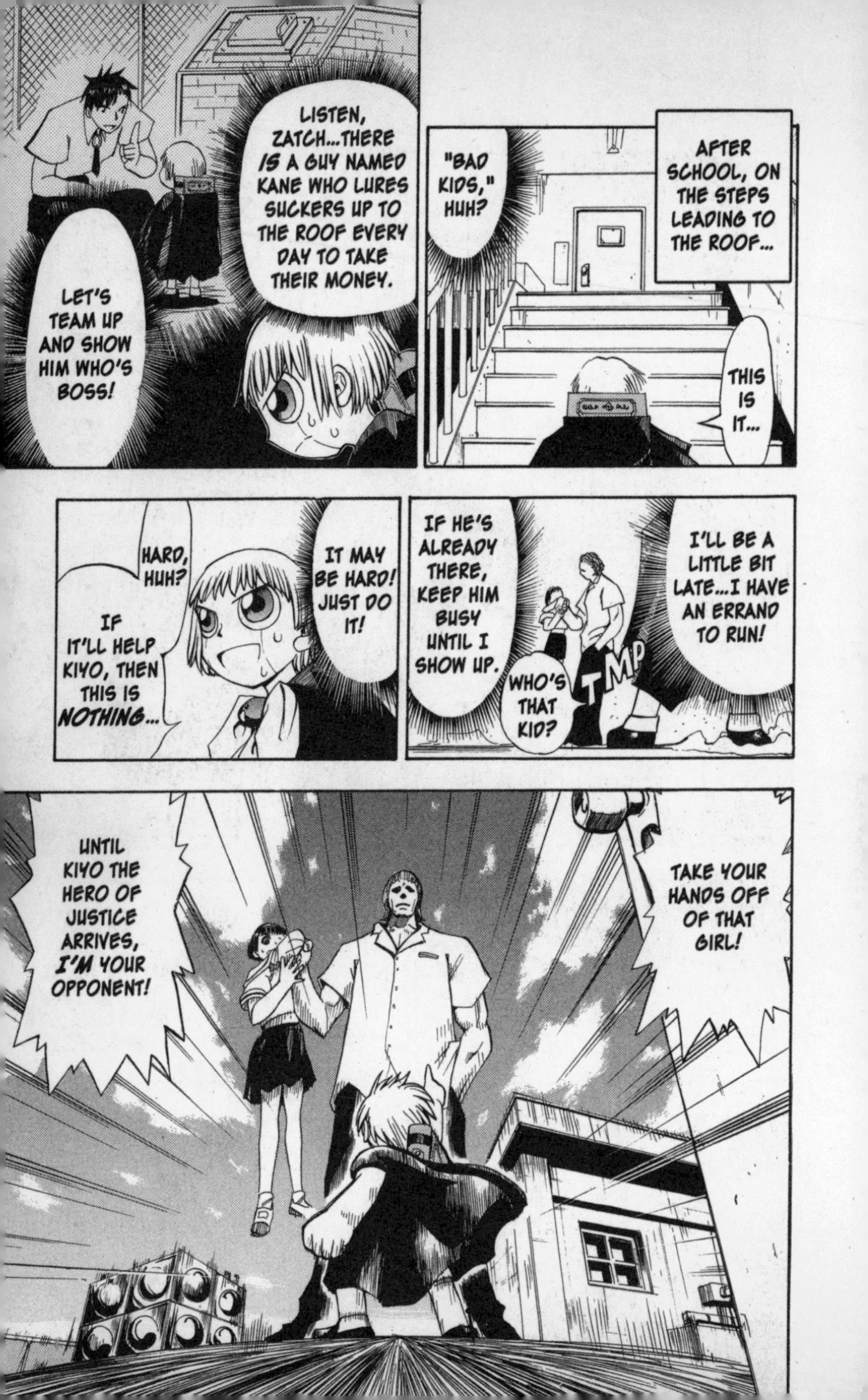
AFTER SCHOOL, ON THE STEPS LEADING TO THE ROOF...
THIS IS IT...
"BAD KIDS," HUH?
LISTEN, ZATCH...THERE *IS* A GUY NAMED KANE WHO LURES SUCKERS UP TO THE ROOF EVERY DAY TO TAKE THEIR MONEY.
LET'S TEAM UP AND SHOW HIM WHO'S BOSS!
I'LL BE A LITTLE BIT LATE...I HAVE AN ERRAND TO RUN!
IF HE'S ALREADY THERE, KEEP HIM BUSY UNTIL I SHOW UP.
TMP
WHO'S THAT KID?
IT MAY BE HARD! JUST DO IT!
HARD, HUH?
IF IT'LL HELP KIYO, THEN THIS IS ***NOTHING***...
TAKE YOUR HANDS OFF OF THAT GIRL!
UNTIL KIYO THE HERO OF JUSTICE ARRIVES, ***I'M*** YOUR OPPONENT!

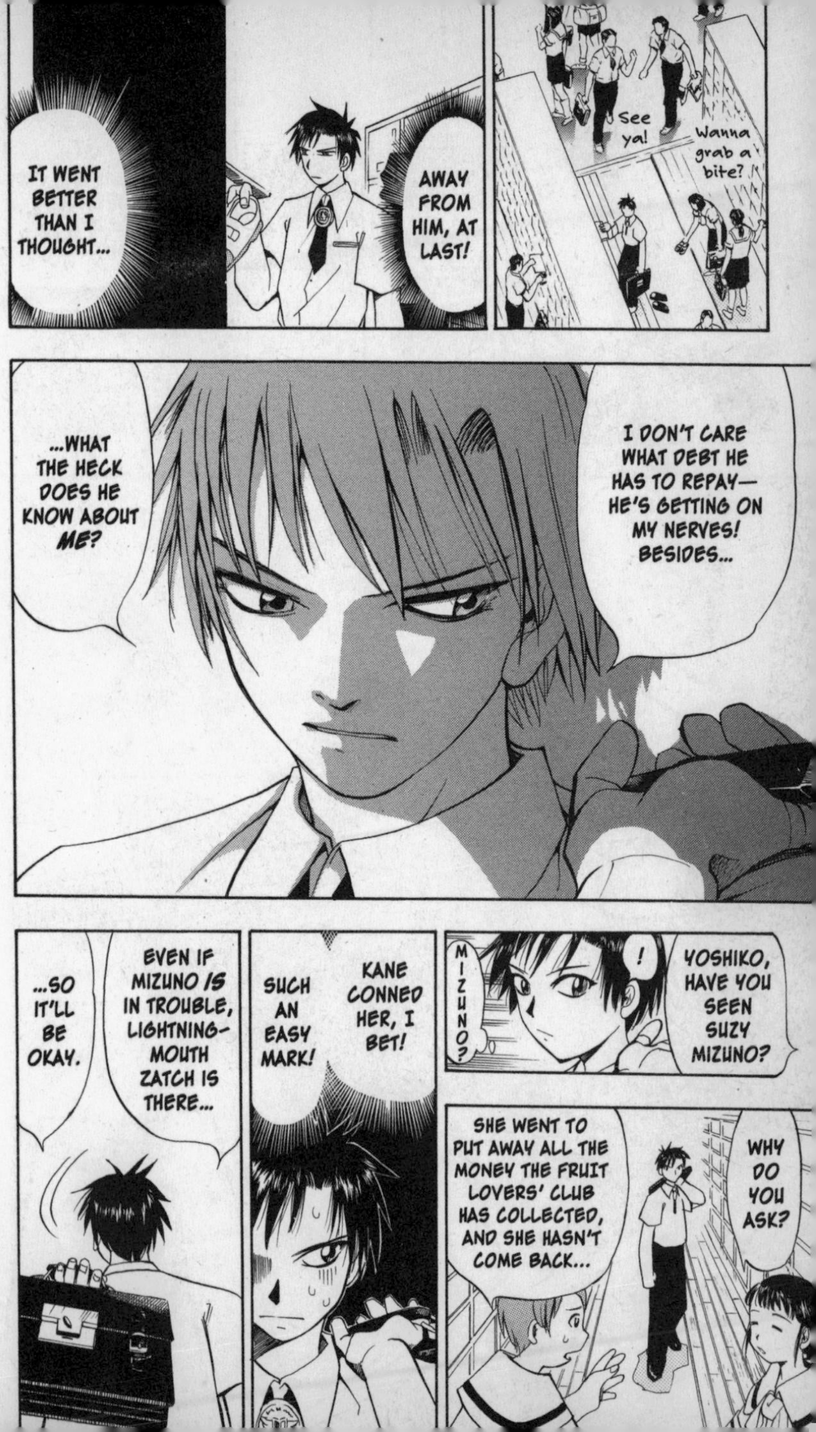
Wanna grab a bite?
See ya!
AWAY FROM HIM, AT LAST!
IT WENT BETTER THAN I THOUGHT...
I DON'T CARE WHAT DEBT HE HAS TO REPAY—HE'S GETTING ON MY NERVES! BESIDES...
...WHAT THE HECK DOES HE KNOW ABOUT *ME*?
YOSHIKO, HAVE YOU SEEN SUZY MIZUNO?
!
MIZUNO?
WHY DO YOU ASK?
SHE WENT TO PUT AWAY ALL THE MONEY THE FRUIT LOVERS' CLUB HAS COLLECTED, AND SHE HASN'T COME BACK...
KANE CONNED HER, I BET!
SUCH AN EASY MARK!
EVEN IF MIZUNO *IS* IN TROUBLE, LIGHTNING-MOUTH ZATCH IS THERE...
...SO IT'LL BE OKAY.

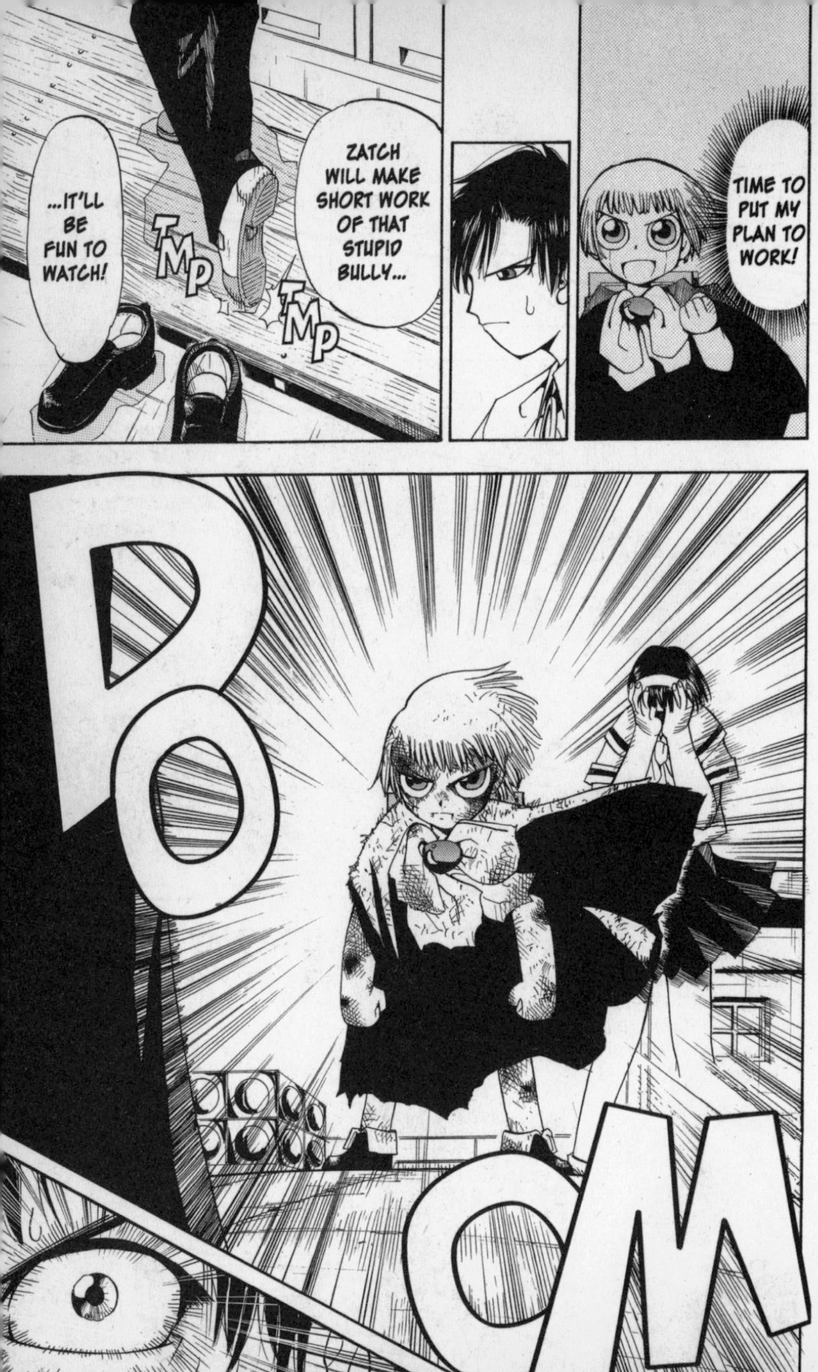
TIME TO PUT MY PLAN TO WORK!
ZATCH WILL MAKE SHORT WORK OF THAT STUPID BULLY...
...IT'LL BE FUN TO WATCH!
TMP
TMP
DOOM

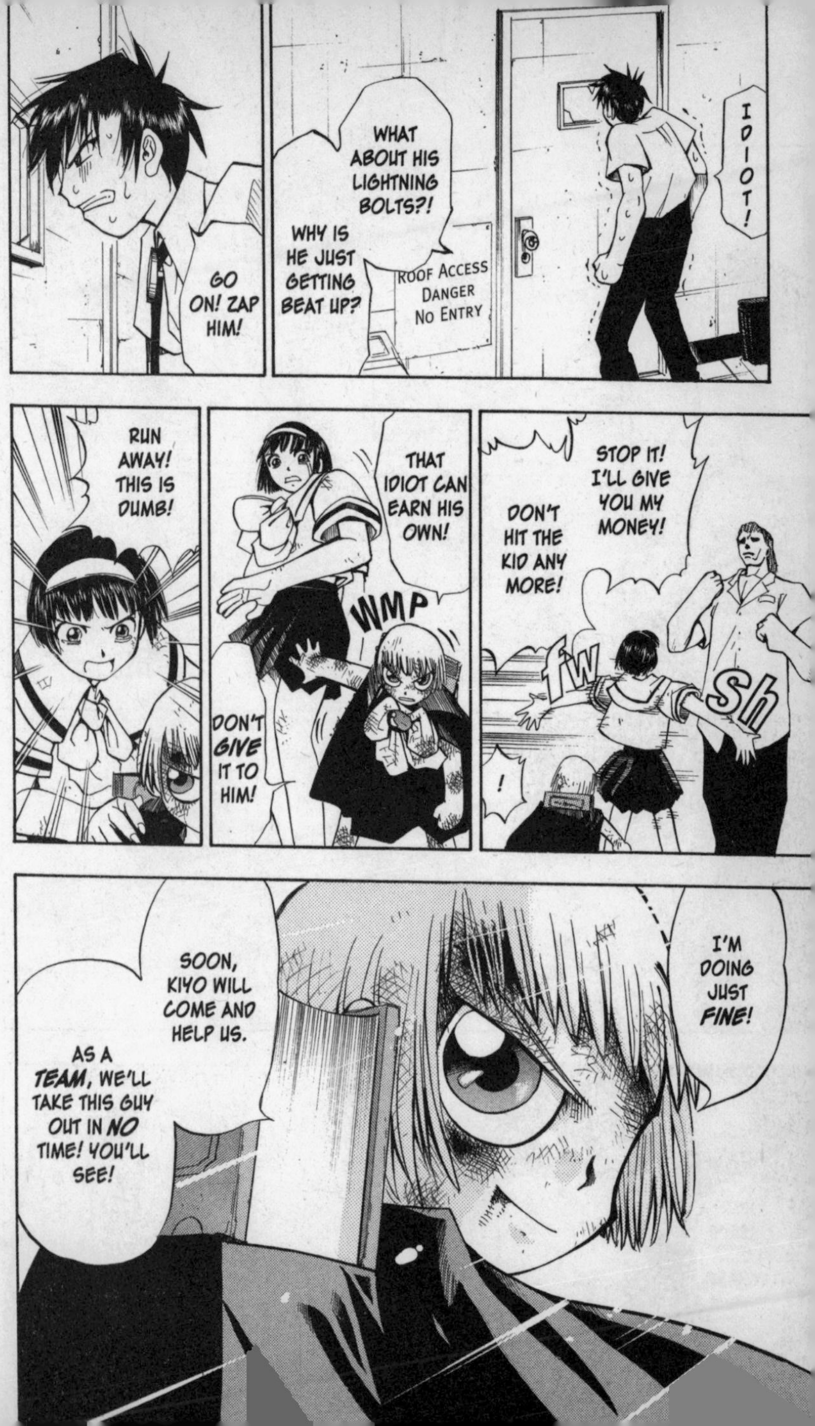
IDIOT!
WHAT ABOUT HIS LIGHTNING BOLTS?!
WHY IS HE JUST GETTING BEAT UP?
ROOF ACCESS DANGER NO ENTRY
GO ON! ZAP HIM!
STOP IT! I'LL GIVE YOU MY MONEY!
DON'T HIT THE KID ANY MORE!
Sh
fw
!
THAT IDIOT CAN EARN HIS OWN!
WMP
DON'T GIVE IT TO HIM!
RUN AWAY! THIS IS DUMB!
I'M DOING JUST FINE!
SOON, KIYO WILL COME AND HELP US.
AS A TEAM, WE'LL TAKE THIS GUY OUT IN NO TIME! YOU'LL SEE!

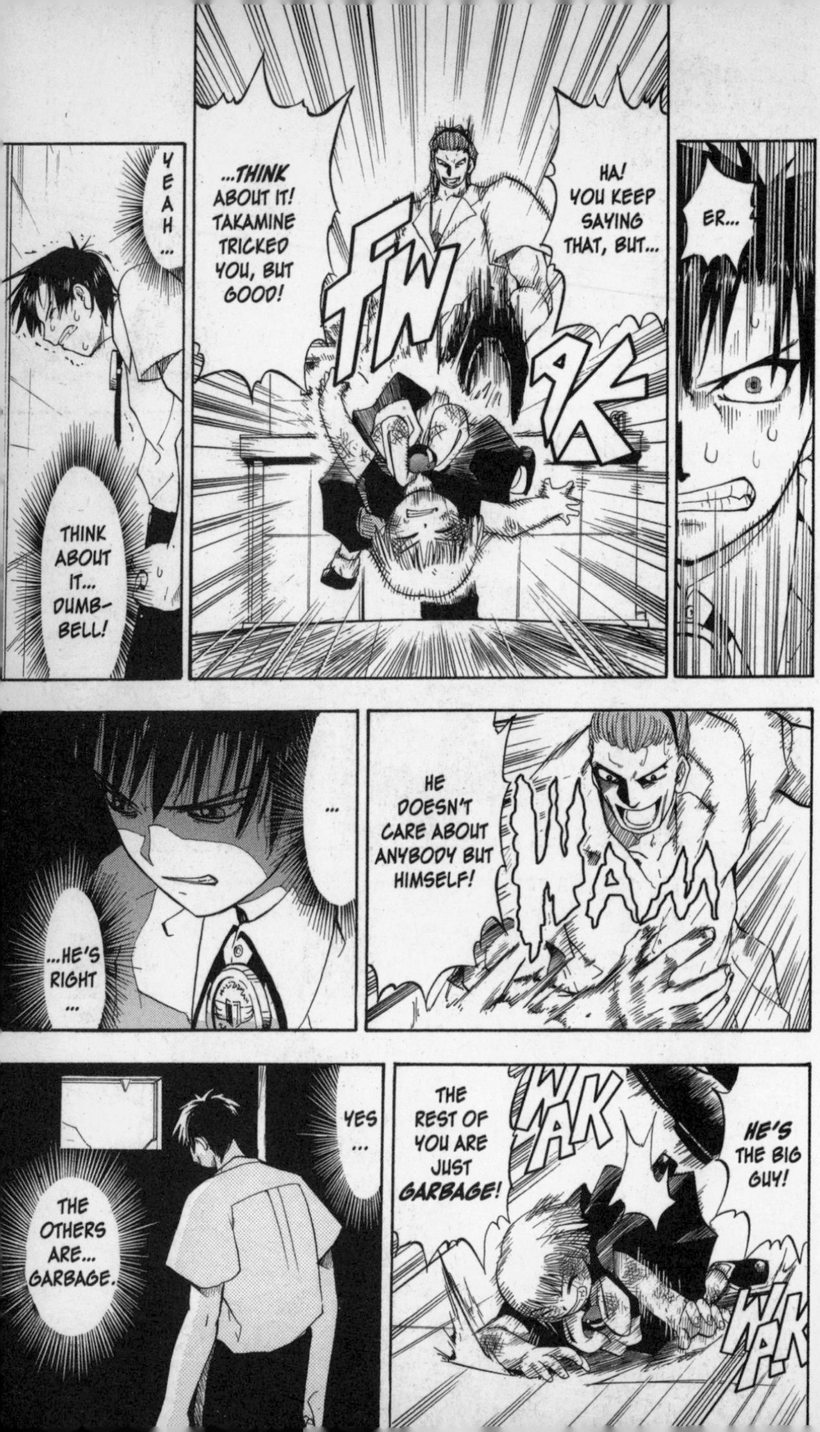
ER...
HA! YOU KEEP SAYING THAT, BUT...
FWAK
...THINK ABOUT IT! TAKAMINE TRICKED YOU, BUT GOOD!
YEAH...
THINK ABOUT IT... DUMB-BELL!
HE DOESN'T CARE ABOUT ANYBODY BUT HIMSELF!
WAM
...
...HE'S RIGHT...
HE'S THE BIG GUY!
WAK
THE REST OF YOU ARE JUST GARBAGE!
WAK
YES...
THE OTHERS ARE... GARBAGE.

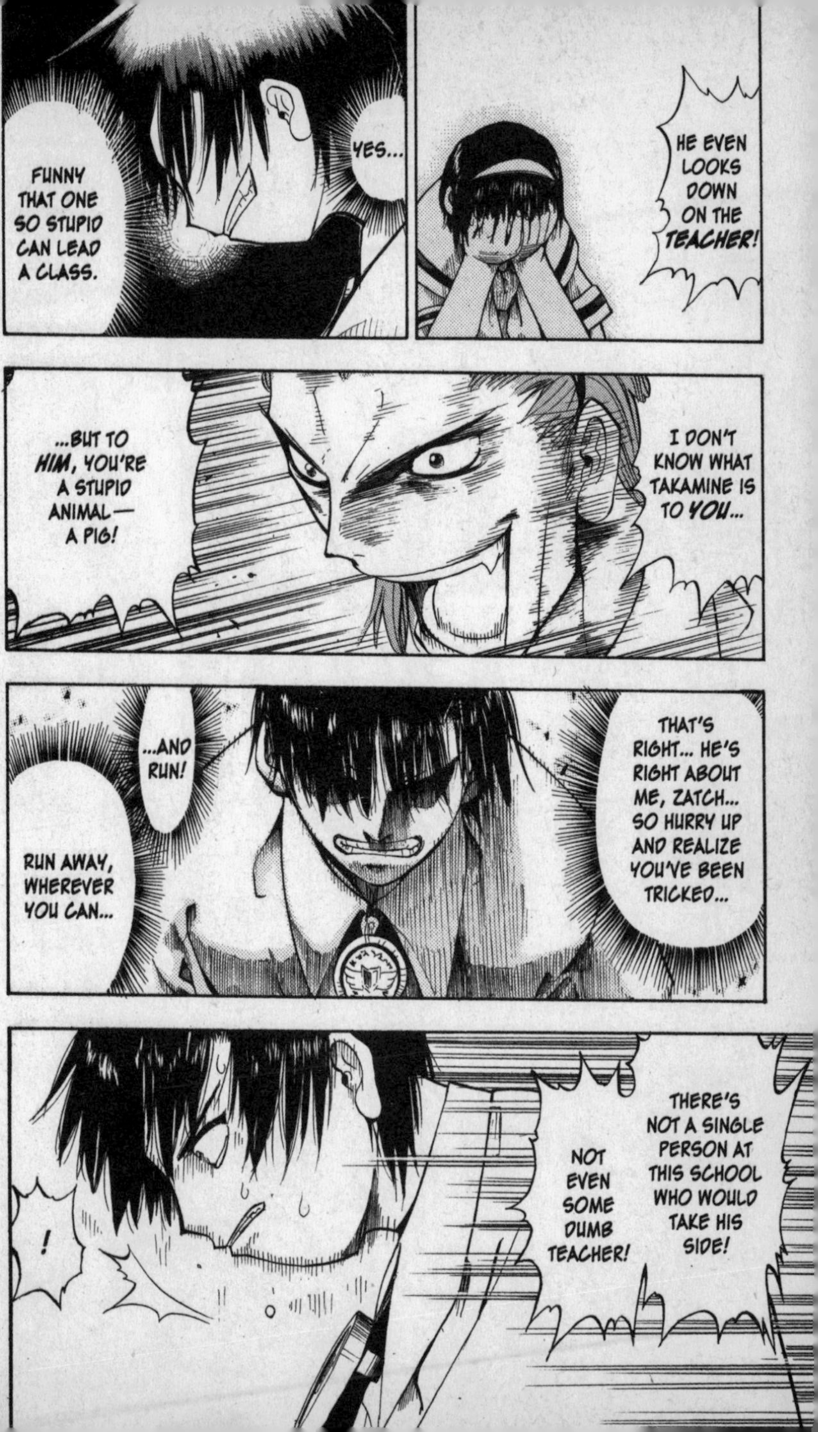
HE EVEN LOOKS DOWN ON THE TEACHER!
YES...
FUNNY THAT ONE SO STUPID CAN LEAD A CLASS.
I DON'T KNOW WHAT TAKAMINE IS TO YOU...
...BUT TO HIM, YOU'RE A STUPID ANIMAL— A PIG!
THAT'S RIGHT... HE'S RIGHT ABOUT ME, ZATCH... SO HURRY UP AND REALIZE YOU'VE BEEN TRICKED...
...AND RUN!
RUN AWAY, WHEREVER YOU CAN...
THERE'S NOT A SINGLE PERSON AT THIS SCHOOL WHO WOULD TAKE HIS SIDE!
NOT EVEN SOME DUMB TEACHER!
!

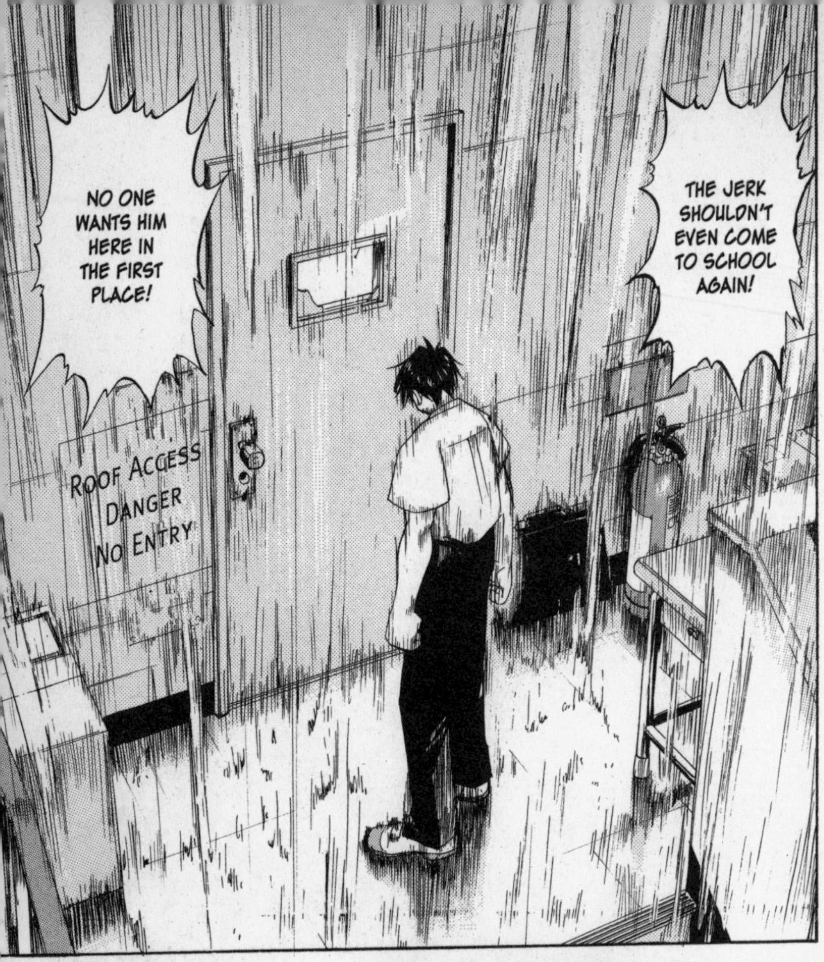
THE JERK SHOULDN'T EVEN COME TO SCHOOL AGAIN!
NO ONE WANTS HIM HERE IN THE FIRST PLACE!
Roof Access
Danger
No Entry

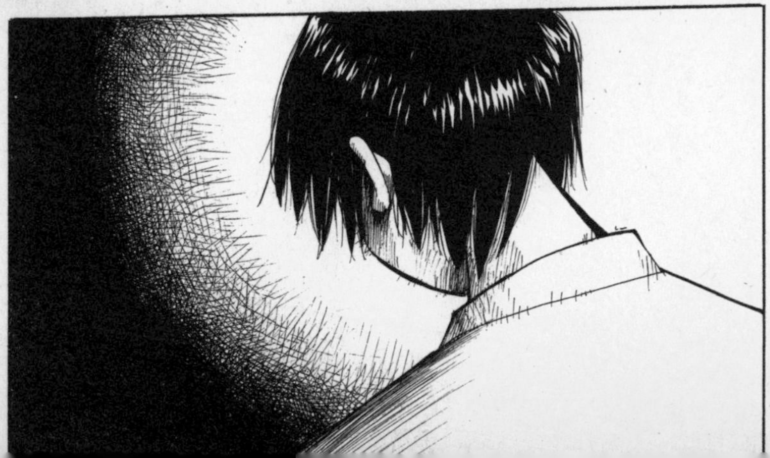

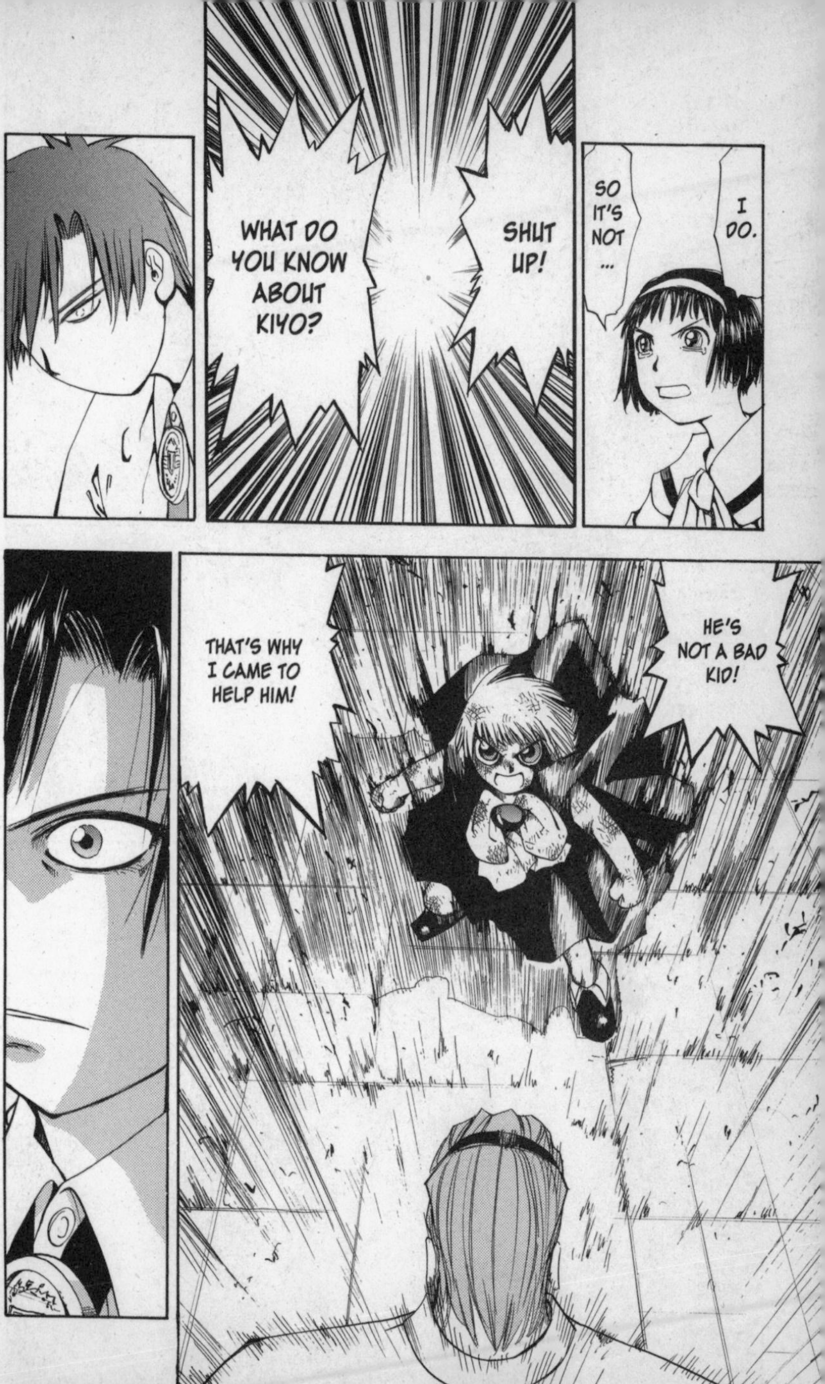
I DO.
SO IT'S NOT ...
SHUT UP!
WHAT DO YOU KNOW ABOUT KIYO?
HE'S NOT A BAD KID!
THAT'S WHY I CAME TO HELP HIM!

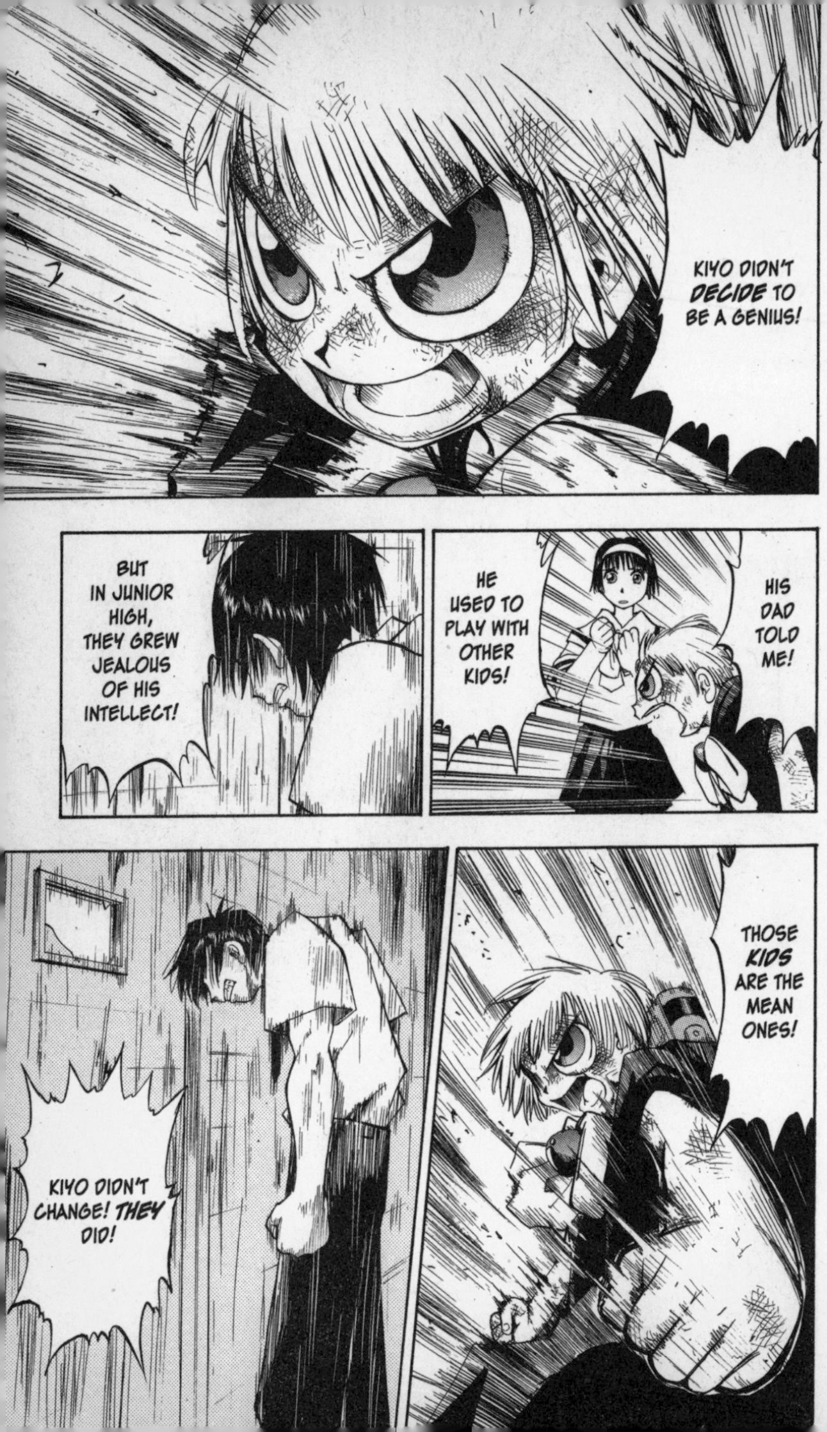
KIYO DIDN'T **DECIDE** TO BE A GENIUS!
HIS DAD TOLD ME!
HE USED TO PLAY WITH OTHER KIDS!
BUT IN JUNIOR HIGH, THEY GREW JEALOUS OF HIS INTELLECT!
THOSE **KIDS** ARE THE MEAN ONES!
KIYO DIDN'T CHANGE! ***THEY*** DID!

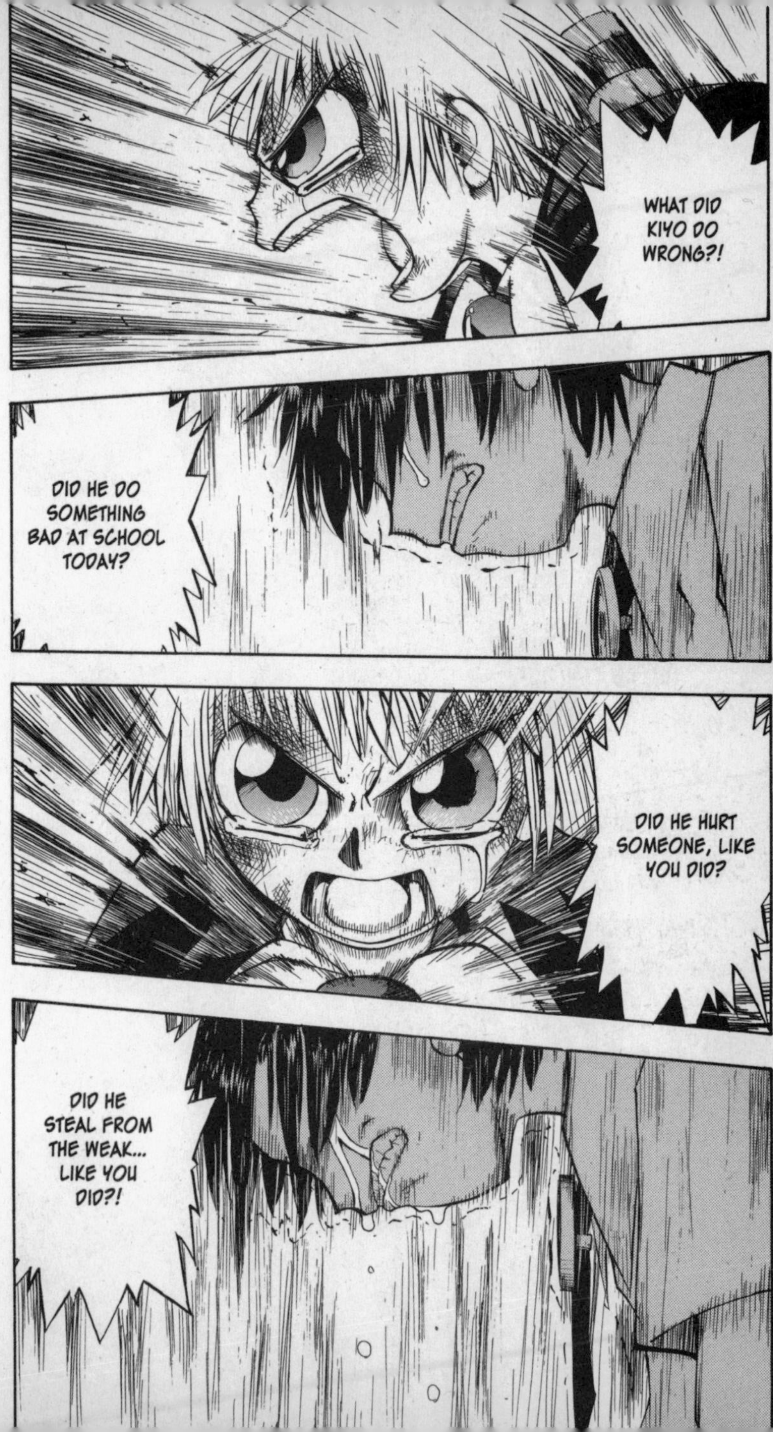
WHAT DID KIYO DO WRONG?!
DID HE DO SOMETHING BAD AT SCHOOL TODAY?
DID HE HURT SOMEONE, LIKE YOU DID?
DID HE STEAL FROM THE WEAK... LIKE YOU DID?!

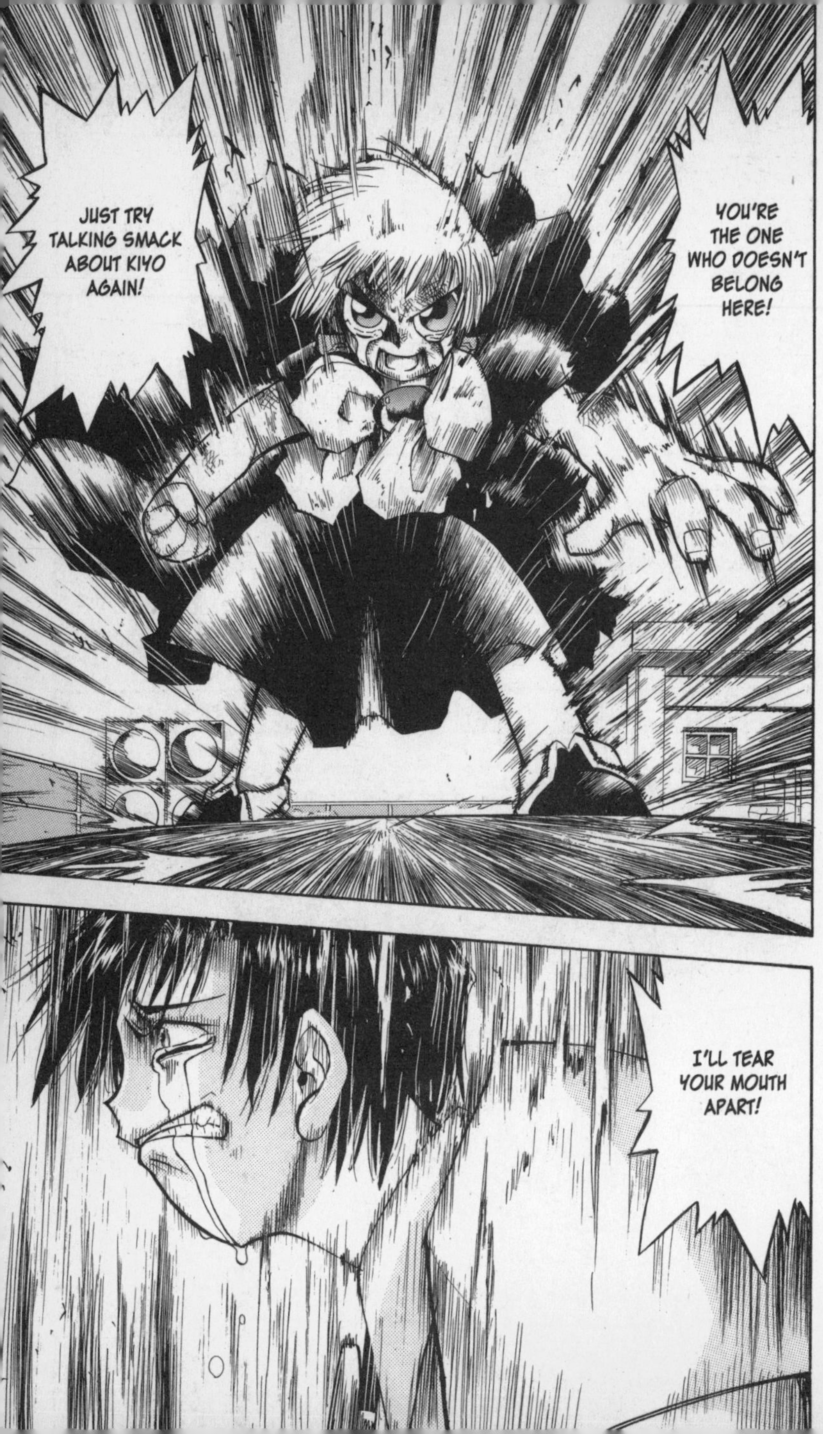
YOU'RE THE ONE WHO DOESN'T BELONG HERE!
JUST TRY TALKING SMACK ABOUT KIYO AGAIN!
I'LL TEAR YOUR MOUTH APART!

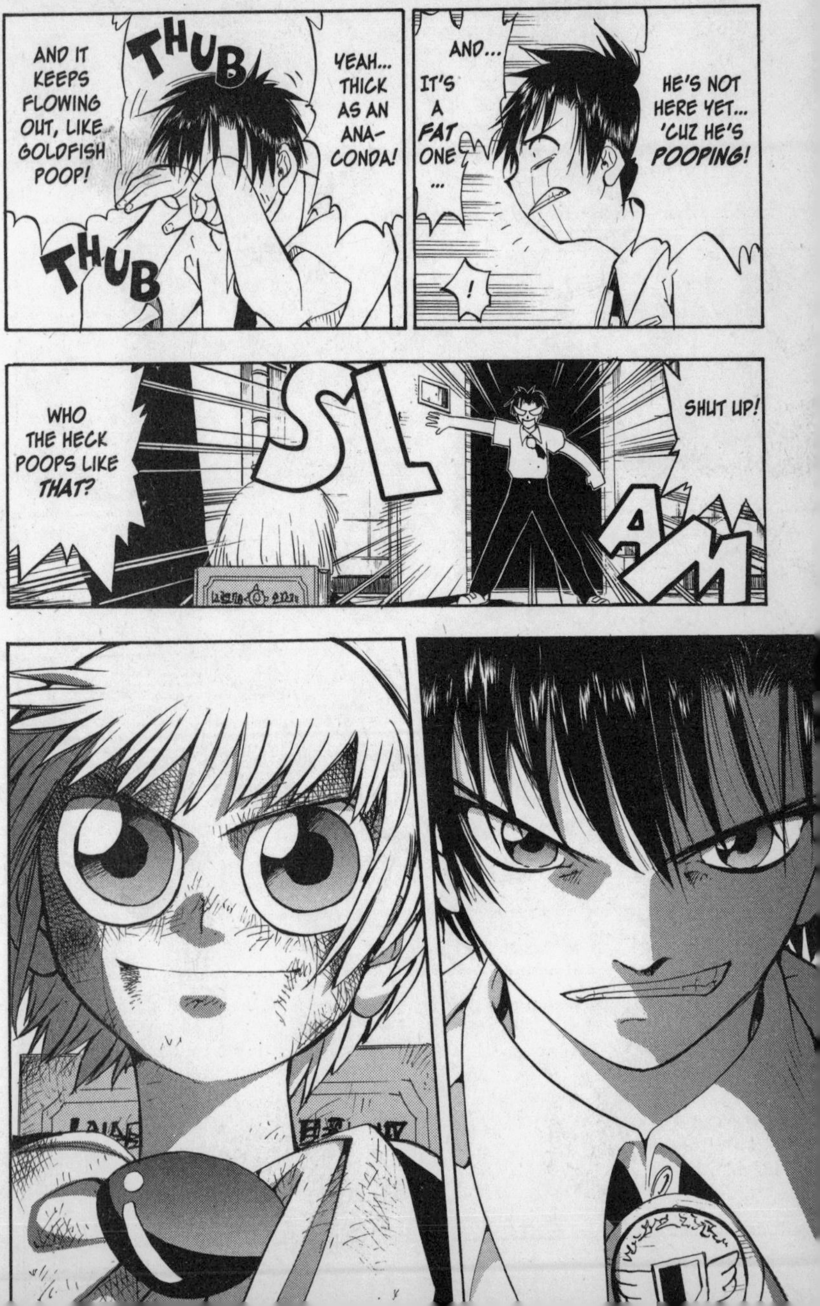
HE'S NOT HERE YET... 'CUZ HE'S POOPING!
AND...
IT'S A FAT ONE ...
!
YEAH... THICK AS AN ANA-CONDA!
THUB
AND IT KEEPS FLOWING OUT, LIKE GOLDFISH POOP!
THUB
SHUT UP!
SLAM
WHO THE HECK POOPS LIKE THAT?

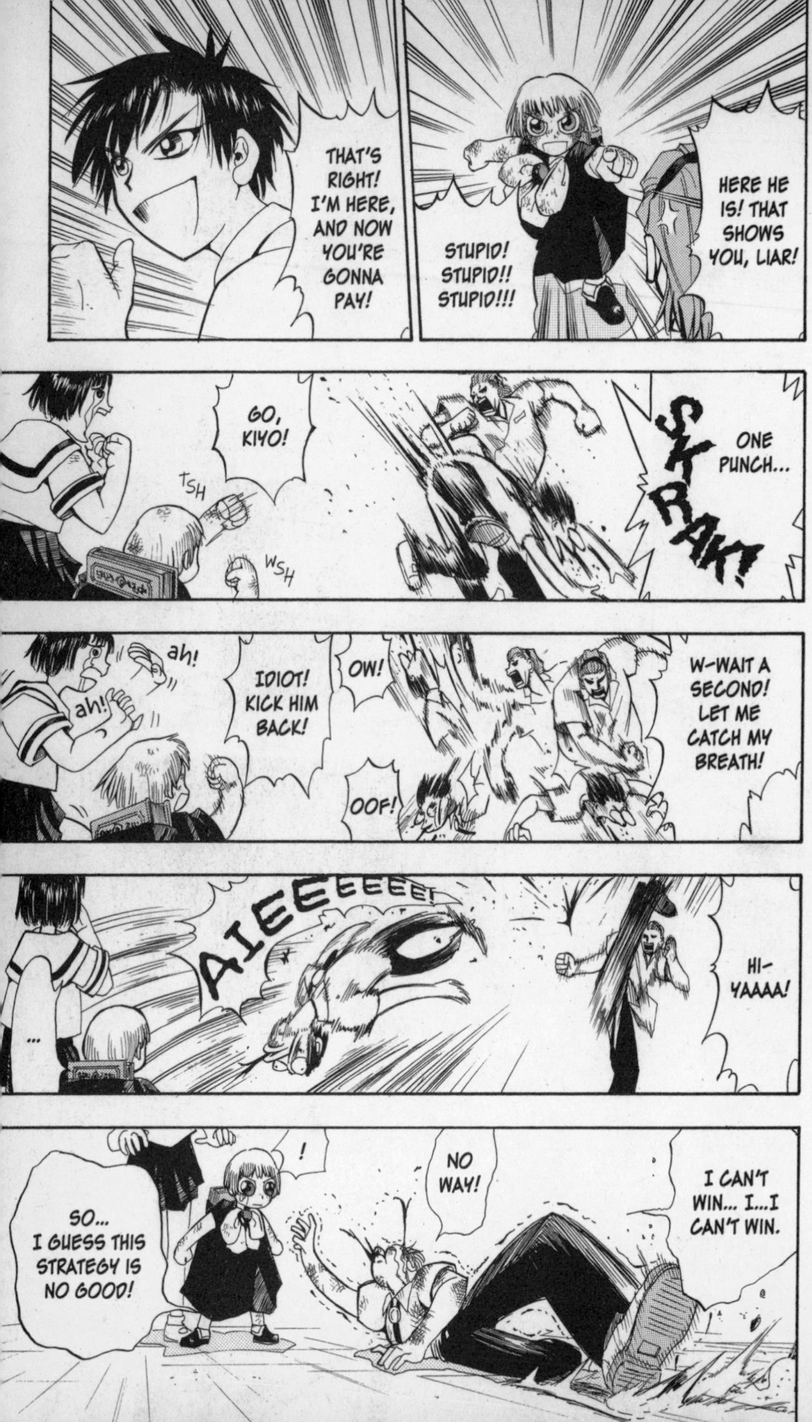
HERE HE IS! THAT SHOWS YOU, LIAR!
STUPID! STUPID!! STUPID!!!
THAT'S RIGHT! I'M HERE, AND NOW YOU'RE GONNA PAY!
ONE PUNCH...
SKRAK!
GO, KIYO!
TSH
WSH
W-WAIT A SECOND! LET ME CATCH MY BREATH!
OW!
OOF!
IDIOT! KICK HIM BACK!
ah!
ah!
HI-YAAAA!
AIEEEEEEE!
...
I CAN'T WIN... I...I CAN'T WIN.
NO WAY!
!
SO... I GUESS THIS STRATEGY IS NO GOOD!

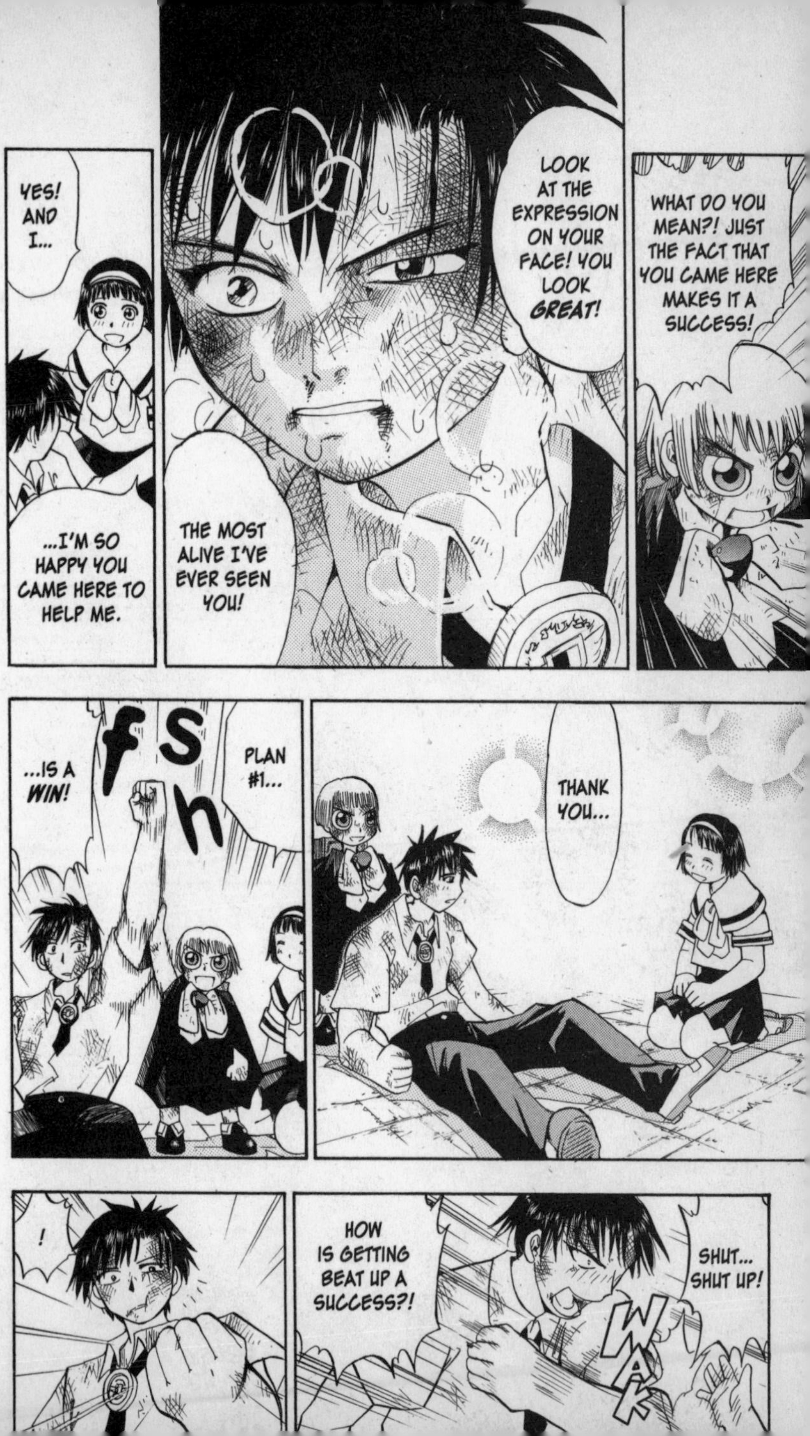
WHAT DO YOU MEAN?! JUST THE FACT THAT YOU CAME HERE MAKES IT A SUCCESS!
LOOK AT THE EXPRESSION ON YOUR FACE! YOU LOOK GREAT!
THE MOST ALIVE I'VE EVER SEEN YOU!
YES! AND I...
...I'M SO HAPPY YOU CAME HERE TO HELP ME.
THANK YOU...
PLAN #1...
fsh
...IS A WIN!
SHUT... SHUT UP!
WAK
HOW IS GETTING BEAT UP A SUCCESS?!
!

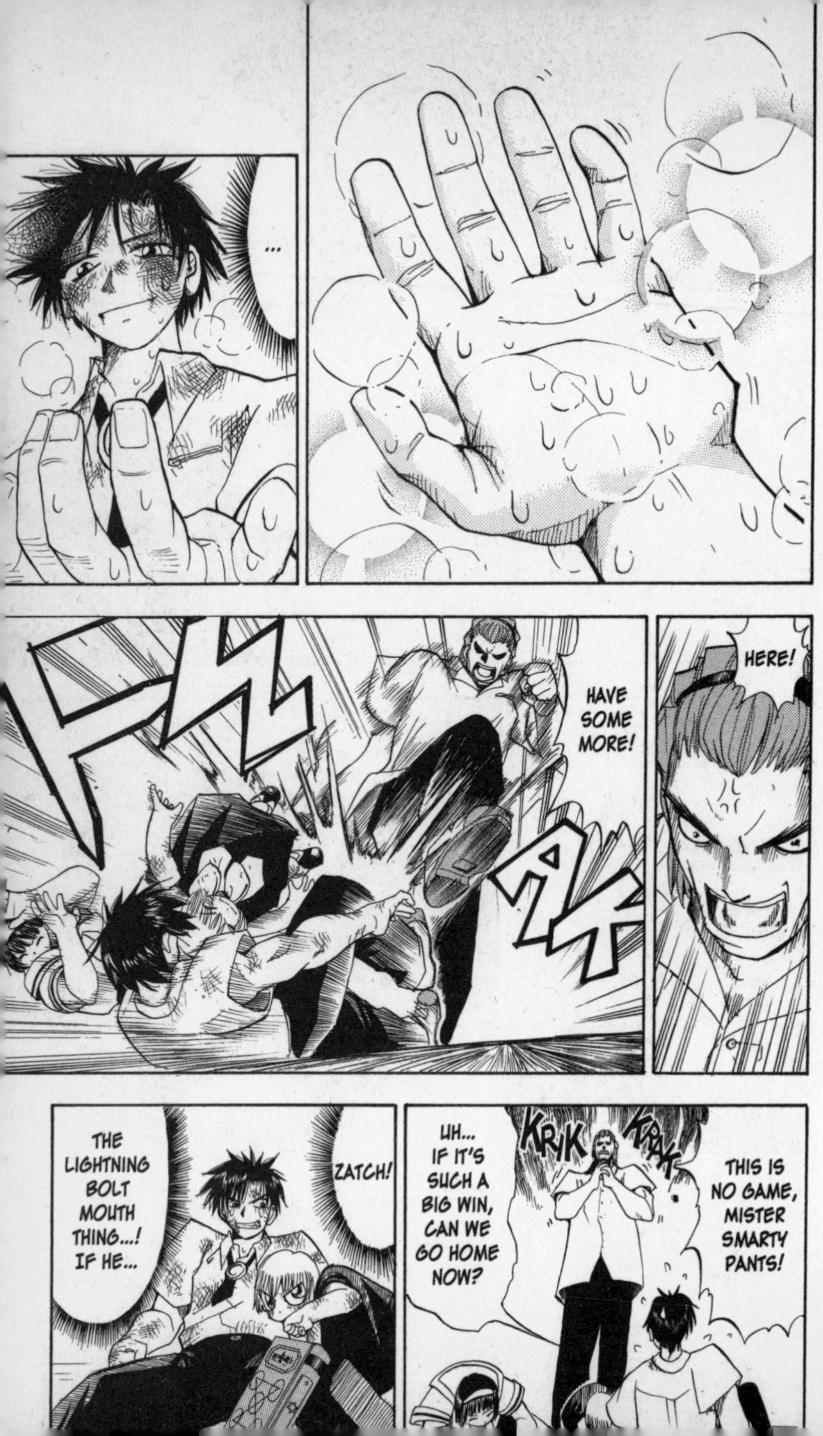
...
HERE!
HAVE SOME MORE!
KRAK
KRIK
THIS IS NO GAME, MISTER SMARTY PANTS!
UH... IF IT'S SUCH A BIG WIN, CAN WE GO HOME NOW?
ZATCH!
THE LIGHTNING BOLT MOUTH THING...! IF HE...

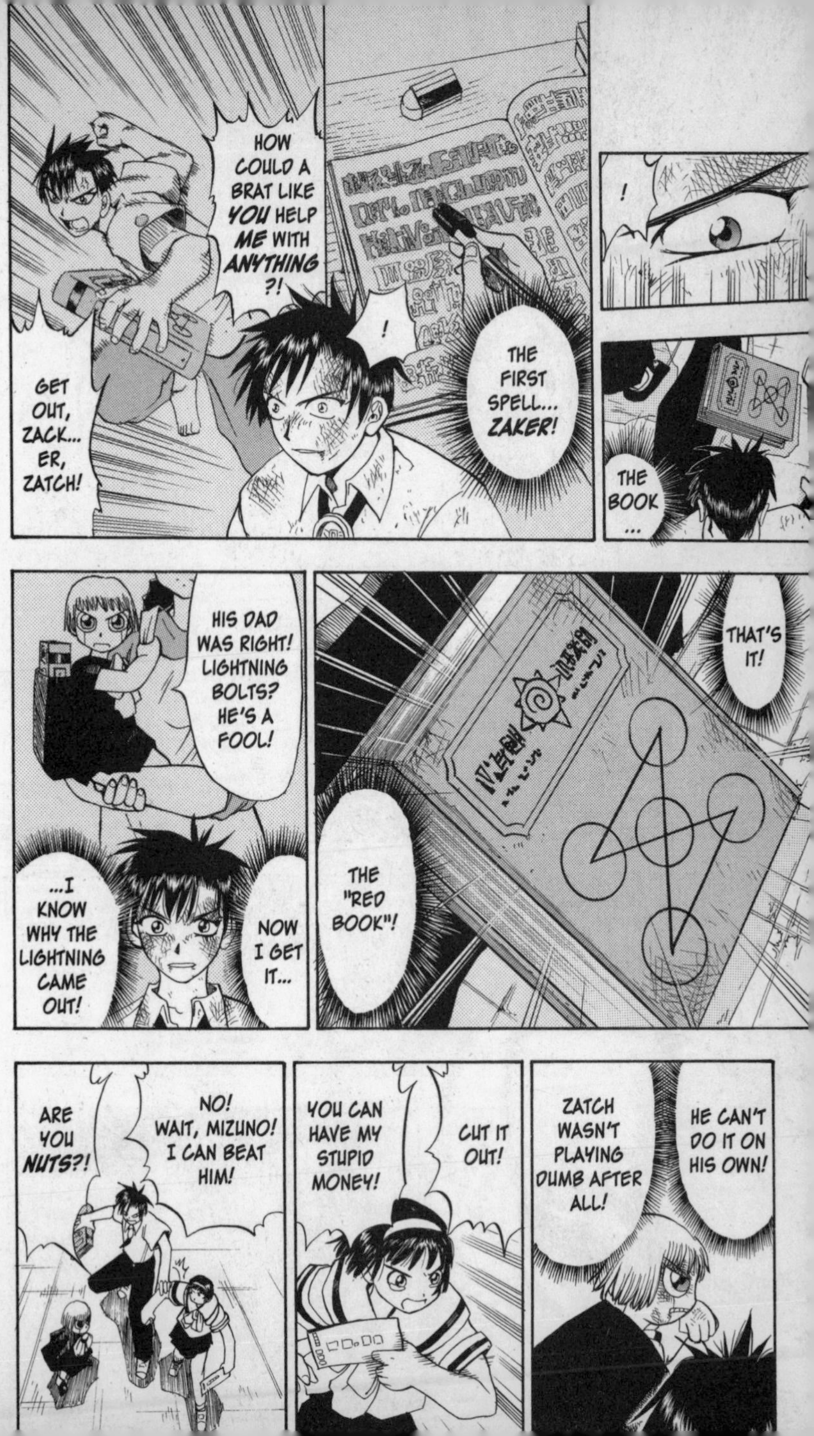
!
THE BOOK...
!
THE FIRST SPELL... ZAKER!
HOW COULD A BRAT LIKE YOU HELP ME WITH ANYTHING?!
GET OUT, ZACK... ER, ZATCH!
THAT'S IT!
THE "RED BOOK"!
HIS DAD WAS RIGHT! LIGHTNING BOLTS? HE'S A FOOL!
NOW I GET IT...
...I KNOW WHY THE LIGHTNING CAME OUT!
HE CAN'T DO IT ON HIS OWN!
ZATCH WASN'T PLAYING DUMB AFTER ALL!
CUT IT OUT!
YOU CAN HAVE MY STUPID MONEY!
NO! WAIT, MIZUNO! I CAN BEAT HIM!
ARE YOU NUTS?!

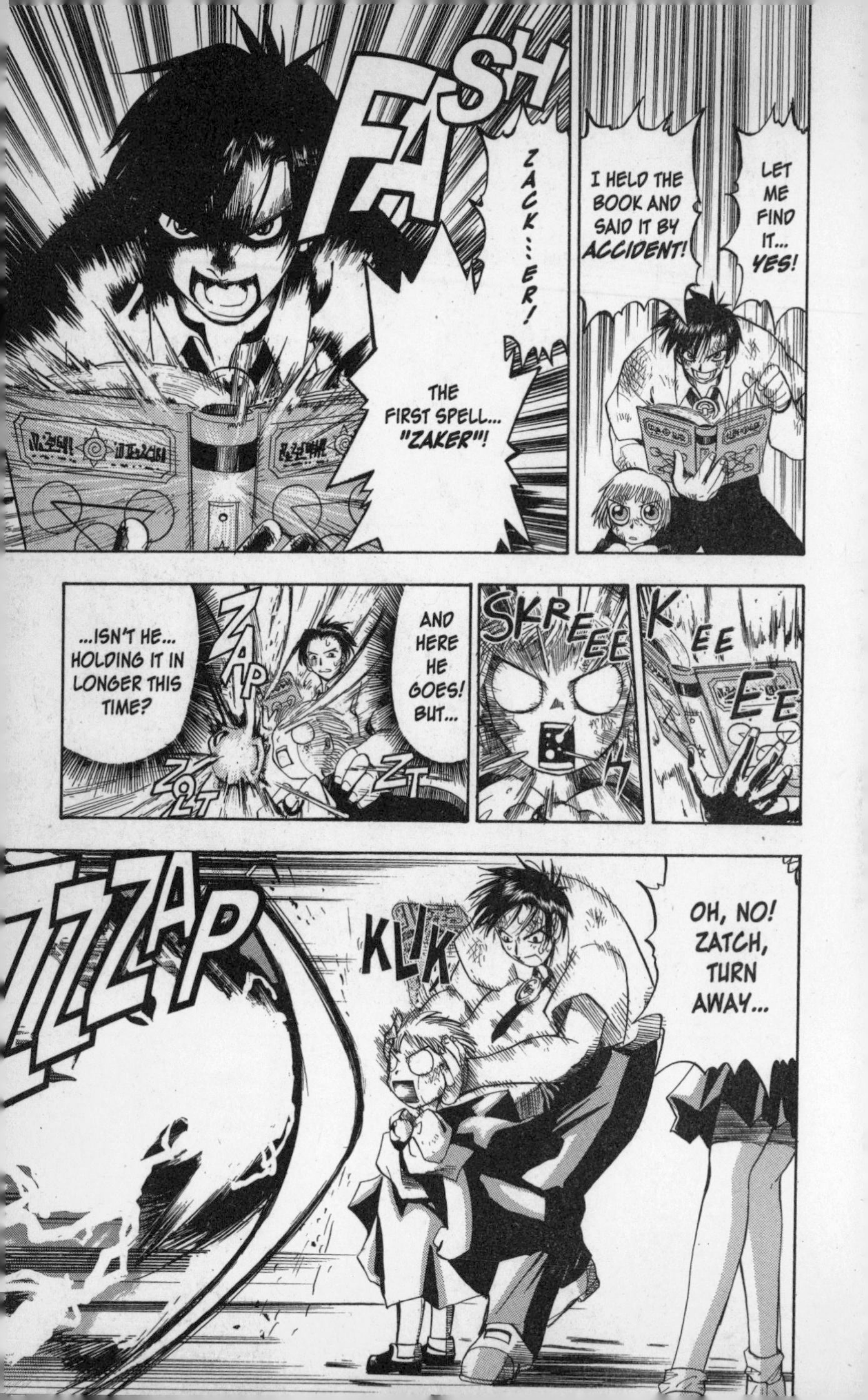
LET ME FIND IT... YES!
I HELD THE BOOK AND SAID IT BY ACCIDENT!
FASH
ZACK... ER!
THE FIRST SPELL... "ZAKER"!
ZAAA
K EE EE
SKREEEE
AND HERE HE GOES! BUT...
...ISN'T HE... HOLDING IT IN LONGER THIS TIME?
ZAP
ZOLT
ZT
OH, NO! ZATCH, TURN AWAY...
KLIK
ZZZAP

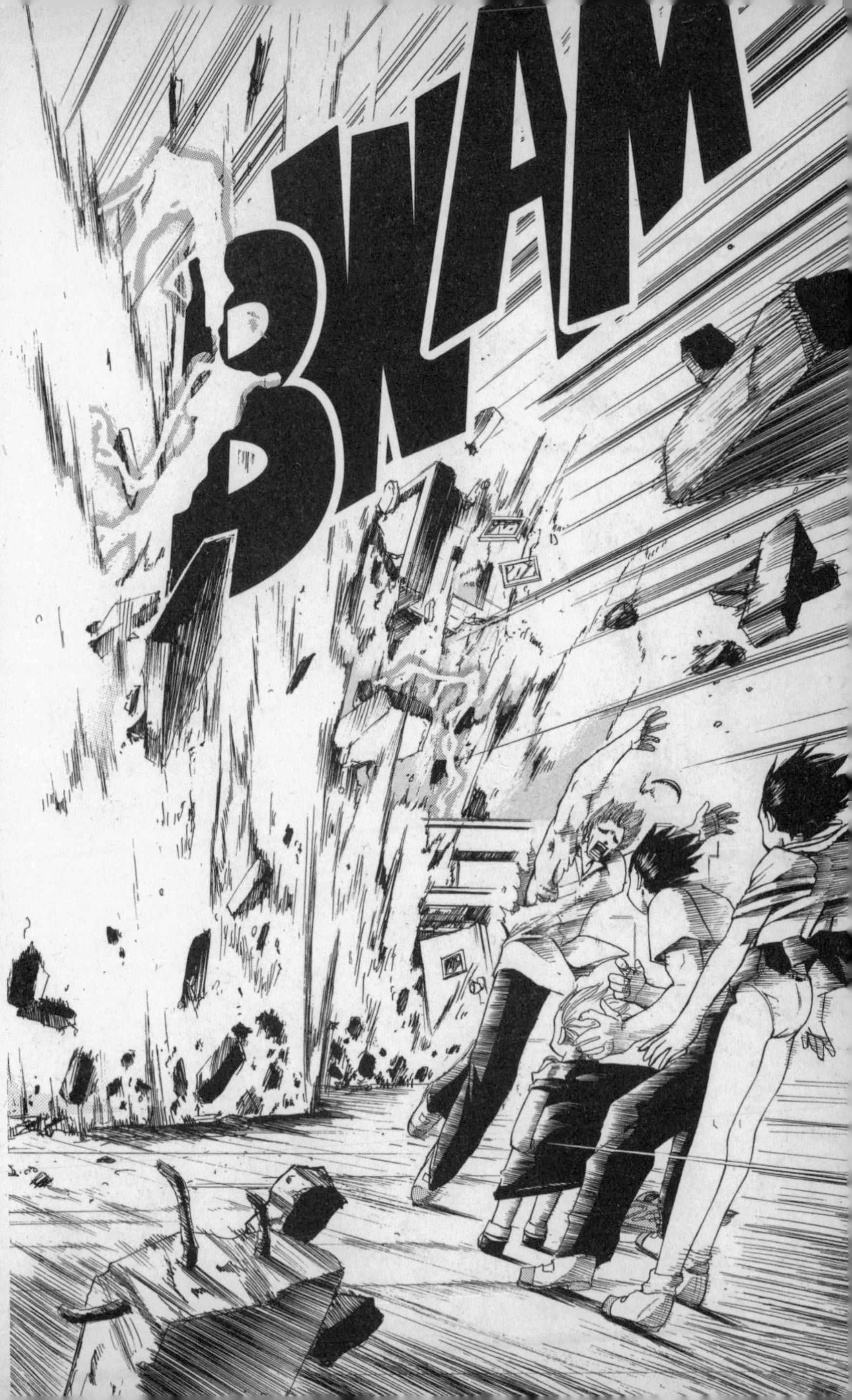
BWAM

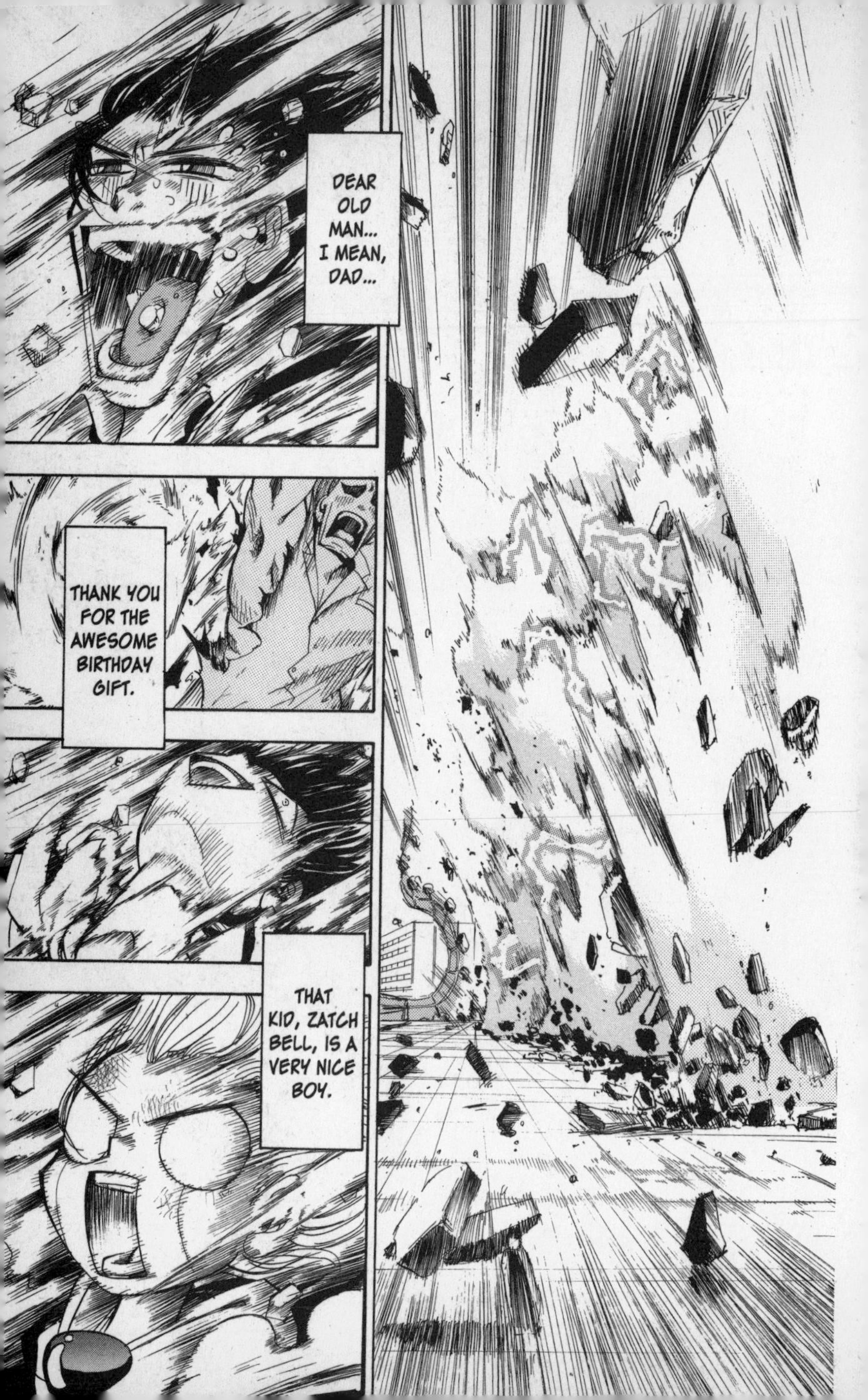
DEAR OLD MAN... I MEAN, DAD...
THANK YOU FOR THE AWESOME BIRTHDAY GIFT.
THAT KID, ZATCH BELL, IS A VERY NICE BOY.

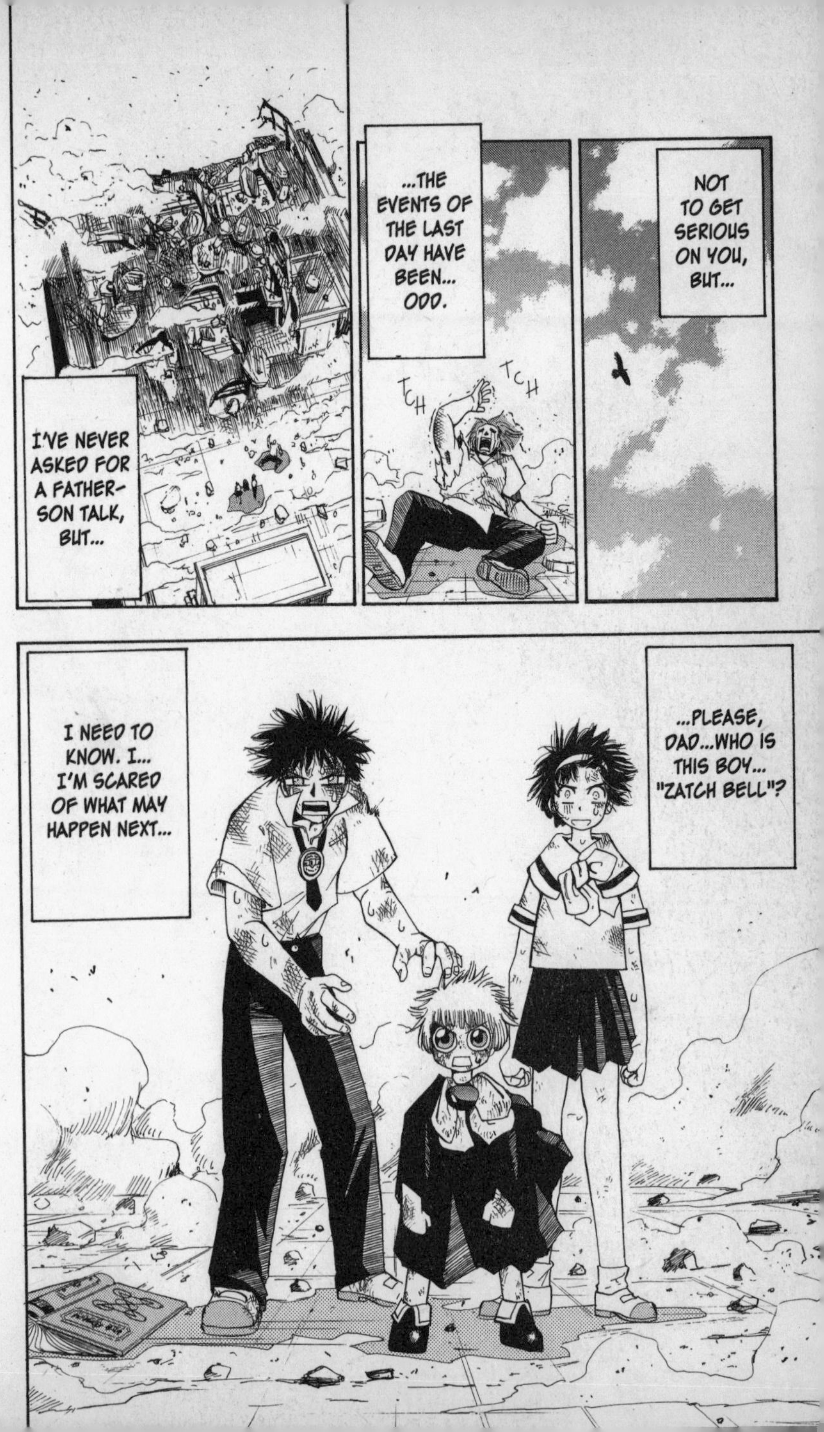
NOT TO GET SERIOUS ON YOU, BUT...
...THE EVENTS OF THE LAST DAY HAVE BEEN... ODD.
TCH
TCH
I'VE NEVER ASKED FOR A FATHER-SON TALK, BUT...
...PLEASE, DAD...WHO IS THIS BOY... "ZATCH BELL"?
I NEED TO KNOW. I... I'M SCARED OF WHAT MAY HAPPEN NEXT...

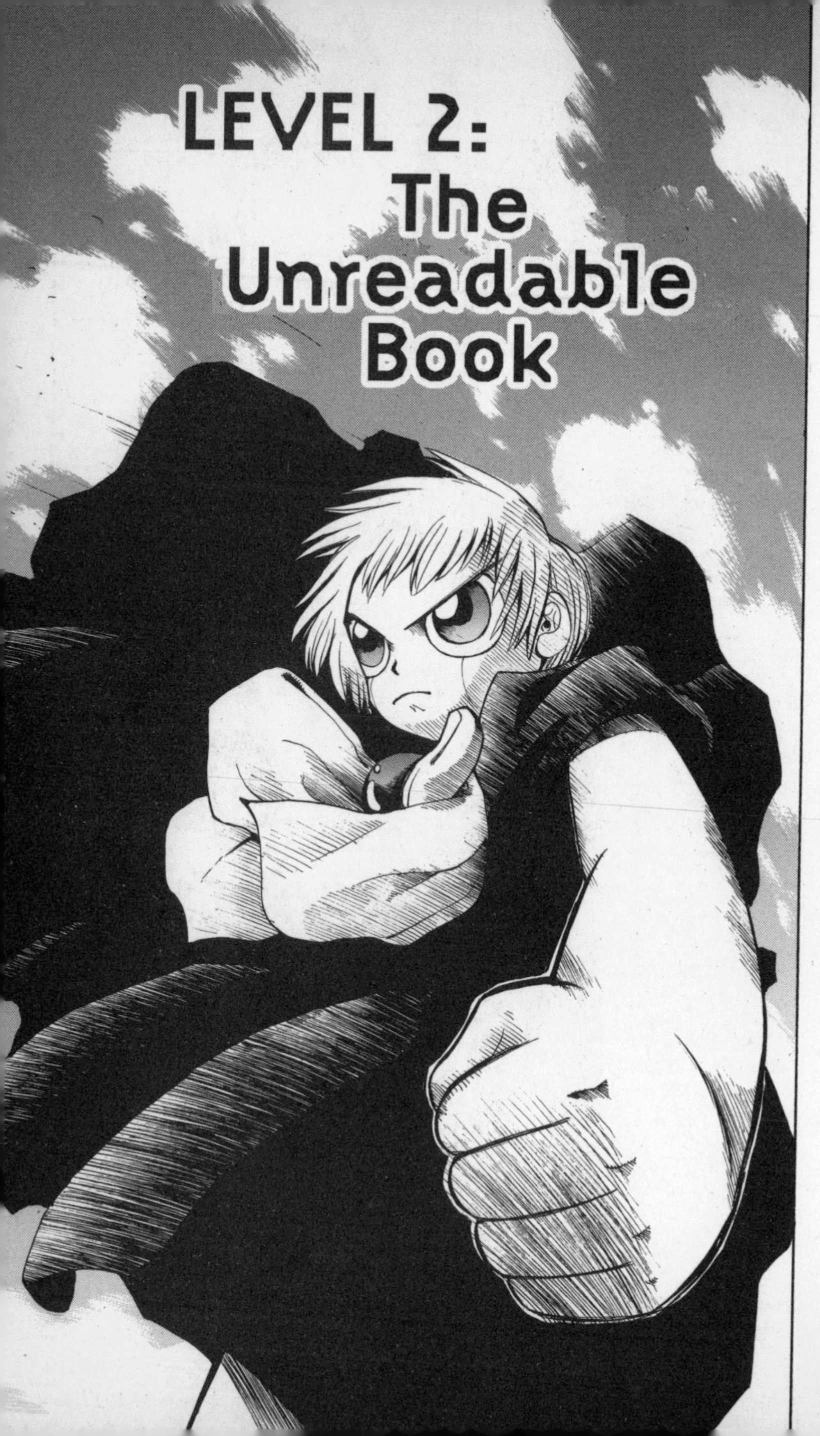
LEVEL 2:
The Unreadable Book

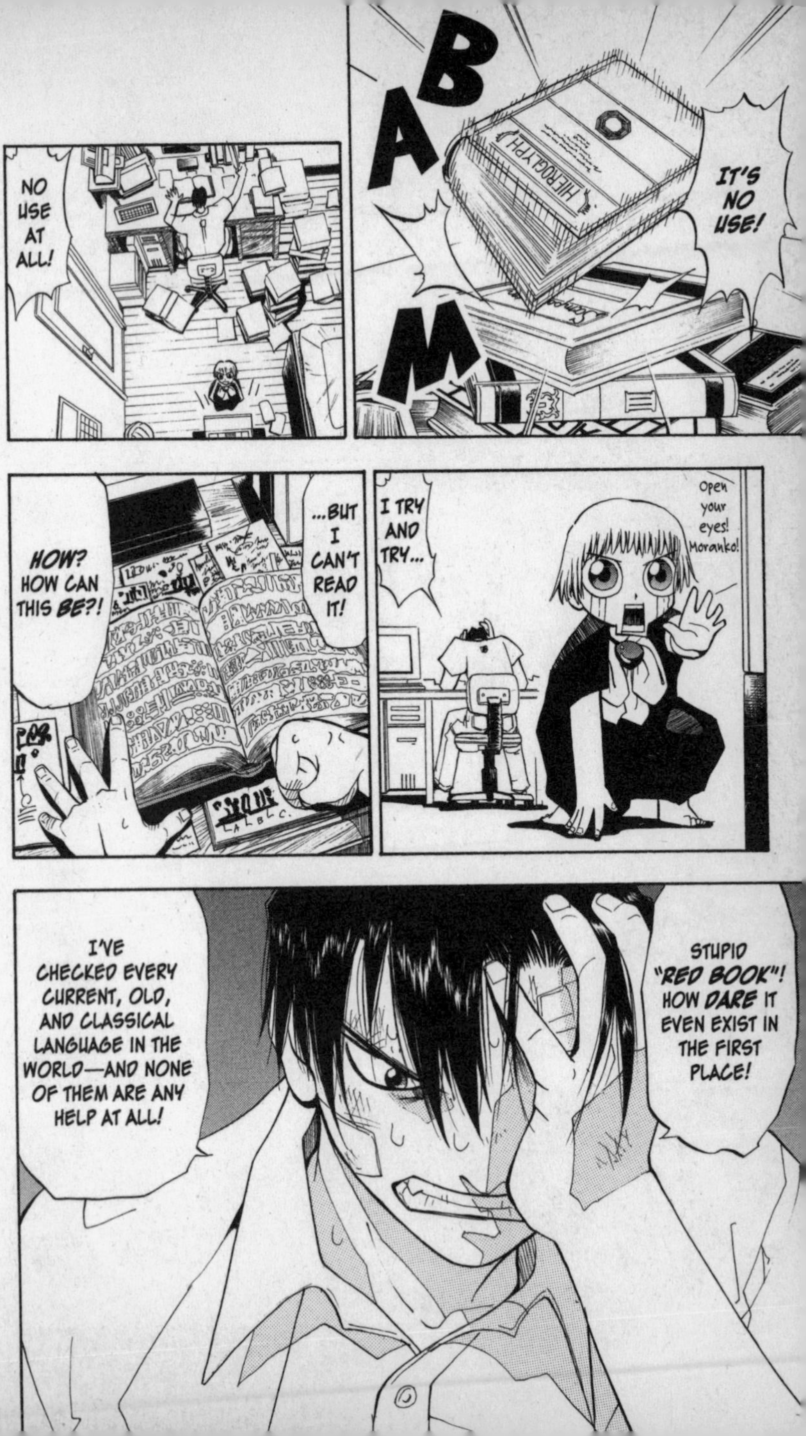
BAM
HIEROGLYPH
IT'S NO USE!
NO USE AT ALL!
Open your eyes! Moranko!
I TRY AND TRY...
...BUT I CAN'T READ IT!
HOW? HOW CAN THIS BE?!
STUPID "RED BOOK"! HOW DARE IT EVEN EXIST IN THE FIRST PLACE!
I'VE CHECKED EVERY CURRENT, OLD, AND CLASSICAL LANGUAGE IN THE WORLD—AND NONE OF THEM ARE ANY HELP AT ALL!

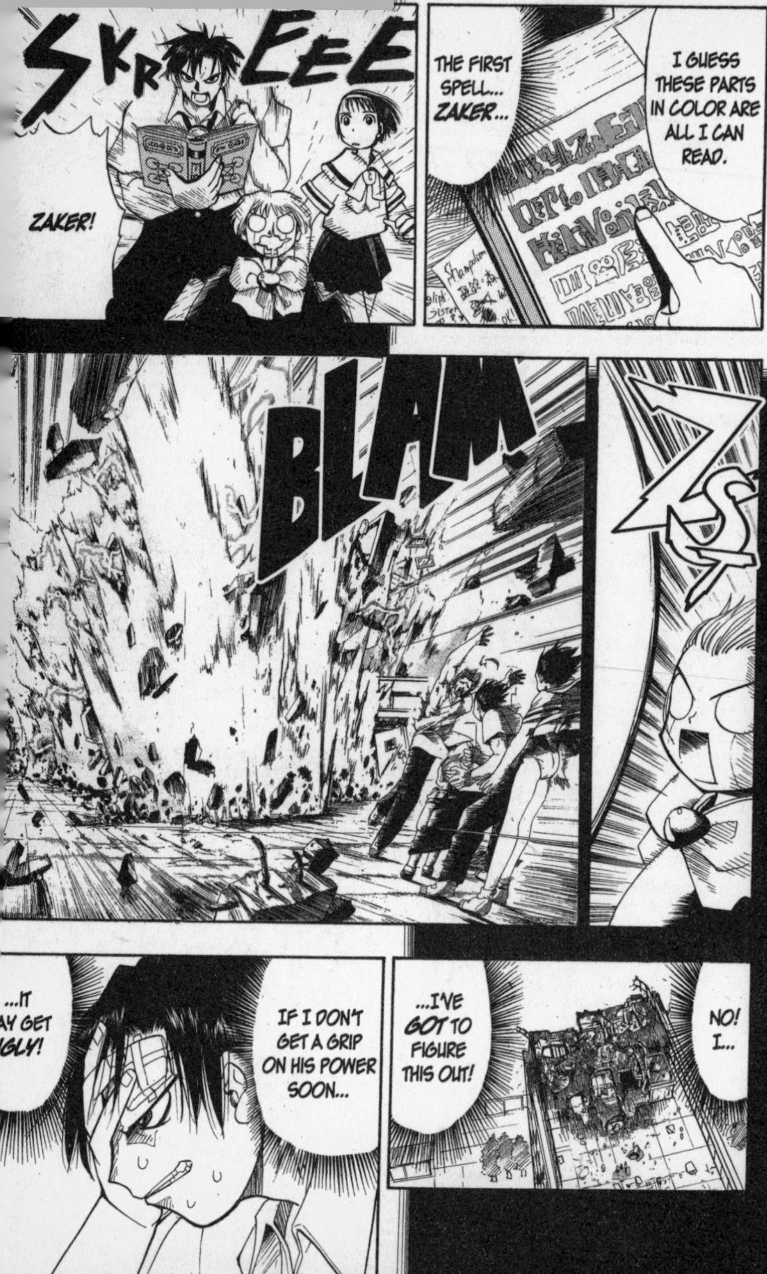

I GUESS THESE PARTS IN COLOR ARE ALL I CAN READ.
THE FIRST SPELL... ZAKER...
SKREEE
ZAKER!
BLAM
NO! I...
...I'VE GOT TO FIGURE THIS OUT!
IF I DON'T GET A GRIP ON HIS POWER SOON...
...IT AY GET GLY!

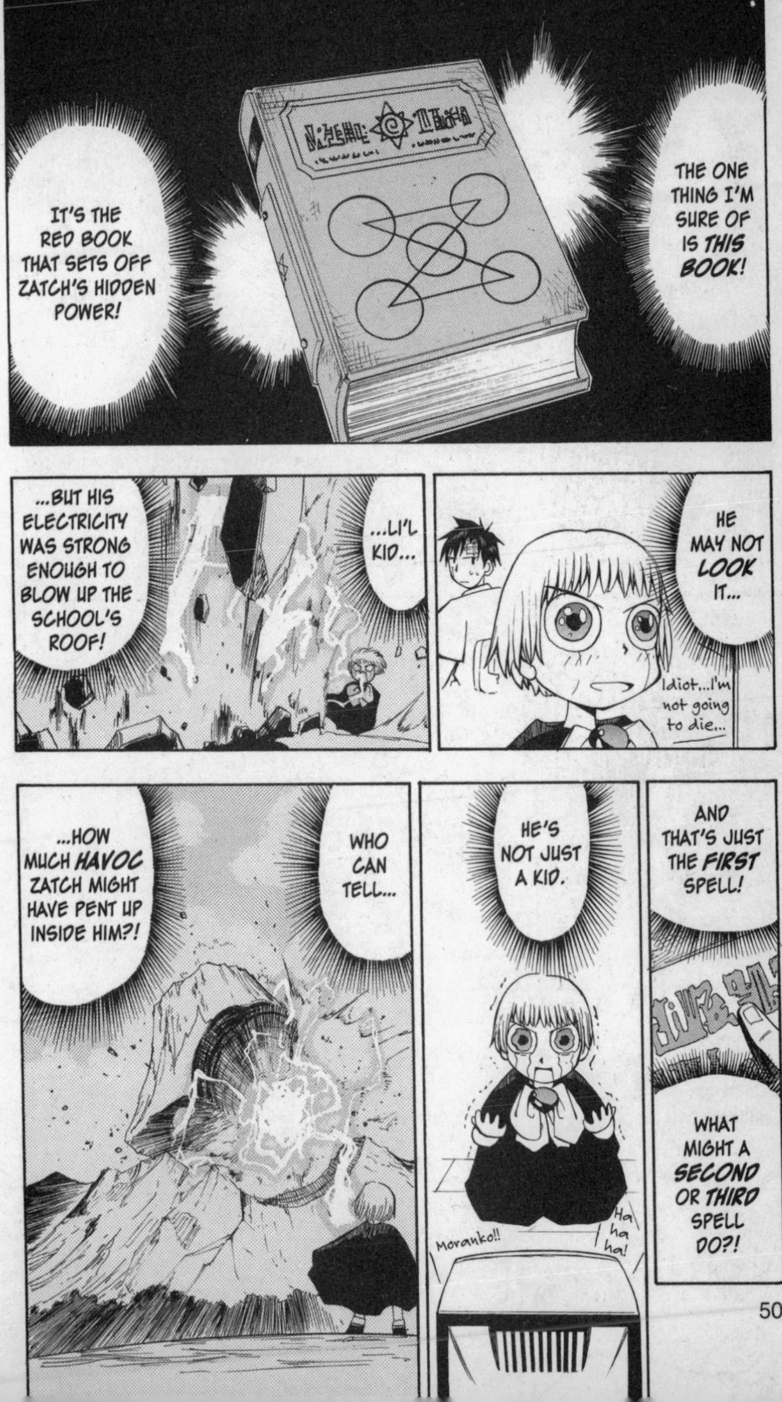
THE ONE THING I'M SURE OF IS THIS BOOK!
IT'S THE RED BOOK THAT SETS OFF ZATCH'S HIDDEN POWER!
HE MAY NOT LOOK IT...
Idiot...I'm not going to die...
...LI'L KID...
...BUT HIS ELECTRICITY WAS STRONG ENOUGH TO BLOW UP THE SCHOOL'S ROOF!
AND THAT'S JUST THE FIRST SPELL!
WHAT MIGHT A SECOND OR THIRD SPELL DO?!
HE'S NOT JUST A KID.
Ha ha ha!
Moranko!!
WHO CAN TELL...
...HOW MUCH HAVOC ZATCH MIGHT HAVE PENT UP INSIDE HIM?!

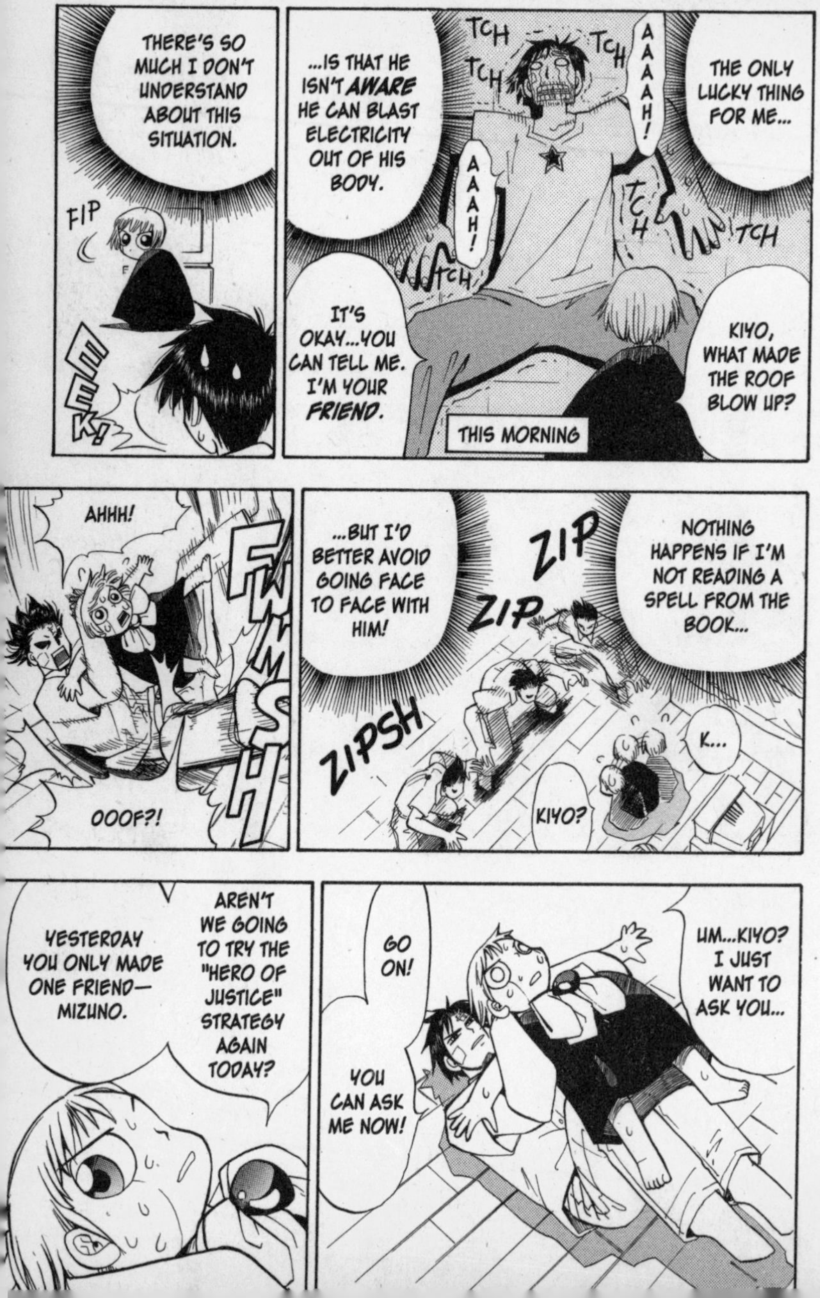
THE ONLY LUCKY THING FOR ME...
AAAAAH!
TCH
TCH
TCH
...IS THAT HE ISN'T AWARE HE CAN BLAST ELECTRICITY OUT OF HIS BODY.
AAAH!
TCH
TCH
TCH
KIYO, WHAT MADE THE ROOF BLOW UP?
IT'S OKAY...YOU CAN TELL ME. I'M YOUR FRIEND.
THIS MORNING
THERE'S SO MUCH I DON'T UNDERSTAND ABOUT THIS SITUATION.
FIP
EEEK!
NOTHING HAPPENS IF I'M NOT READING A SPELL FROM THE BOOK...
ZIP
...BUT I'D BETTER AVOID GOING FACE TO FACE WITH HIM!
ZIP
ZIPSH
K...
KIYO?
AHHH!
FWUMSH
OOOF?!
UM...KIYO? I JUST WANT TO ASK YOU...
GO ON!
YOU CAN ASK ME NOW!
AREN'T WE GOING TO TRY THE "HERO OF JUSTICE" STRATEGY AGAIN TODAY?
YESTERDAY YOU ONLY MADE ONE FRIEND—MIZUNO.

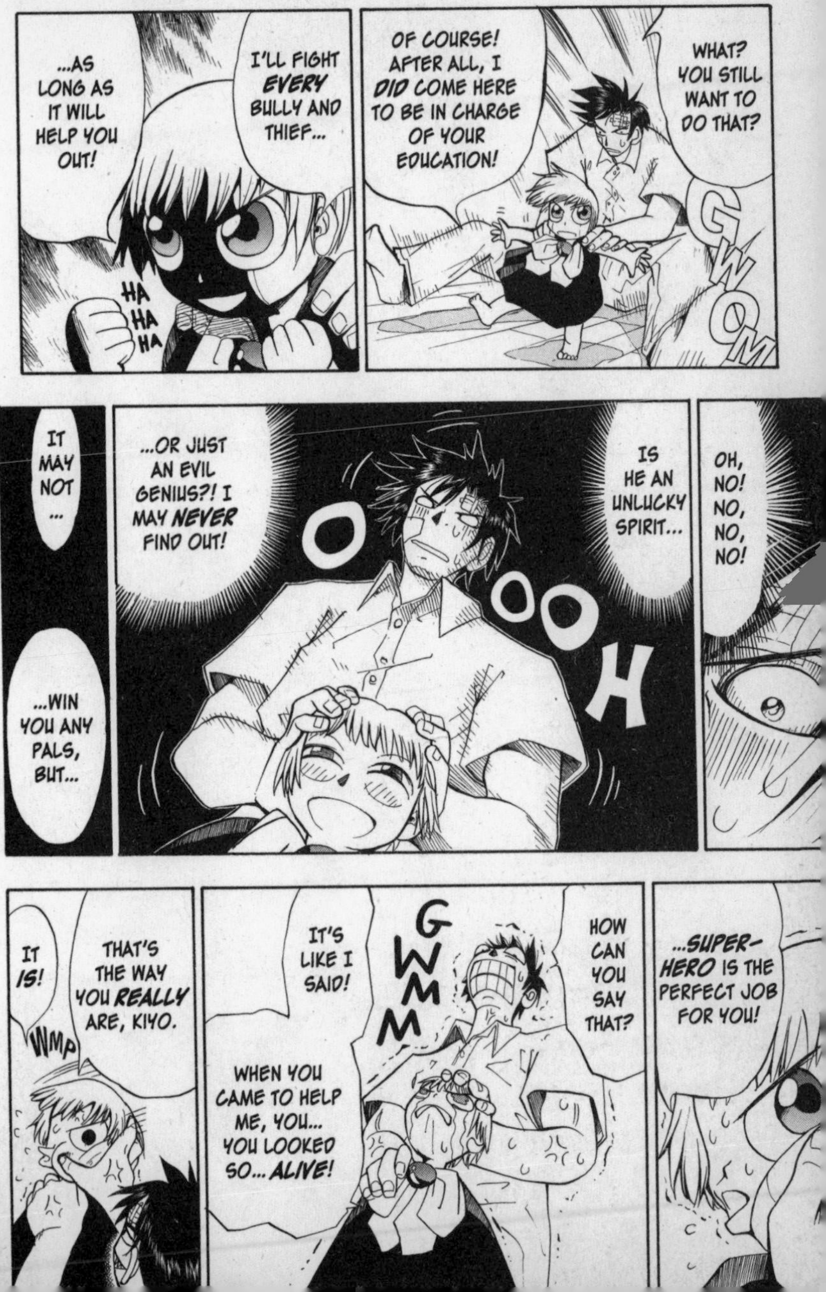
WHAT? YOU STILL WANT TO DO THAT?
GWOM
OF COURSE! AFTER ALL, I DID COME HERE TO BE IN CHARGE OF YOUR EDUCATION!
I'LL FIGHT EVERY BULLY AND THIEF...
...AS LONG AS IT WILL HELP YOU OUT!
HA HA HA
OH, NO! NO, NO, NO!
IS HE AN UNLUCKY SPIRIT...
...OR JUST AN EVIL GENIUS?! I MAY NEVER FIND OUT!
OOOH
IT MAY NOT ...
...WIN YOU ANY PALS, BUT...
...SUPER-HERO IS THE PERFECT JOB FOR YOU!
HOW CAN YOU SAY THAT?
GWMM
IT'S LIKE I SAID!
WHEN YOU CAME TO HELP ME, YOU... YOU LOOKED SO... ALIVE!
THAT'S THE WAY YOU REALLY ARE, KIYO.
IT IS!
WMP

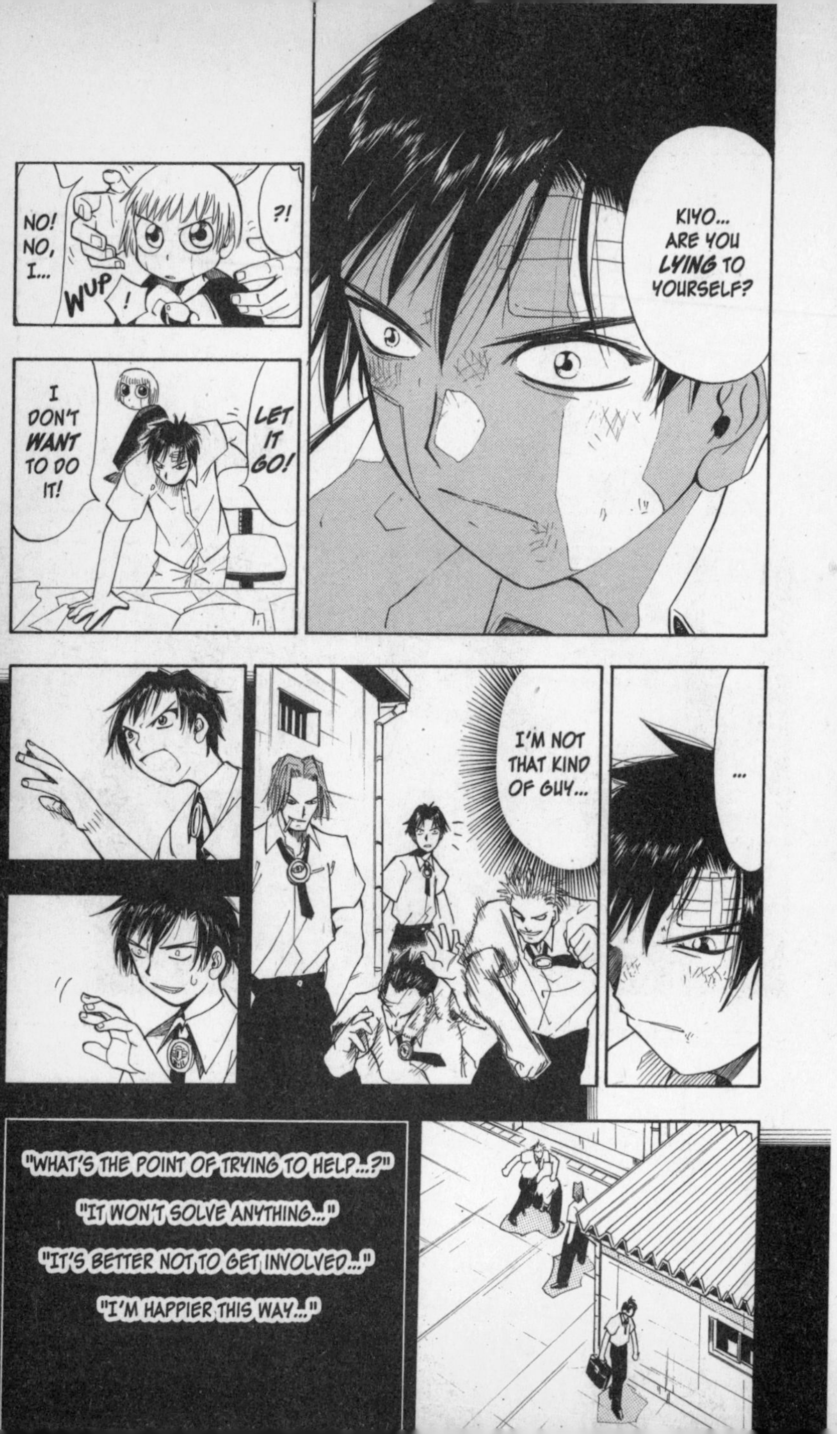
KIYO... ARE YOU LYING TO YOURSELF?
?!
NO! NO, I...
!
WUP
LET IT GO!
I DON'T WANT TO DO IT!
...
I'M NOT THAT KIND OF GUY...
"WHAT'S THE POINT OF TRYING TO HELP...?"
"IT WON'T SOLVE ANYTHING..."
"IT'S BETTER NOT TO GET INVOLVED..."
"I'M HAPPIER THIS WAY..."

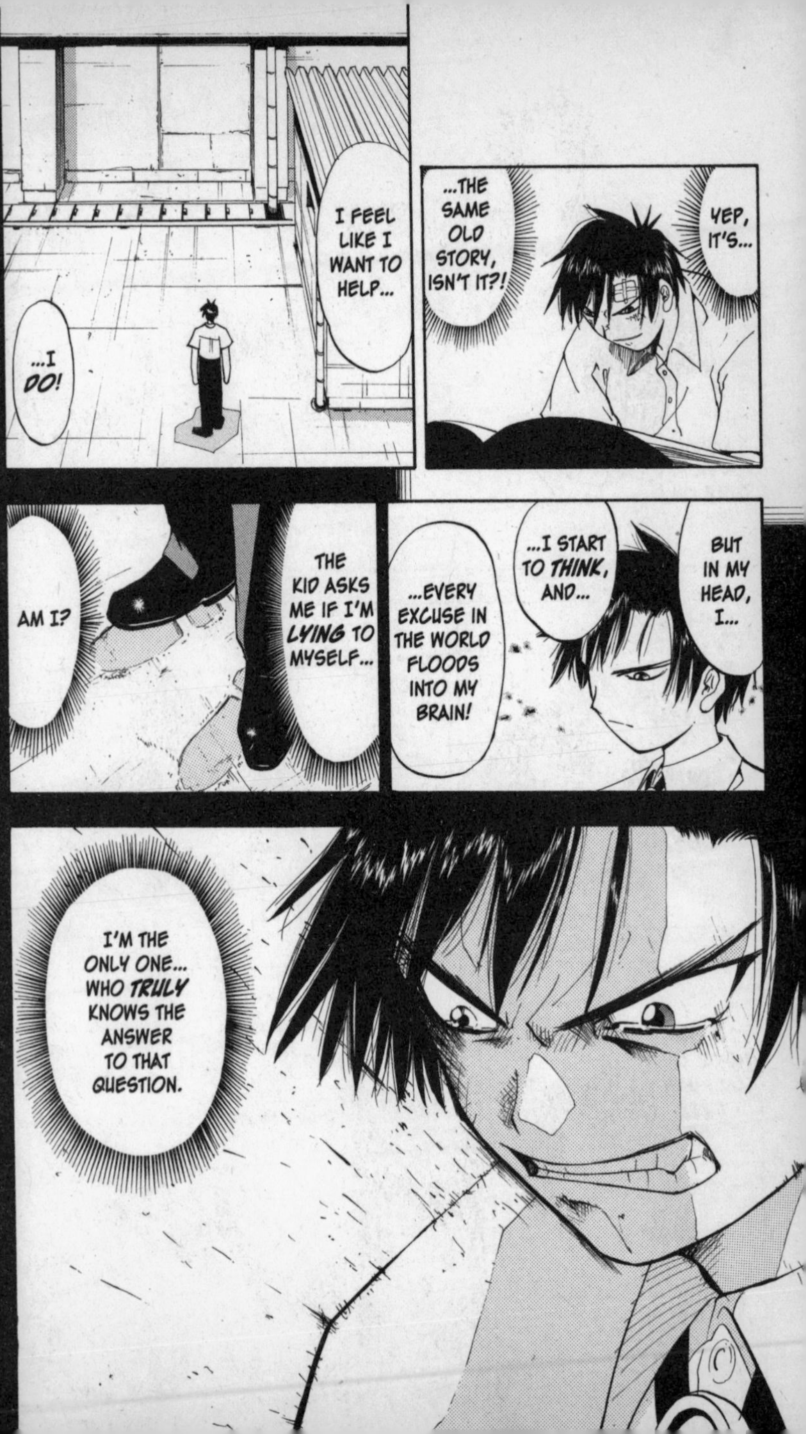
YEP, IT'S...
...THE SAME OLD STORY, ISN'T IT?!
I FEEL LIKE I WANT TO HELP...
...I *DO*!
BUT IN MY HEAD, I...
...I START TO *THINK*, AND...
...EVERY EXCUSE IN THE WORLD FLOODS INTO MY BRAIN!
THE KID ASKS ME IF I'M *LYING* TO MYSELF...
AM I?
I'M THE ONLY ONE... WHO *TRULY* KNOWS THE ANSWER TO THAT QUESTION.

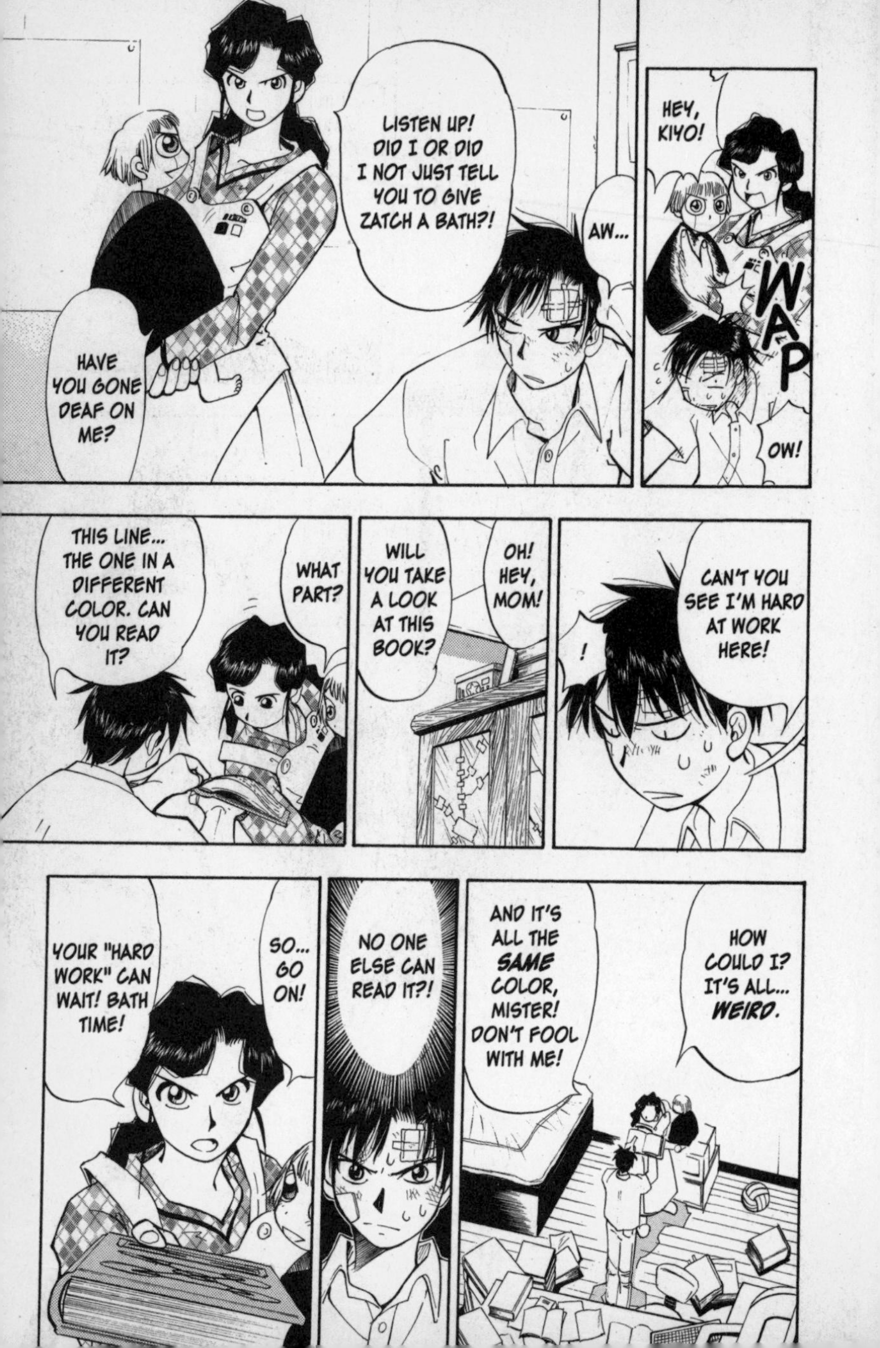
HEY, KIYO!
WAP
OW!
AW...
LISTEN UP! DID I OR DID I NOT JUST TELL YOU TO GIVE ZATCH A BATH?!
HAVE YOU GONE DEAF ON ME?
CAN'T YOU SEE I'M HARD AT WORK HERE!
!
OH! HEY, MOM!
WILL YOU TAKE A LOOK AT THIS BOOK?
WHAT PART?
THIS LINE... THE ONE IN A DIFFERENT COLOR. CAN YOU READ IT?
HOW COULD I? IT'S ALL... **WEIRD**.
AND IT'S ALL THE **SAME** COLOR, MISTER! DON'T FOOL WITH ME!
NO ONE ELSE CAN READ IT?!
SO... GO ON!
YOUR "HARD WORK" CAN WAIT! BATH TIME!

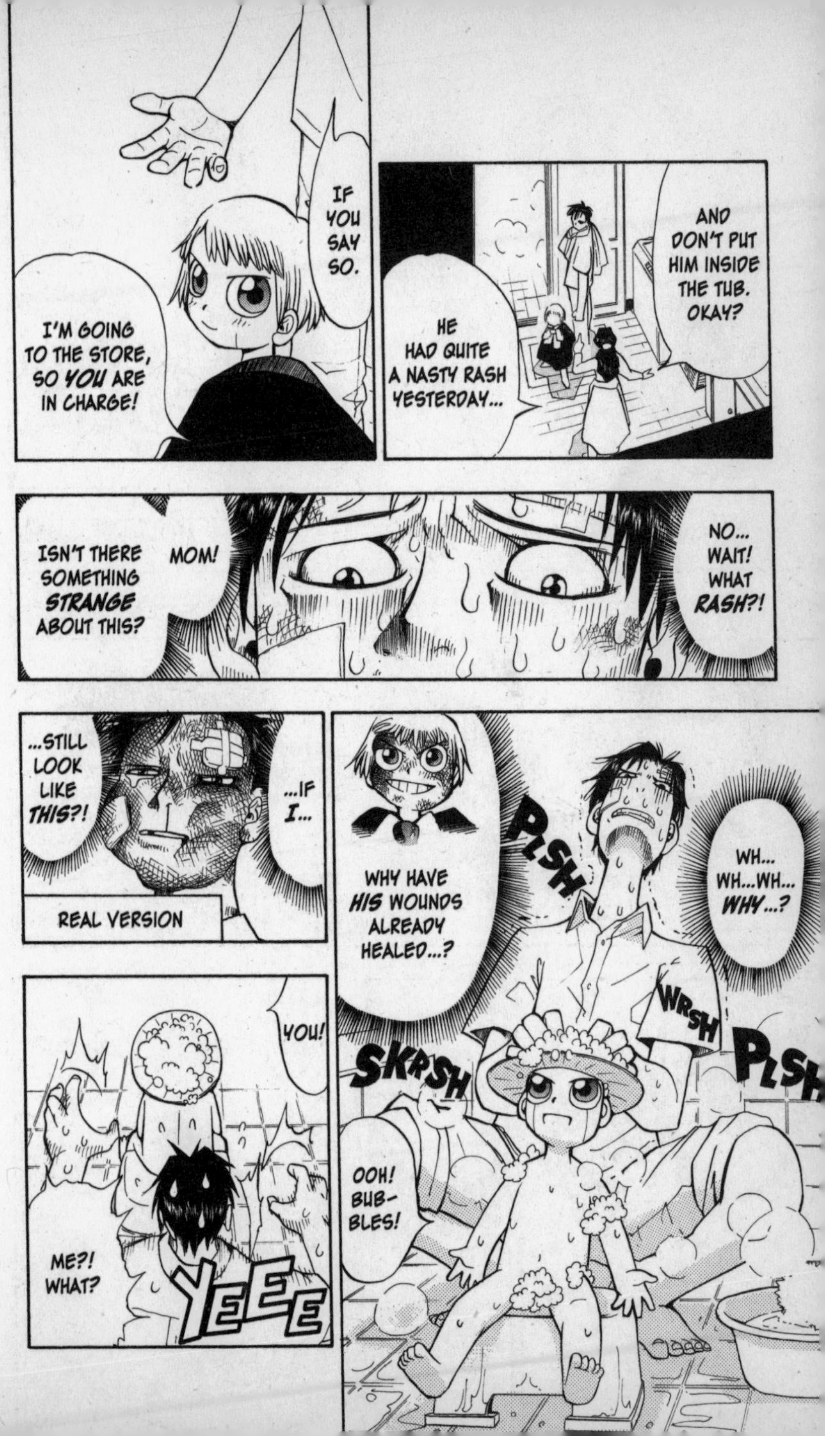
AND DON'T PUT HIM INSIDE THE TUB. OKAY?
HE HAD QUITE A NASTY RASH YESTERDAY...
IF YOU SAY SO.
I'M GOING TO THE STORE, SO YOU ARE IN CHARGE!
NO... WAIT! WHAT RASH?!
MOM!
ISN'T THERE SOMETHING STRANGE ABOUT THIS?
WH... WH...WH... WHY...?
PLSH
WHY HAVE HIS WOUNDS ALREADY HEALED...?
WRSH
PLSH
SKRSH
OOH! BUB-BLES!
...IF I...
...STILL LOOK LIKE THIS?!
REAL VERSION
YOU!
ME?! WHAT?
YEEE

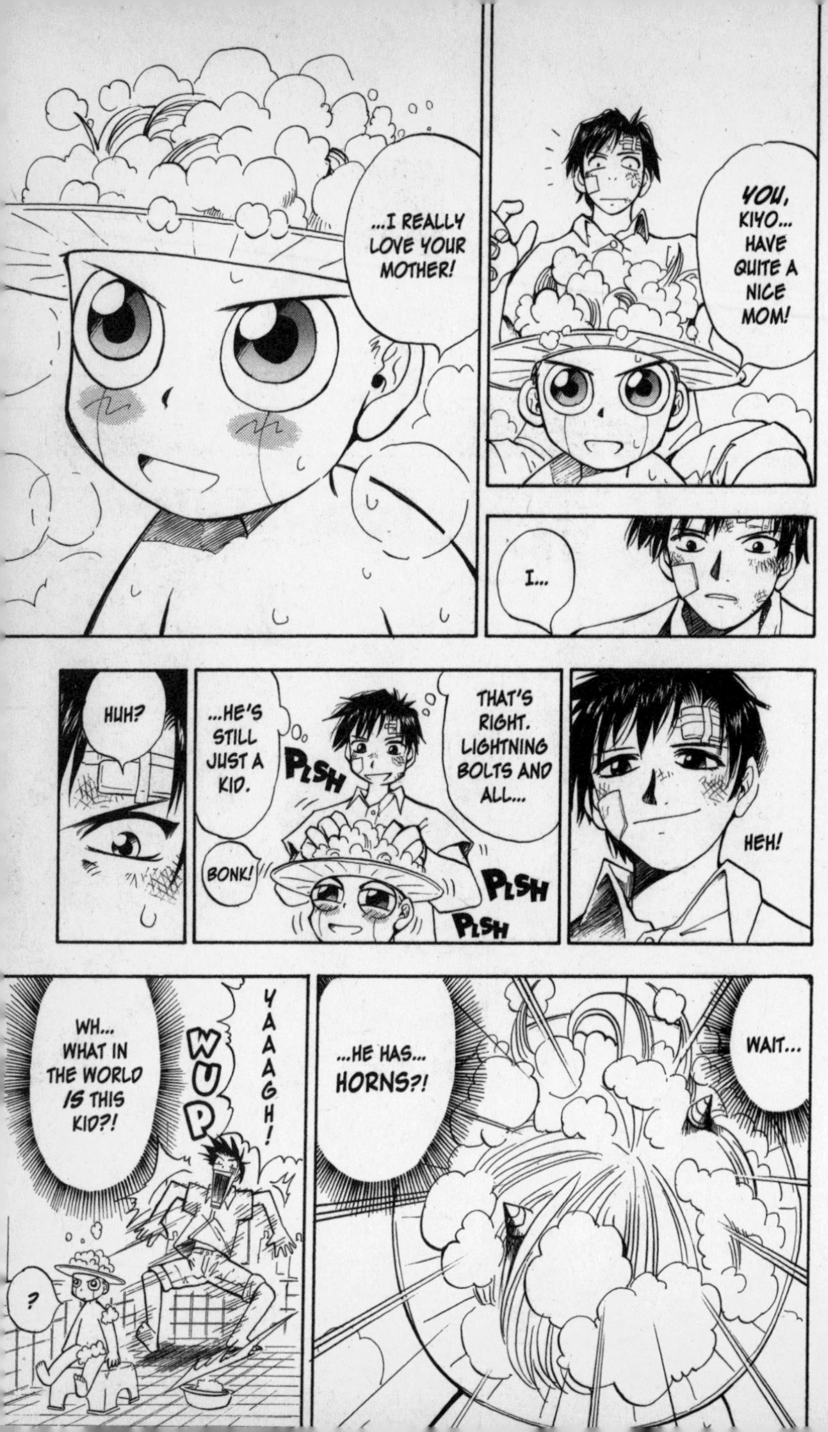
YOU, KIYO... HAVE QUITE A NICE MOM!
I...
...I REALLY LOVE YOUR MOTHER!
HEH!
THAT'S RIGHT. LIGHTNING BOLTS AND ALL...
...HE'S STILL JUST A KID.
PLSH
BONK!
PLSH
PLSH
HUH?
WAIT...
...HE HAS... HORNS?!
YAAAAGH!
WUP
WH... WHAT IN THE WORLD *IS* THIS KID?!
?

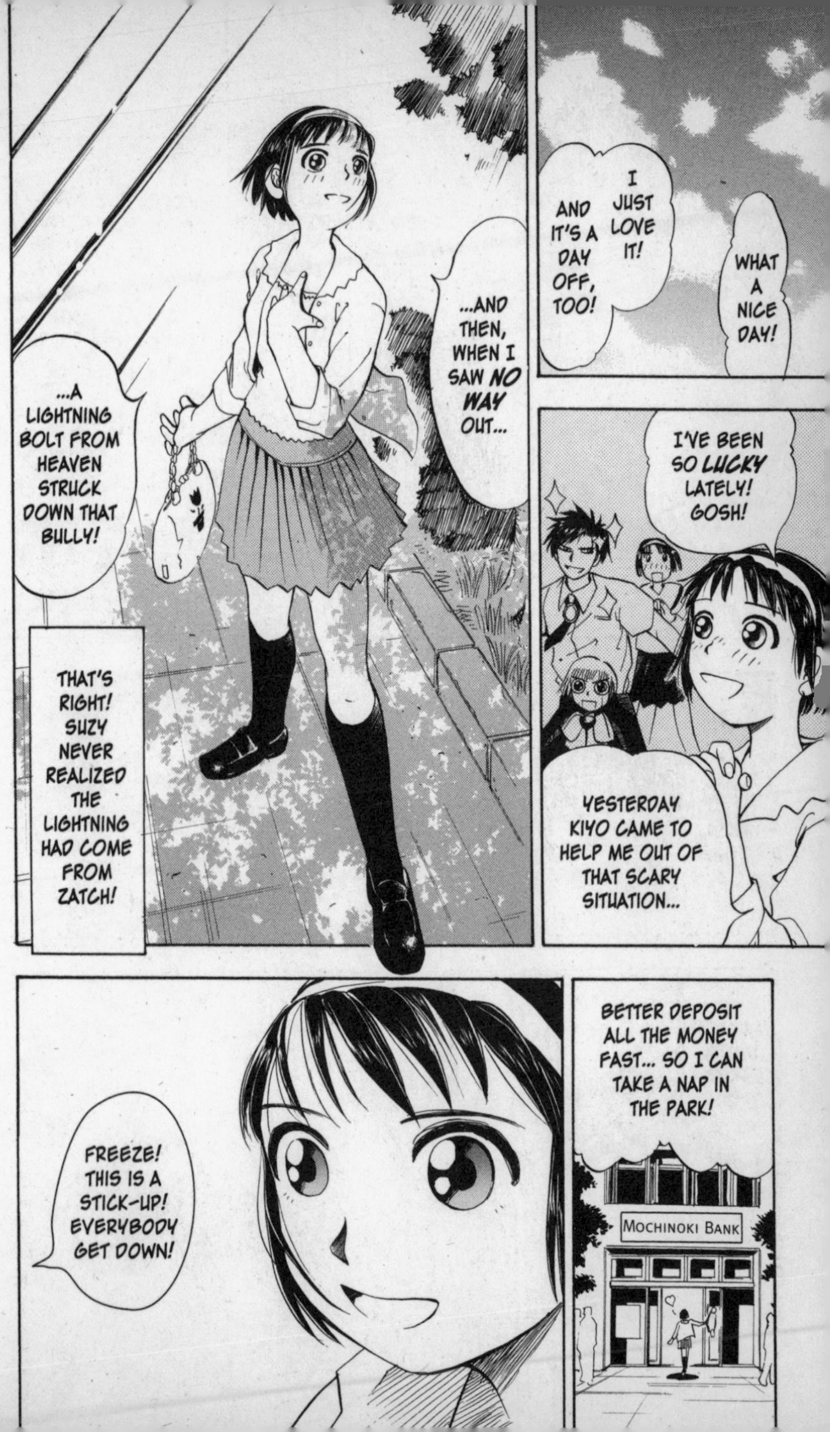
WHAT A NICE DAY!
I JUST LOVE IT!
AND IT'S A DAY OFF, TOO!
I'VE BEEN SO LUCKY LATELY! GOSH!
YESTERDAY KIYO CAME TO HELP ME OUT OF THAT SCARY SITUATION...
...AND THEN, WHEN I SAW NO WAY OUT...
...A LIGHTNING BOLT FROM HEAVEN STRUCK DOWN THAT BULLY!
THAT'S RIGHT! SUZY NEVER REALIZED THE LIGHTNING HAD COME FROM ZATCH!
BETTER DEPOSIT ALL THE MONEY FAST... SO I CAN TAKE A NAP IN THE PARK!
MOCHINOKI BANK
FREEZE! THIS IS A STICK-UP! EVERYBODY GET DOWN!

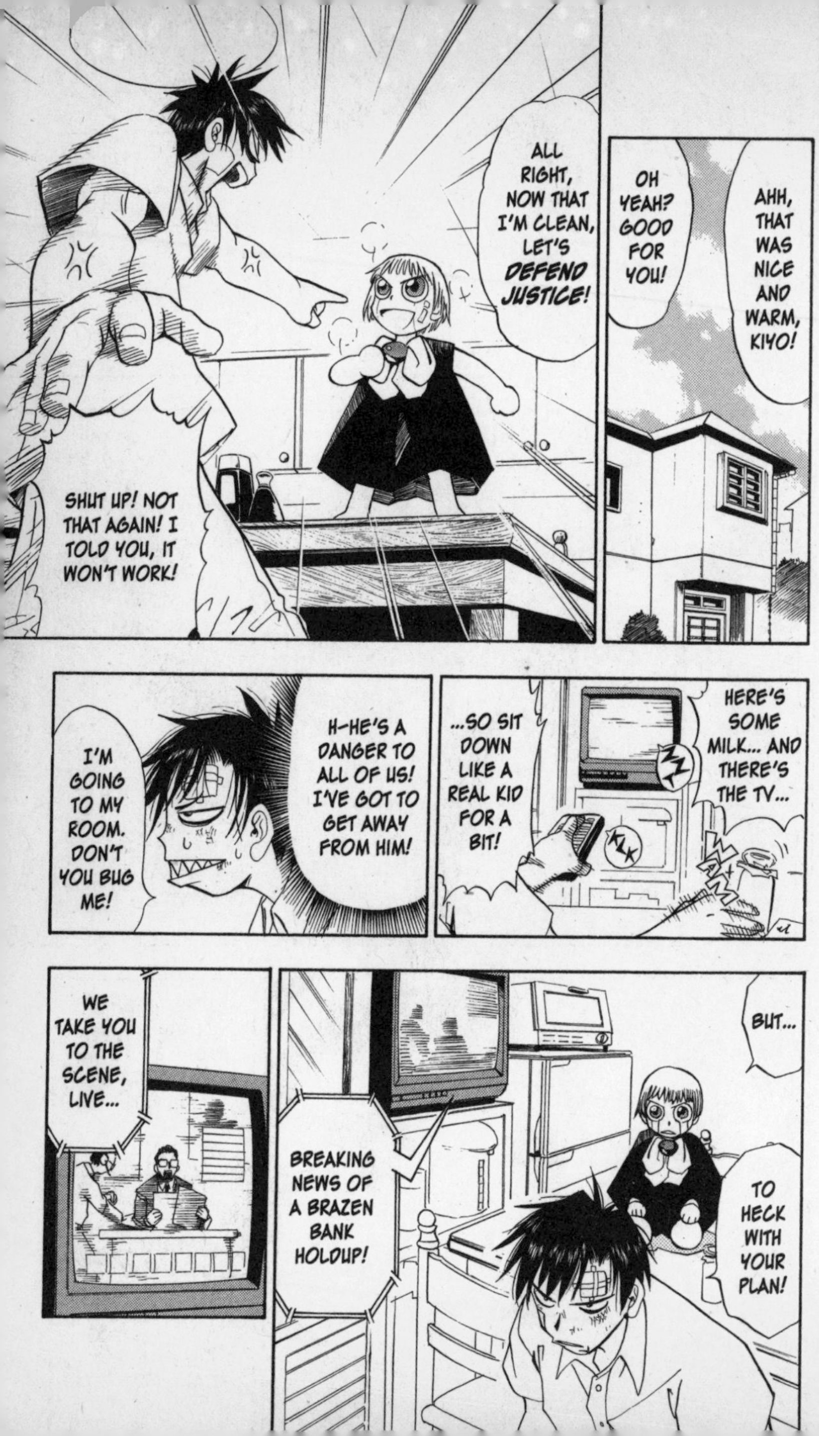
AHH, THAT WAS NICE AND WARM, KIYO!
OH YEAH? GOOD FOR YOU!
ALL RIGHT, NOW THAT I'M CLEAN, LET'S DEFEND JUSTICE!
SHUT UP! NOT THAT AGAIN! I TOLD YOU, IT WON'T WORK!
HERE'S SOME MILK... AND THERE'S THE TV...
WAM
KLK
...SO SIT DOWN LIKE A REAL KID FOR A BIT!
H-HE'S A DANGER TO ALL OF US! I'VE GOT TO GET AWAY FROM HIM!
I'M GOING TO MY ROOM. DON'T YOU BUG ME!
BUT...
TO HECK WITH YOUR PLAN!
BREAKING NEWS OF A BRAZEN BANK HOLDUP!
WE TAKE YOU TO THE SCENE, LIVE...

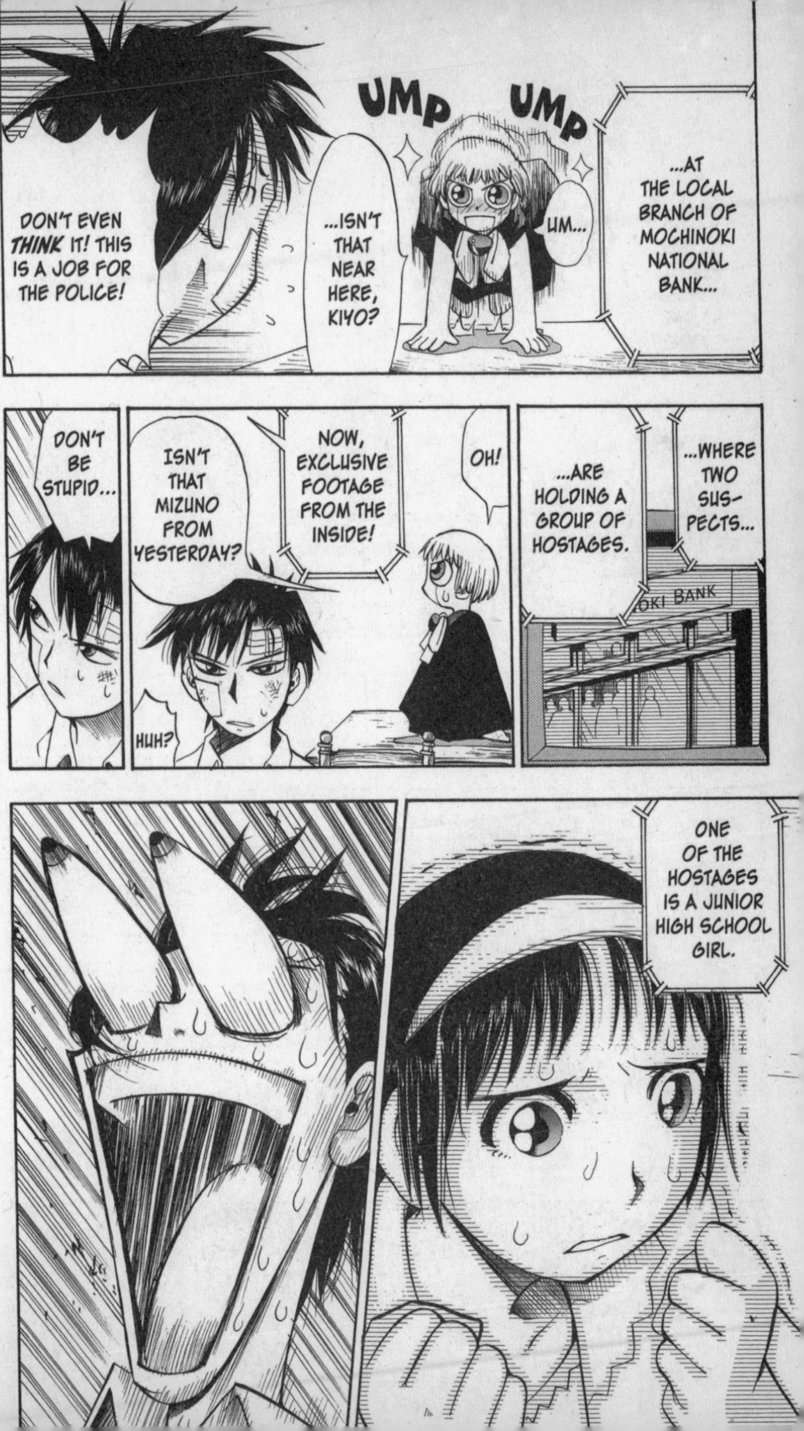
...AT THE LOCAL BRANCH OF MOCHINOKI NATIONAL BANK...
UMP UMP
UM...
...ISN'T THAT NEAR HERE, KIYO?
DON'T EVEN *THINK* IT! THIS IS A JOB FOR THE POLICE!
...WHERE TWO SUS-PECTS...
...ARE HOLDING A GROUP OF HOSTAGES.
OKI BANK
OH!
NOW, EXCLUSIVE FOOTAGE FROM THE INSIDE!
ISN'T THAT MIZUNO FROM YESTERDAY?
HUH?
DON'T BE STUPID...
ONE OF THE HOSTAGES IS A JUNIOR HIGH SCHOOL GIRL.

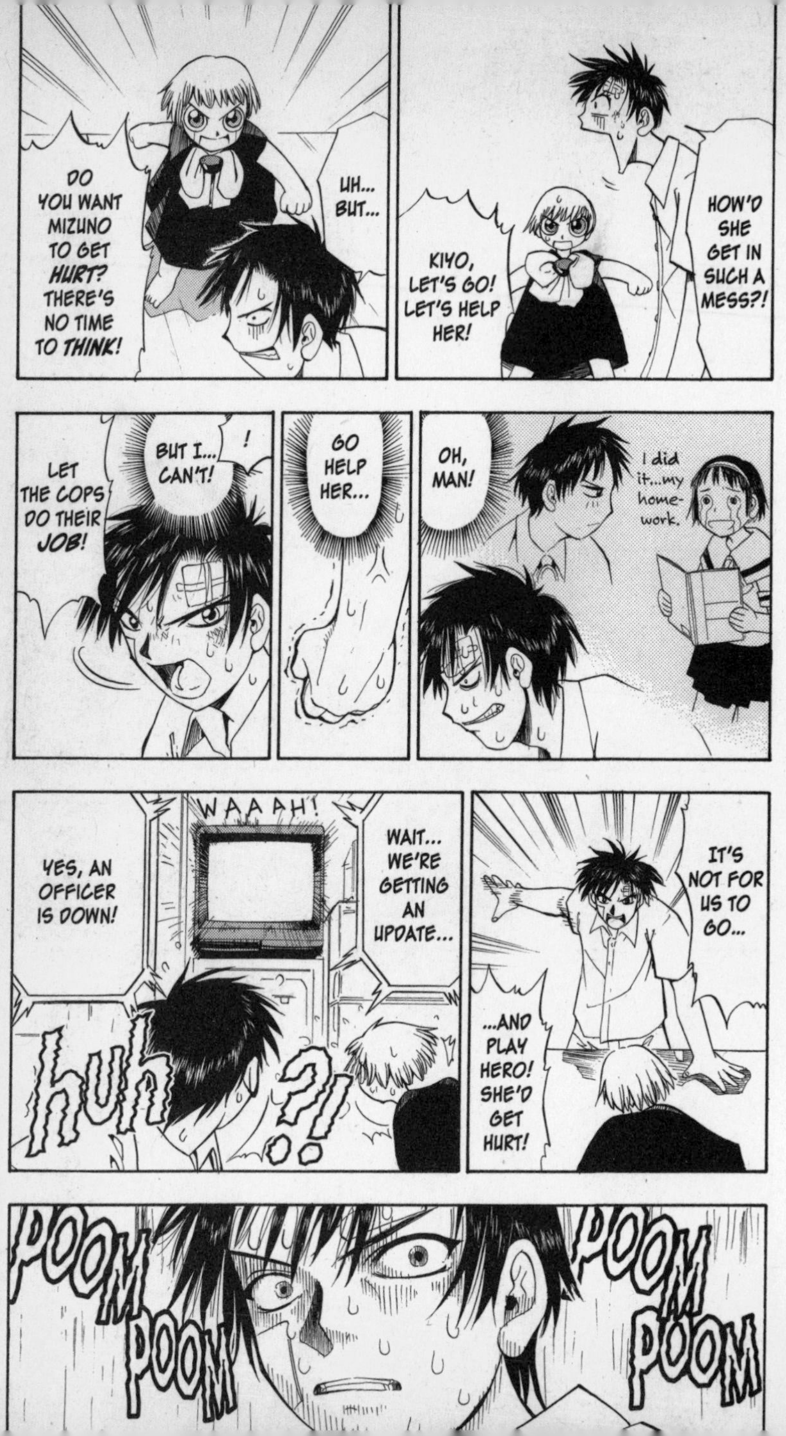

HOW'D SHE GET IN SUCH A MESS?!
KIYO, LET'S GO! LET'S HELP HER!
UH... BUT...
DO YOU WANT MIZUNO TO GET HURT? THERE'S NO TIME TO THINK!
I did it...my home-work.
OH, MAN!
GO HELP HER...
!
BUT I... CAN'T!
LET THE COPS DO THEIR JOB!
IT'S NOT FOR US TO GO...
...AND PLAY HERO! SHE'D GET HURT!
WAIT... WE'RE GETTING AN UPDATE...
WAAAH!
YES, AN OFFICER IS DOWN!
huh?!
POOM
POOM
POOM
POOM

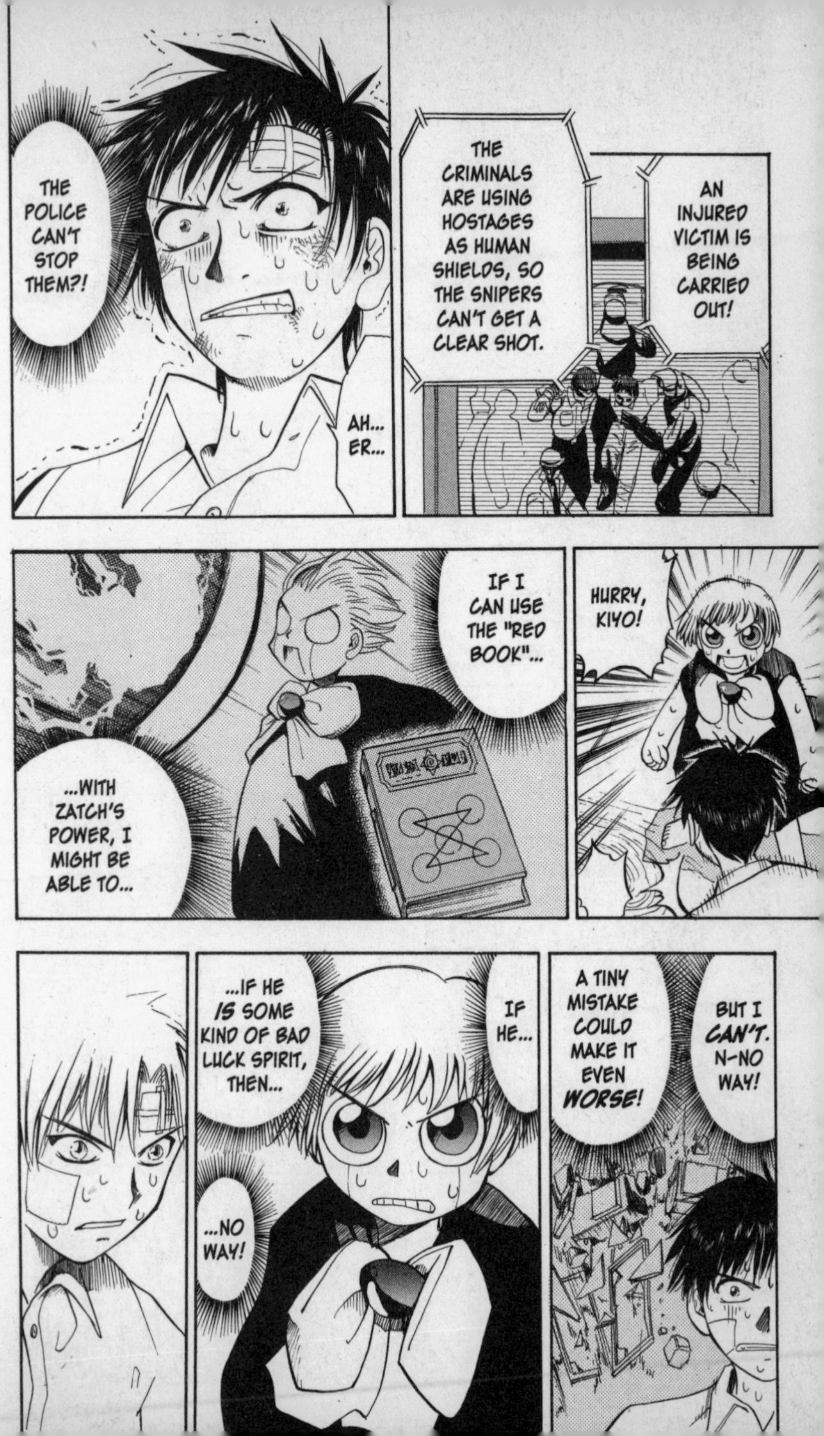
AN INJURED VICTIM IS BEING CARRIED OUT!
THE CRIMINALS ARE USING HOSTAGES AS HUMAN SHIELDS, SO THE SNIPERS CAN'T GET A CLEAR SHOT.
THE POLICE CAN'T STOP THEM?!
AH... ER...
HURRY, KIYO!
IF I CAN USE THE "RED BOOK"...
...WITH ZATCH'S POWER, I MIGHT BE ABLE TO...
BUT I *CAN'T*. N-NO WAY!
A TINY MISTAKE COULD MAKE IT EVEN *WORSE*!
IF HE...
...IF HE *IS* SOME KIND OF BAD LUCK SPIRIT, THEN...
...NO WAY!

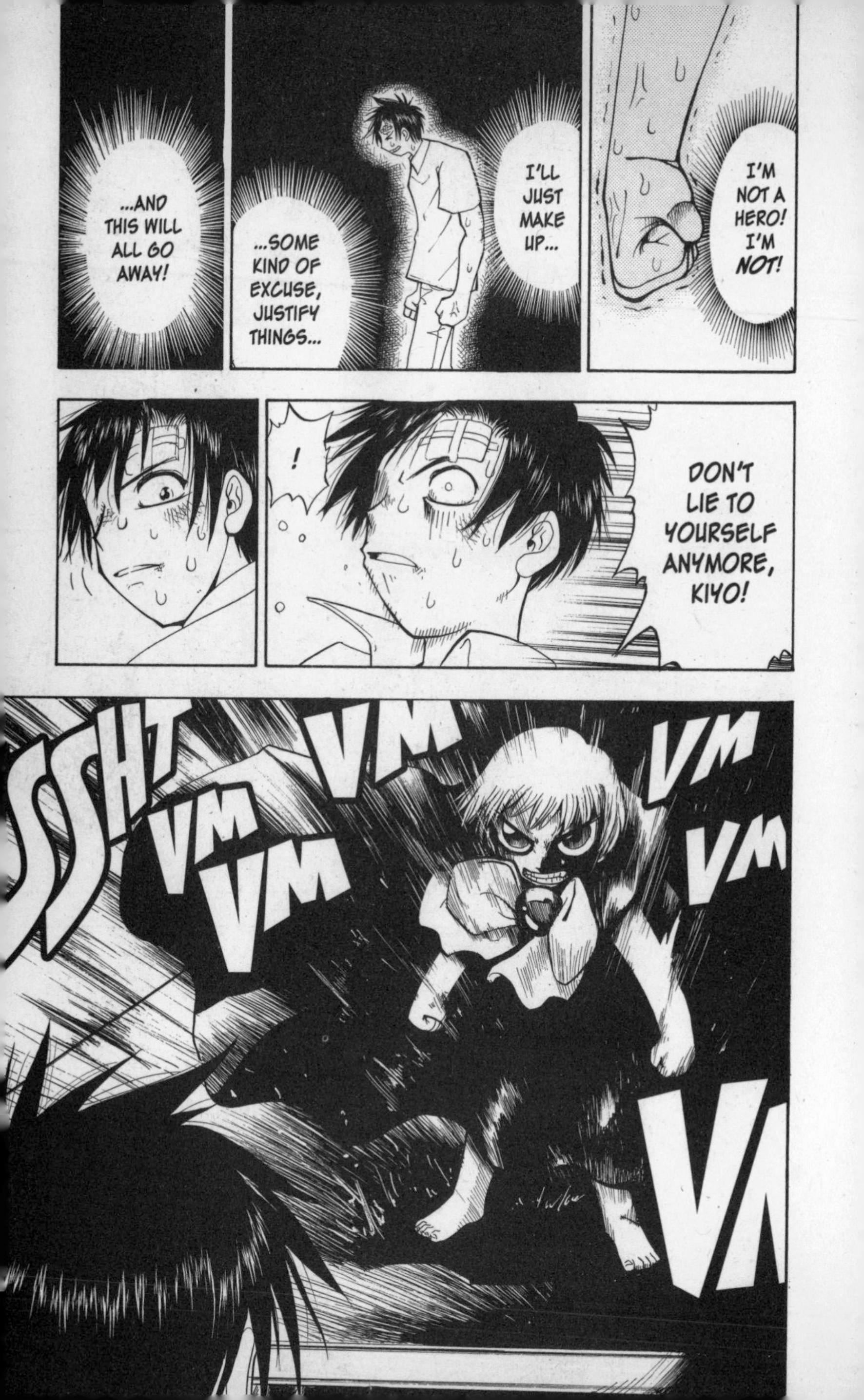
I'M NOT A HERO! I'M NOT!
I'LL JUST MAKE UP...
...SOME KIND OF EXCUSE, JUSTIFY THINGS...
...AND THIS WILL ALL GO AWAY!
DON'T LIE TO YOURSELF ANYMORE, KIYO!
!
VM
VM
VM
VM
VM
SSHT
VM
VM

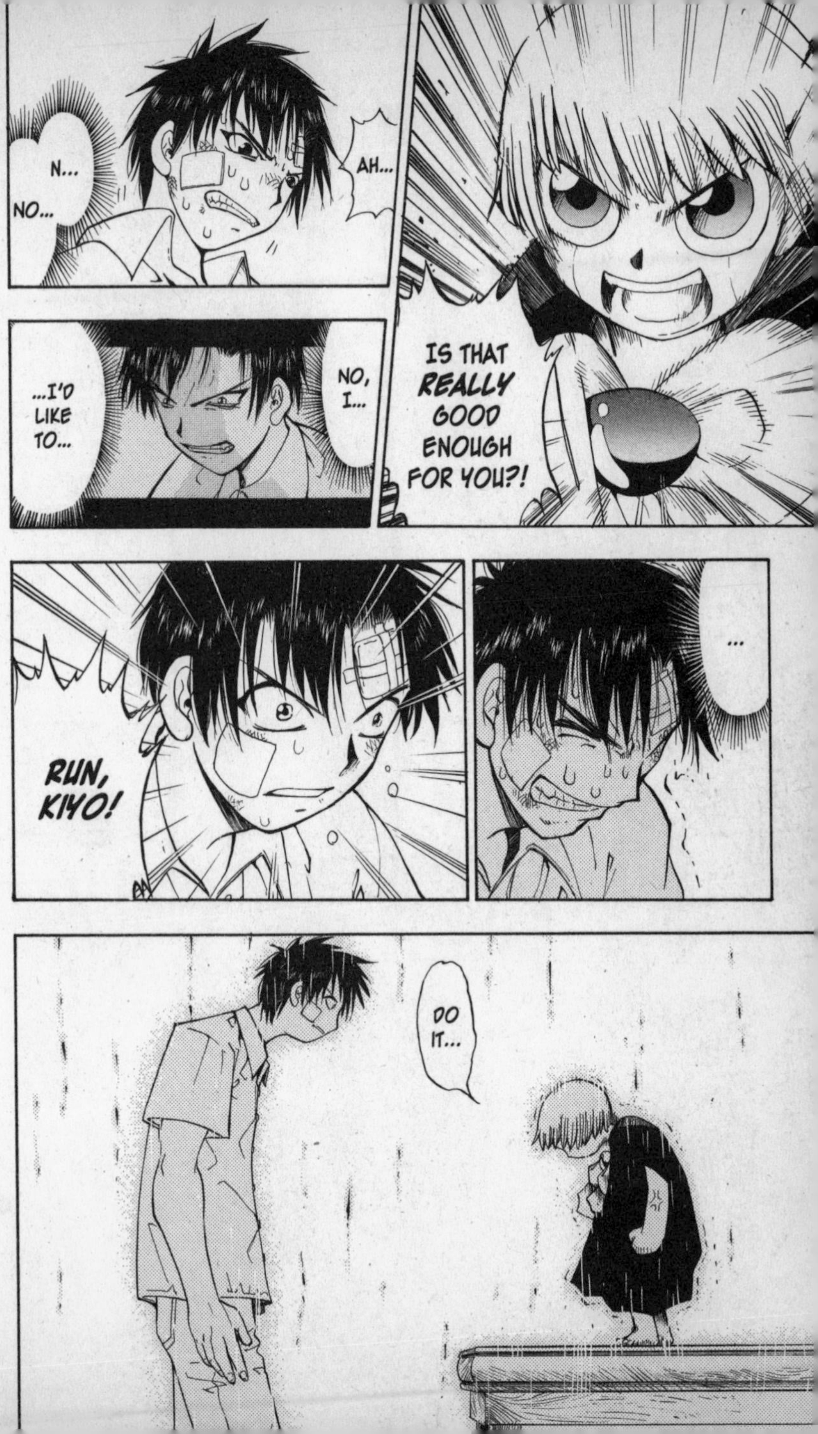
IS THAT REALLY GOOD ENOUGH FOR YOU?!
AH...
N... NO...
NO, I...
...I'D LIKE TO...
...
RUN, KIYO!
DO IT...

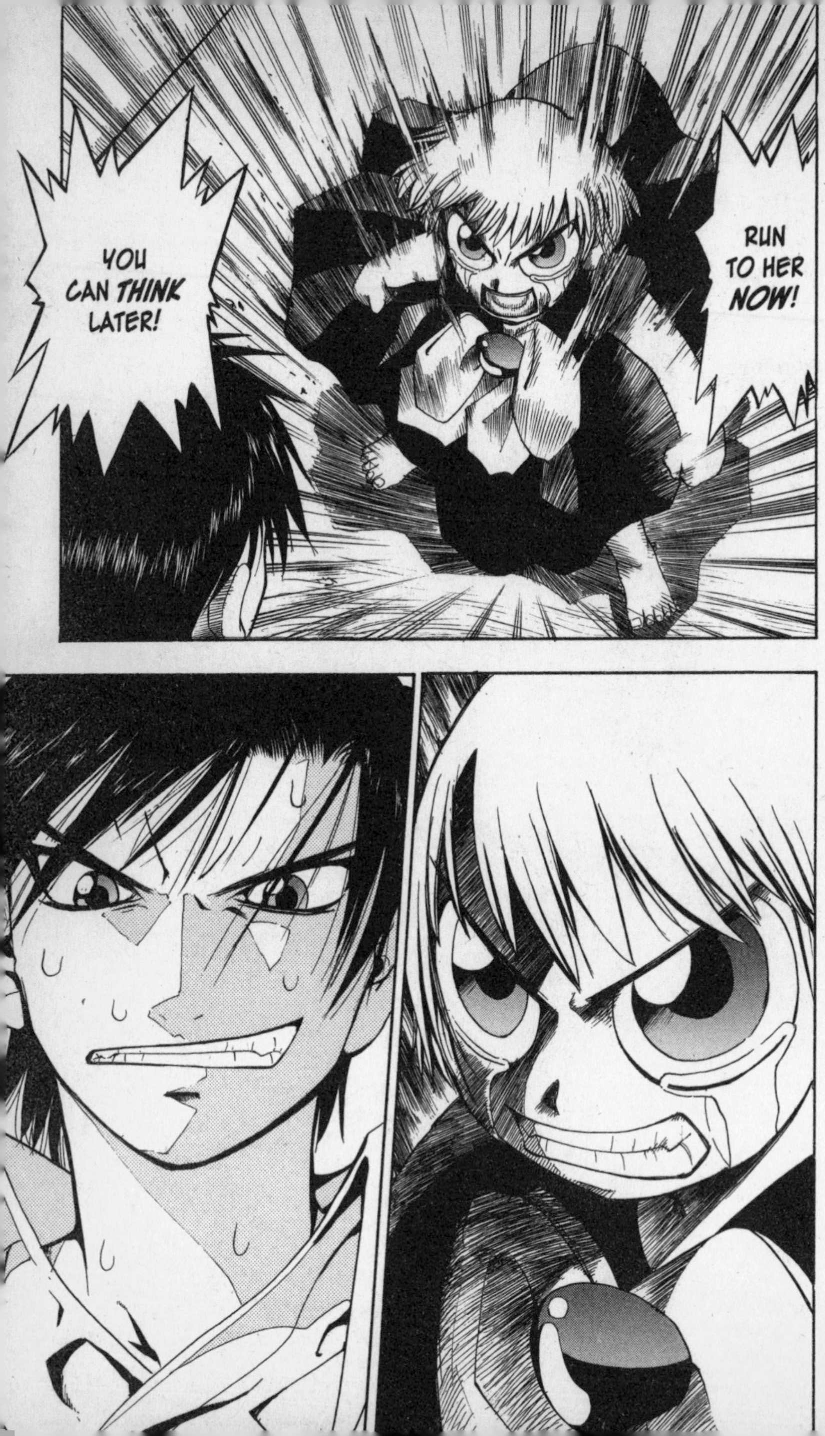
RUN TO HER NOW!
YOU CAN THINK LATER!

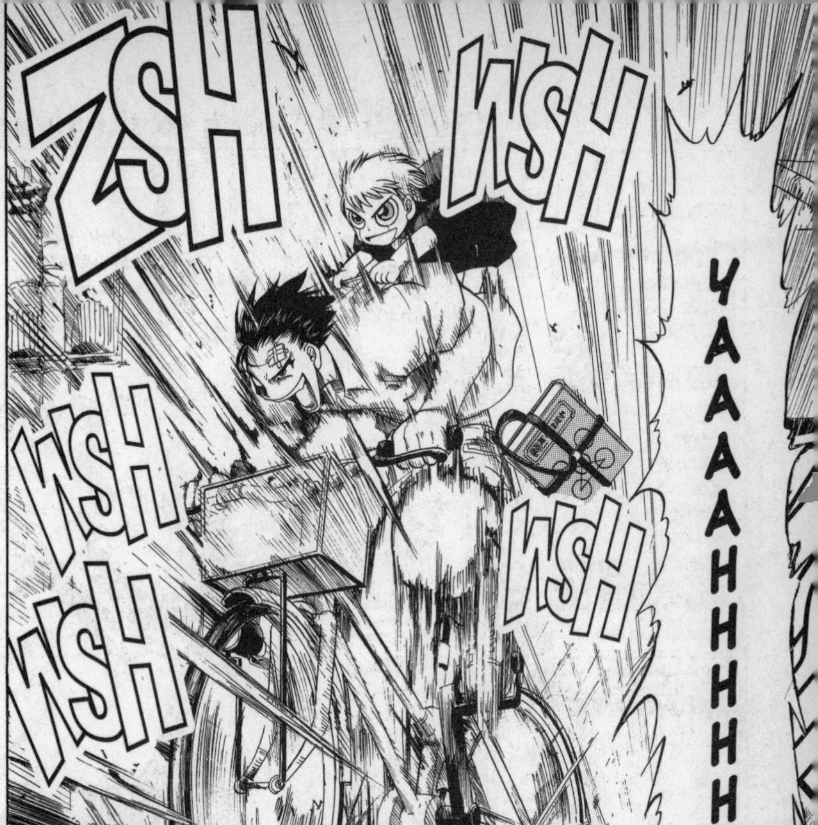
YAAAAHHHHHH!
WSH
ZSH
WSH
WSH
WSH
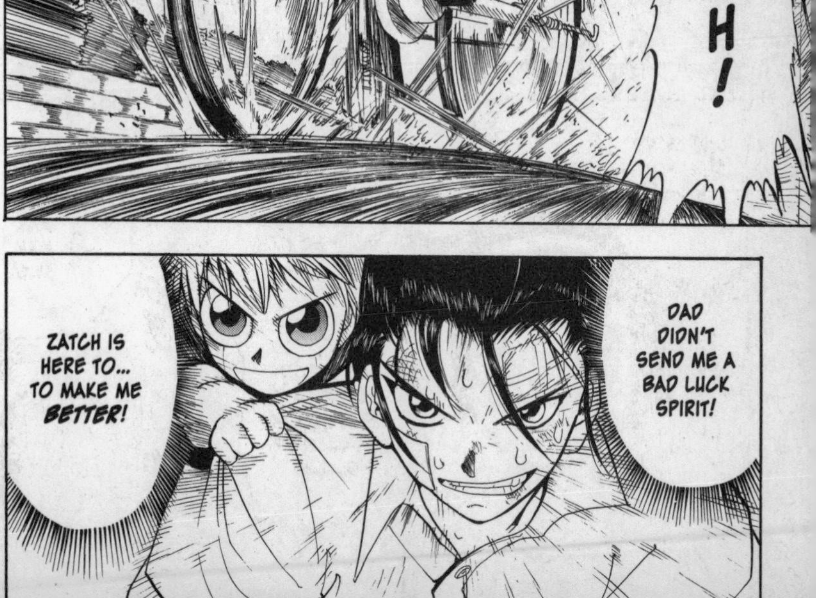
DAD DIDN'T SEND ME A BAD LUCK SPIRIT!
ZATCH IS HERE TO... TO MAKE ME *BETTER!*

LEVEL 3: A Shock to the Heart

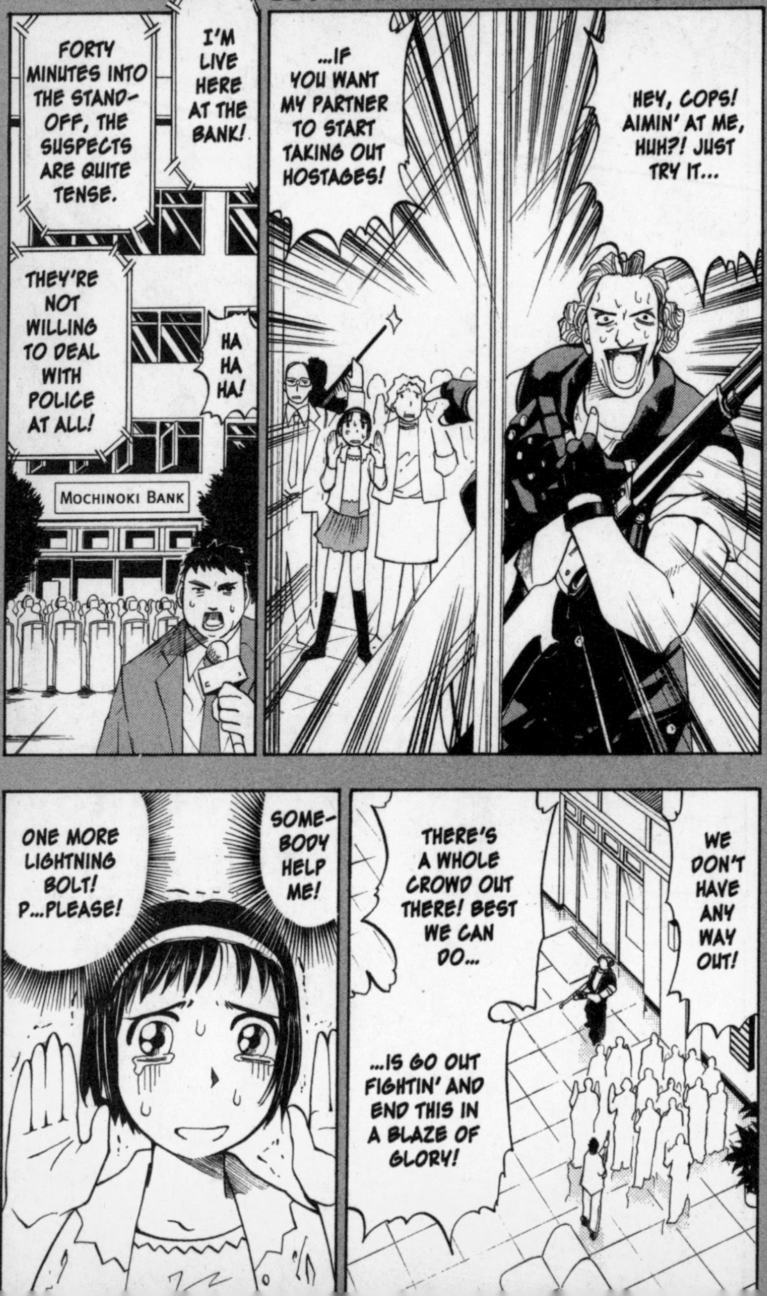
HEY, COPS! AIMIN' AT ME, HUH?! JUST TRY IT...
...IF YOU WANT MY PARTNER TO START TAKING OUT HOSTAGES!
I'M LIVE HERE AT THE BANK!
FORTY MINUTES INTO THE STAND-OFF, THE SUSPECTS ARE QUITE TENSE.
HA HA HA!
THEY'RE NOT WILLING TO DEAL WITH POLICE AT ALL!
MOCHINOKI BANK
WE DON'T HAVE ANY WAY OUT!
THERE'S A WHOLE CROWD OUT THERE! BEST WE CAN DO...
...IS GO OUT FIGHTIN' AND END THIS IN A BLAZE OF GLORY!
SOMEBODY HELP ME!
ONE MORE LIGHTNING BOLT! P...PLEASE!

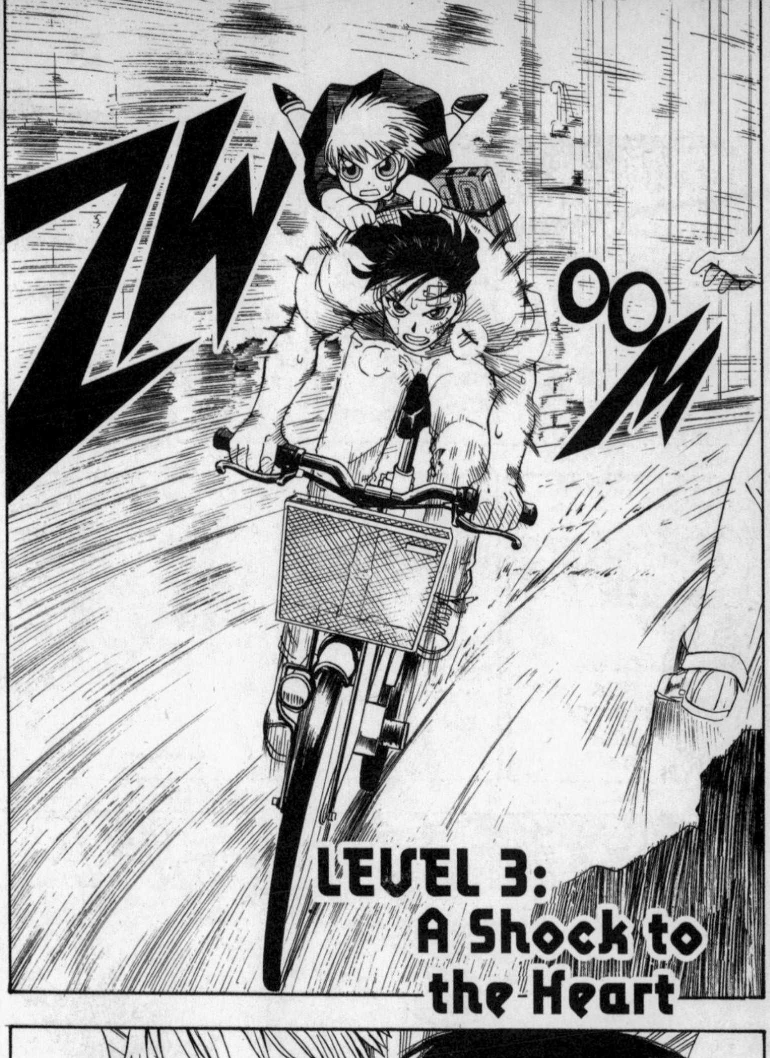
ZWOOM

LEVEL 3: A Shock to the Heart

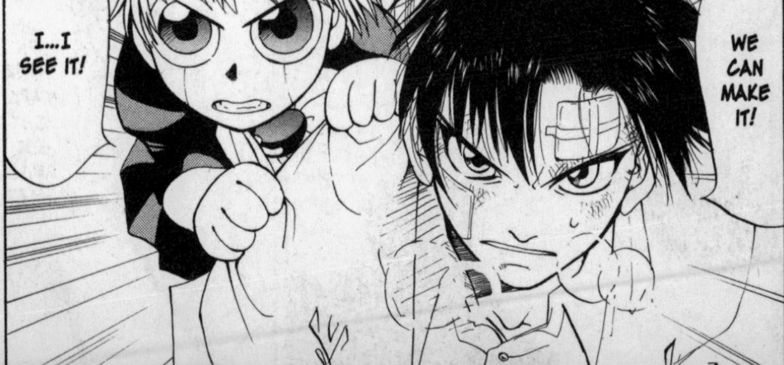
WE CAN MAKE IT!
I...I SEE IT!

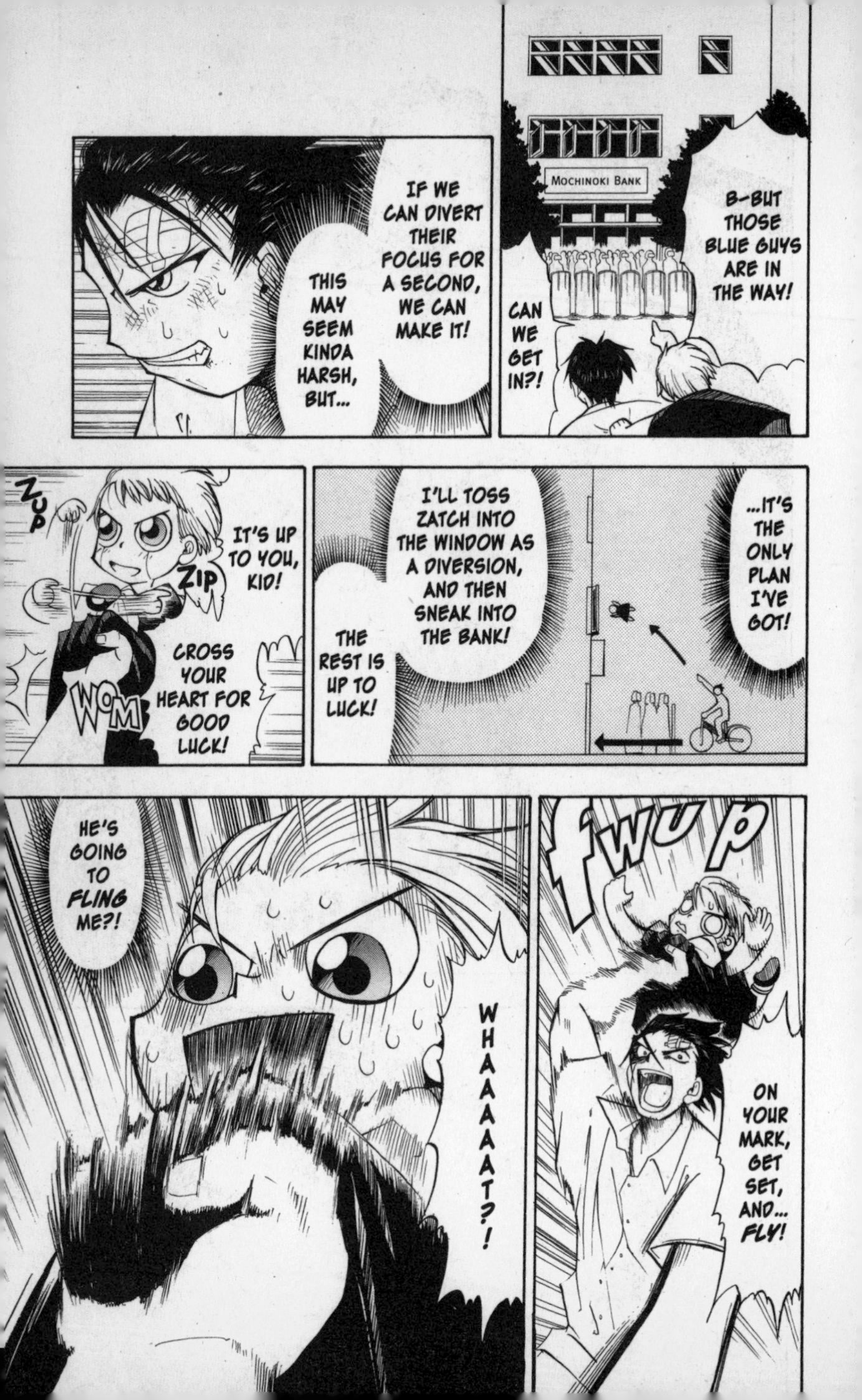
MOCHINOKI BANK
B-BUT THOSE BLUE GUYS ARE IN THE WAY!
CAN WE GET IN?!
IF WE CAN DIVERT THEIR FOCUS FOR A SECOND, WE CAN MAKE IT!
THIS MAY SEEM KINDA HARSH, BUT...
...IT'S THE ONLY PLAN I'VE GOT!
I'LL TOSS ZATCH INTO THE WINDOW AS A DIVERSION, AND THEN SNEAK INTO THE BANK!
THE REST IS UP TO LUCK!
IT'S UP TO YOU, KID!
ZUP
ZIP
WOM
CROSS YOUR HEART FOR GOOD LUCK!
fwup
ON YOUR MARK, GET SET, AND... FLY!
WHAAAAAAT?!
HE'S GOING TO FLING ME?!

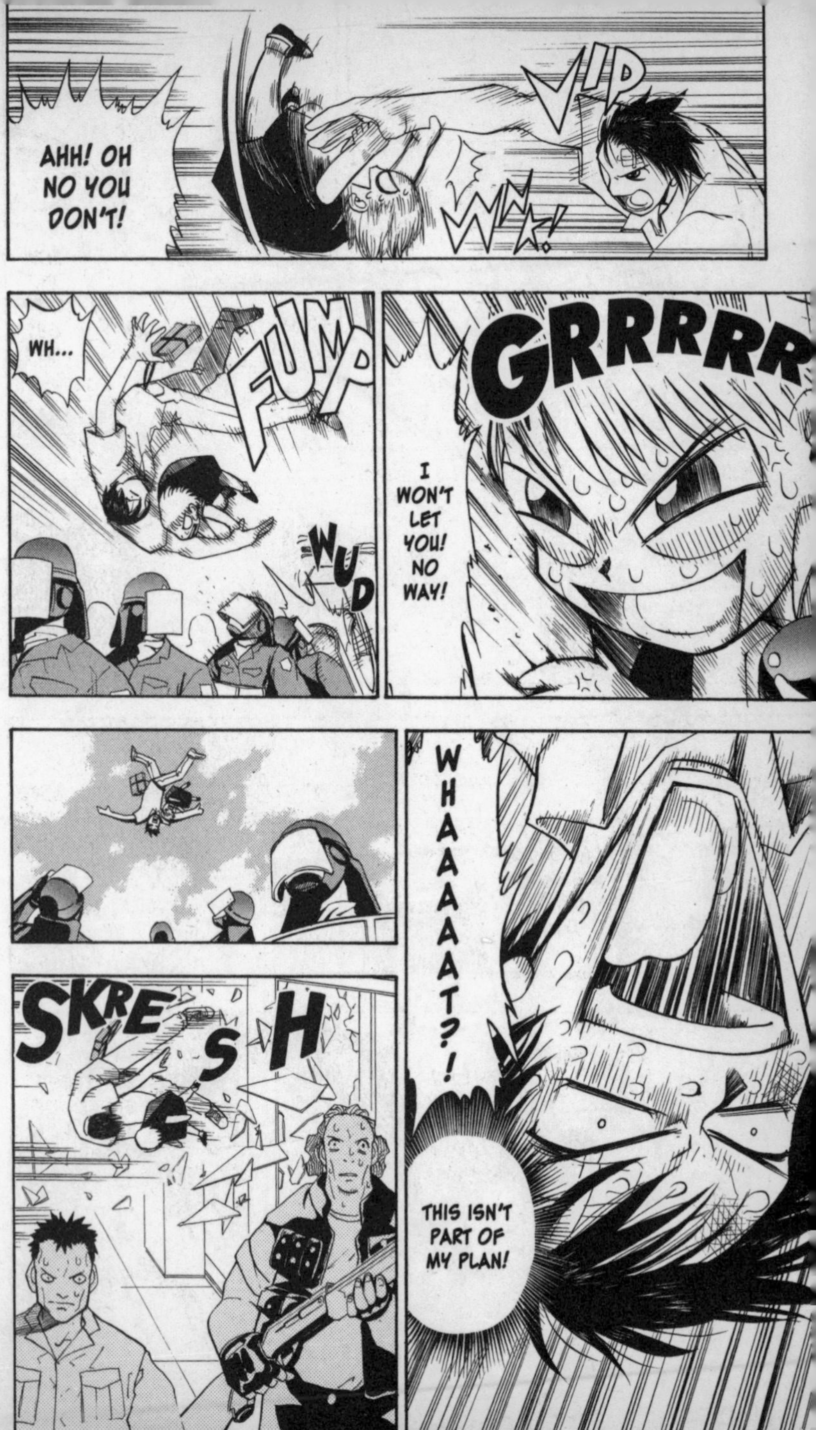
VIP
WNNK!
AHH! OH NO YOU DON'T!
GRRRRRR
I WON'T LET YOU! NO WAY!
WH...
FUMP
WUD
WHAAAAAT?!
THIS ISN'T PART OF MY PLAN!
SKRESH

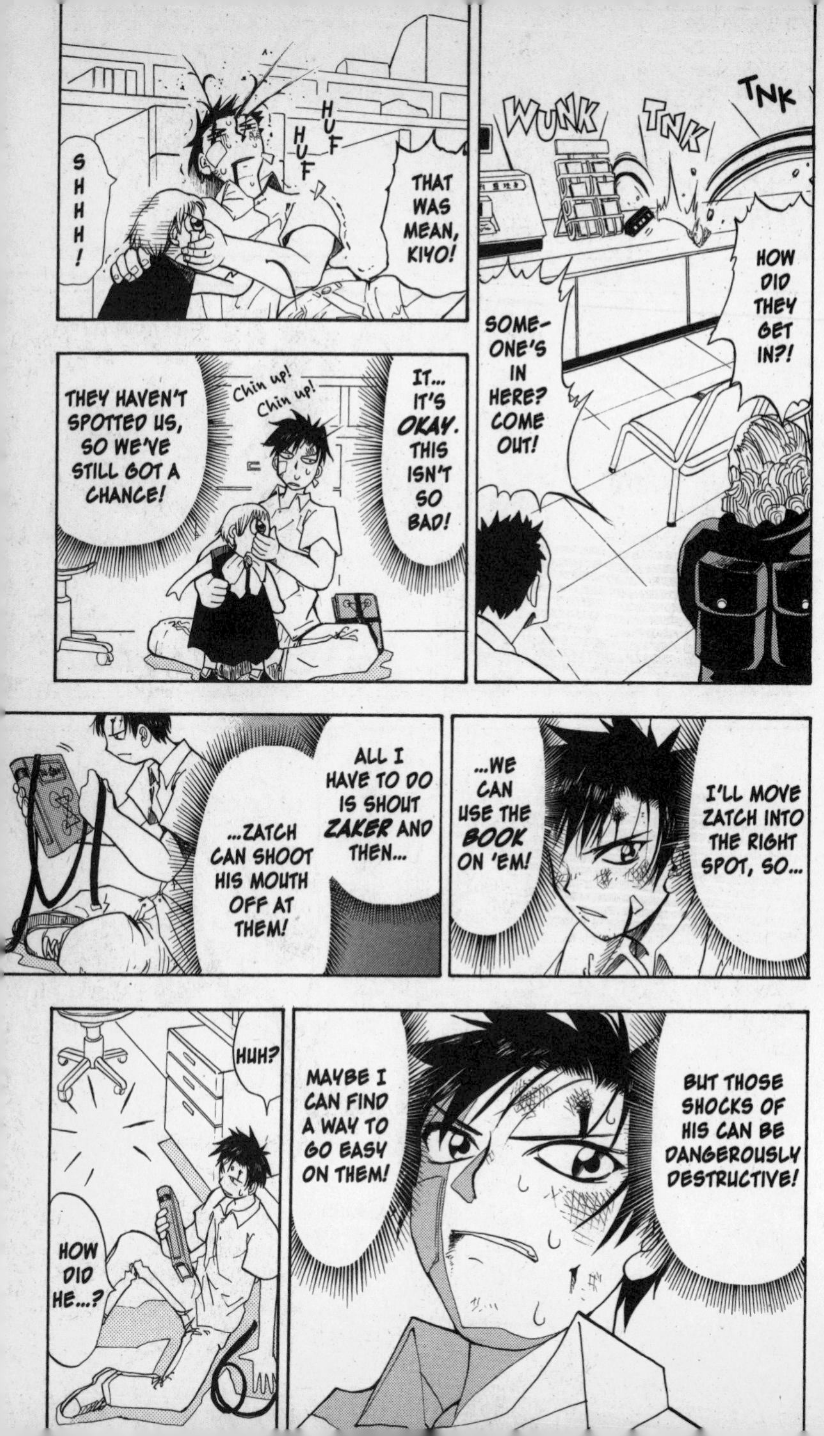
TNK
TNK
WUNK
HOW DID THEY GET IN?!
SOME-ONE'S IN HERE? COME OUT!
THAT WAS MEAN, KIYO!
HUF HUF
SHHHH!
IT... IT'S OKAY. THIS ISN'T SO BAD!
Chin up! Chin up!
THEY HAVEN'T SPOTTED US, SO WE'VE STILL GOT A CHANCE!
I'LL MOVE ZATCH INTO THE RIGHT SPOT, SO...
...WE CAN USE THE BOOK ON 'EM!
ALL I HAVE TO DO IS SHOUT ZAKER AND THEN...
...ZATCH CAN SHOOT HIS MOUTH OFF AT THEM!
BUT THOSE SHOCKS OF HIS CAN BE DANGEROUSLY DESTRUCTIVE!
MAYBE I CAN FIND A WAY TO GO EASY ON THEM!
HUH?
HOW DID HE...?

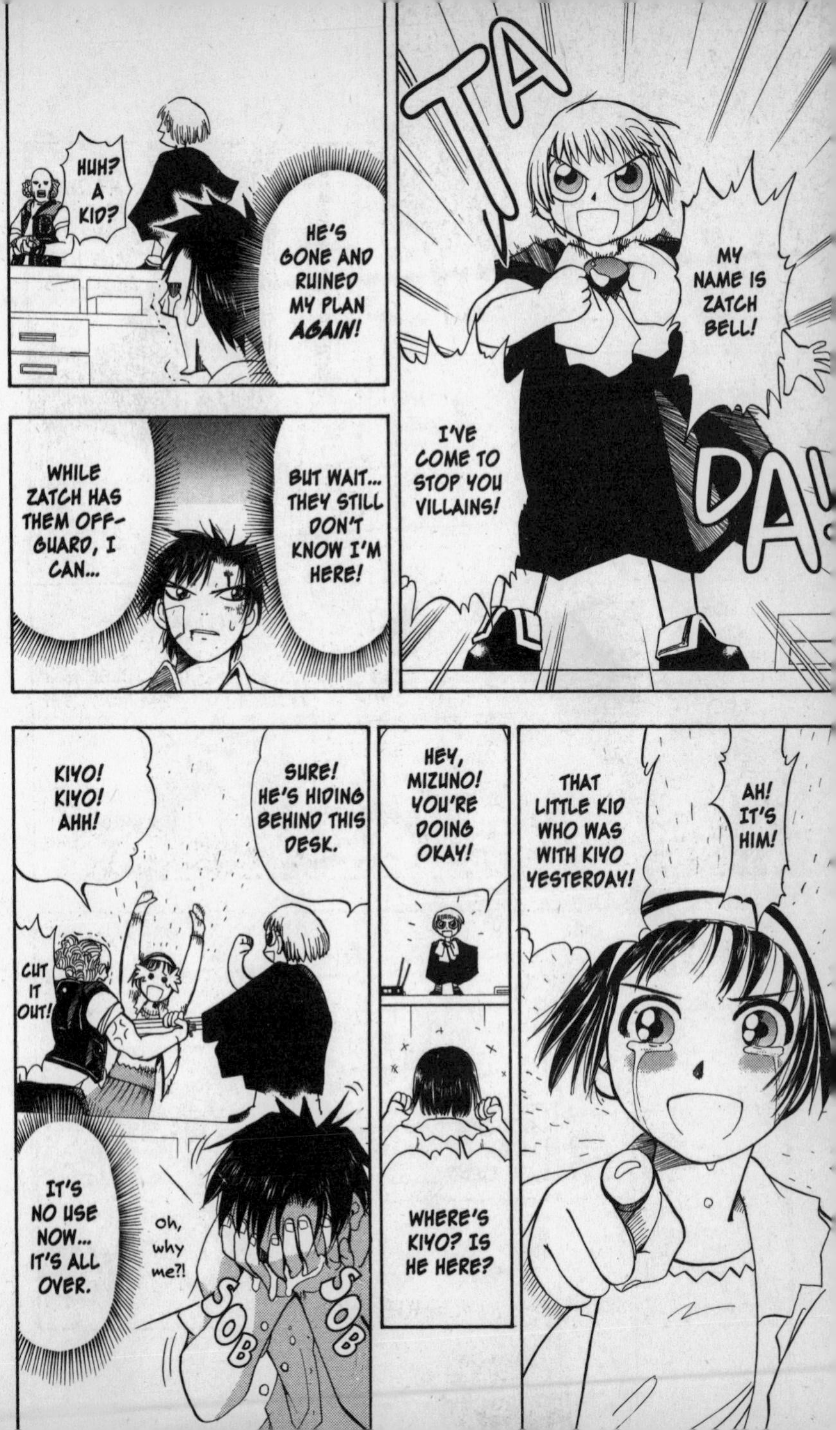
TA
MY NAME IS ZATCH BELL!
DA!
I'VE COME TO STOP YOU VILLAINS!
HE'S GONE AND RUINED MY PLAN AGAIN!
HUH? A KID?
BUT WAIT... THEY STILL DON'T KNOW I'M HERE!
WHILE ZATCH HAS THEM OFF-GUARD, I CAN...
AH! IT'S HIM!
THAT LITTLE KID WHO WAS WITH KIYO YESTERDAY!
HEY, MIZUNO! YOU'RE DOING OKAY!
WHERE'S KIYO? IS HE HERE?
SURE! HE'S HIDING BEHIND THIS DESK.
KIYO! KIYO! AHH!
CUT IT OUT!
IT'S NO USE NOW... IT'S ALL OVER.
oh, why me?!
SOB
SOB

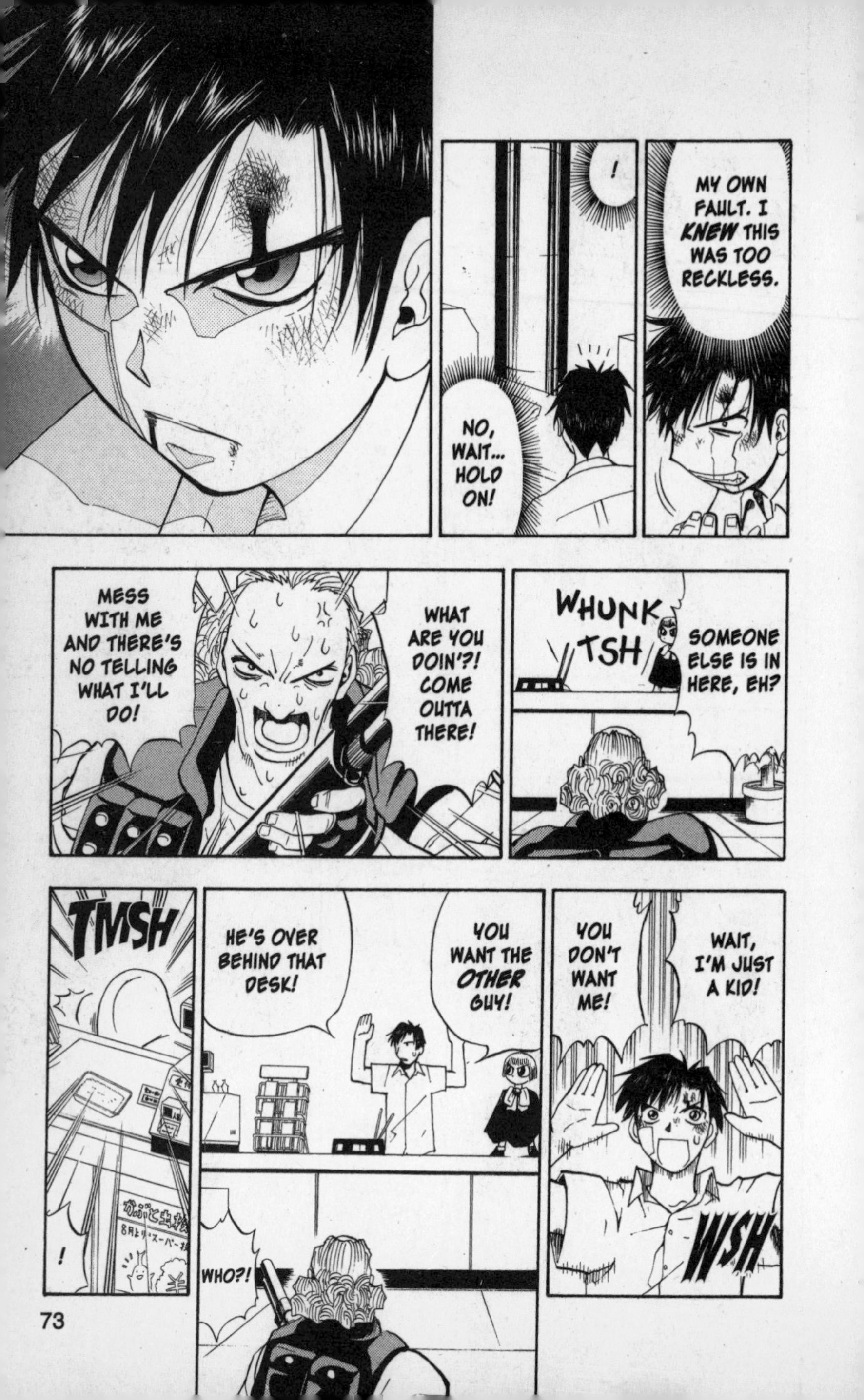
MY OWN FAULT. I KNEW THIS WAS TOO RECKLESS.
!
NO, WAIT... HOLD ON!
WHUNK
TSH
SOMEONE ELSE IS IN HERE, EH?
WHAT ARE YOU DOIN'?! COME OUTTA THERE!
MESS WITH ME AND THERE'S NO TELLING WHAT I'LL DO!
WAIT, I'M JUST A KID!
YOU DON'T WANT ME!
WSH
YOU WANT THE OTHER GUY!
HE'S OVER BEHIND THAT DESK!
WHO?!
TMSH
!

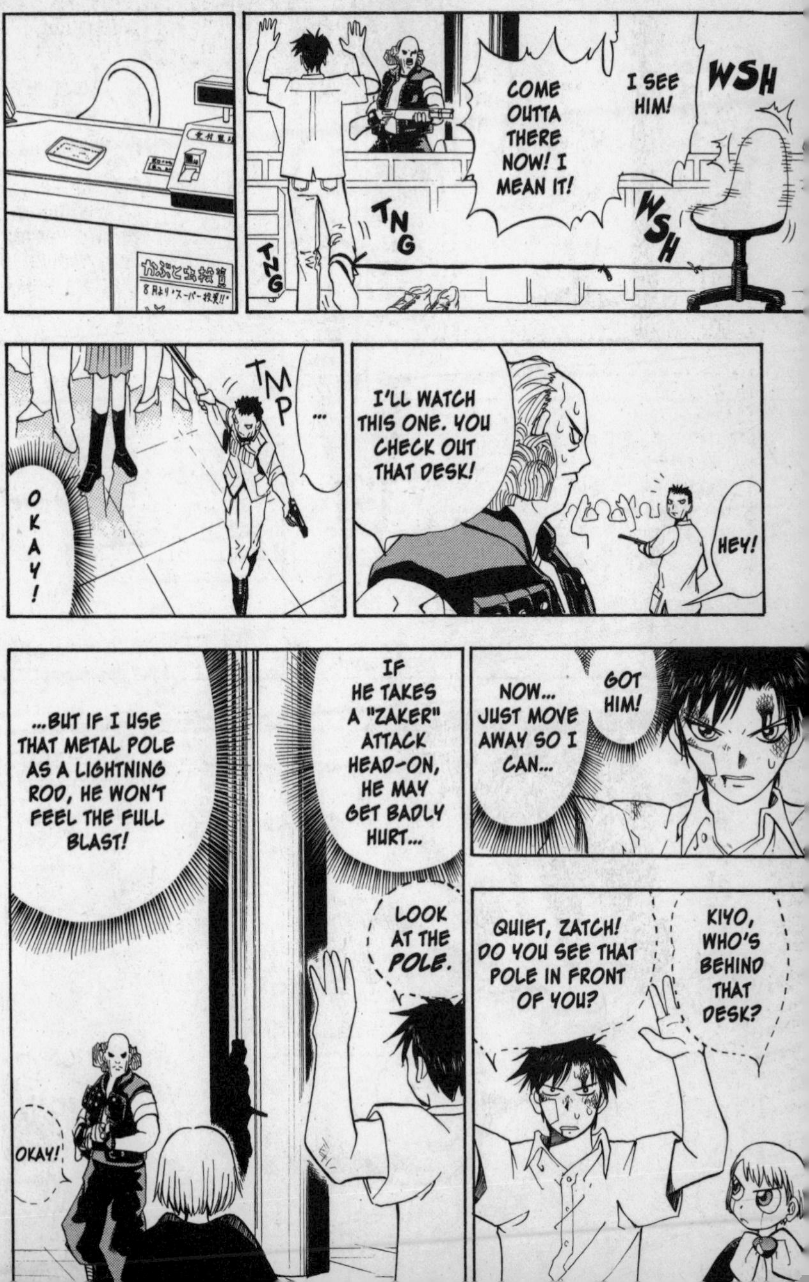
WSH
I SEE HIM!
WSH
COME OUTTA THERE NOW! I MEAN IT!
TNG
TNG
かぶと虫投資
HEY!
I'LL WATCH THIS ONE. YOU CHECK OUT THAT DESK!
...
TMP
OKAY!
GOT HIM!
NOW... JUST MOVE AWAY SO I CAN...
KIYO, WHO'S BEHIND THAT DESK?
QUIET, ZATCH! DO YOU SEE THAT POLE IN FRONT OF YOU?
IF HE TAKES A "ZAKER" ATTACK HEAD-ON, HE MAY GET BADLY HURT...
...BUT IF I USE THAT METAL POLE AS A LIGHTNING ROD, HE WON'T FEEL THE FULL BLAST!
LOOK AT THE POLE.
OKAY!

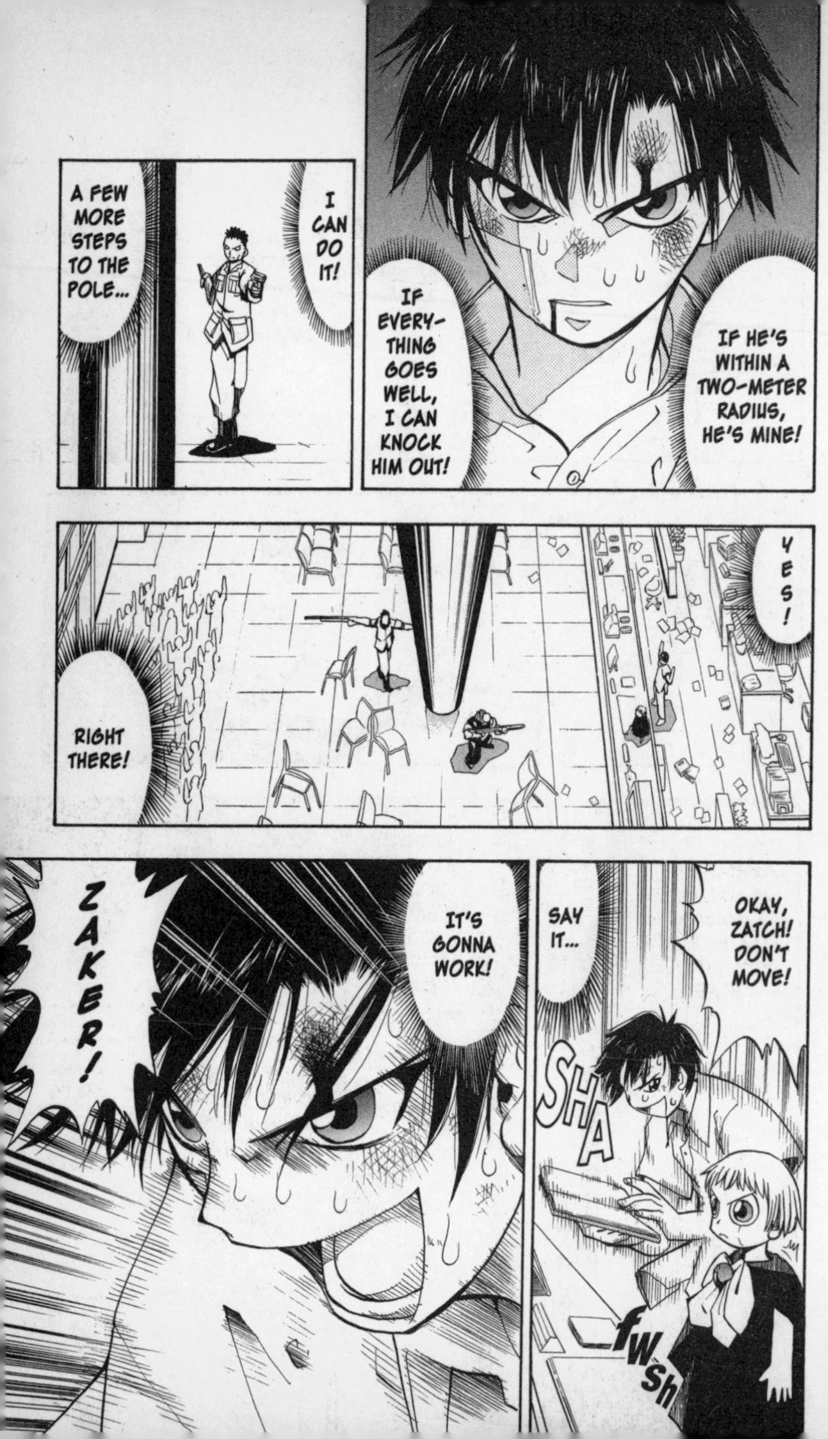
IF HE'S WITHIN A TWO-METER RADIUS, HE'S MINE!
IF EVERYTHING GOES WELL, I CAN KNOCK HIM OUT!
I CAN DO IT!
A FEW MORE STEPS TO THE POLE...
YES!
RIGHT THERE!
OKAY, ZATCH! DON'T MOVE!
SAY IT...
SHA
fwsh
IT'S GONNA WORK!
ZAKER!

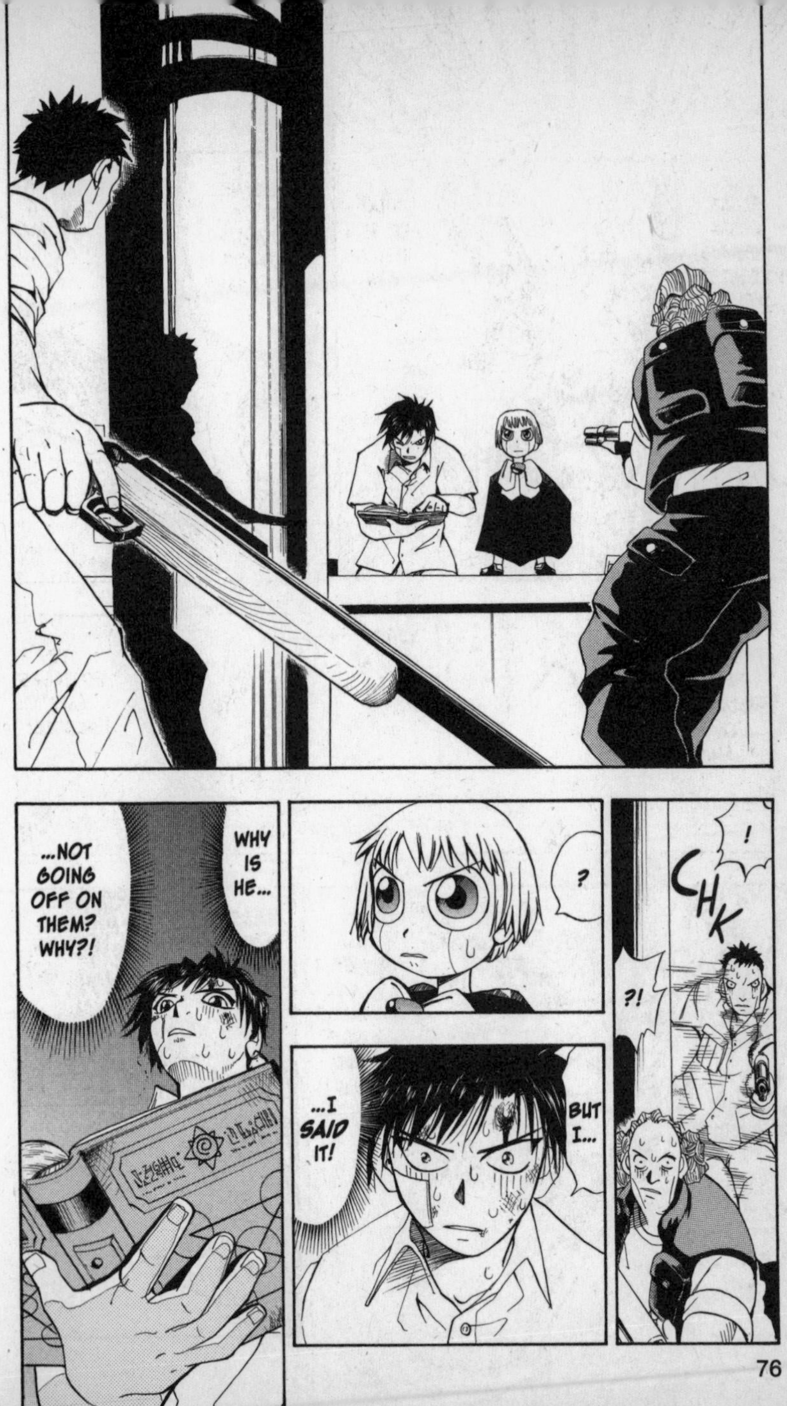
!
CHK
?!
?
BUT I...
...I SAID IT!
WHY IS HE...
...NOT GOING OFF ON THEM? WHY?!

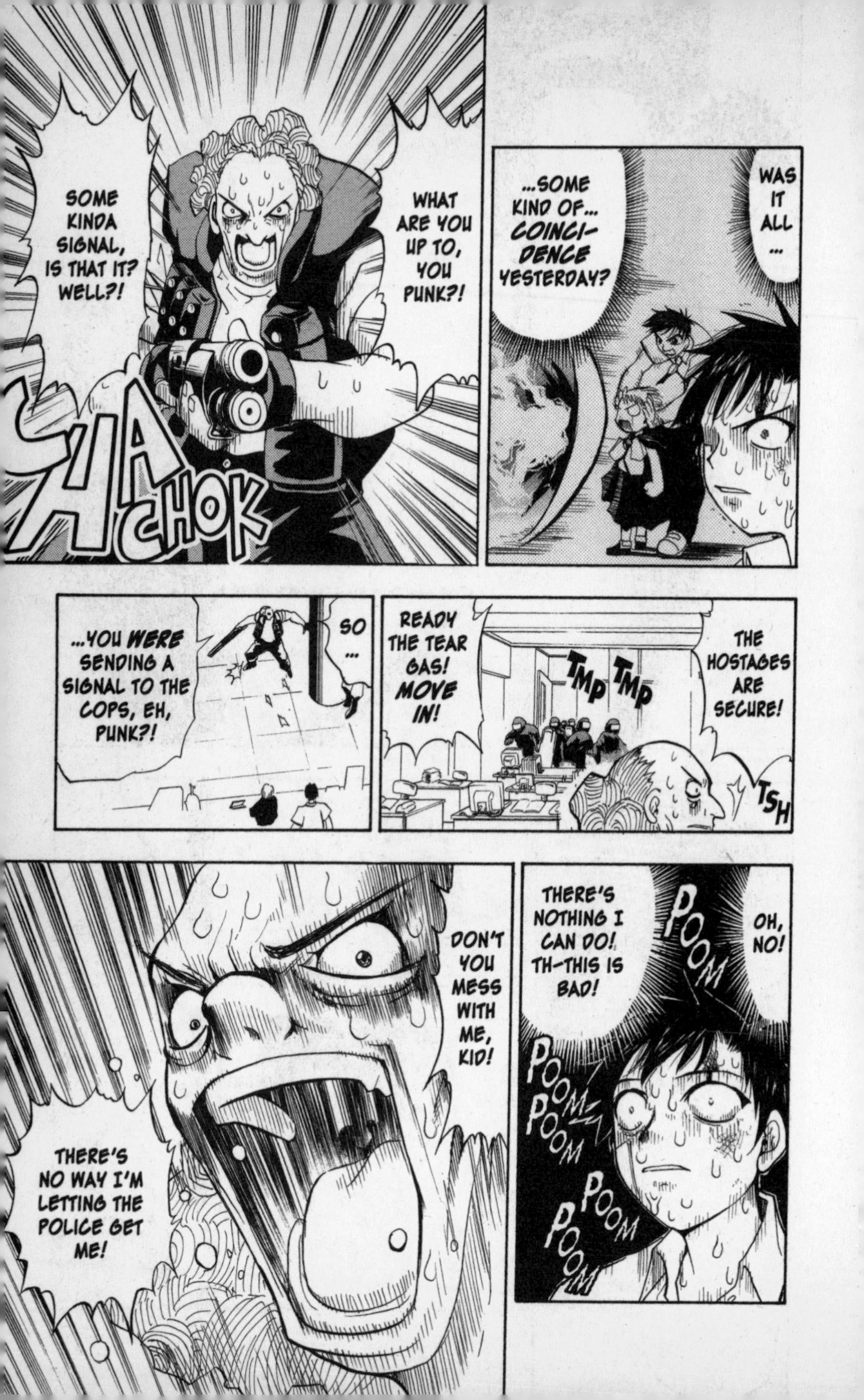
WAS IT ALL...
...SOME KIND OF... COINCIDENCE YESTERDAY?
WHAT ARE YOU UP TO, YOU PUNK?!
SOME KINDA SIGNAL, IS THAT IT? WELL?!
CHA CHOK
THE HOSTAGES ARE SECURE!
READY THE TEAR GAS! MOVE IN!
TMP TMP
TSH
SO...
...YOU WERE SENDING A SIGNAL TO THE COPS, EH, PUNK?!
OH, NO!
THERE'S NOTHING I CAN DO! TH-THIS IS BAD!
POOM POOM POOM POOM POOM POOM
DON'T YOU MESS WITH ME, KID!
THERE'S NO WAY I'M LETTING THE POLICE GET ME!

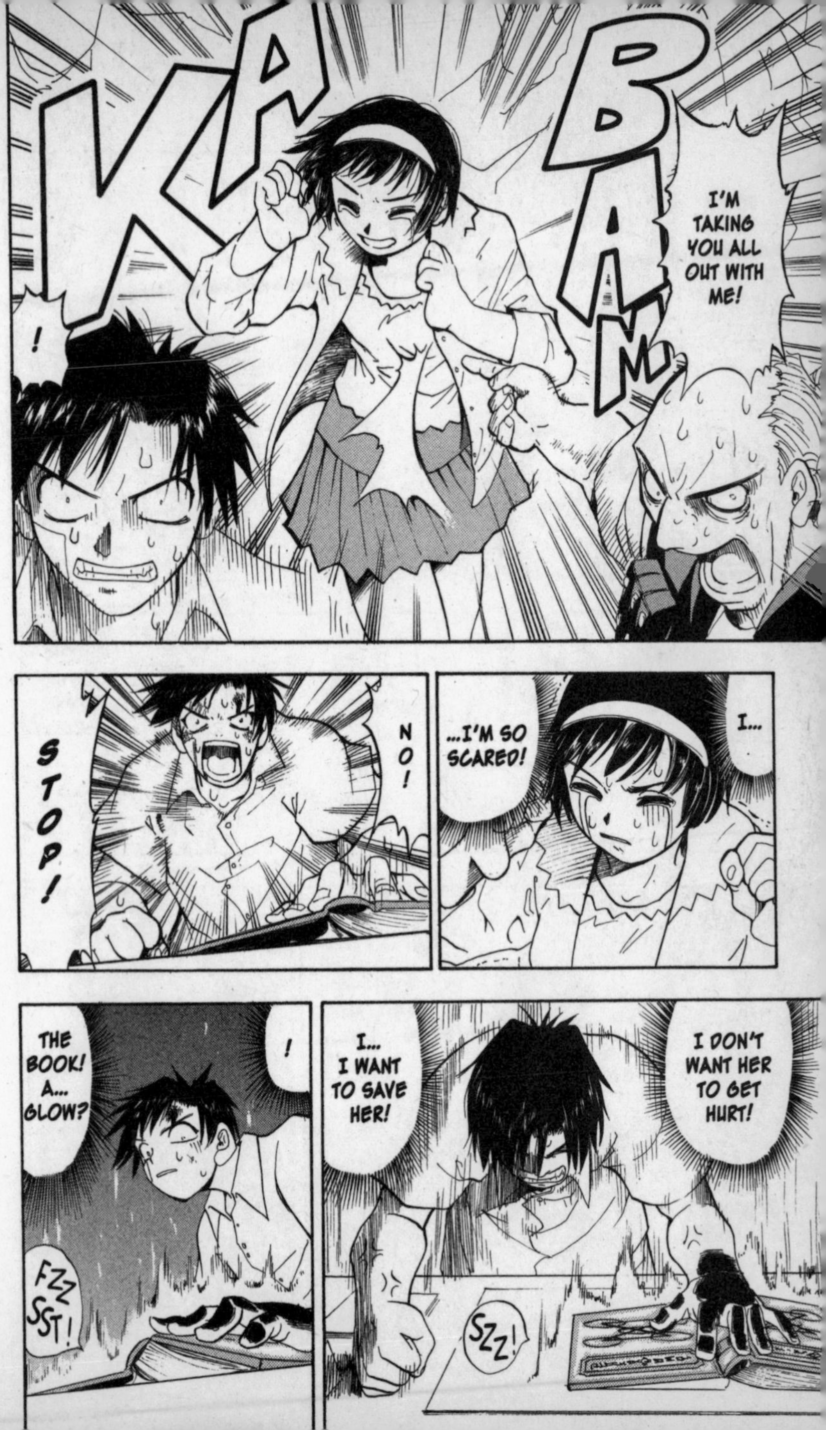
KABAM
I'M TAKING YOU ALL OUT WITH ME!
!
I...
...I'M SO SCARED!
NO!
STOP!
I DON'T WANT HER TO GET HURT!
I... I WANT TO SAVE HER!
SZZ!
!
THE BOOK! A... GLOW?
FZZ SST!

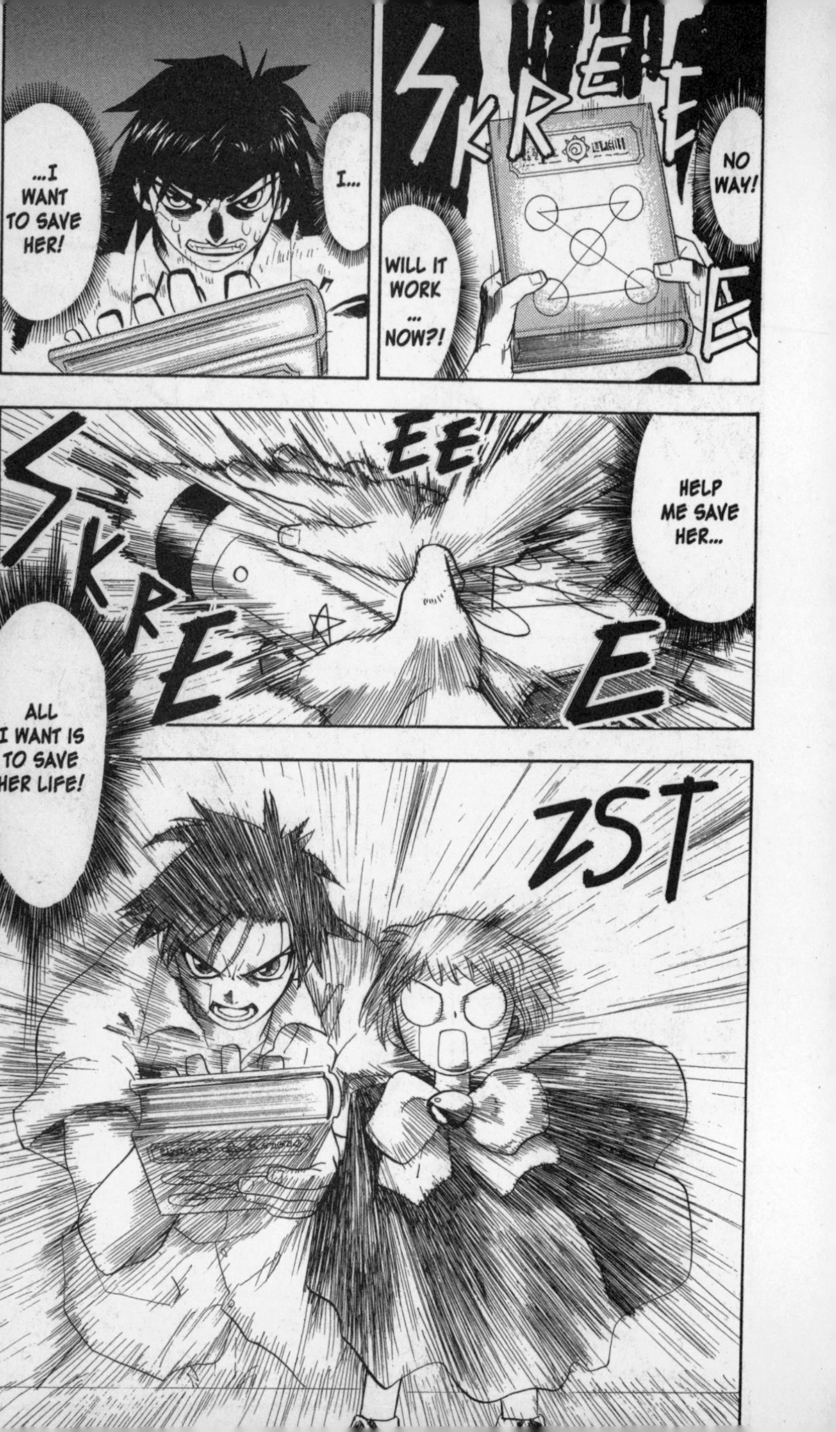
SKREEE
NO WAY!
WILL IT WORK ... NOW?!
I...
...I WANT TO SAVE HER!
HELP ME SAVE HER...
SKREEEE
ALL I WANT IS TO SAVE HER LIFE!
ZST

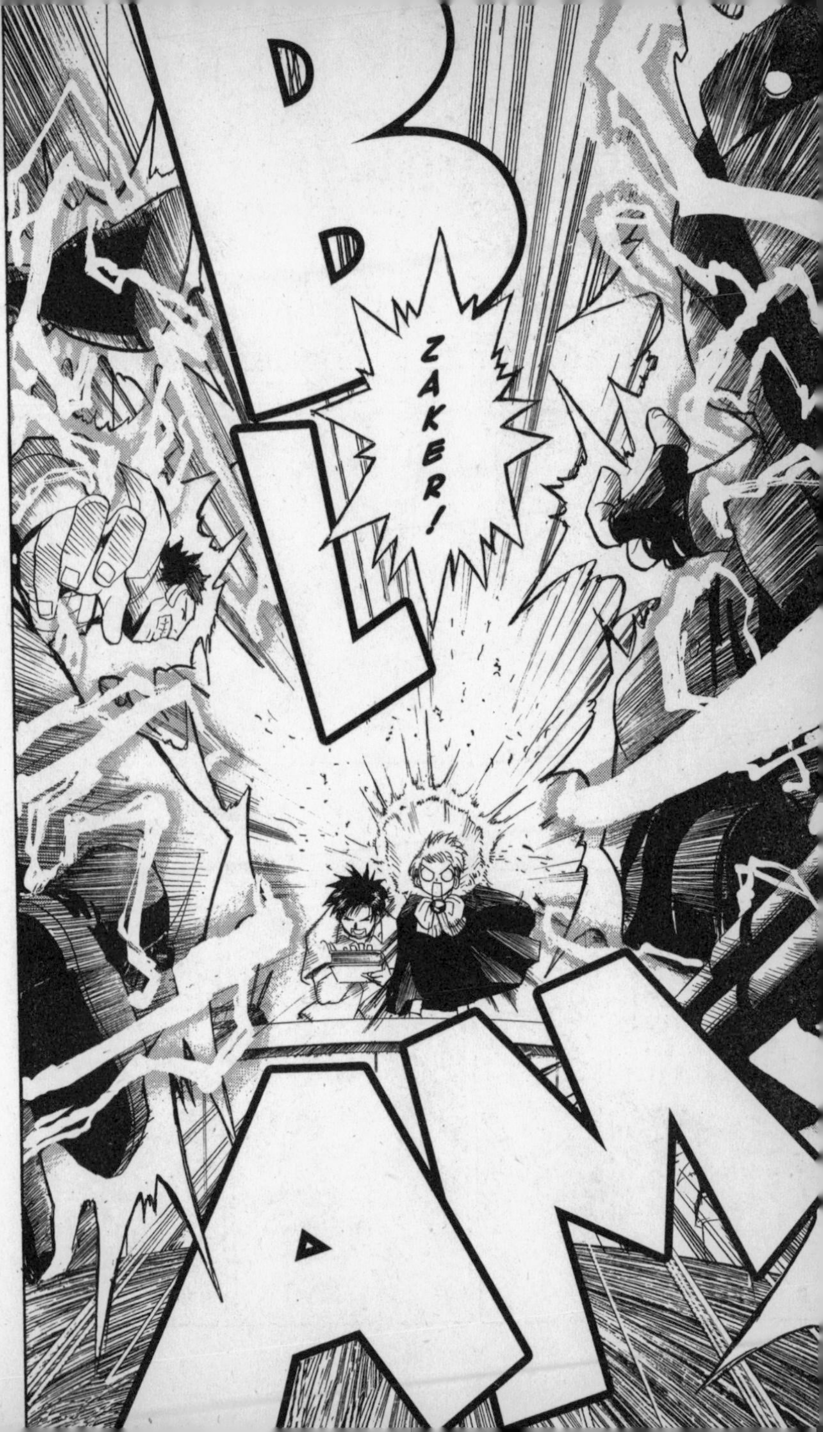
ZAKER!
BLAM

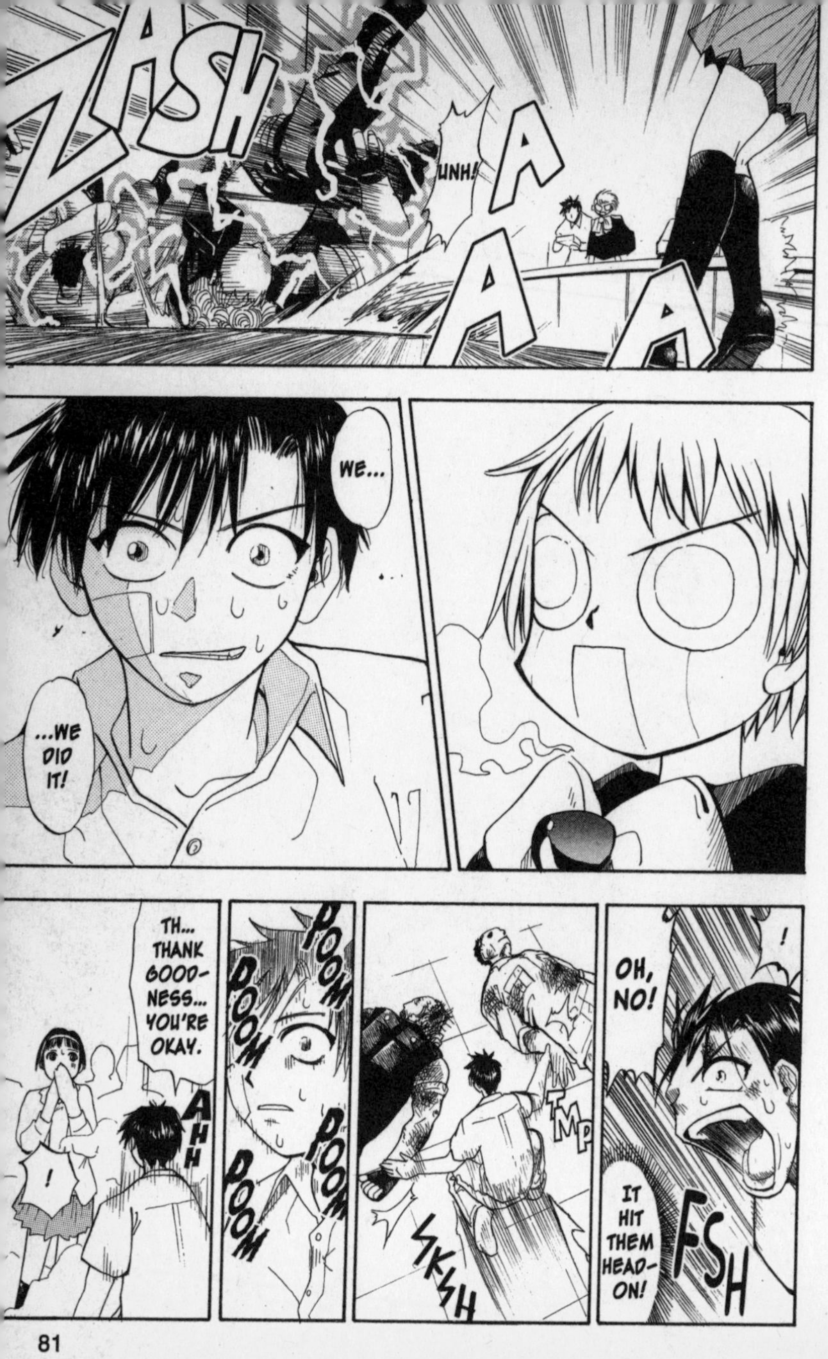
AAA
UNH!
ZASH
WE...
...WE DID IT!
!
OH, NO!
IT HIT THEM HEAD-ON!
FSH
TMP
SKSH
POOM
POOM
POOM
POOM
POOM
TH... THANK GOODNESS... YOU'RE OKAY.
AHH
!

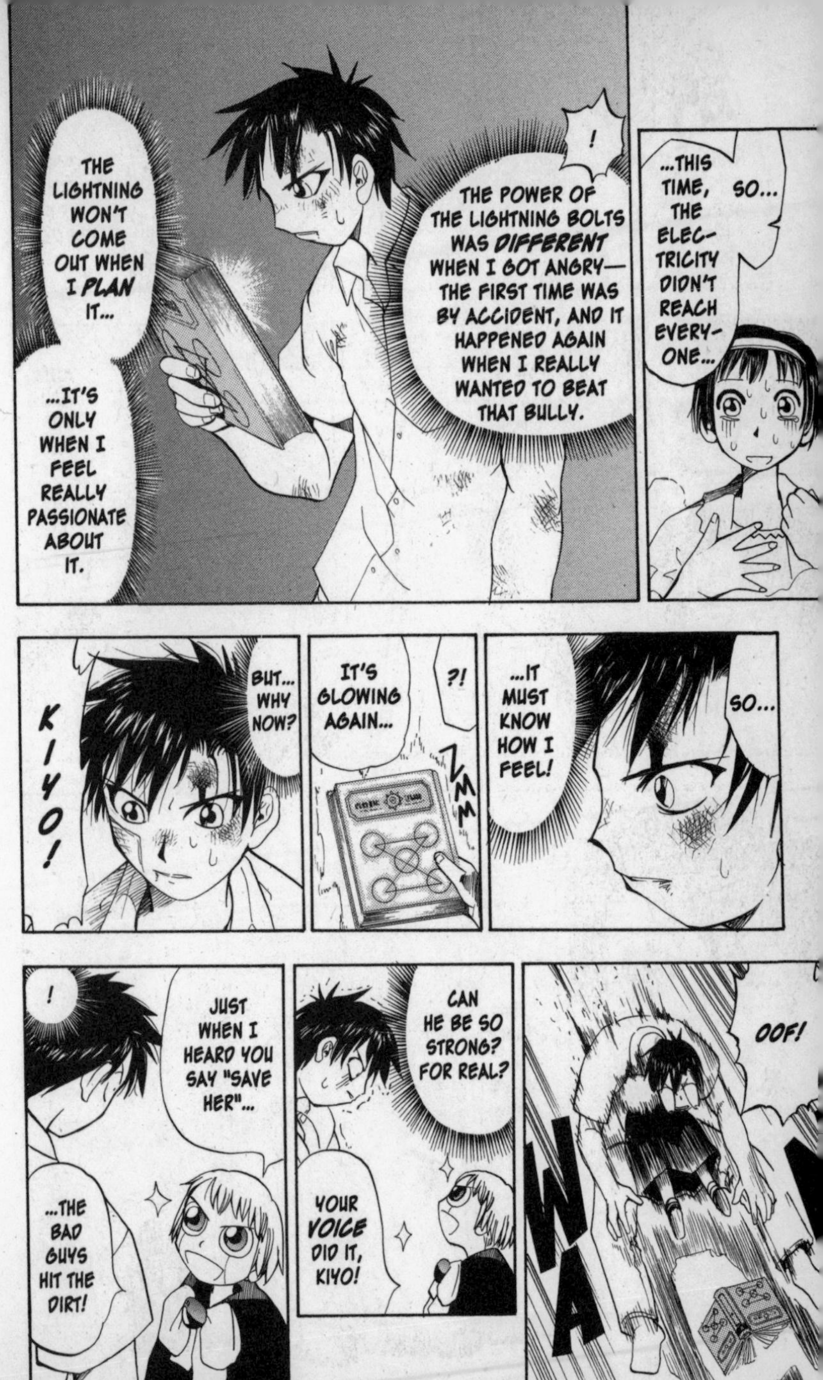
SO...
...THIS TIME, THE ELECTRICITY DIDN'T REACH EVERYONE...
!
THE POWER OF THE LIGHTNING BOLTS WAS *DIFFERENT* WHEN I GOT ANGRY—THE FIRST TIME WAS BY ACCIDENT, AND IT HAPPENED AGAIN WHEN I REALLY WANTED TO BEAT THAT BULLY.
THE LIGHTNING WON'T COME OUT WHEN I *PLAN* IT...
...IT'S ONLY WHEN I FEEL REALLY PASSIONATE ABOUT IT.
SO...
...IT MUST KNOW HOW I FEEL!
?!
IT'S GLOWING AGAIN...
ZMM
BUT... WHY NOW?
KIYO!
OOF!
WA
CAN HE BE SO STRONG? FOR REAL?
YOUR *VOICE* DID IT, KIYO!
JUST WHEN I HEARD YOU SAY "SAVE HER"...
!
...THE BAD GUYS HIT THE DIRT!

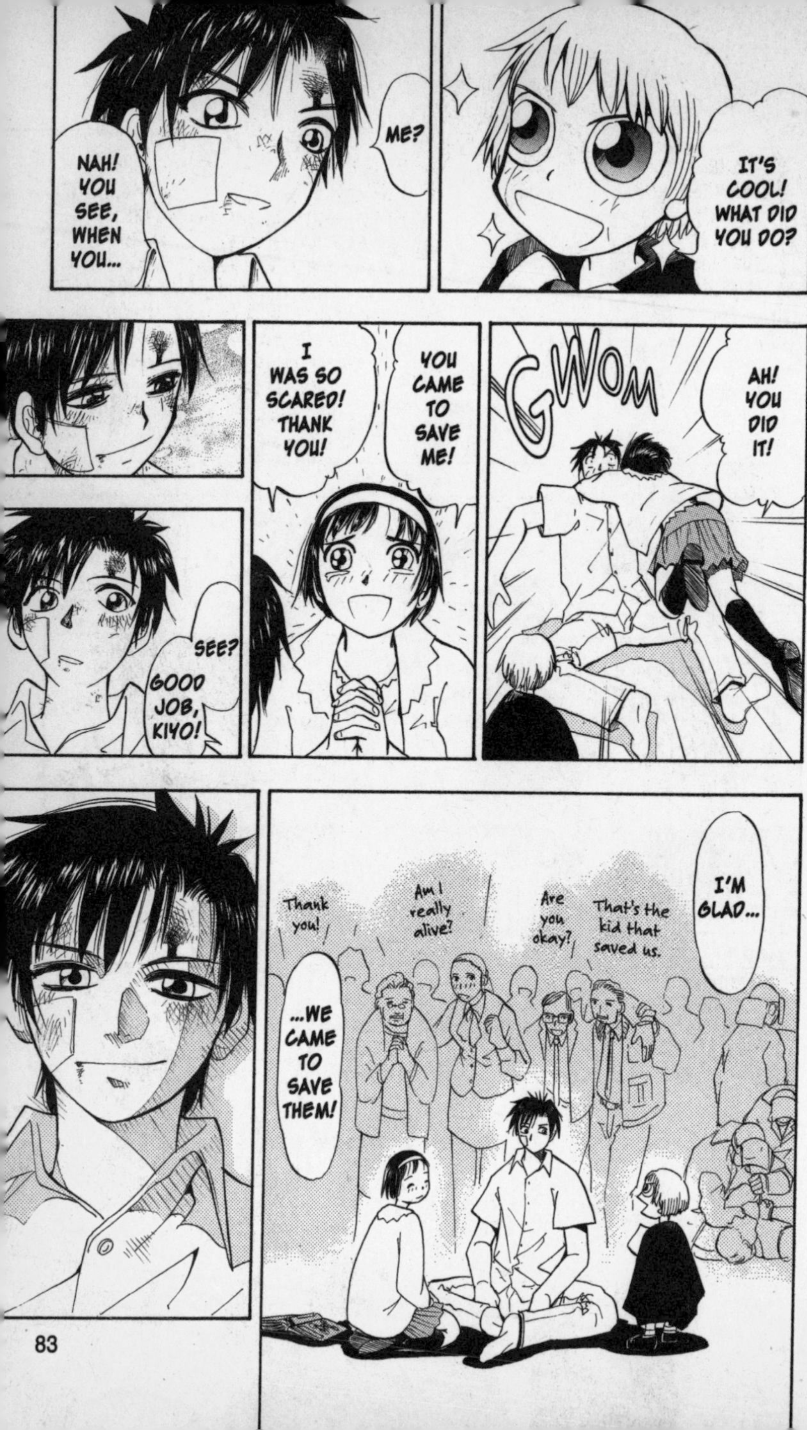
IT'S COOL! WHAT DID YOU DO?
ME?
NAH! YOU SEE, WHEN YOU...
AH! YOU DID IT!
GWOM
YOU CAME TO SAVE ME!
I WAS SO SCARED! THANK YOU!
SEE?
GOOD JOB, KIYO!
I'M GLAD...
That's the kid that saved us.
Are you okay?
Am I really alive?
Thank you!
...WE CAME TO SAVE THEM!

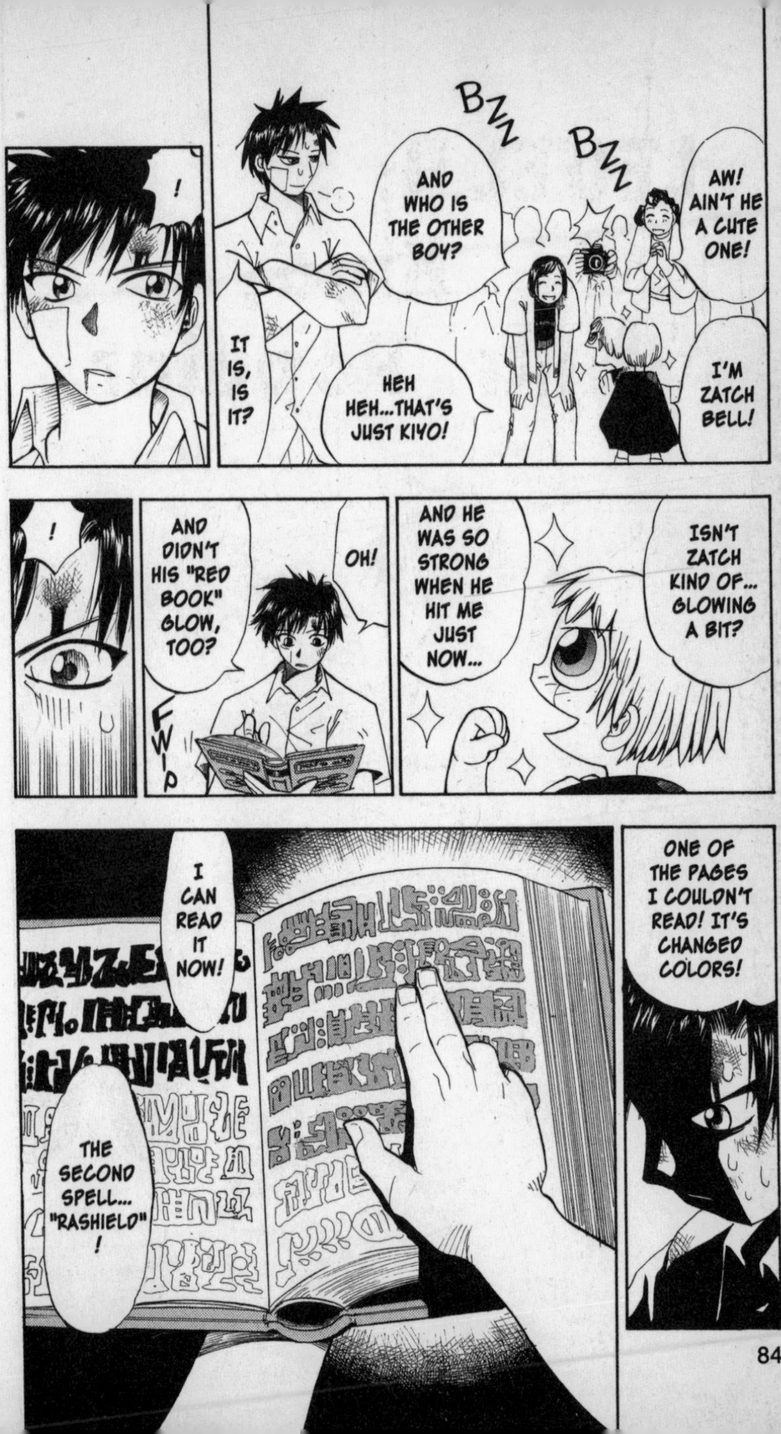
AW! AIN'T HE A CUTE ONE!
BZZ
BZZ
AND WHO IS THE OTHER BOY?
I'M ZATCH BELL!
HEH HEH...THAT'S JUST KIYO!
IT IS, IS IT?
!
ISN'T ZATCH KIND OF... GLOWING A BIT?
AND HE WAS SO STRONG WHEN HE HIT ME JUST NOW...
OH!
AND DIDN'T HIS "RED BOOK" GLOW, TOO?
FWIP
!
ONE OF THE PAGES I COULDN'T READ! IT'S CHANGED COLORS!
I CAN READ IT NOW!
THE SECOND SPELL... "RASHIELD"!

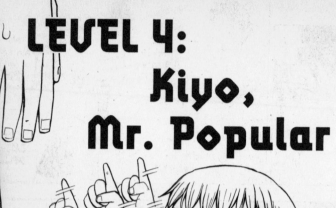

LEVEL 4:
Kiyo,
Mr. Popular

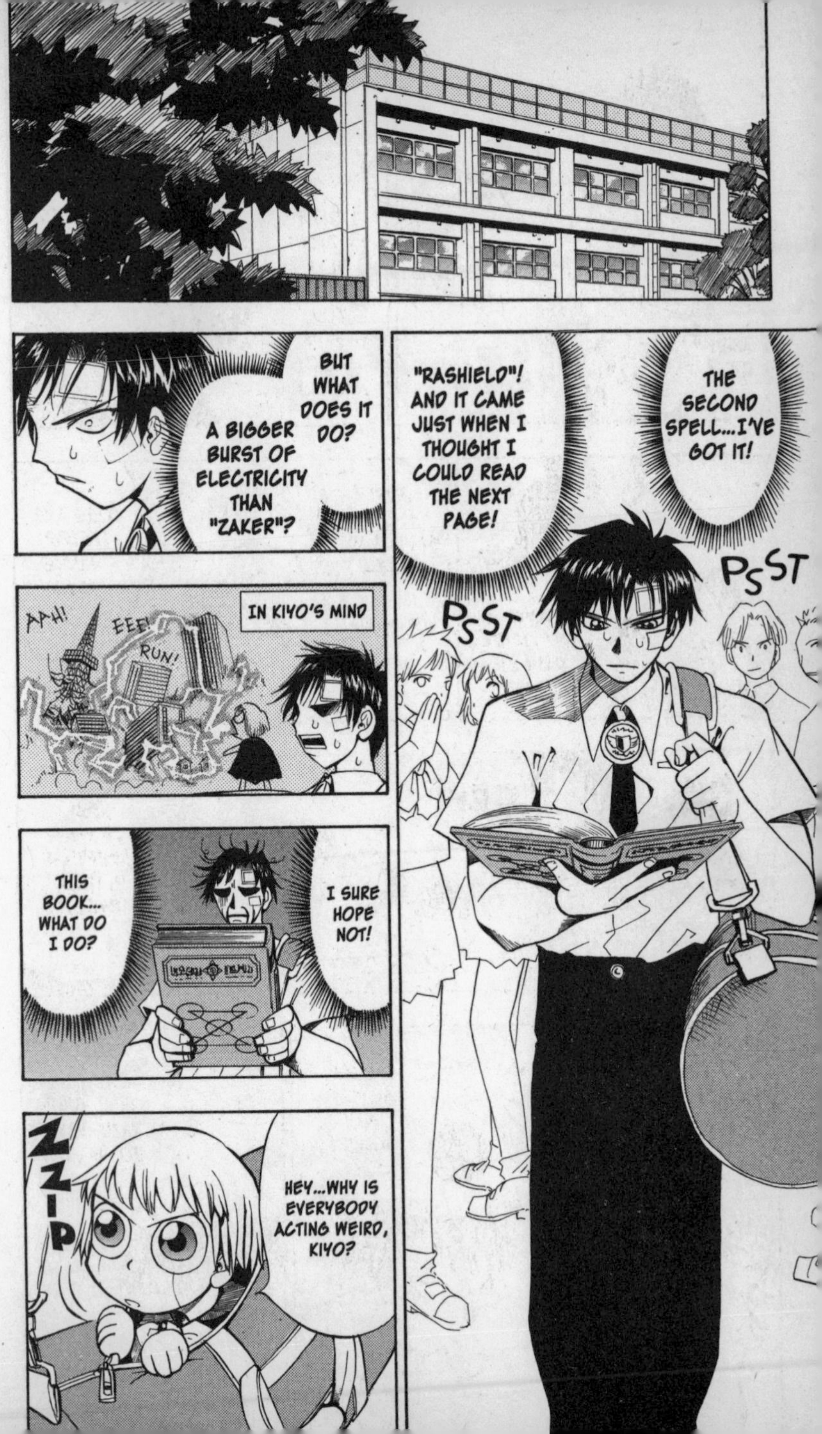
THE SECOND SPELL...I'VE GOT IT!
"RASHIELD"! AND IT CAME JUST WHEN I THOUGHT I COULD READ THE NEXT PAGE!
PSST
PSST
BUT WHAT DOES IT DO?
A BIGGER BURST OF ELECTRICITY THAN "ZAKER"?
IN KIYO'S MIND
APH!
EEE!
RUN!
I SURE HOPE NOT!
THIS BOOK... WHAT DO I DO?
ZZIP
HEY...WHY IS EVERYBODY ACTING WEIRD, KIYO?

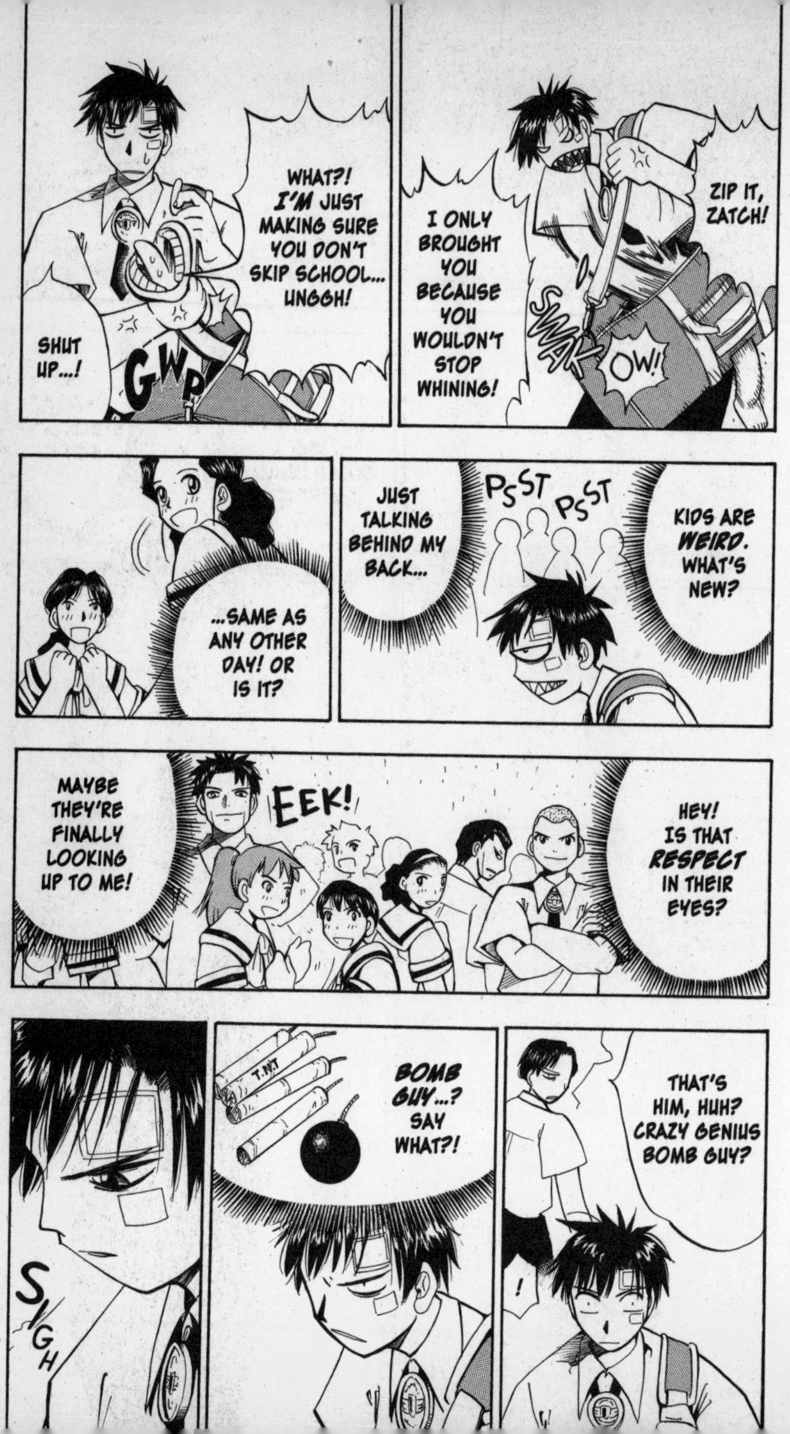
ZIP IT, ZATCH!
I ONLY BROUGHT YOU BECAUSE YOU WOULDN'T STOP WHINING!
SWAK
OW!
WHAT?! I'M JUST MAKING SURE YOU DON'T SKIP SCHOOL... UNGGH!
SHUT UP...!
GWP
KIDS ARE WEIRD. WHAT'S NEW?
PSST PSST
JUST TALKING BEHIND MY BACK...
...SAME AS ANY OTHER DAY! OR IS IT?
HEY! IS THAT RESPECT IN THEIR EYES?
EEK!
MAYBE THEY'RE FINALLY LOOKING UP TO ME!
THAT'S HIM, HUH? CRAZY GENIUS BOMB GUY?
!
BOMB GUY...? SAY WHAT?!
T.N.T
SIGH

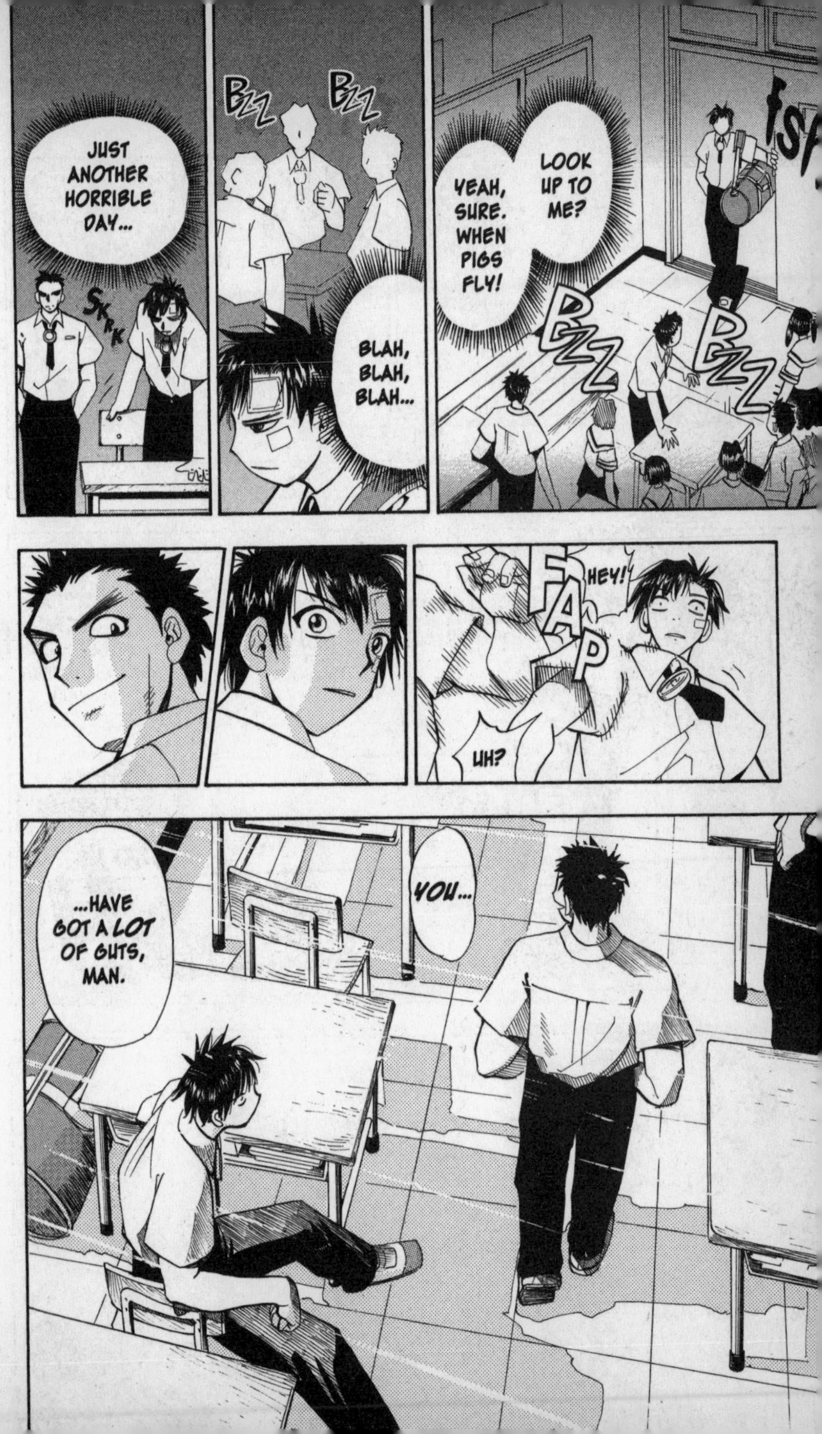
LOOK UP TO ME?
YEAH, SURE. WHEN PIGS FLY!
BZZ
BZZ
BZZ
BZZ
BLAH, BLAH, BLAH...
JUST ANOTHER HORRIBLE DAY...
SKRK
HEY!
FAP
UH?
YOU...
...HAVE GOT A LOT OF GUTS, MAN.

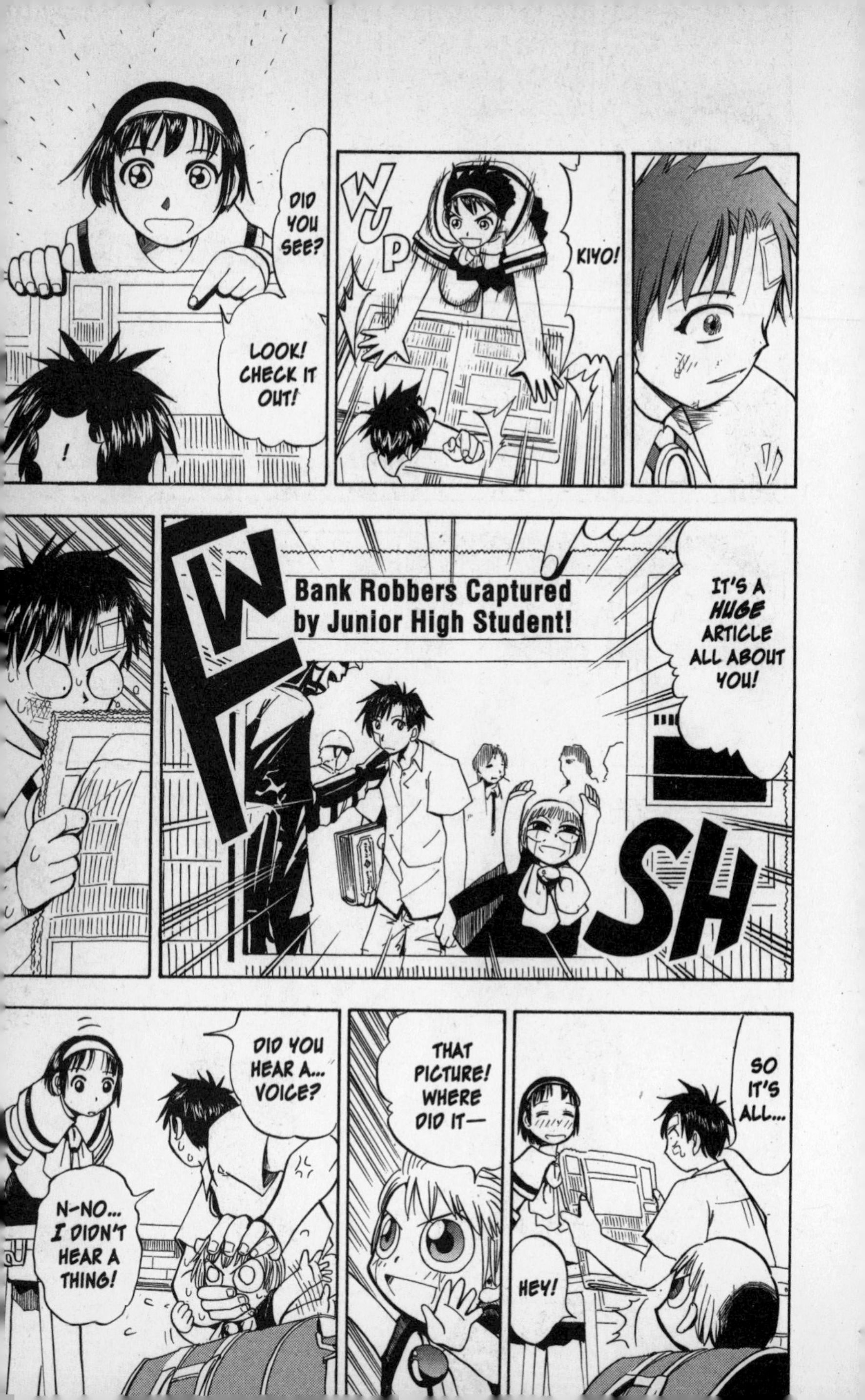
WUP
KIYO!
DID YOU SEE?
LOOK! CHECK IT OUT!
!
IT'S A HUGE ARTICLE ALL ABOUT YOU!
Bank Robbers Captured by Junior High Student!
FWSH
SO IT'S ALL...
HEY!
THAT PICTURE! WHERE DID IT—
DID YOU HEAR A... VOICE?
N-NO... I DIDN'T HEAR A THING!

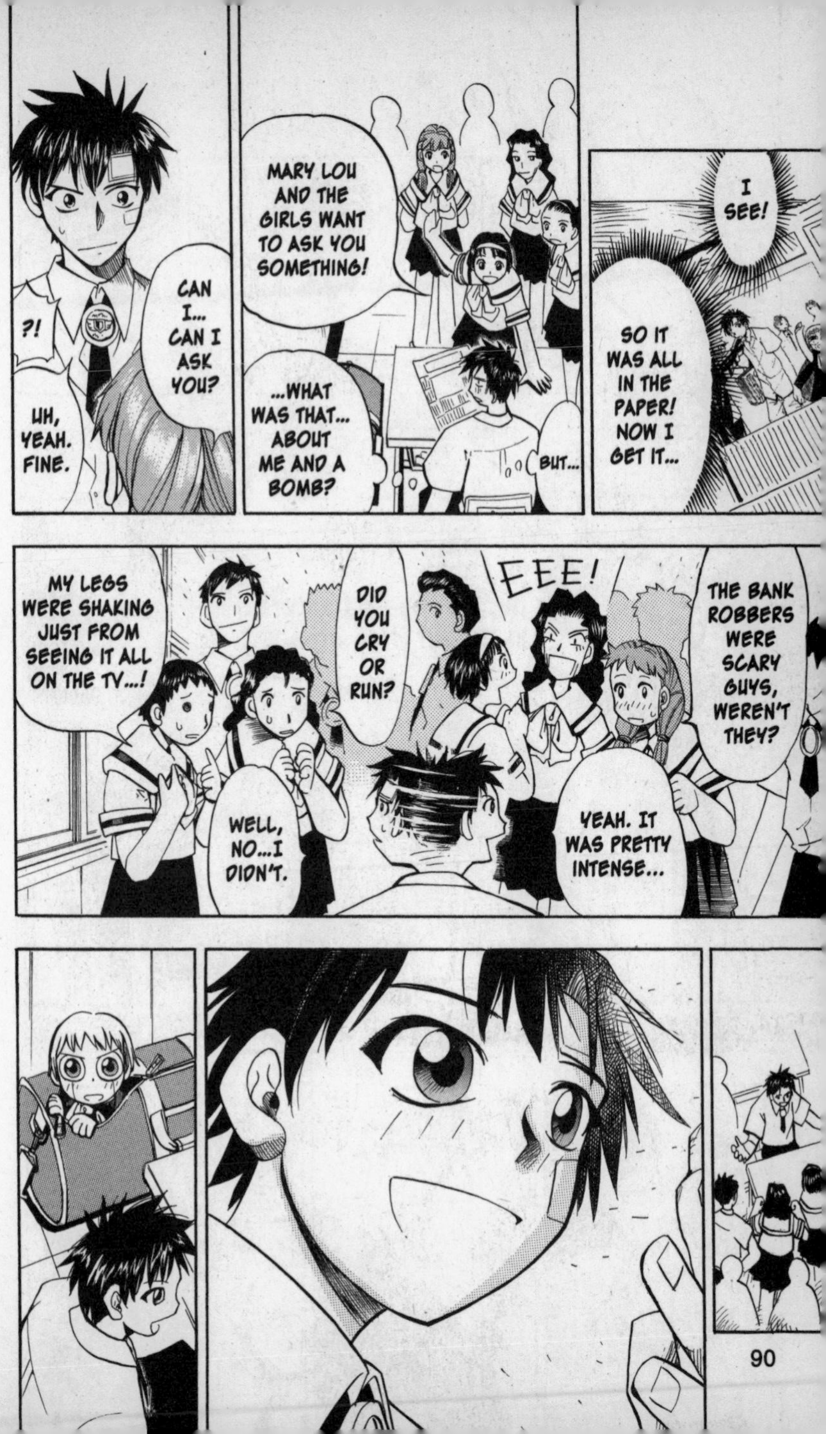
I SEE!
SO IT WAS ALL IN THE PAPER! NOW I GET IT...
MARY LOU AND THE GIRLS WANT TO ASK YOU SOMETHING!
BUT...
...WHAT WAS THAT... ABOUT ME AND A BOMB?
CAN I... CAN I ASK YOU?
?!
UH, YEAH. FINE.
THE BANK ROBBERS WERE SCARY GUYS, WEREN'T THEY?
EEE!
YEAH. IT WAS PRETTY INTENSE...
DID YOU CRY OR RUN?
WELL, NO...I DIDN'T.
MY LEGS WERE SHAKING JUST FROM SEEING IT ALL ON THE TV...!

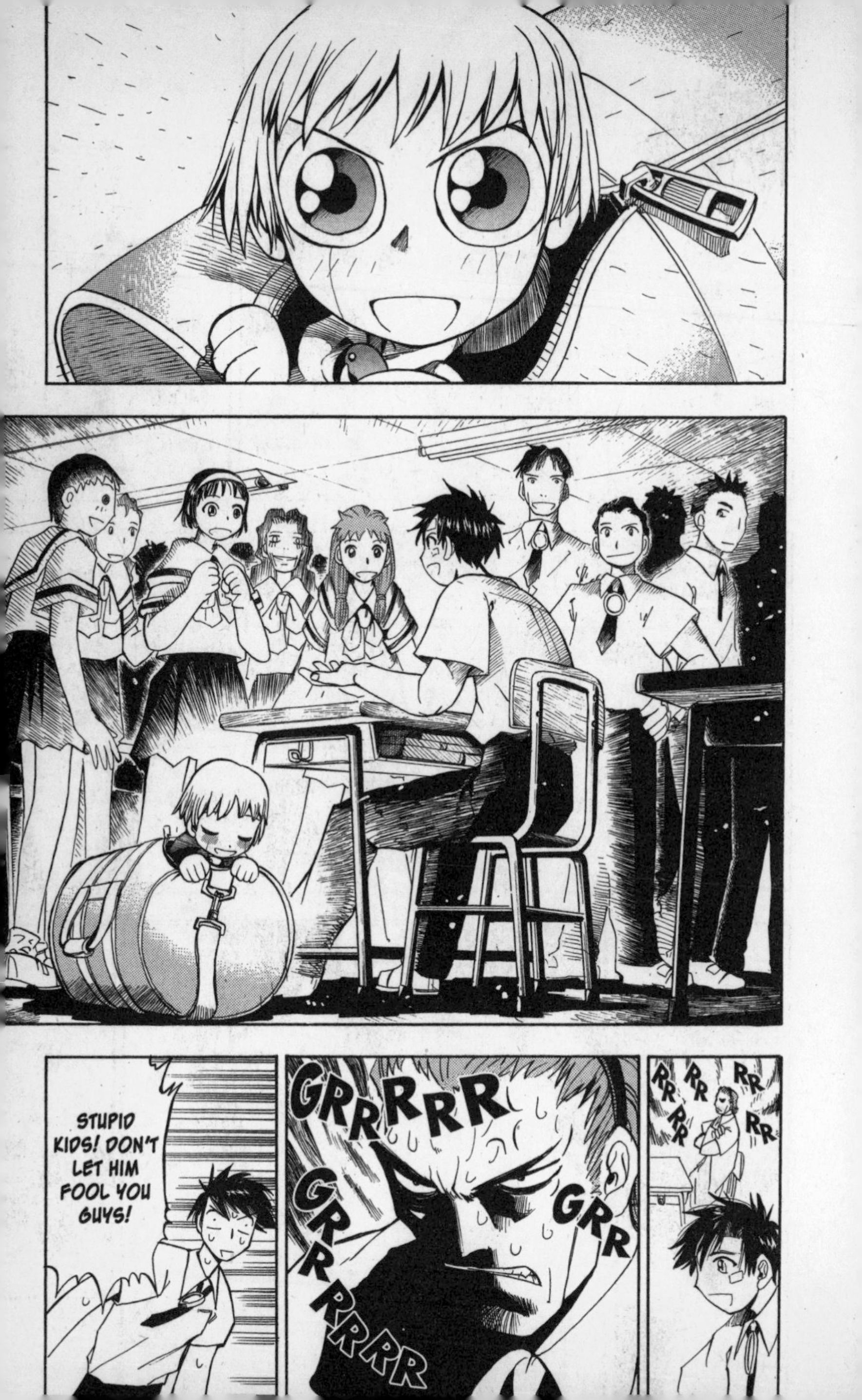
RR RR RR RR RR
GRRRRR
GRR
GRRRRRR
STUPID KIDS! DON'T LET HIM FOOL YOU GUYS!

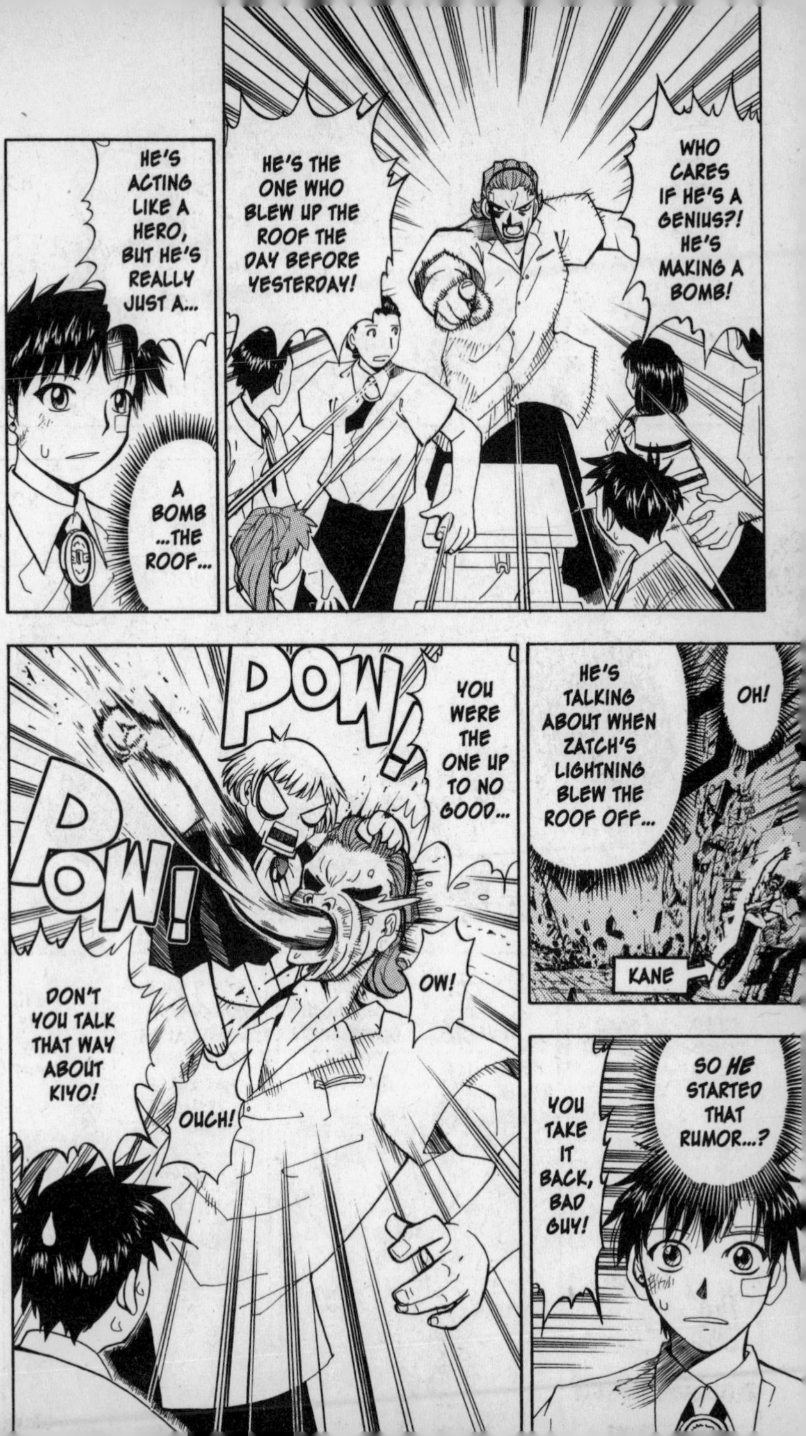
WHO CARES IF HE'S A GENIUS?! HE'S MAKING A BOMB!
HE'S THE ONE WHO BLEW UP THE ROOF THE DAY BEFORE YESTERDAY!
HE'S ACTING LIKE A HERO, BUT HE'S REALLY JUST A...
A BOMB ...THE ROOF...
OH!
HE'S TALKING ABOUT WHEN ZATCH'S LIGHTNING BLEW THE ROOF OFF...
KANE
SO HE STARTED THAT RUMOR...?
YOU TAKE IT BACK, BAD GUY!
POW!
YOU WERE THE ONE UP TO NO GOOD...
POW!
OW!
DON'T YOU TALK THAT WAY ABOUT KIYO!
OUCH!

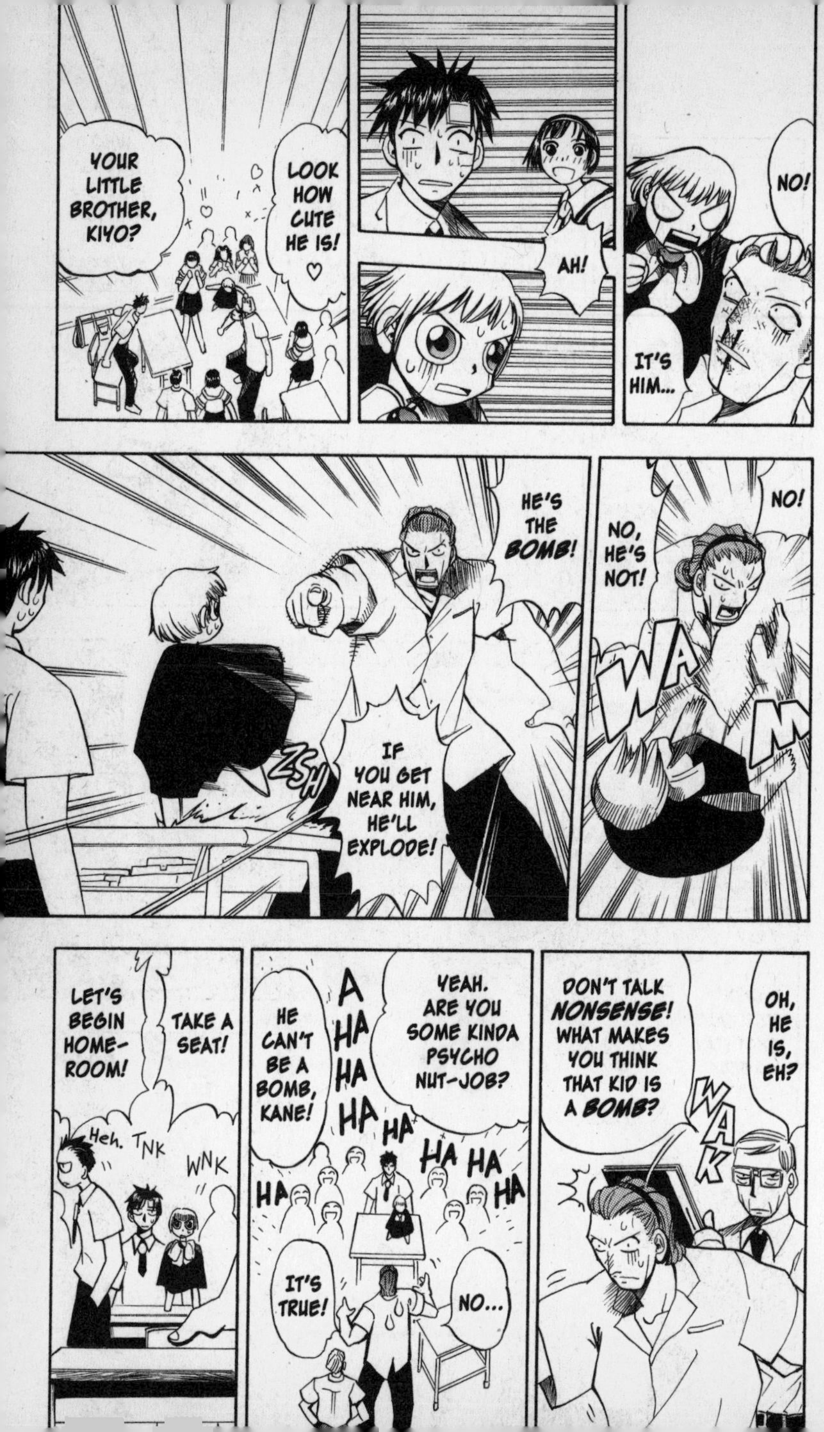
NO!
IT'S HIM...
AH!
LOOK HOW CUTE HE IS! ♡
YOUR LITTLE BROTHER, KIYO?
NO!
NO, HE'S NOT!
WAM
HE'S THE BOMB!
IF YOU GET NEAR HIM, HE'LL EXPLODE!
ZSH
OH, HE IS, EH?
DON'T TALK NONSENSE! WHAT MAKES YOU THINK THAT KID IS A BOMB?
WAK
YEAH. ARE YOU SOME KINDA PSYCHO NUT-JOB?
A HA HA HA
HE CAN'T BE A BOMB, KANE!
HA HA HA HA HA
NO...
IT'S TRUE!
TAKE A SEAT!
LET'S BEGIN HOME-ROOM!
WNK
Heh. TNK

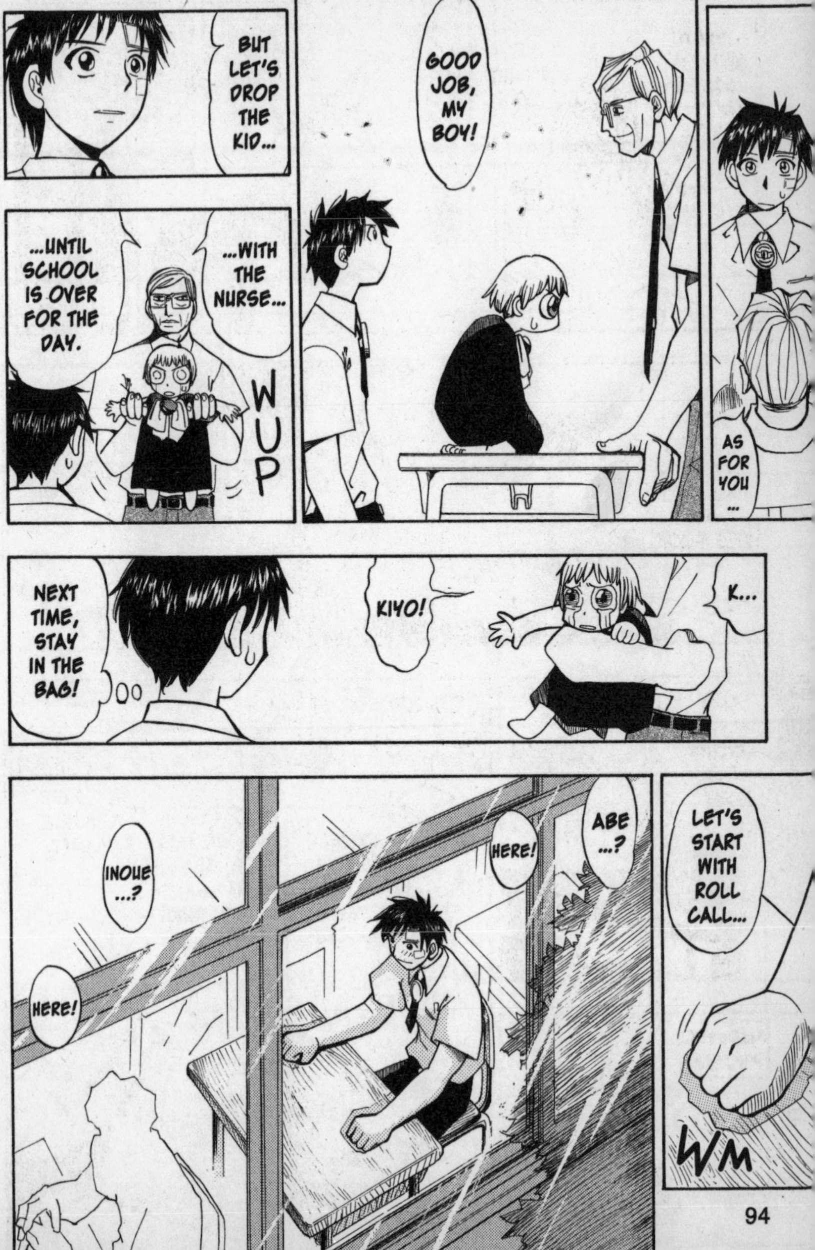
AS FOR YOU ...
GOOD JOB, MY BOY!
BUT LET'S DROP THE KID...
...WITH THE NURSE...
...UNTIL SCHOOL IS OVER FOR THE DAY.
WUP
K...
KIYO!
NEXT TIME, STAY IN THE BAG!
LET'S START WITH ROLL CALL...
WM
ABE ...?
HERE!
INOUE ...?
HERE!

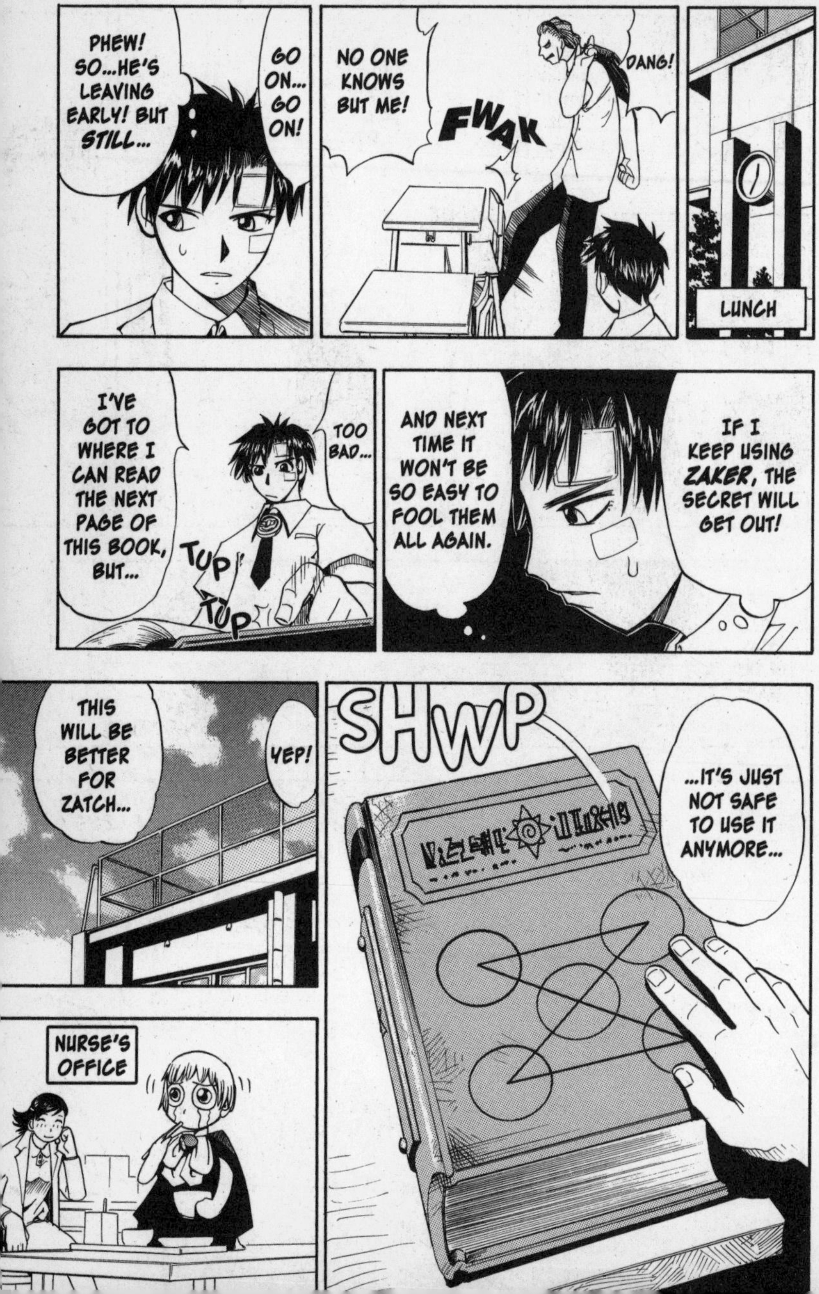
LUNCH
DANG!
NO ONE KNOWS BUT ME!
FWAK
GO ON... GO ON!
PHEW! SO...HE'S LEAVING EARLY! BUT STILL...
IF I KEEP USING ZAKER, THE SECRET WILL GET OUT!
AND NEXT TIME IT WON'T BE SO EASY TO FOOL THEM ALL AGAIN.
TOO BAD...
I'VE GOT TO WHERE I CAN READ THE NEXT PAGE OF THIS BOOK, BUT...
TUP
TUP
...IT'S JUST NOT SAFE TO USE IT ANYMORE...
SHWP
YEP!
THIS WILL BE BETTER FOR ZATCH...
NURSE'S OFFICE

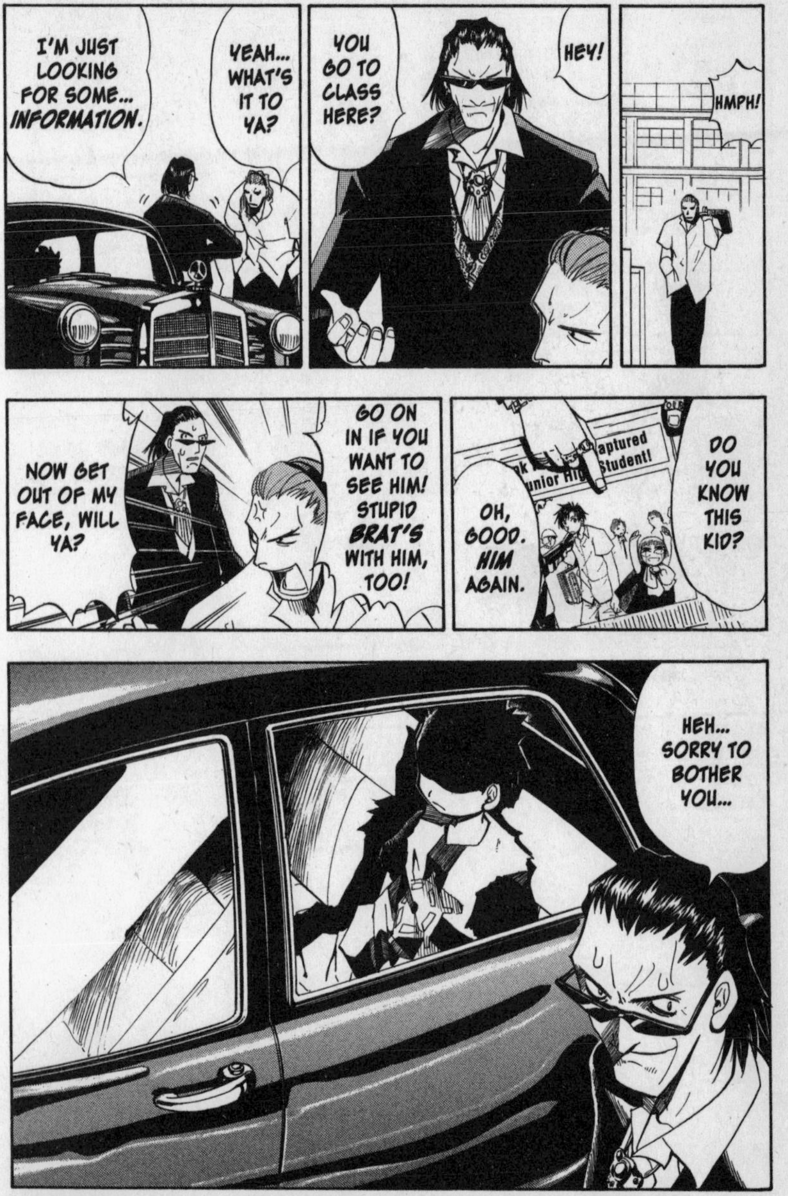
HMPH!
HEY!
YOU GO TO CLASS HERE?
YEAH... WHAT'S IT TO YA?
I'M JUST LOOKING FOR SOME... *INFORMATION.*
DO YOU KNOW THIS KID?
OH, GOOD. *HIM* AGAIN.
GO ON IN IF YOU WANT TO SEE HIM! STUPID *BRAT'S* WITH HIM, TOO!
NOW GET OUT OF MY FACE, WILL YA?
HEH... SORRY TO BOTHER YOU...

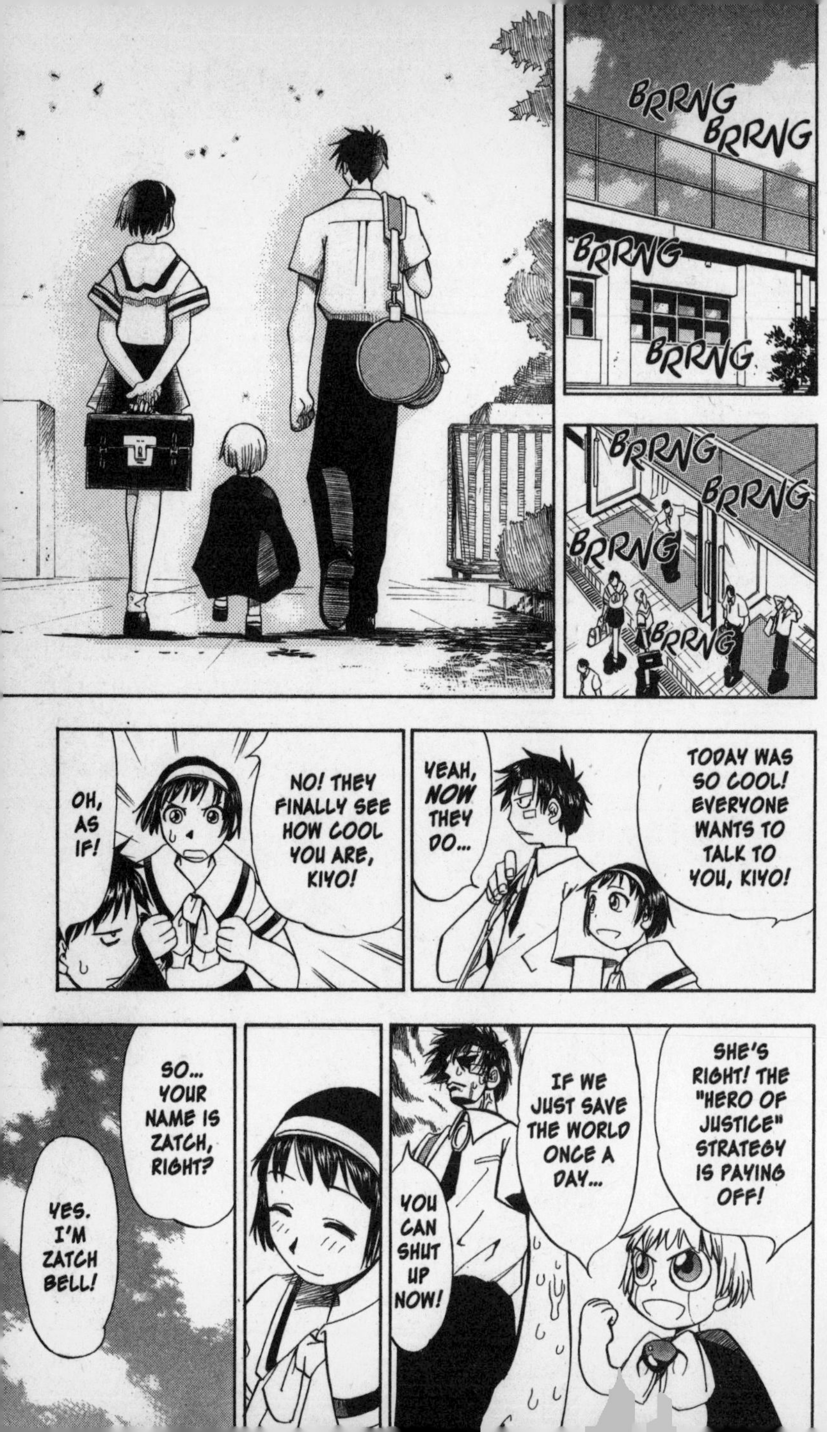
BRRNG
BRRNG
BRRNG
BRRNG
BRRNG
BRRNG
BRRNG
BRRNG
TODAY WAS SO COOL! EVERYONE WANTS TO TALK TO YOU, KIYO!
YEAH, NOW THEY DO...
NO! THEY FINALLY SEE HOW COOL YOU ARE, KIYO!
OH, AS IF!
SHE'S RIGHT! THE "HERO OF JUSTICE" STRATEGY IS PAYING OFF!
IF WE JUST SAVE THE WORLD ONCE A DAY...
YOU CAN SHUT UP NOW!
SO... YOUR NAME IS ZATCH, RIGHT?
YES. I'M ZATCH BELL!

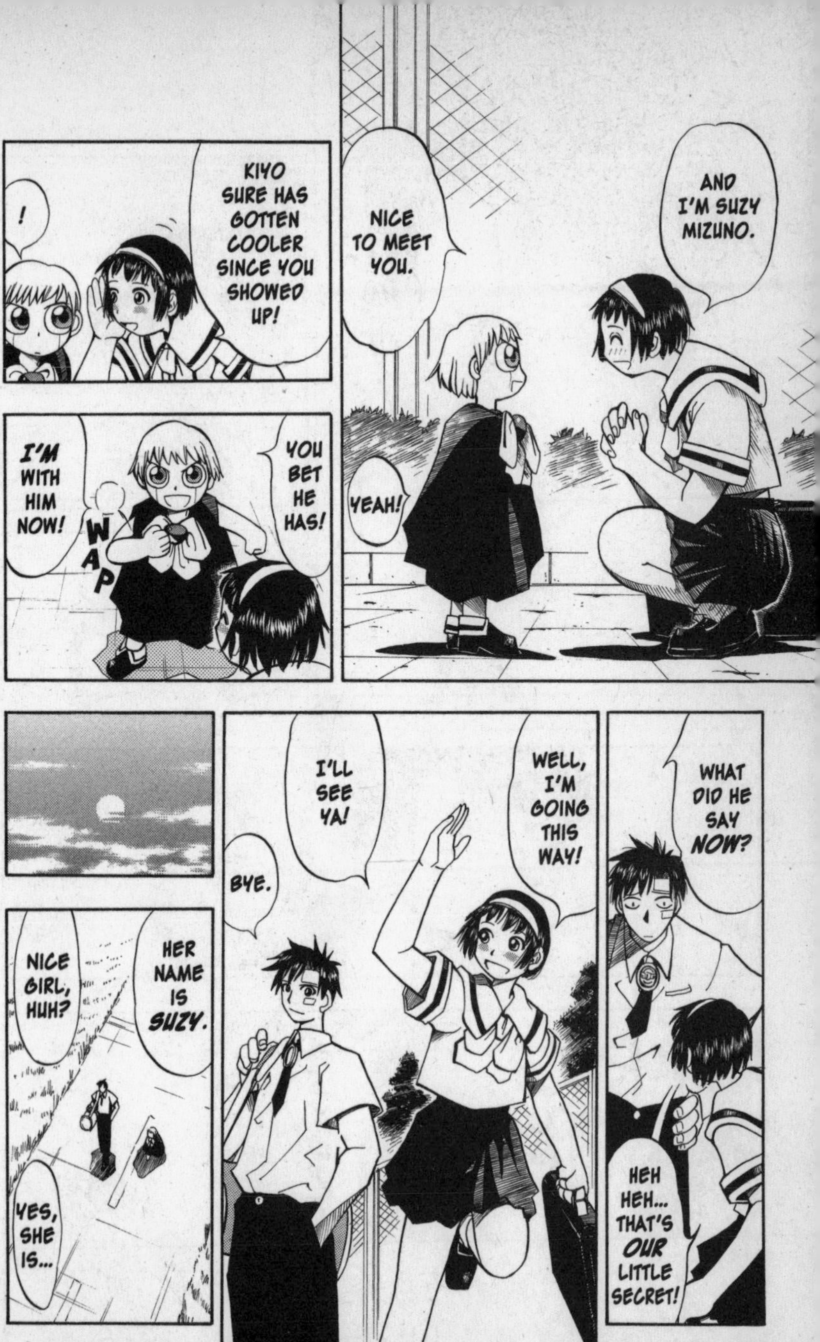
AND I'M SUZY MIZUNO.
NICE TO MEET YOU.
YEAH!
KIYO SURE HAS GOTTEN COOLER SINCE YOU SHOWED UP!
!
YOU BET HE HAS!
I'M WITH HIM NOW!
WAP
WHAT DID HE SAY NOW?
HEH HEH... THAT'S OUR LITTLE SECRET!
WELL, I'M GOING THIS WAY!
I'LL SEE YA!
BYE.
HER NAME IS SUZY.
NICE GIRL, HUH?
YES, SHE IS...

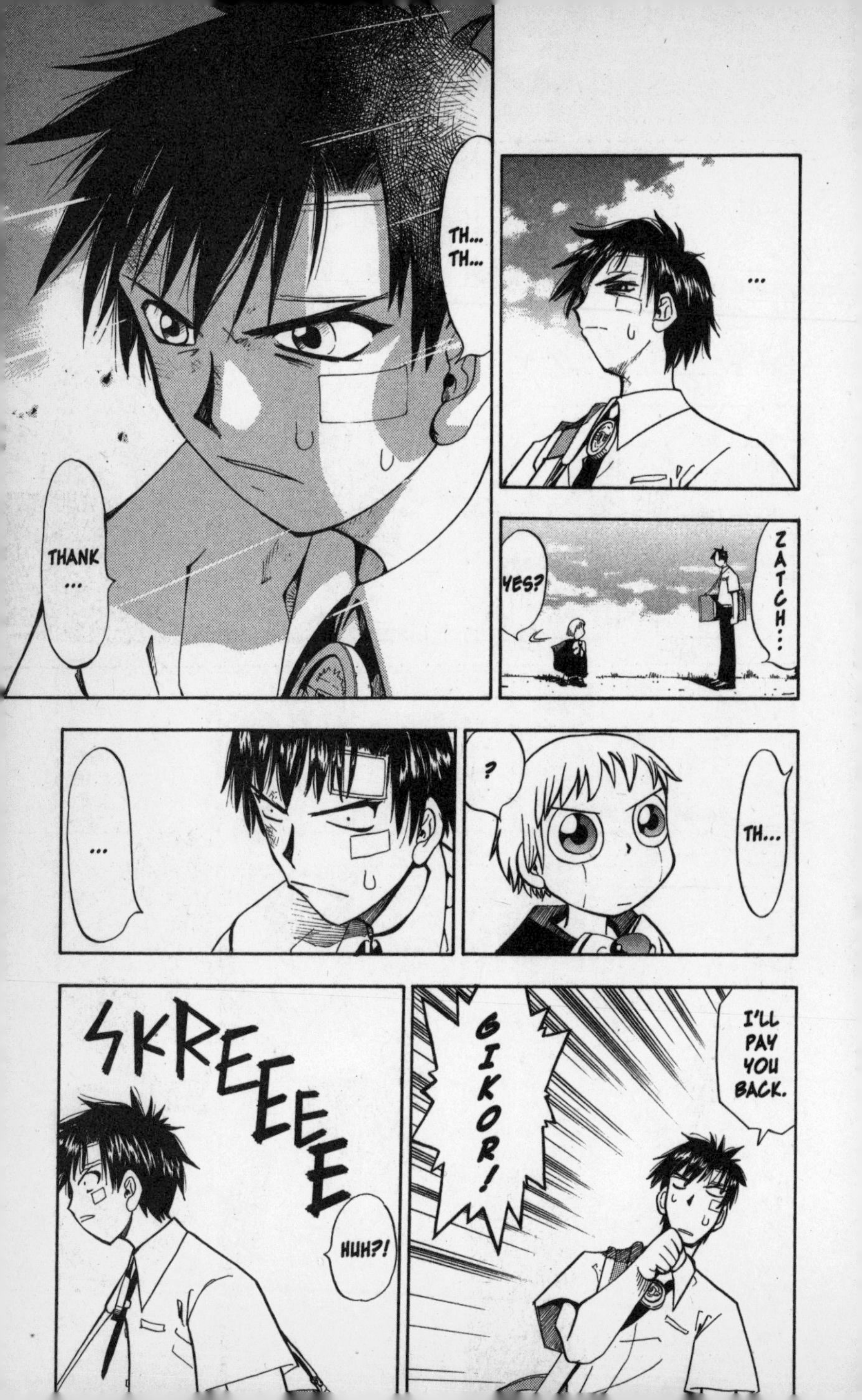
...
ZATCH...
YES?
TH...
TH...
THANK
...
TH...
?
...
I'LL PAY YOU BACK.
GIKOR!
SKREEEEE
HUH?!

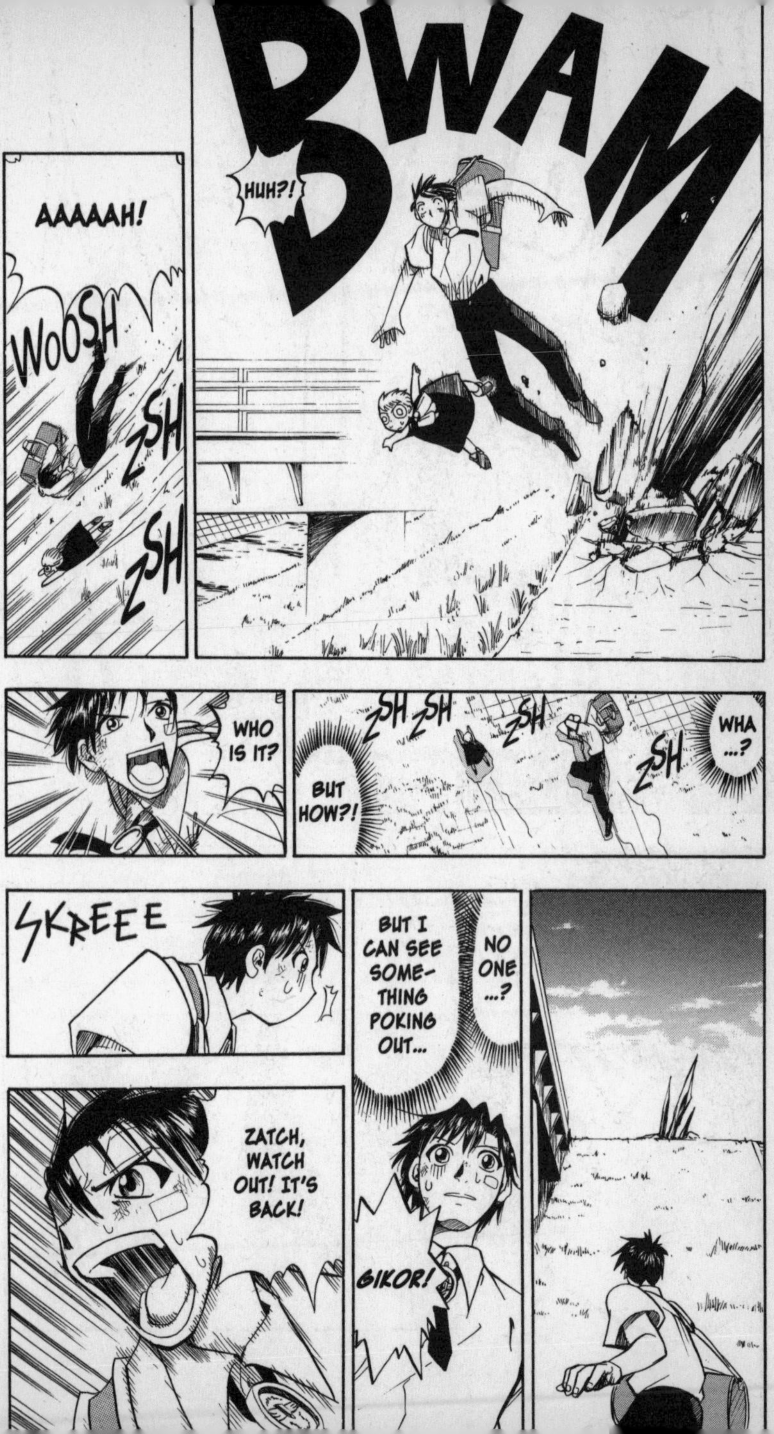
BWAM
HUH?!
AAAAAH!
WOOSH
ZSH
ZSH
WHA ...?
ZSH
ZSH
ZSH
ZSH
BUT HOW?!
WHO IS IT?
NO ONE ...?
BUT I CAN SEE SOME-THING POKING OUT...
GIKOR!
SKREEE
ZATCH, WATCH OUT! IT'S BACK!

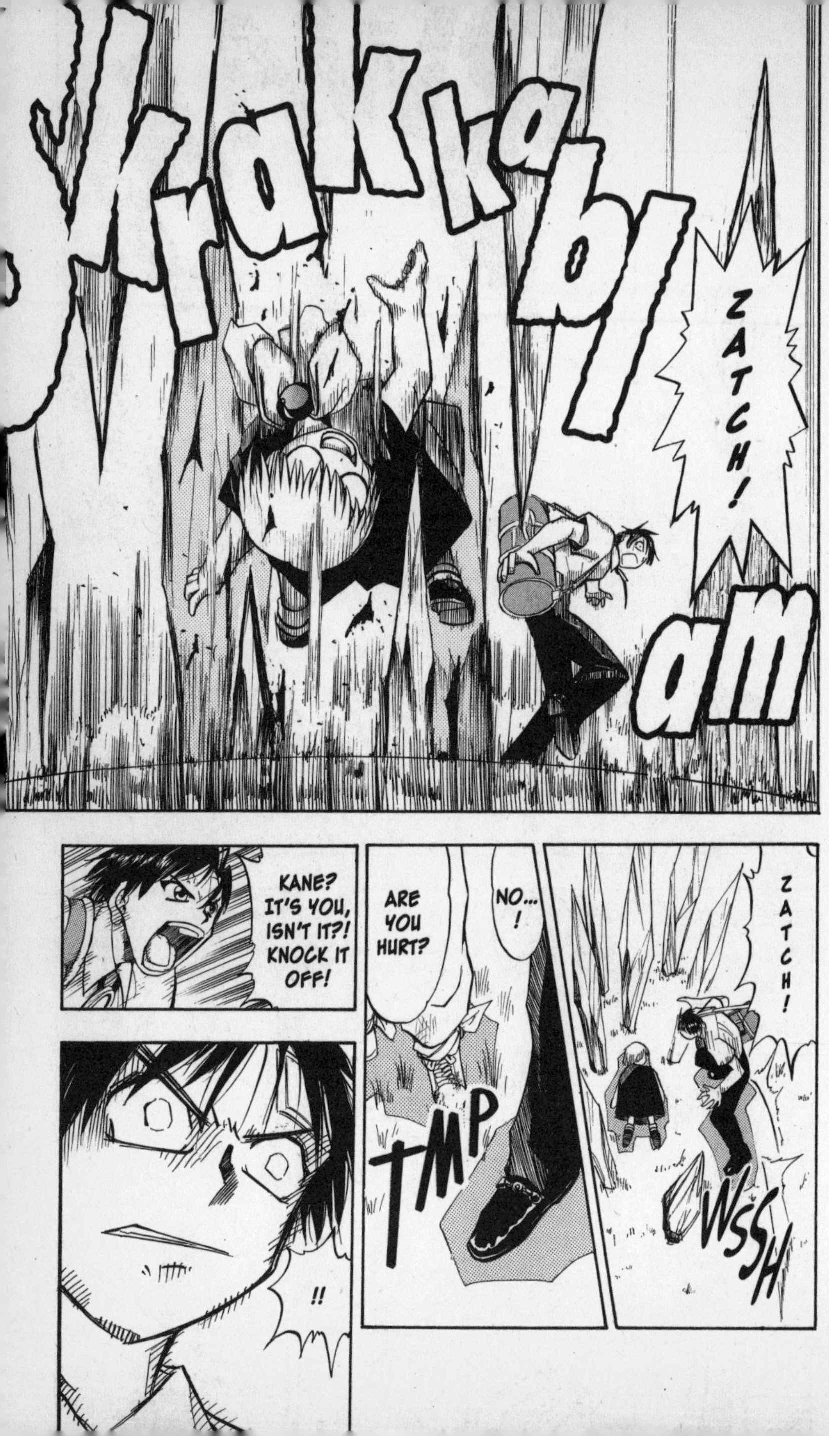
KRAKKABLAM
ZATCH!
ZATCH!
WSSH
NO... !
ARE YOU HURT?
TMP
KANE? IT'S YOU, ISN'T IT?! KNOCK IT OFF!
!!

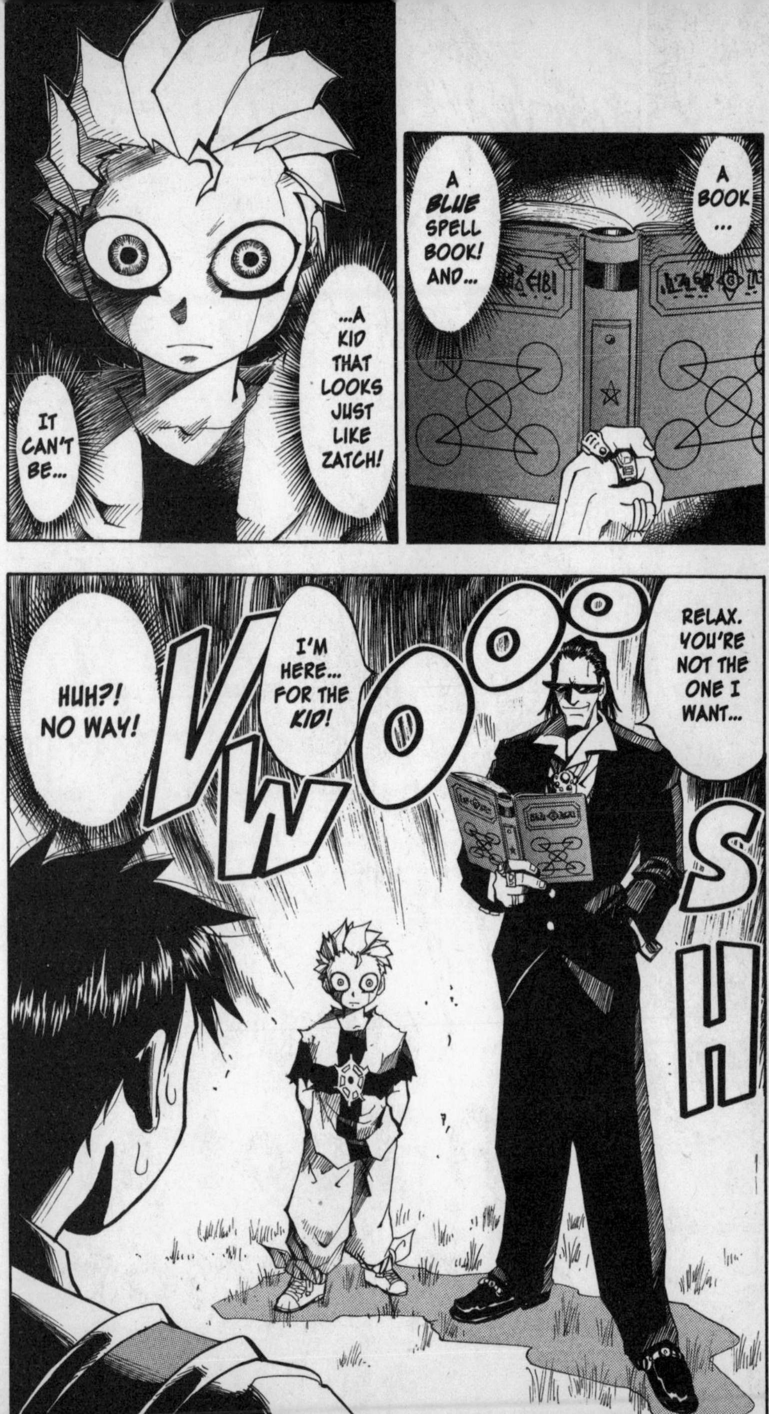
A BOOK...
A BLUE SPELL BOOK! AND...
...A KID THAT LOOKS JUST LIKE ZATCH!
IT CAN'T BE...
RELAX. YOU'RE NOT THE ONE I WANT...
I'M HERE... FOR THE KID!
HUH?! NO WAY!
VWOOOOSH

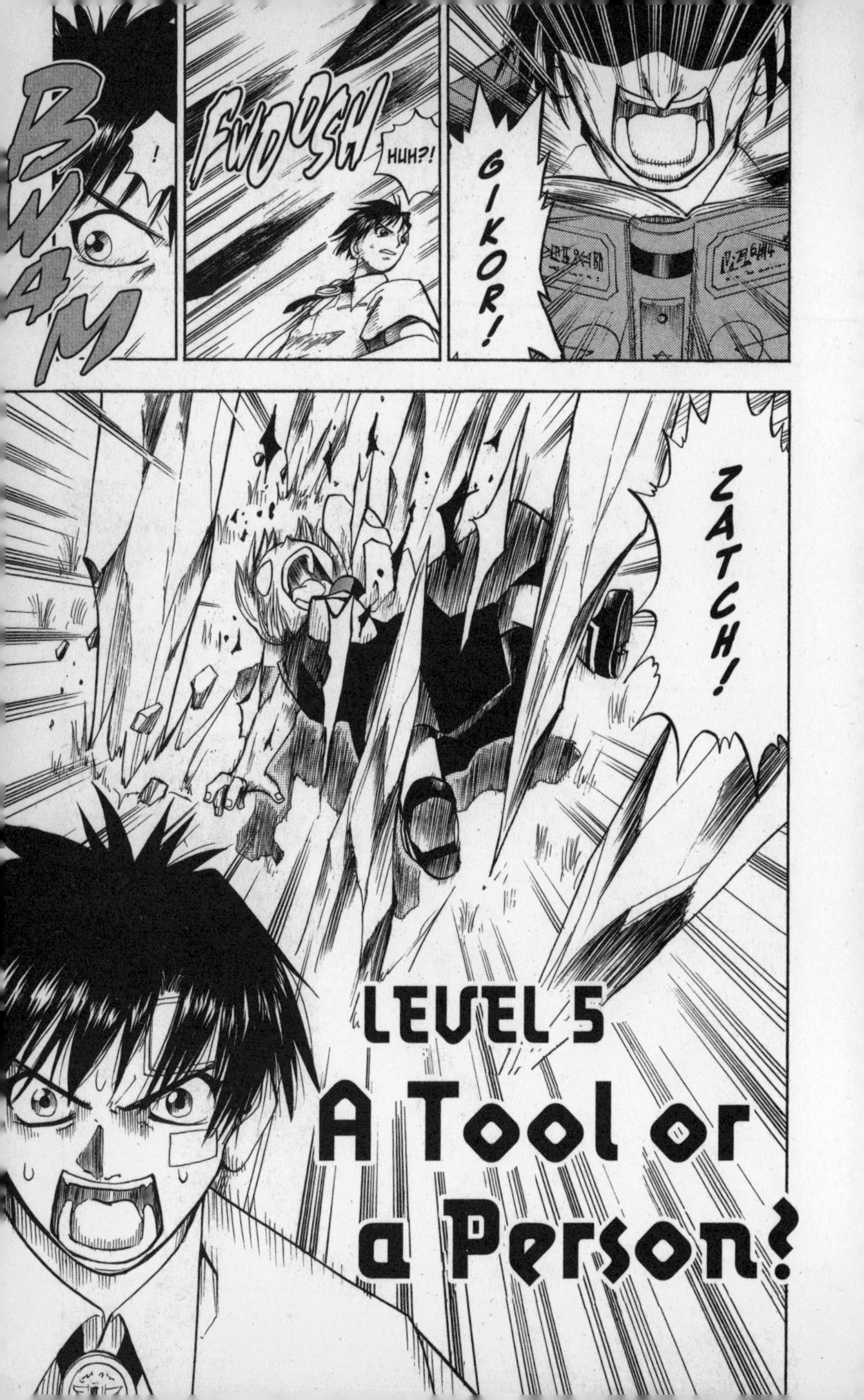
GIKOR!
FWOOSH
HUH?!
!
BWAM
ZATCH!
LEVEL 5
A Tool or a Person?

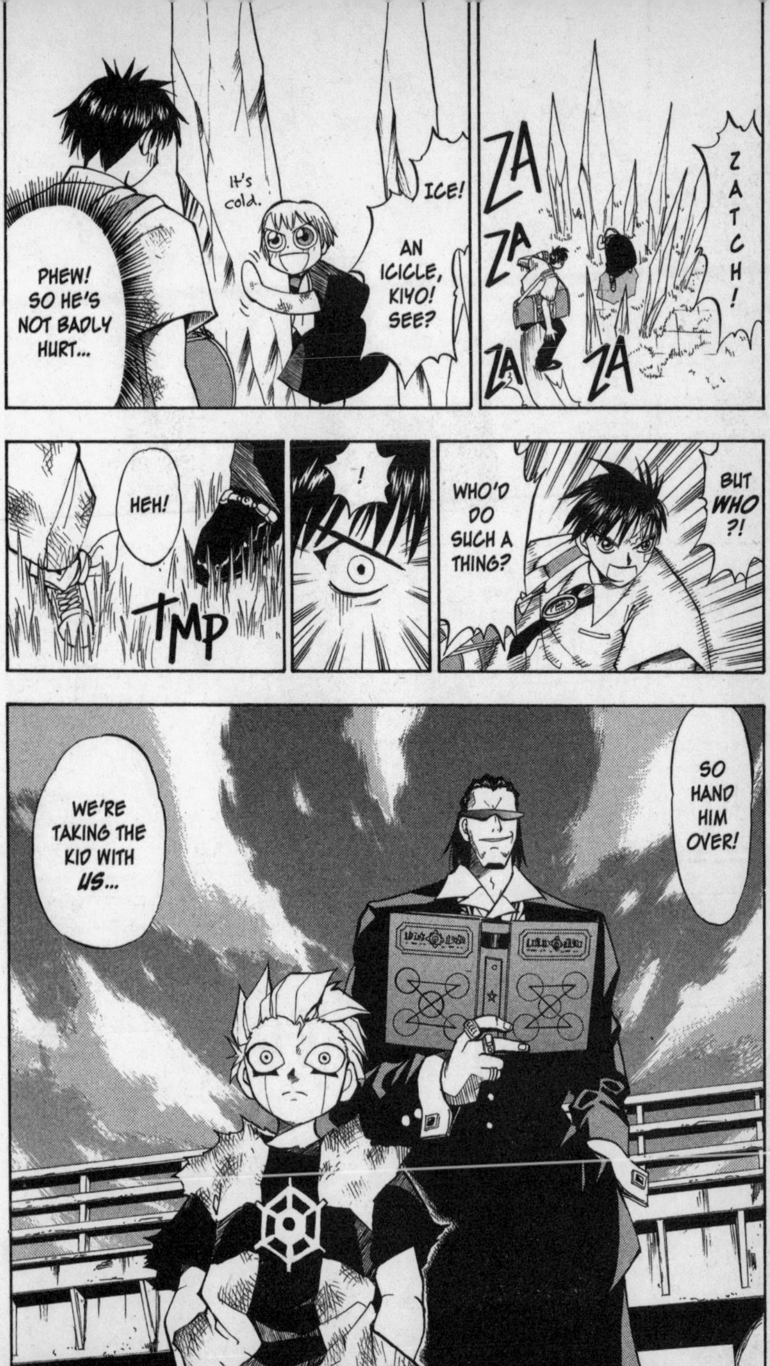
ZATCH!
ZA
ZA
ZA
ZA
ICE!
It's cold.
AN ICICLE, KIYO! SEE?
PHEW! SO HE'S NOT BADLY HURT...
BUT WHO?!
WHO'D DO SUCH A THING?
!
HEH!
TMP
WE'RE TAKING THE KID WITH US...
SO HAND HIM OVER!

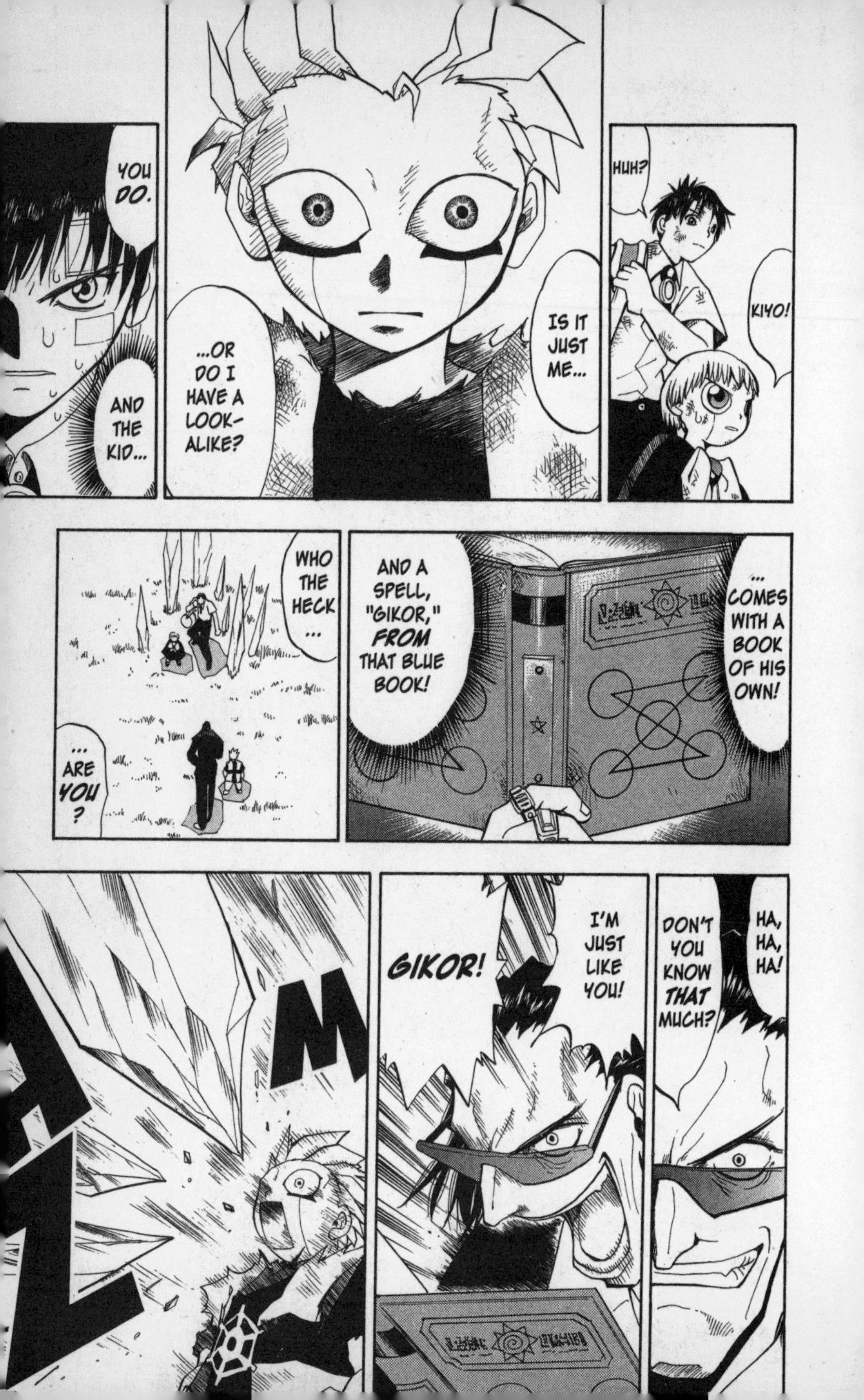
HUH?
KIYO!
IS IT JUST ME...
...OR DO I HAVE A LOOK-ALIKE?
YOU DO.
AND THE KID...
...COMES WITH A BOOK OF HIS OWN!
AND A SPELL, "GIKOR," *FROM* THAT BLUE BOOK!
WHO THE HECK ...
... ARE *YOU* ?
HA, HA, HA!
DON'T YOU KNOW *THAT* MUCH?
I'M JUST LIKE YOU!
GIKOR!
M

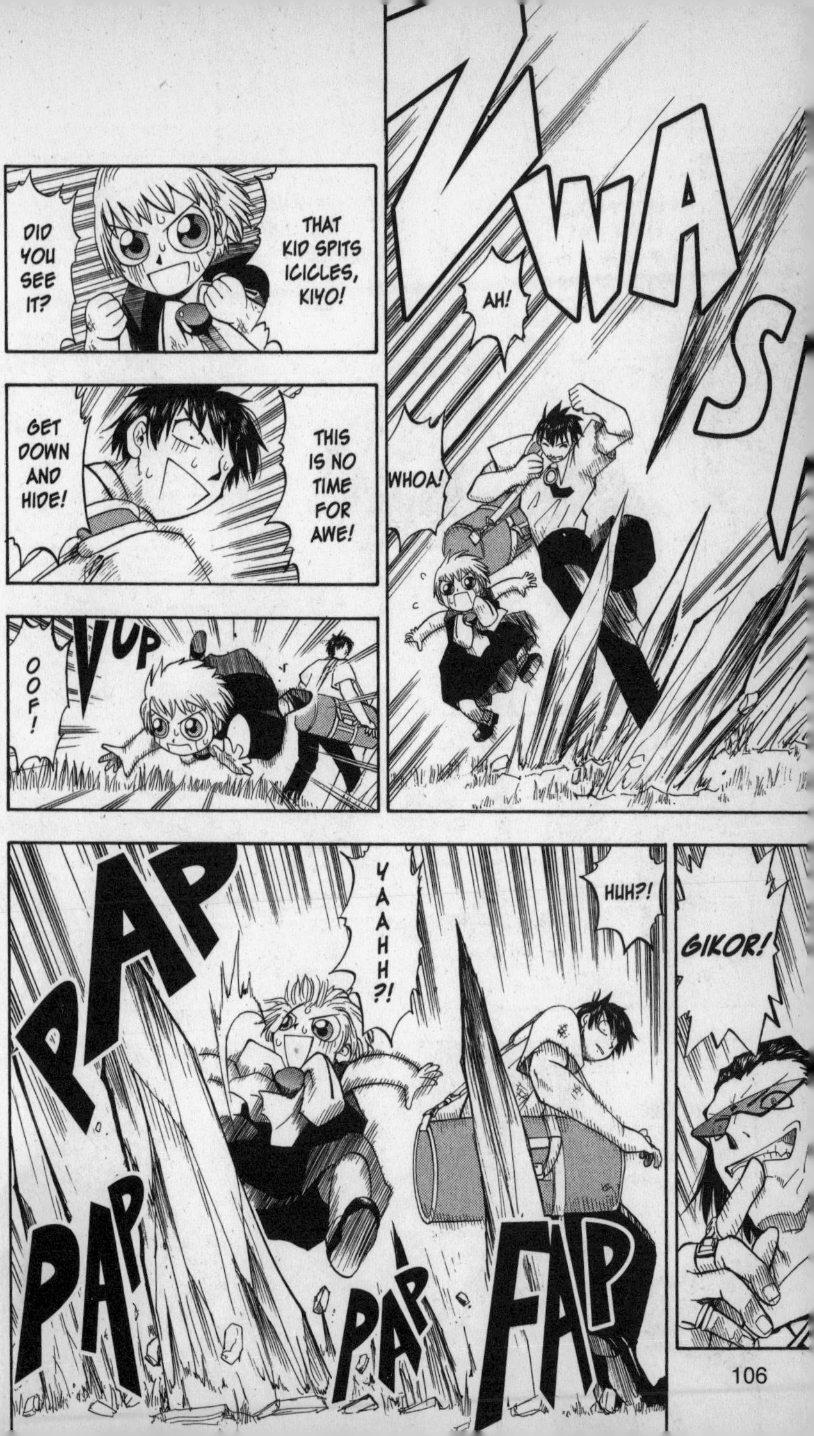
WAS
AH!
WHOA!
THAT KID SPITS ICICLES, KIYO!
DID YOU SEE IT?
THIS IS NO TIME FOR AWE!
GET DOWN AND HIDE!
VUP
OOF!
HUH?!
GIKOR!
YAAHH?!
PAP
PAP
PAP
PAP
FAP

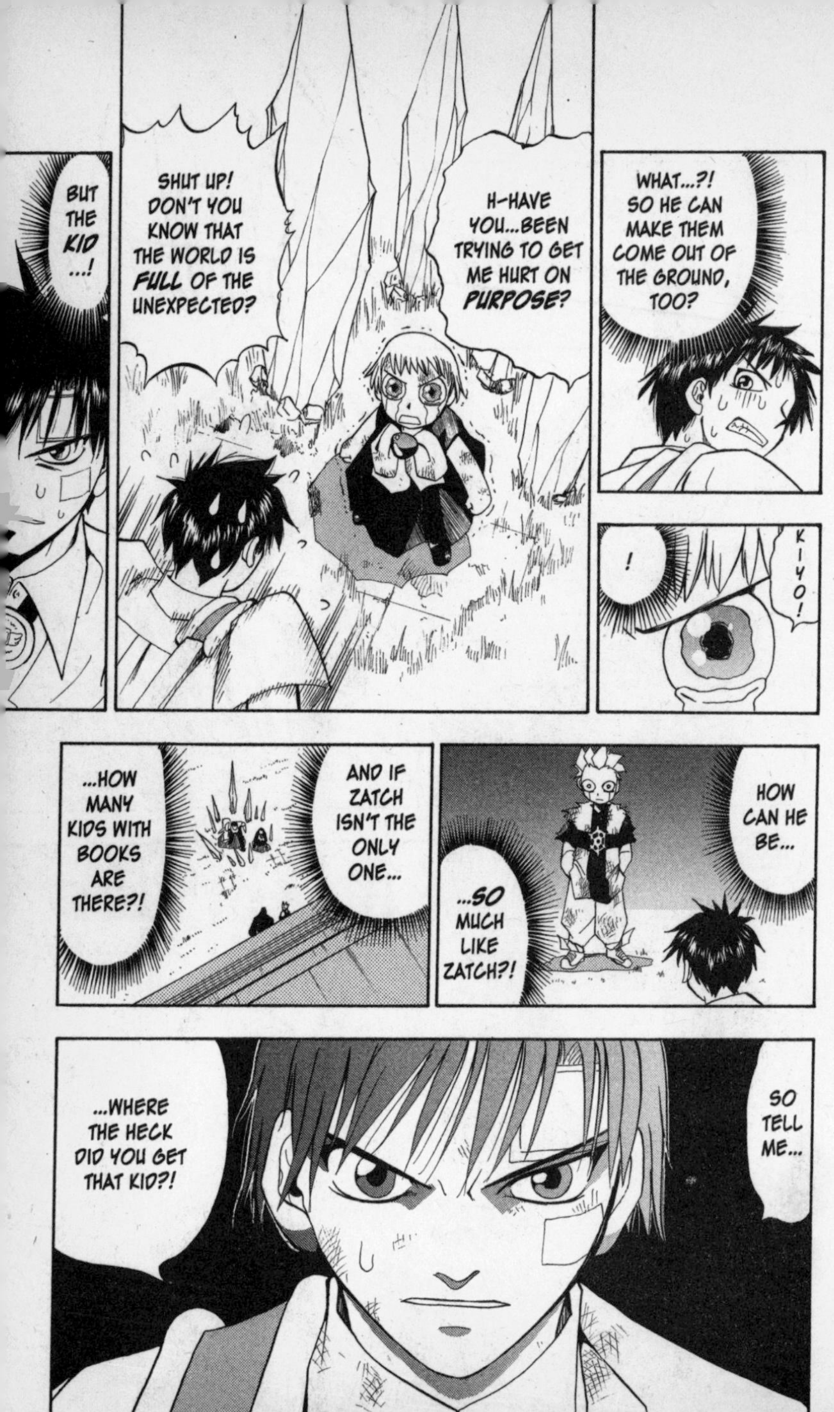
WHAT...?! SO HE CAN MAKE THEM COME OUT OF THE GROUND, TOO?
!
KIYO!
H-HAVE YOU...BEEN TRYING TO GET ME HURT ON PURPOSE?
SHUT UP! DON'T YOU KNOW THAT THE WORLD IS FULL OF THE UNEXPECTED?
BUT THE KID ...!
HOW CAN HE BE...
...SO MUCH LIKE ZATCH?!
AND IF ZATCH ISN'T THE ONLY ONE...
...HOW MANY KIDS WITH BOOKS ARE THERE?!
SO TELL ME...
...WHERE THE HECK DID YOU GET THAT KID?!

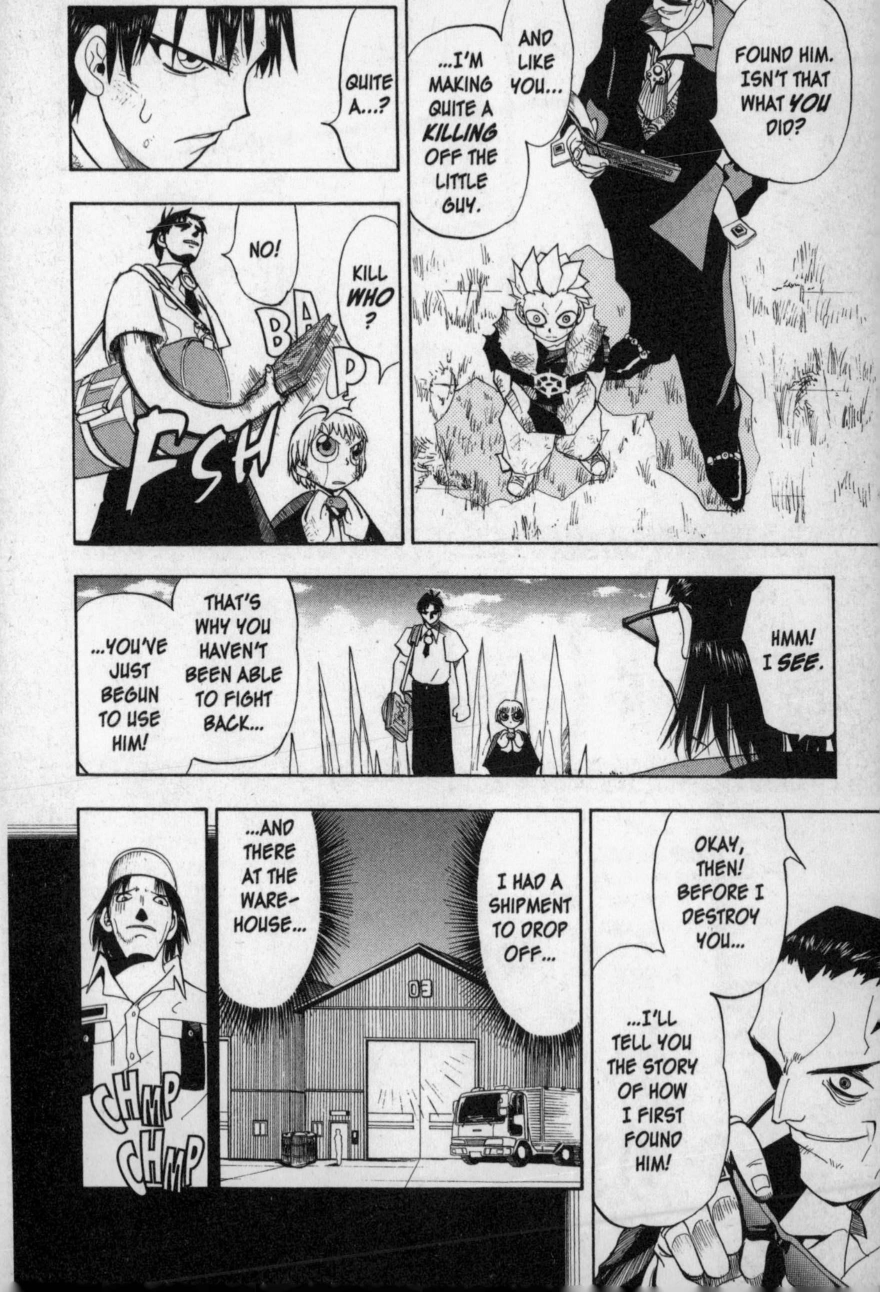
FOUND HIM. ISN'T THAT WHAT YOU DID?
AND LIKE YOU...
...I'M MAKING QUITE A KILLING OFF THE LITTLE GUY.
QUITE A...?
KILL WHO?
NO!
BAP
FSH
HMM! I SEE.
THAT'S WHY YOU HAVEN'T BEEN ABLE TO FIGHT BACK...
...YOU'VE JUST BEGUN TO USE HIM!
OKAY, THEN! BEFORE I DESTROY YOU...
...I'LL TELL YOU THE STORY OF HOW I FIRST FOUND HIM!
I HAD A SHIPMENT TO DROP OFF...
...AND THERE AT THE WARE-HOUSE...
CHMP CHMP

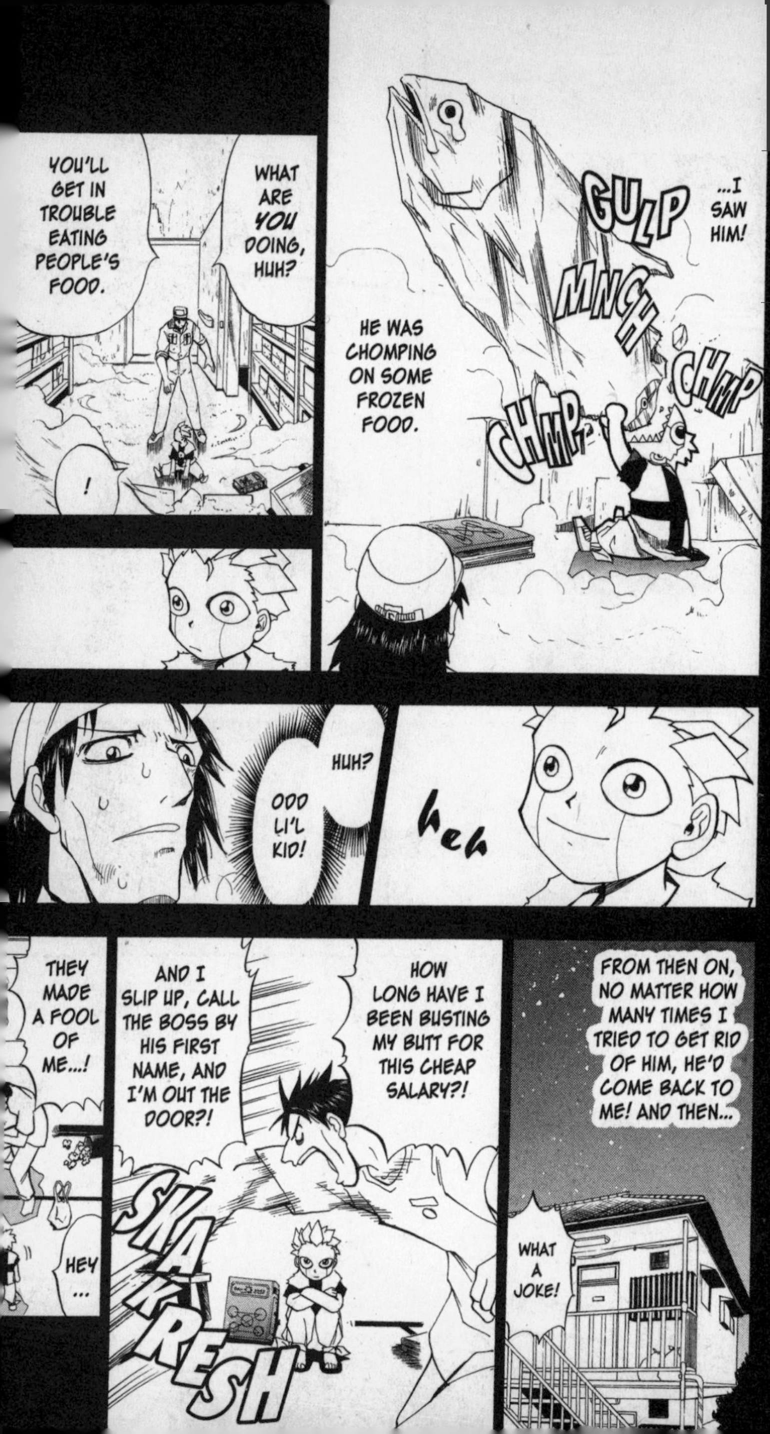
...I SAW HIM!
GULP
MNCH
CHMP
CHMP
HE WAS CHOMPING ON SOME FROZEN FOOD.
WHAT ARE *YOU* DOING, HUH?
YOU'LL GET IN TROUBLE EATING PEOPLE'S FOOD.
!
heh
HUH?
ODD LI'L KID!
FROM THEN ON, NO MATTER HOW MANY TIMES I TRIED TO GET RID OF HIM, HE'D COME BACK TO ME! AND THEN...
WHAT A JOKE!
HOW LONG HAVE I BEEN BUSTING MY BUTT FOR THIS CHEAP SALARY?!
AND I SLIP UP, CALL THE BOSS BY HIS FIRST NAME, AND I'M OUT THE DOOR?!
SKAKRESH
THEY MADE A FOOL OF ME...!
HEY ...

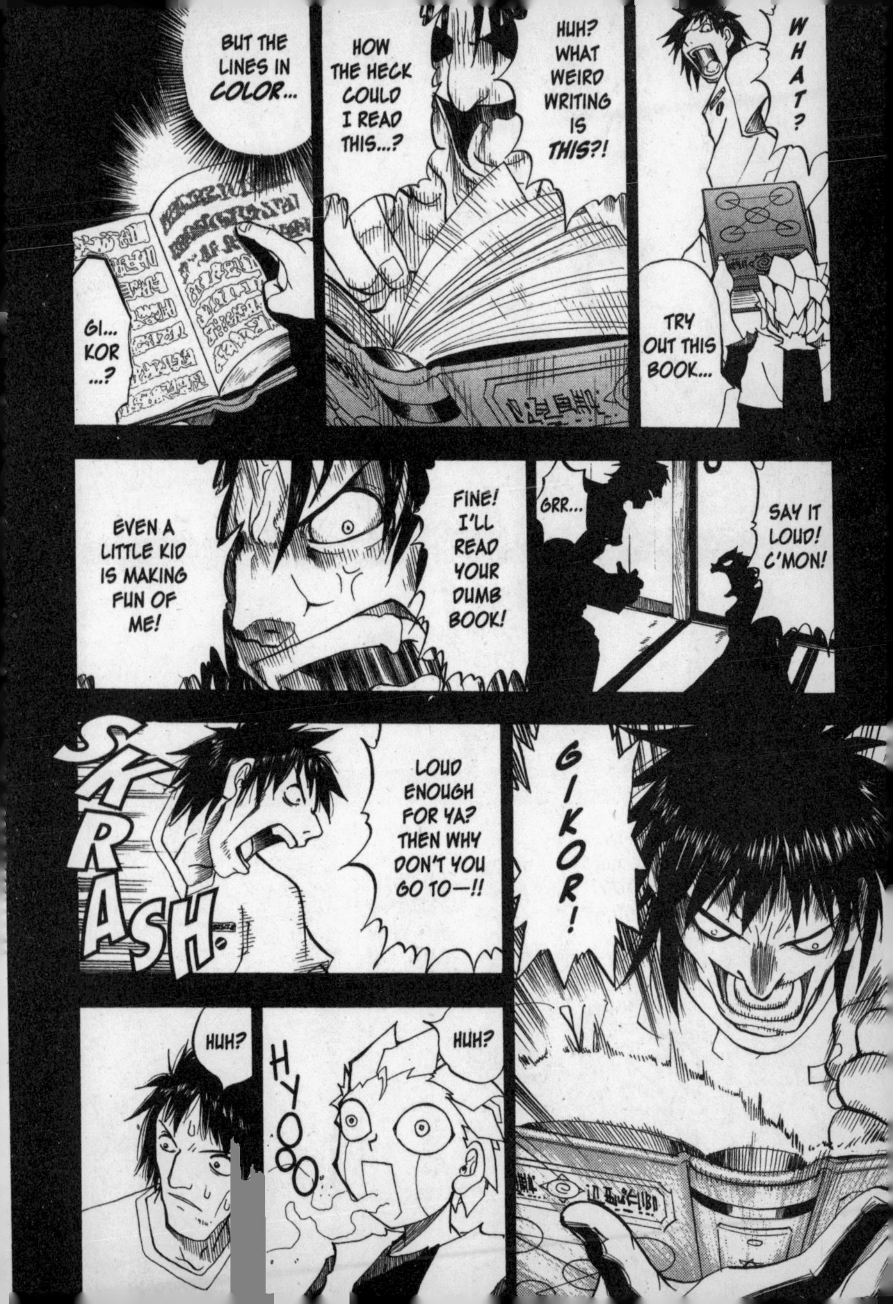
WHAT?
TRY OUT THIS BOOK...
HUH? WHAT WEIRD WRITING IS THIS?!
HOW THE HECK COULD I READ THIS...?
BUT THE LINES IN COLOR...
GI... KOR ...?
SAY IT LOUD! C'MON!
GRR...
FINE! I'LL READ YOUR DUMB BOOK!
EVEN A LITTLE KID IS MAKING FUN OF ME!
GIKOR!
LOUD ENOUGH FOR YA? THEN WHY DON'T YOU GO TO—!!
SKRASH
HUH?
HYOOO
HUH?

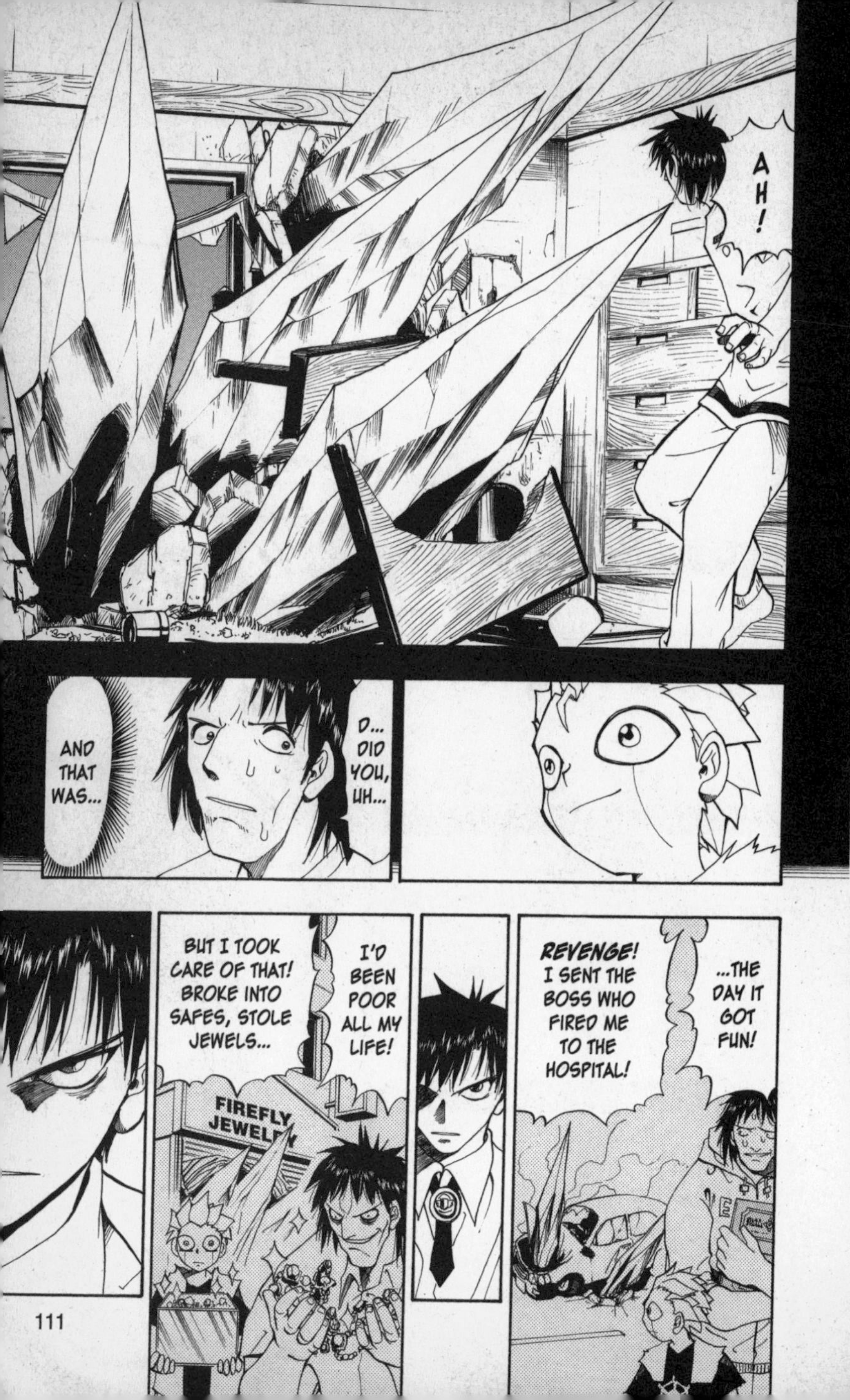
AH!
D... DID YOU, UH...
AND THAT WAS...
...THE DAY IT GOT FUN!
REVENGE! I SENT THE BOSS WHO FIRED ME TO THE HOSPITAL!
I'D BEEN POOR ALL MY LIFE!
BUT I TOOK CARE OF THAT! BROKE INTO SAFES, STOLE JEWELS...
FIREFLY JEWELR

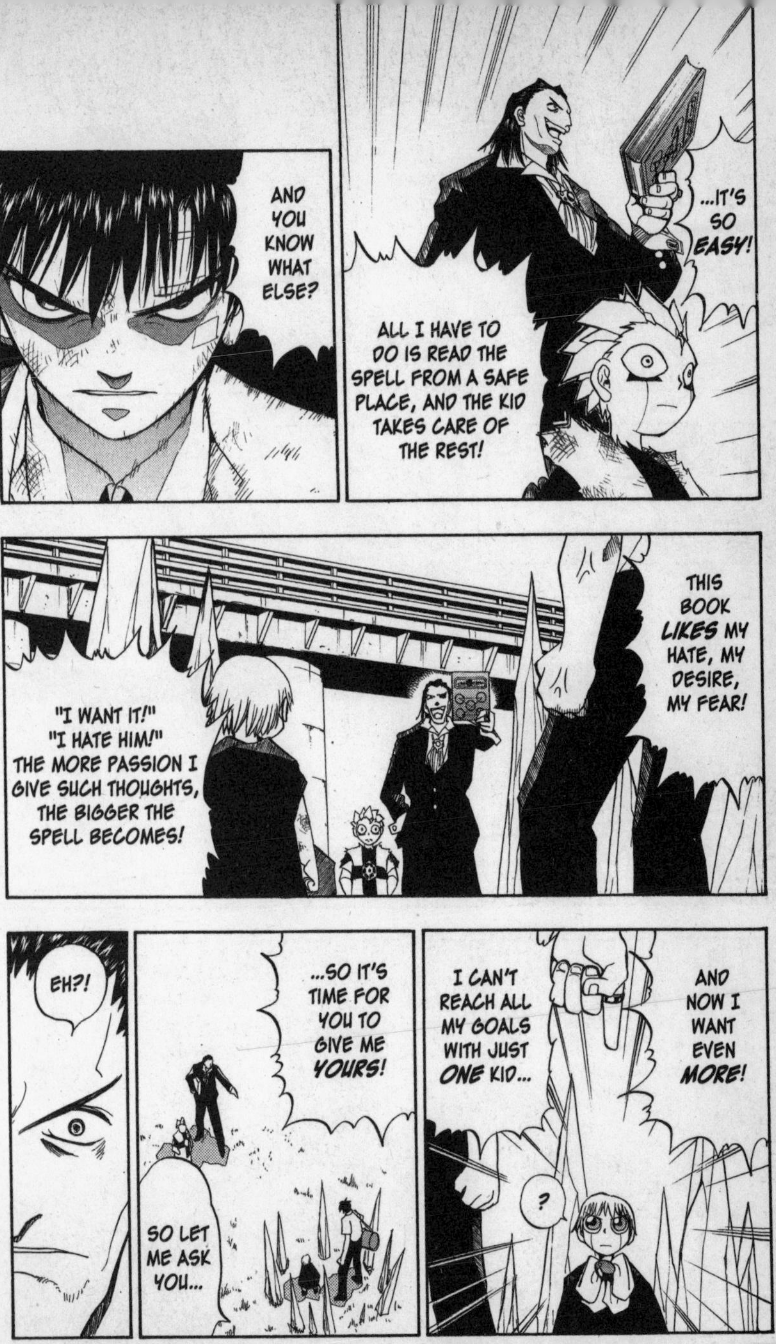

...IT'S SO EASY!
ALL I HAVE TO DO IS READ THE SPELL FROM A SAFE PLACE, AND THE KID TAKES CARE OF THE REST!
AND YOU KNOW WHAT ELSE?
THIS BOOK LIKES MY HATE, MY DESIRE, MY FEAR!
"I WANT IT!" "I HATE HIM!" THE MORE PASSION I GIVE SUCH THOUGHTS, THE BIGGER THE SPELL BECOMES!
AND NOW I WANT EVEN MORE!
I CAN'T REACH ALL MY GOALS WITH JUST ONE KID...
?
...SO IT'S TIME FOR YOU TO GIVE ME YOURS!
SO LET ME ASK YOU...
EH?!

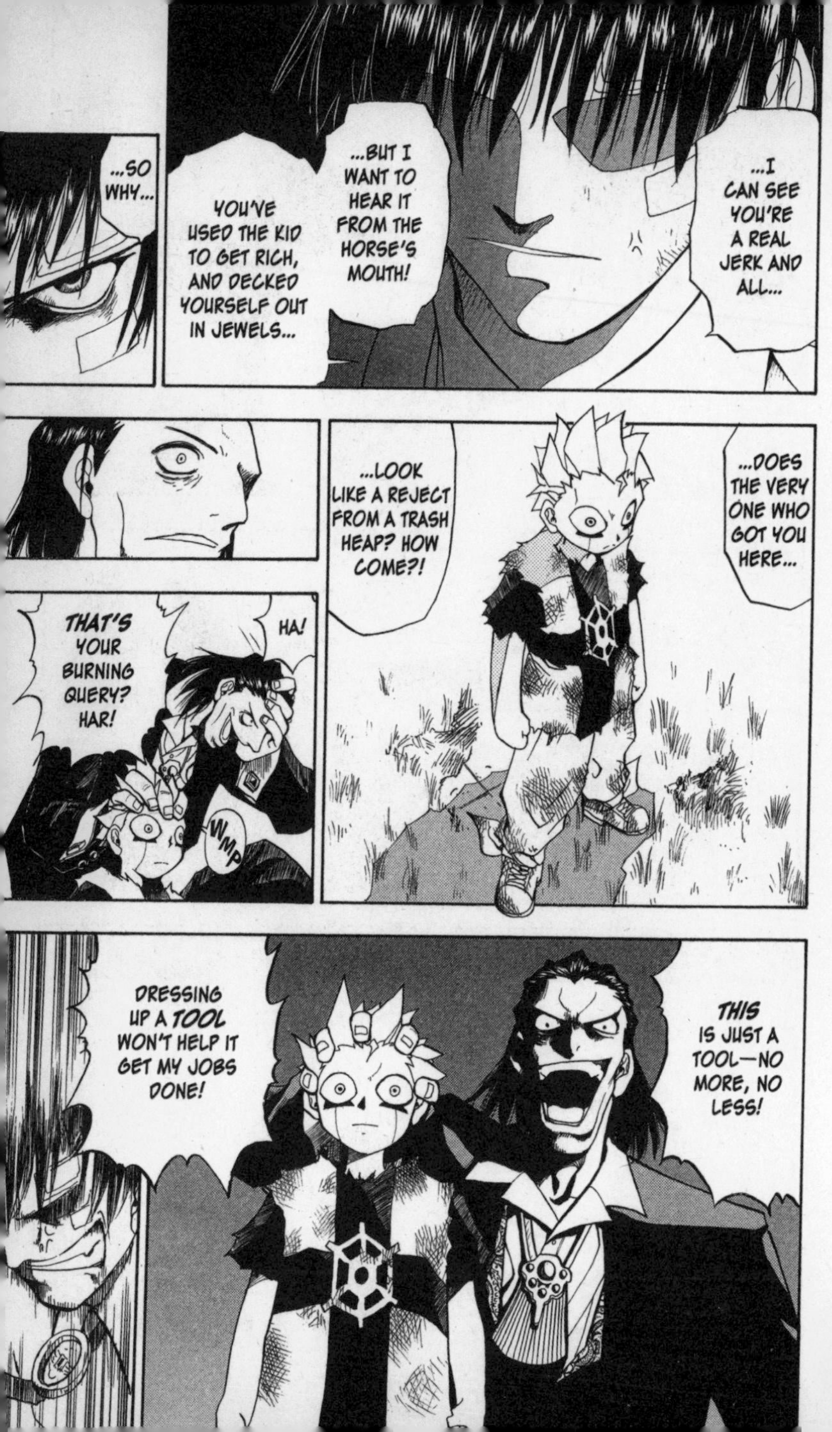

...I CAN SEE YOU'RE A REAL JERK AND ALL...
...BUT I WANT TO HEAR IT FROM THE HORSE'S MOUTH!
YOU'VE USED THE KID TO GET RICH, AND DECKED YOURSELF OUT IN JEWELS...
...SO WHY...
...DOES THE VERY ONE WHO GOT YOU HERE...
...LOOK LIKE A REJECT FROM A TRASH HEAP? HOW COME?!
HA!
THAT'S YOUR BURNING QUERY? HAR!
WMP
THIS IS JUST A TOOL—NO MORE, NO LESS!
DRESSING UP A *TOOL* WON'T HELP IT GET MY JOBS DONE!

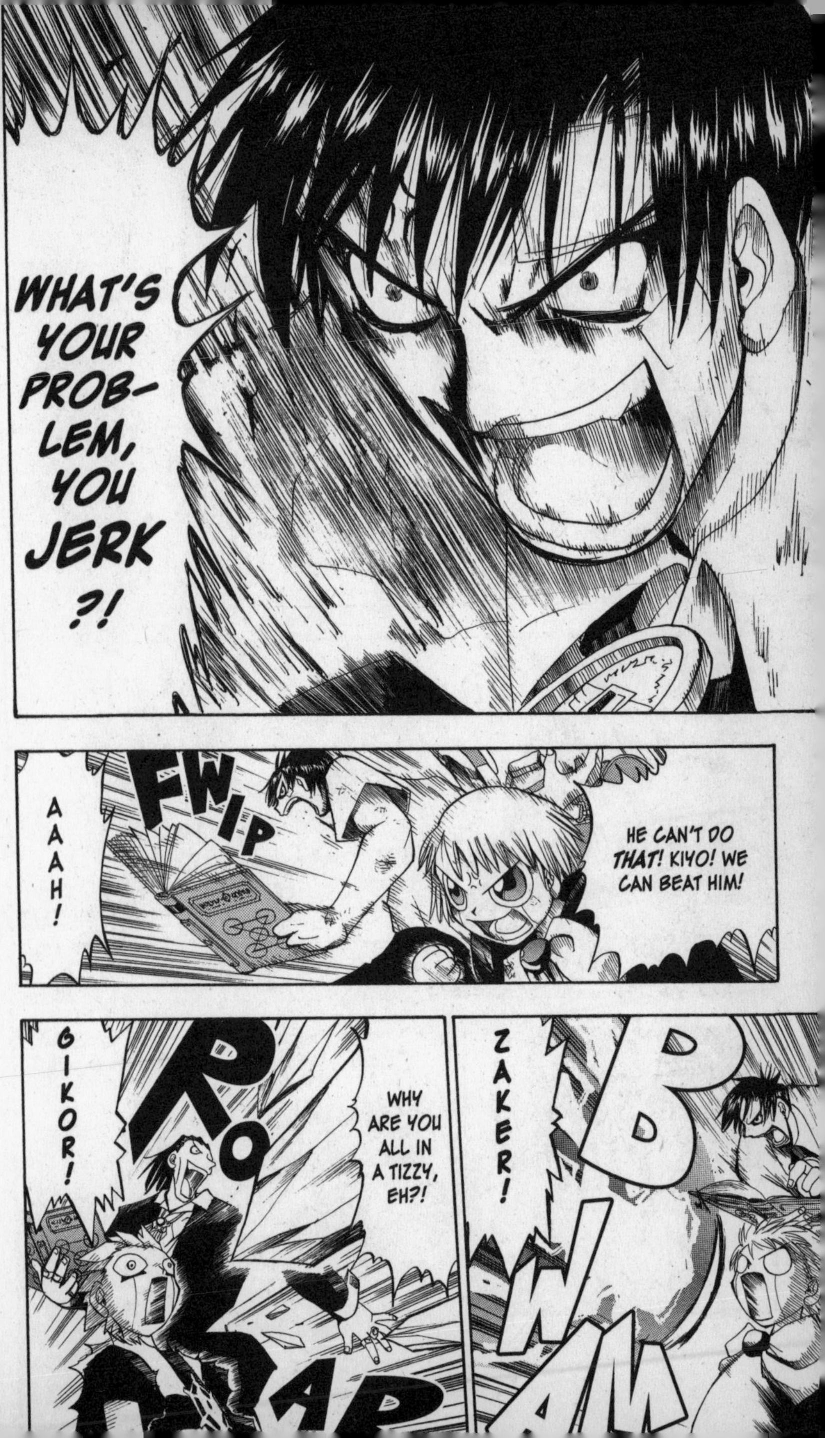
WHAT'S YOUR PROB-LEM, YOU JERK ?!
HE CAN'T DO THAT! KIYO! WE CAN BEAT HIM!
FWIP
AAAAH!
ZAKER!
WHY ARE YOU ALL IN A TIZZY, EH?!
GIKOR!

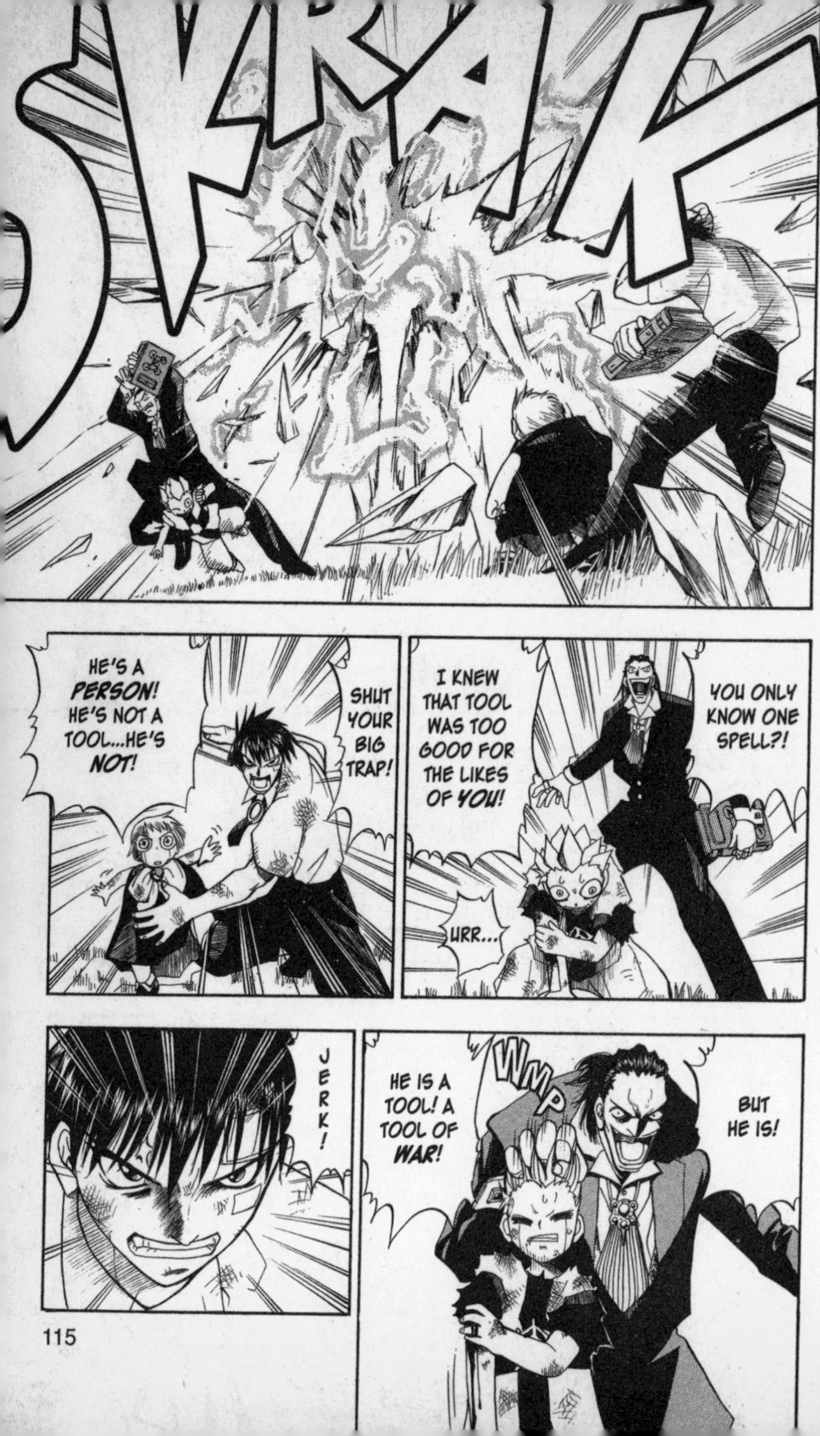
SKRAK
YOU ONLY KNOW ONE SPELL?!
I KNEW THAT TOOL WAS TOO GOOD FOR THE LIKES OF YOU!
URR...
SHUT YOUR BIG TRAP!
HE'S A PERSON! HE'S NOT A TOOL...HE'S NOT!
BUT HE IS!
WMP
HE IS A TOOL! A TOOL OF WAR!
JERK!

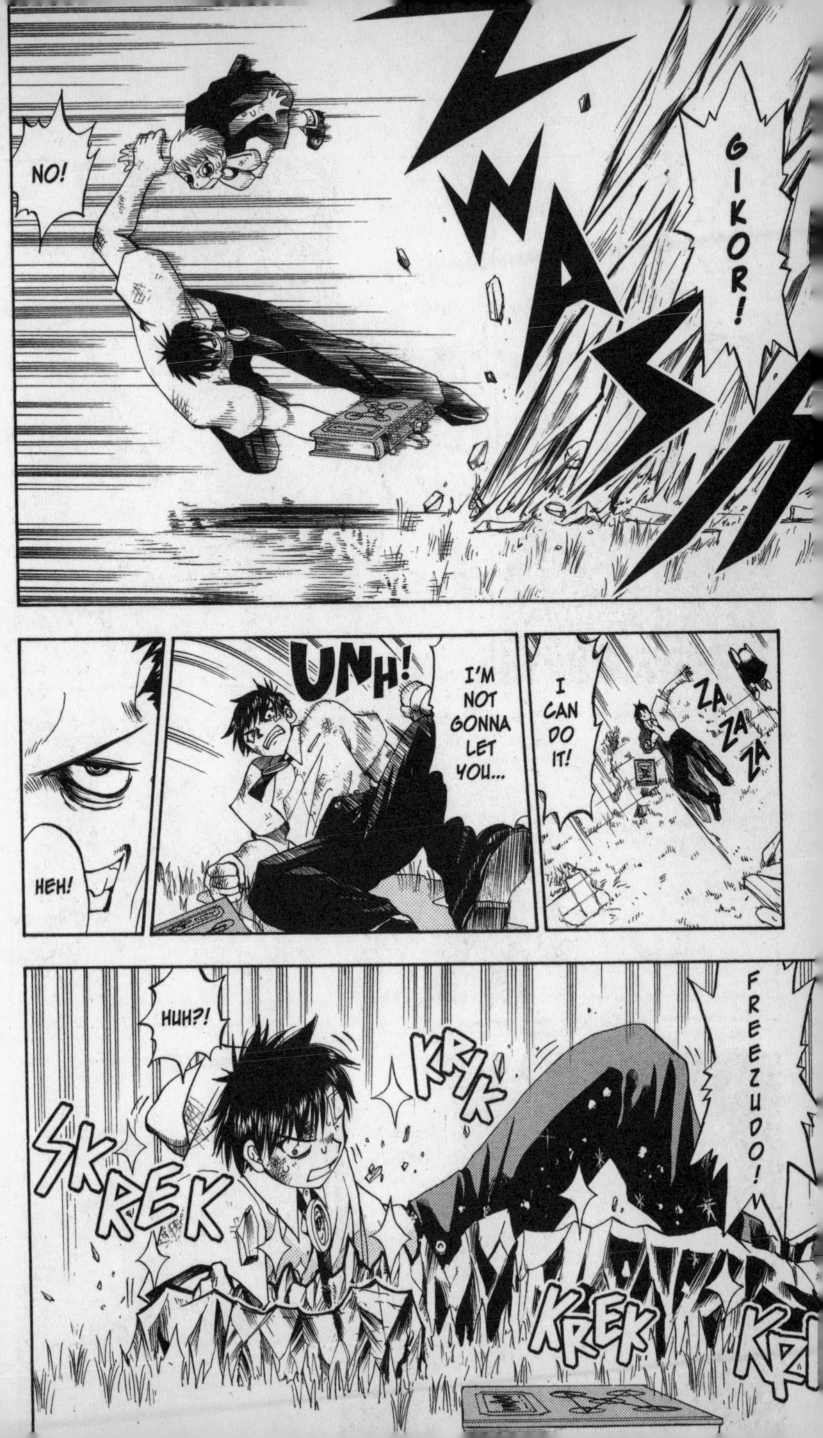
GIKOR!
ZASH
NO!
I CAN DO IT!
ZA ZA ZA
I'M NOT GONNA LET YOU...
UNH!
HEH!
FREEZUDOO!
KRYK
HUH?!
SKREK
KREK

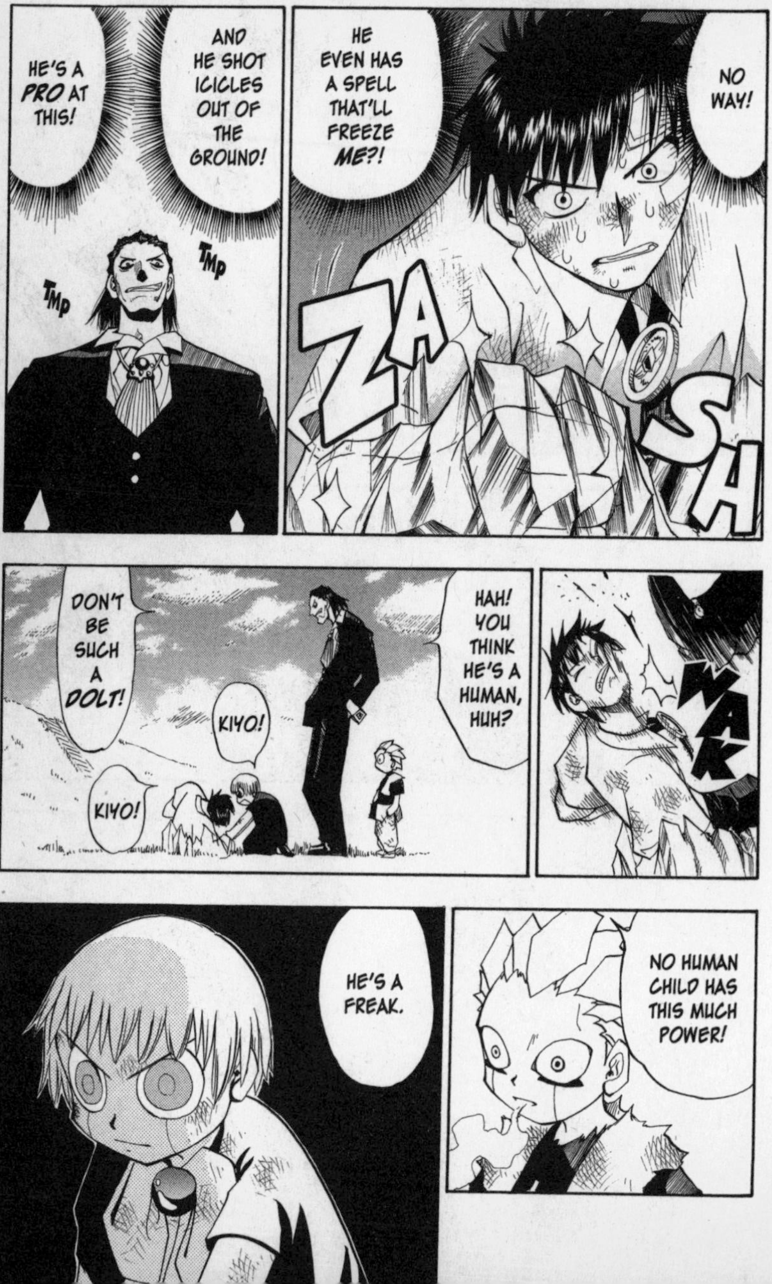
NO WAY!
HE EVEN HAS A SPELL THAT'LL FREEZE ME?!
ZA
SH
AND HE SHOT ICICLES OUT OF THE GROUND!
HE'S A PRO AT THIS!
TMP
TMP
WAK
HAH! YOU THINK HE'S A HUMAN, HUH?
KIYO!
DON'T BE SUCH A DOLT!
KIYO!
NO HUMAN CHILD HAS THIS MUCH POWER!
HE'S A FREAK.

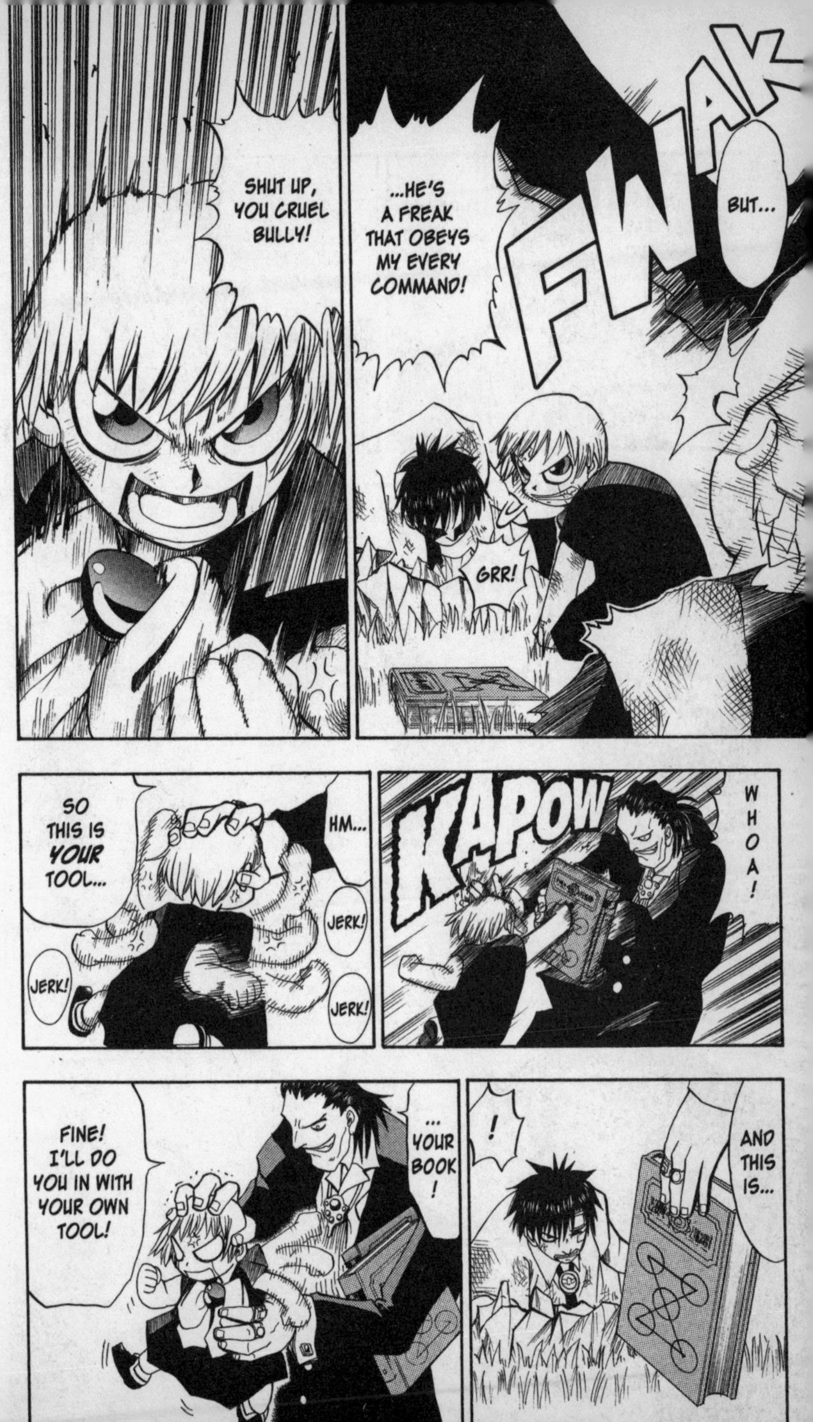
BUT...
FWAK
...HE'S A FREAK THAT OBEYS MY EVERY COMMAND!
GRR!
SHUT UP, YOU CRUEL BULLY!
WHOA!
KAPOW
HM...
SO THIS IS *YOUR* TOOL...
JERK!
JERK!
JERK!
AND THIS IS...
!
...YOUR BOOK!
FINE! I'LL DO YOU IN WITH YOUR OWN TOOL!

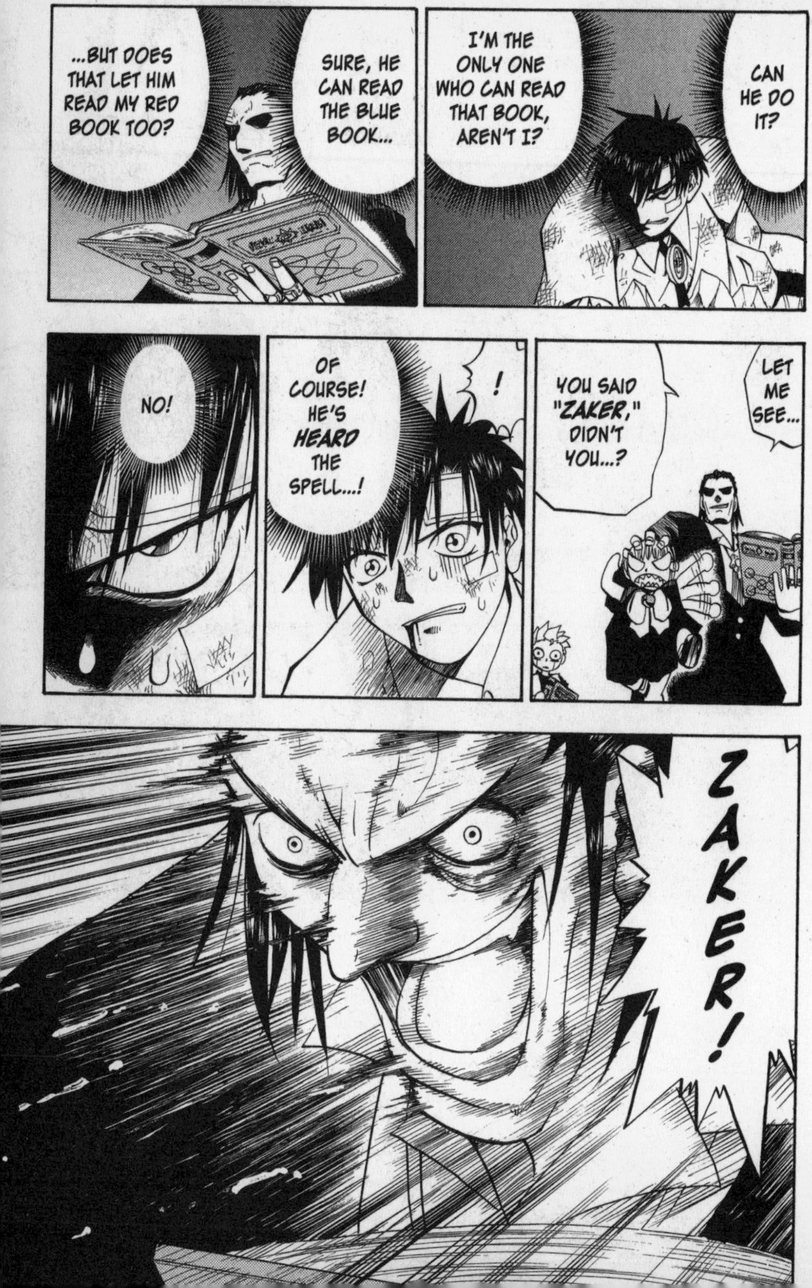
CAN HE DO IT?
I'M THE ONLY ONE WHO CAN READ THAT BOOK, AREN'T I?
SURE, HE CAN READ THE BLUE BOOK...
...BUT DOES THAT LET HIM READ MY RED BOOK TOO?
LET ME SEE...
YOU SAID "ZAKER," DIDN'T YOU...?
!
OF COURSE! HE'S HEARD THE SPELL...!
NO!
ZAKER!

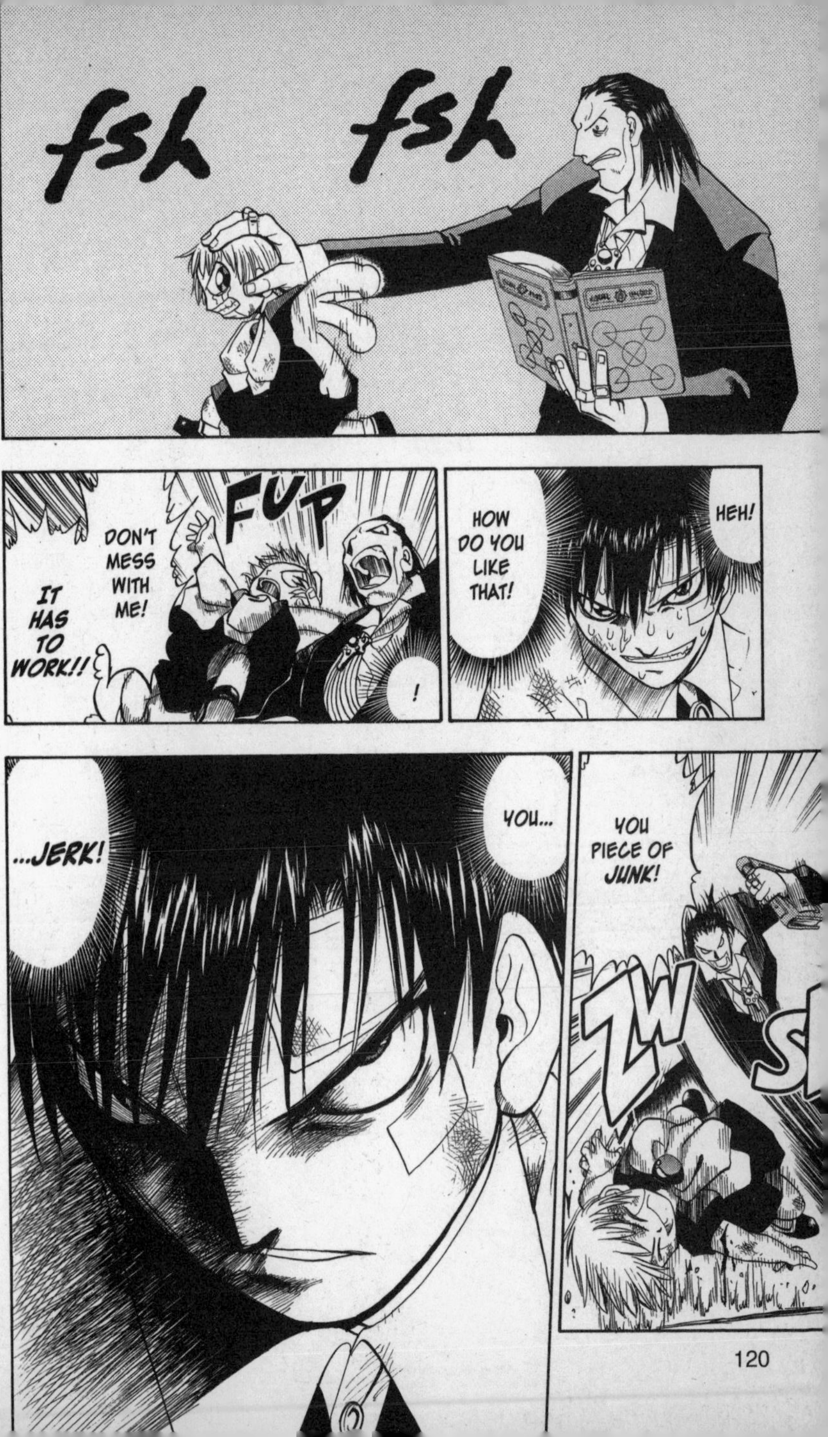
fsh
fsh
HEH!
HOW DO YOU LIKE THAT!
FUP
DON'T MESS WITH ME!
IT HAS TO WORK!!
!
YOU PIECE OF JUNK!
ZW
YOU...
...JERK!

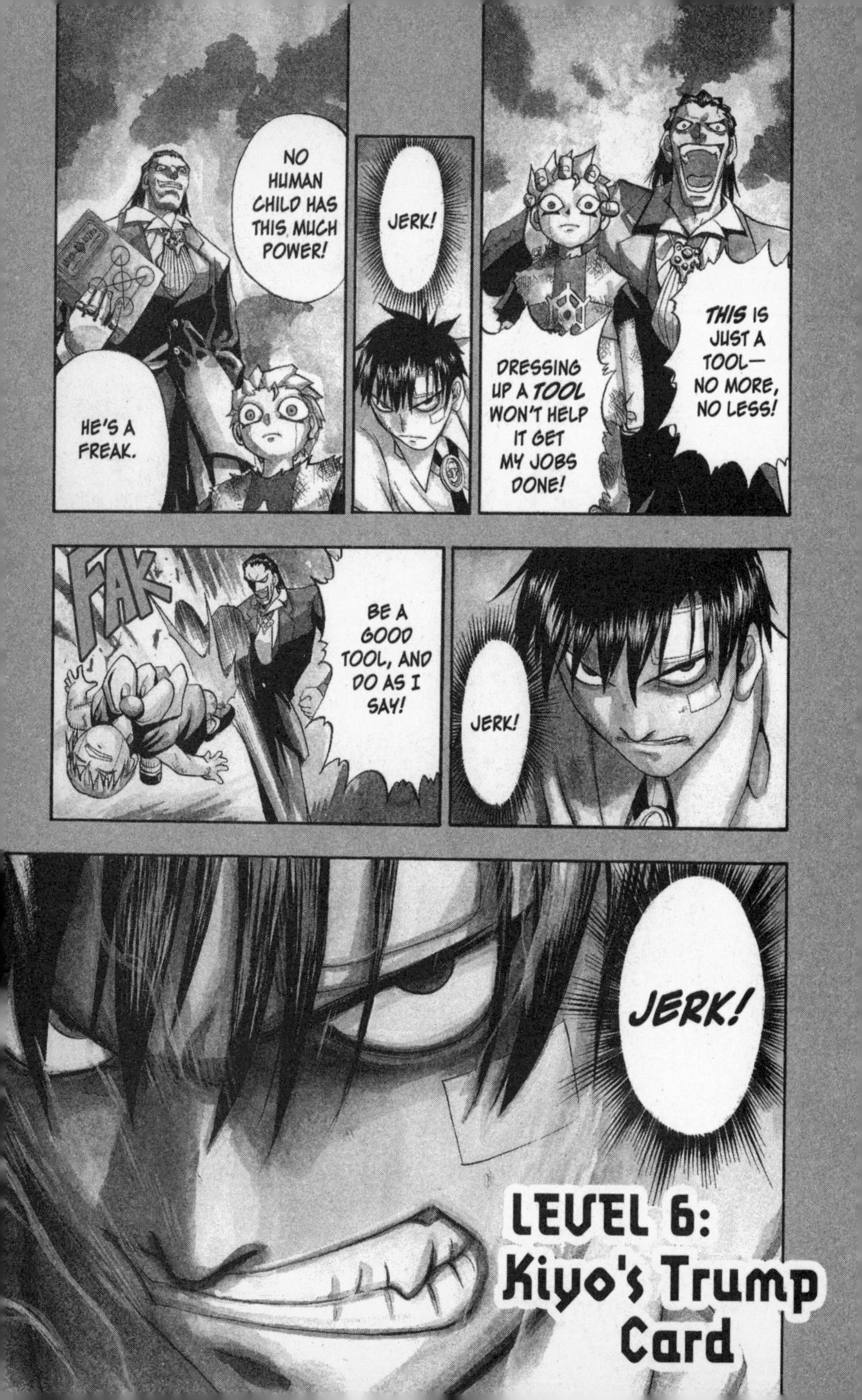
THIS IS JUST A TOOL— NO MORE, NO LESS!
DRESSING UP A TOOL WON'T HELP IT GET MY JOBS DONE!
JERK!
NO HUMAN CHILD HAS THIS MUCH POWER!
HE'S A FREAK.
JERK!
BE A GOOD TOOL, AND DO AS I SAY!
FAK
JERK!
LEVEL 6: Kiyo's Trump Card

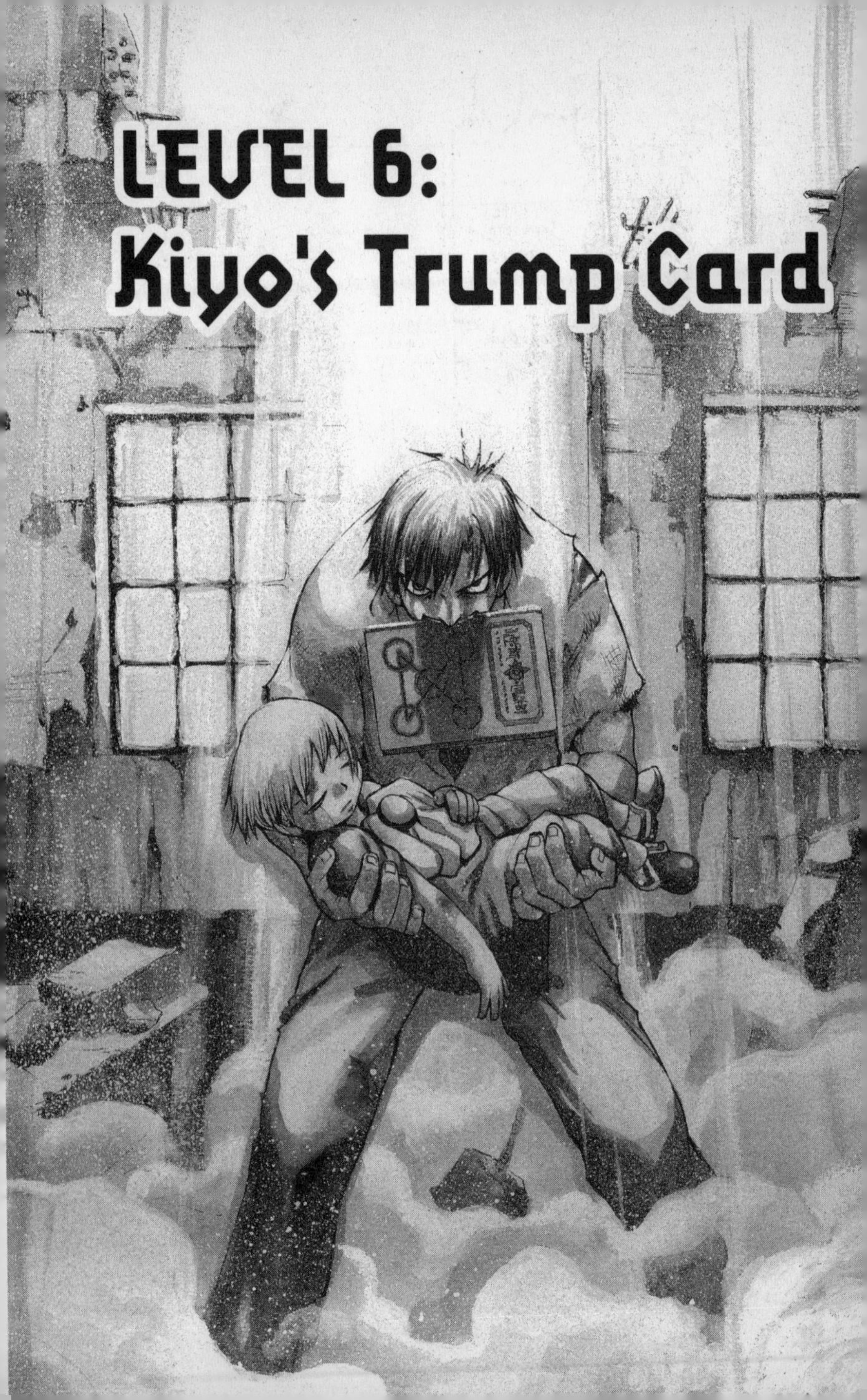
LEVEL 6:
Kiyo's Trump Card

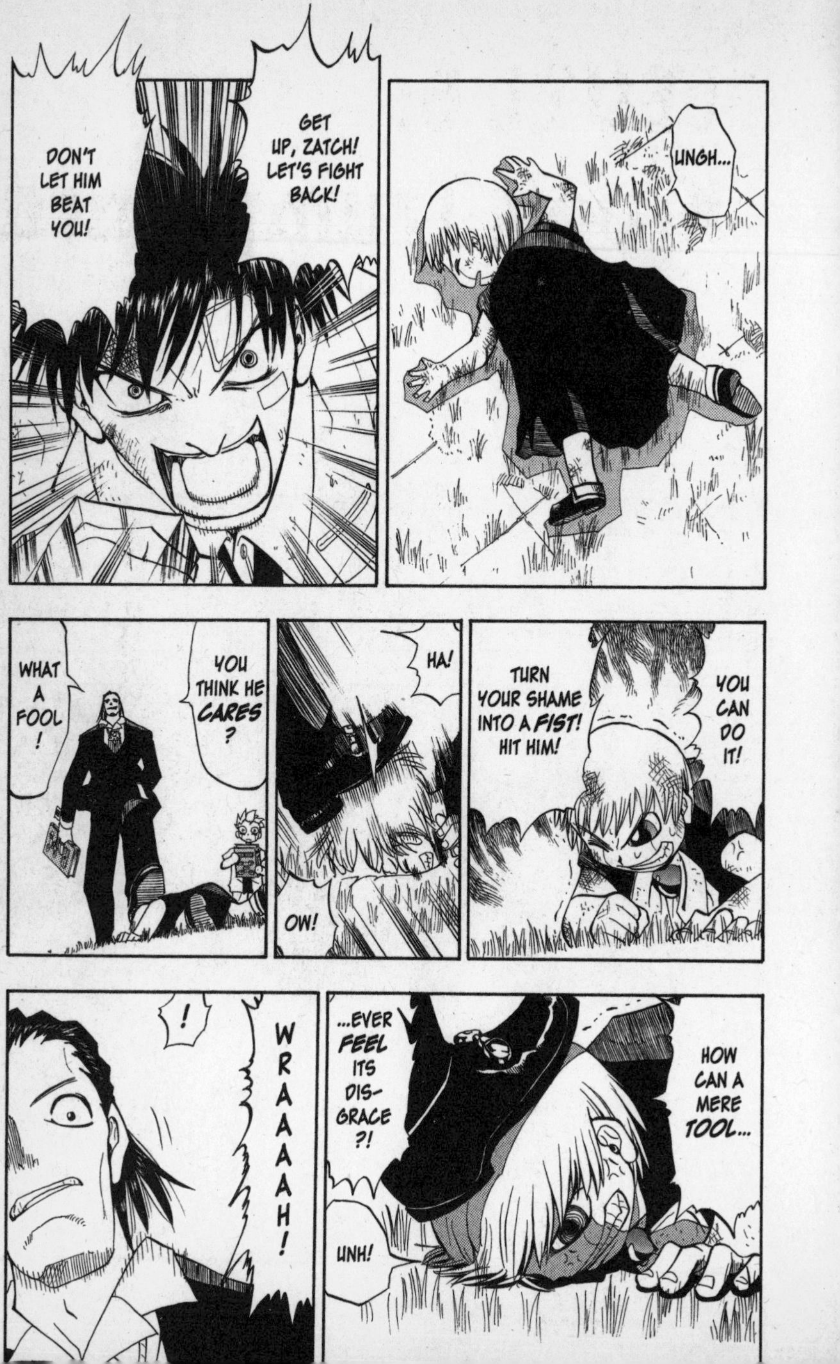
UNGH...
GET UP, ZATCH! LET'S FIGHT BACK!
DON'T LET HIM BEAT YOU!
YOU CAN DO IT!
TURN YOUR SHAME INTO A FIST! HIT HIM!
HA!
OW!
YOU THINK HE CARES?
WHAT A FOOL!
HOW CAN A MERE TOOL...
...EVER FEEL ITS DIS-GRACE?!
UNH!
WRAAAAH!
!

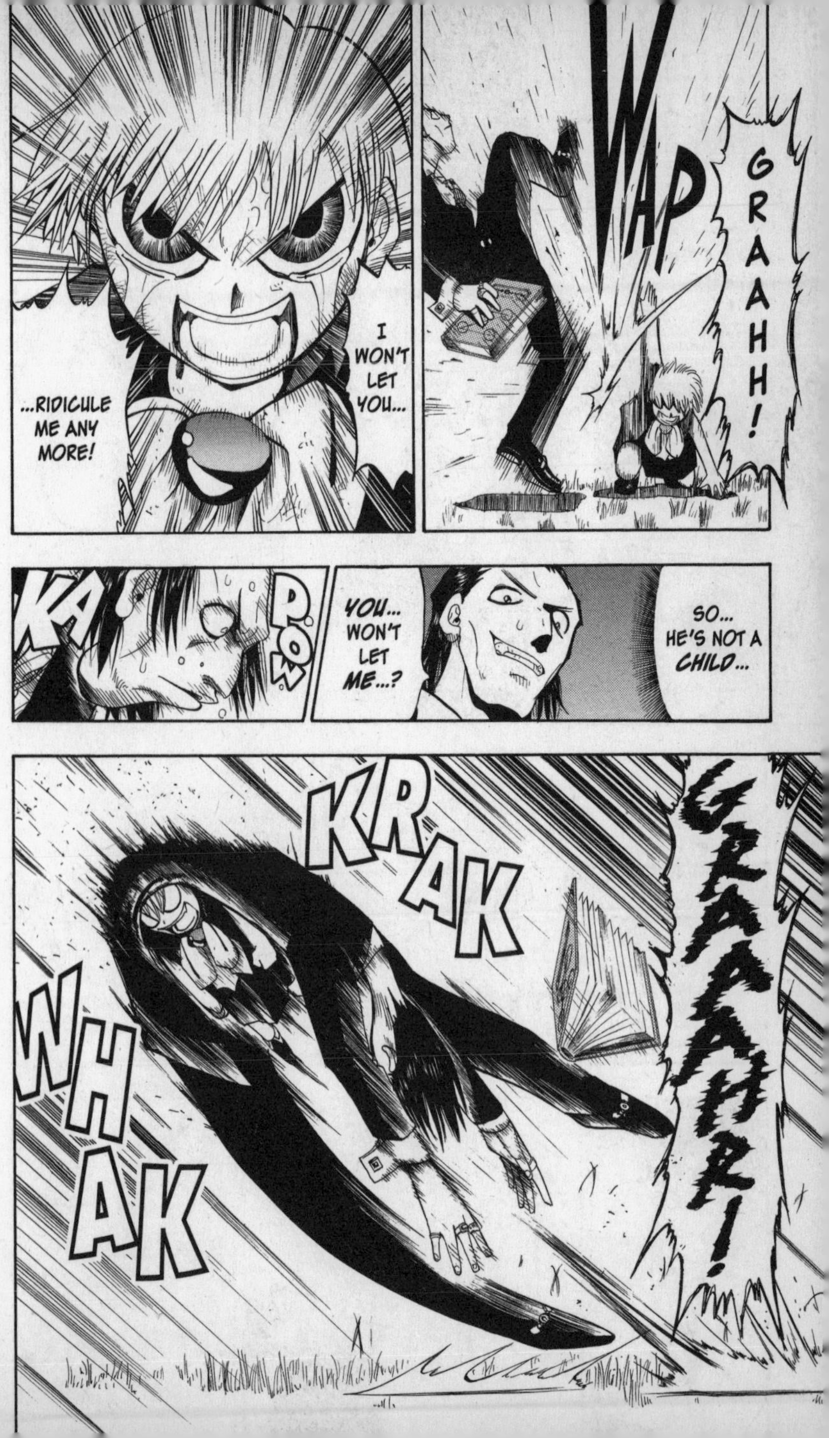
WAP
GRAAHH!
I WON'T LET YOU...
...RIDICULE ME ANY MORE!
SO... HE'S NOT A CHILD...
YOU... WON'T LET ME...?
KA
POW
GRAAAHR!
KRAK
WHAK

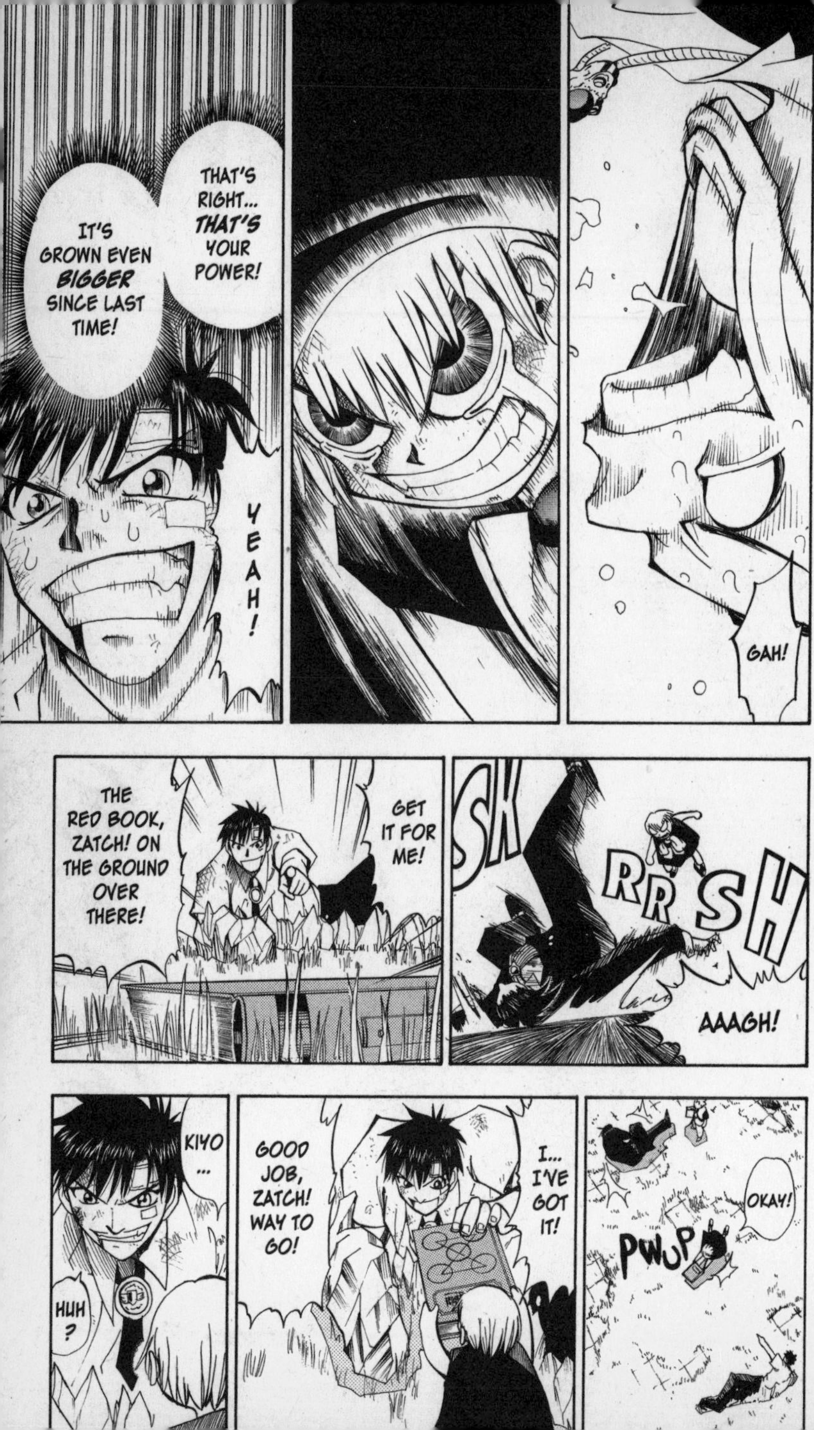
GAH!
THAT'S RIGHT... THAT'S YOUR POWER!
IT'S GROWN EVEN BIGGER SINCE LAST TIME!
YEAH!
SK
RRRSH
AAAGH!
GET IT FOR ME!
THE RED BOOK, ZATCH! ON THE GROUND OVER THERE!
OKAY!
PWUP
I... I'VE GOT IT!
GOOD JOB, ZATCH! WAY TO GO!
KIYO...
HUH?

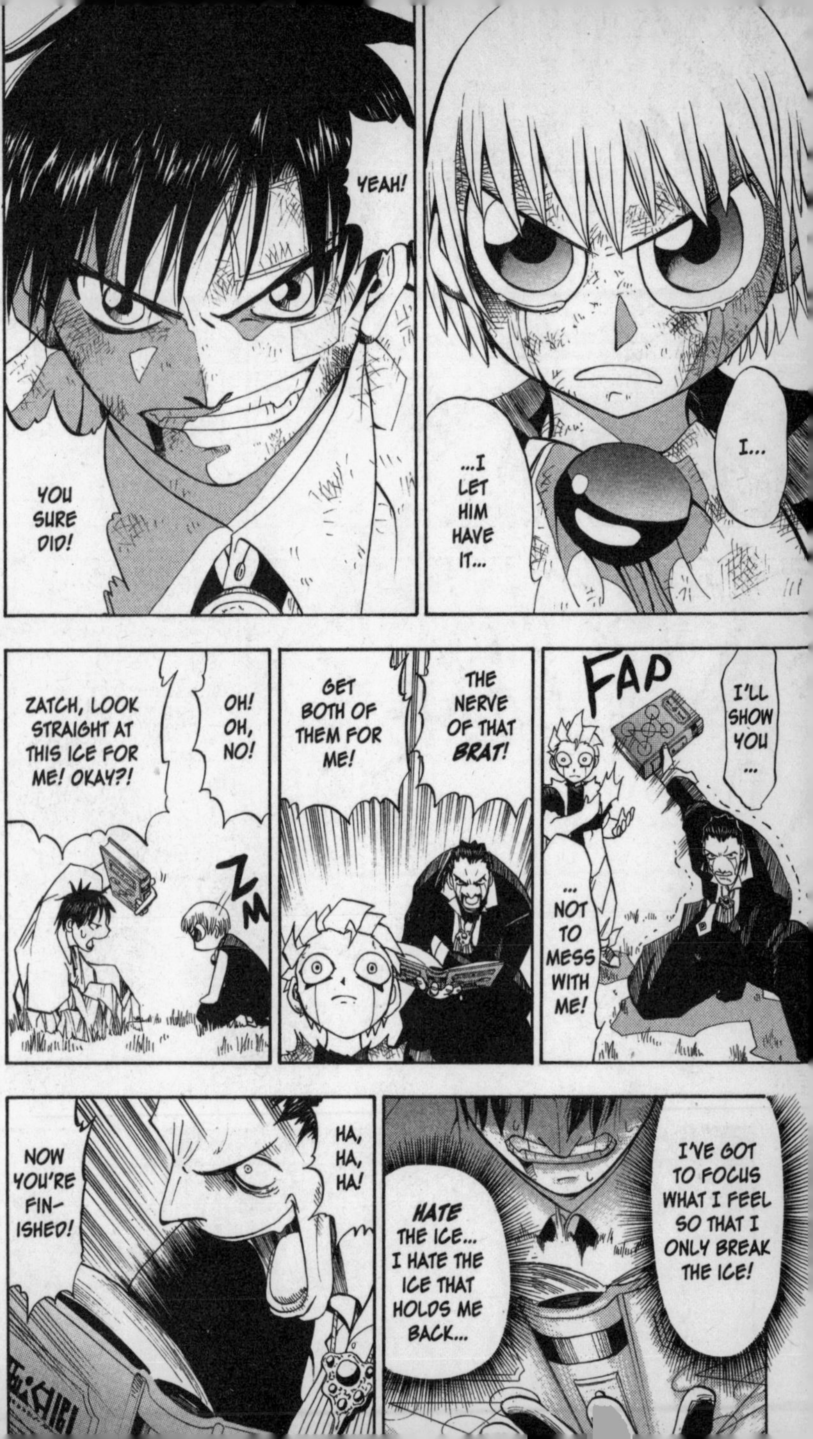
I...
...I LET HIM HAVE IT...
YEAH!
YOU SURE DID!
FAP
I'LL SHOW YOU ...
... NOT TO MESS WITH ME!
THE NERVE OF THAT *BRAT!*
GET BOTH OF THEM FOR ME!
OH! OH, NO!
ZATCH, LOOK STRAIGHT AT THIS ICE FOR ME! OKAY?!
ZM
I'VE GOT TO FOCUS WHAT I FEEL SO THAT I ONLY BREAK THE ICE!
HATE THE ICE... I HATE THE ICE THAT HOLDS ME BACK...
HA, HA, HA!
NOW YOU'RE FIN-ISHED!

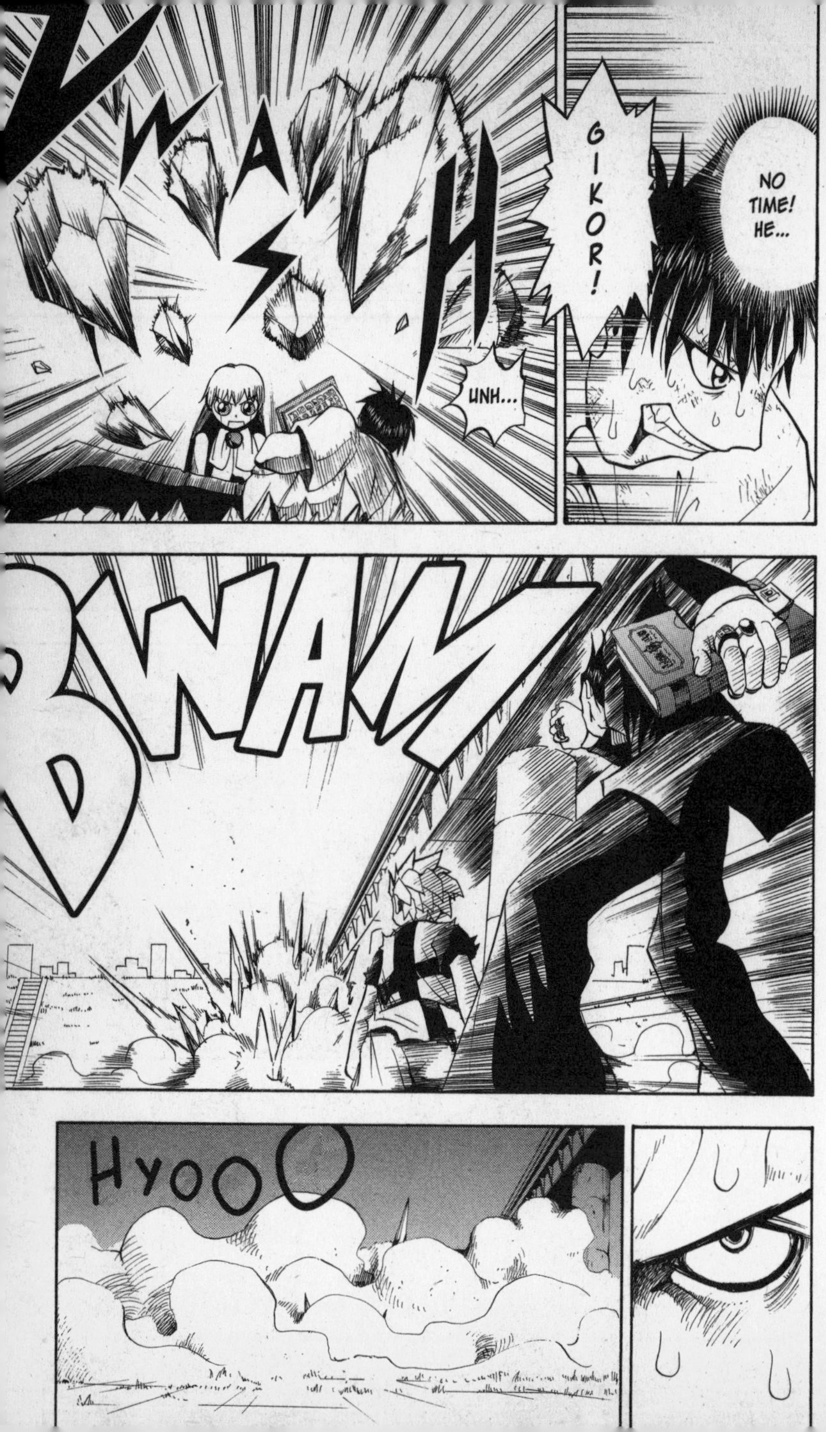

NO TIME! HE...
GIKOR!
KWASH
UNH...
BWAM
HYOOO

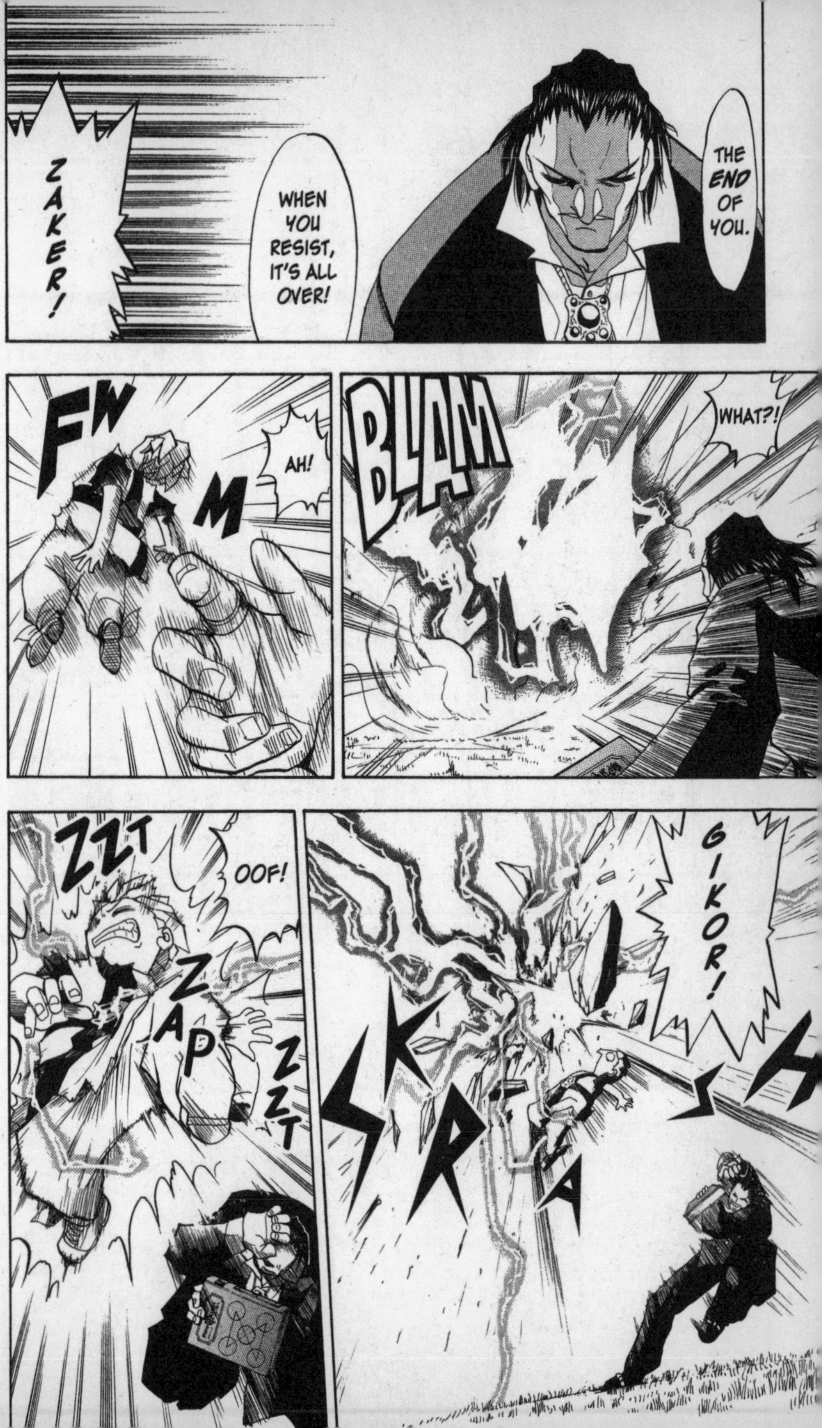
THE END OF YOU.
WHEN YOU RESIST, IT'S ALL OVER!
ZAKER!
WHAT?!
BLAM
AH!
FWM
GIKOR!
SKRA
OOF!
ZZZT
ZAP
ZZZT

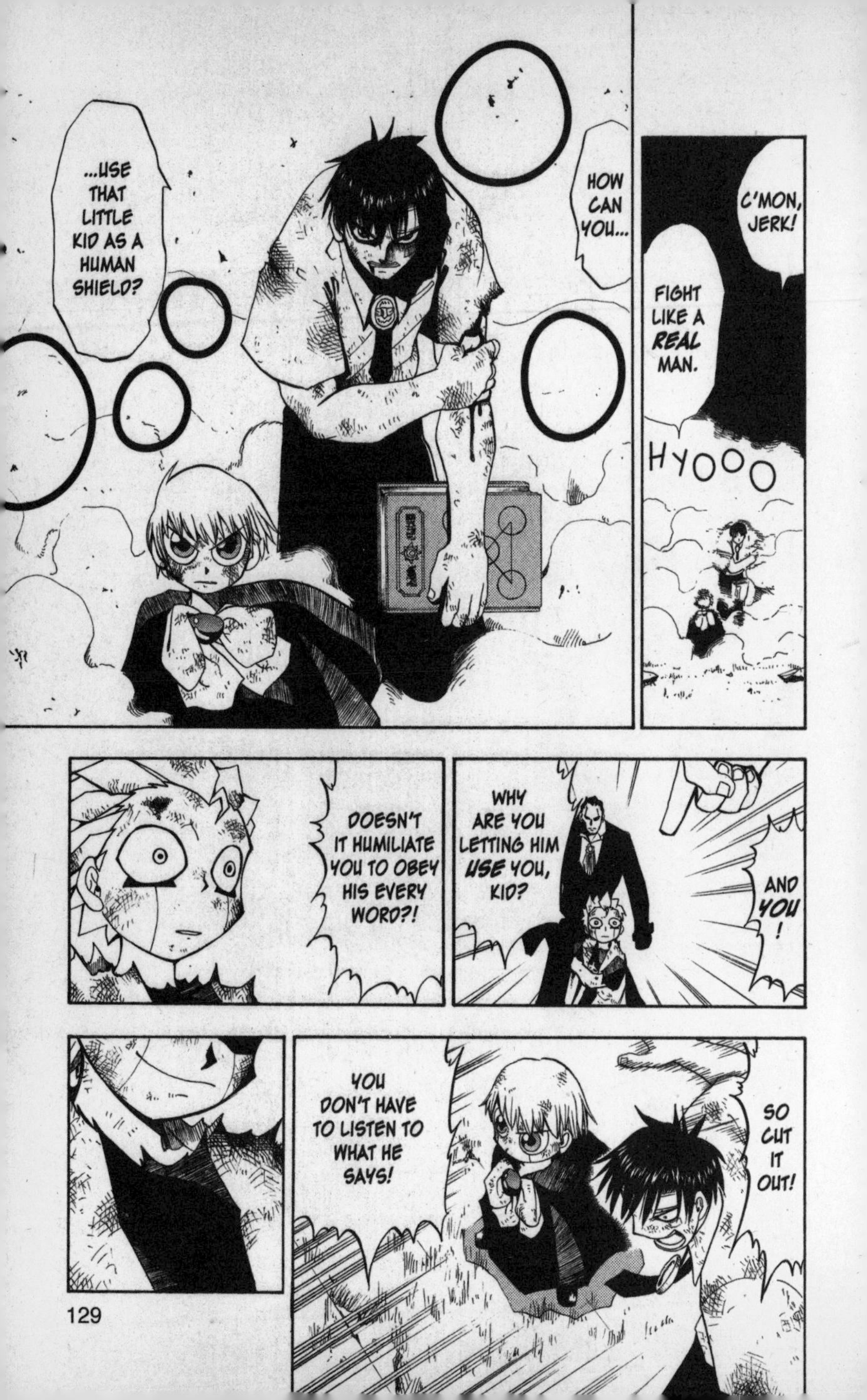
C'MON, JERK!
FIGHT LIKE A REAL MAN.
HYOOO
HOW CAN YOU...
...USE THAT LITTLE KID AS A HUMAN SHIELD?
AND YOU!
WHY ARE YOU LETTING HIM USE YOU, KID?
DOESN'T IT HUMILIATE YOU TO OBEY HIS EVERY WORD?!
SO CUT IT OUT!
YOU DON'T HAVE TO LISTEN TO WHAT HE SAYS!

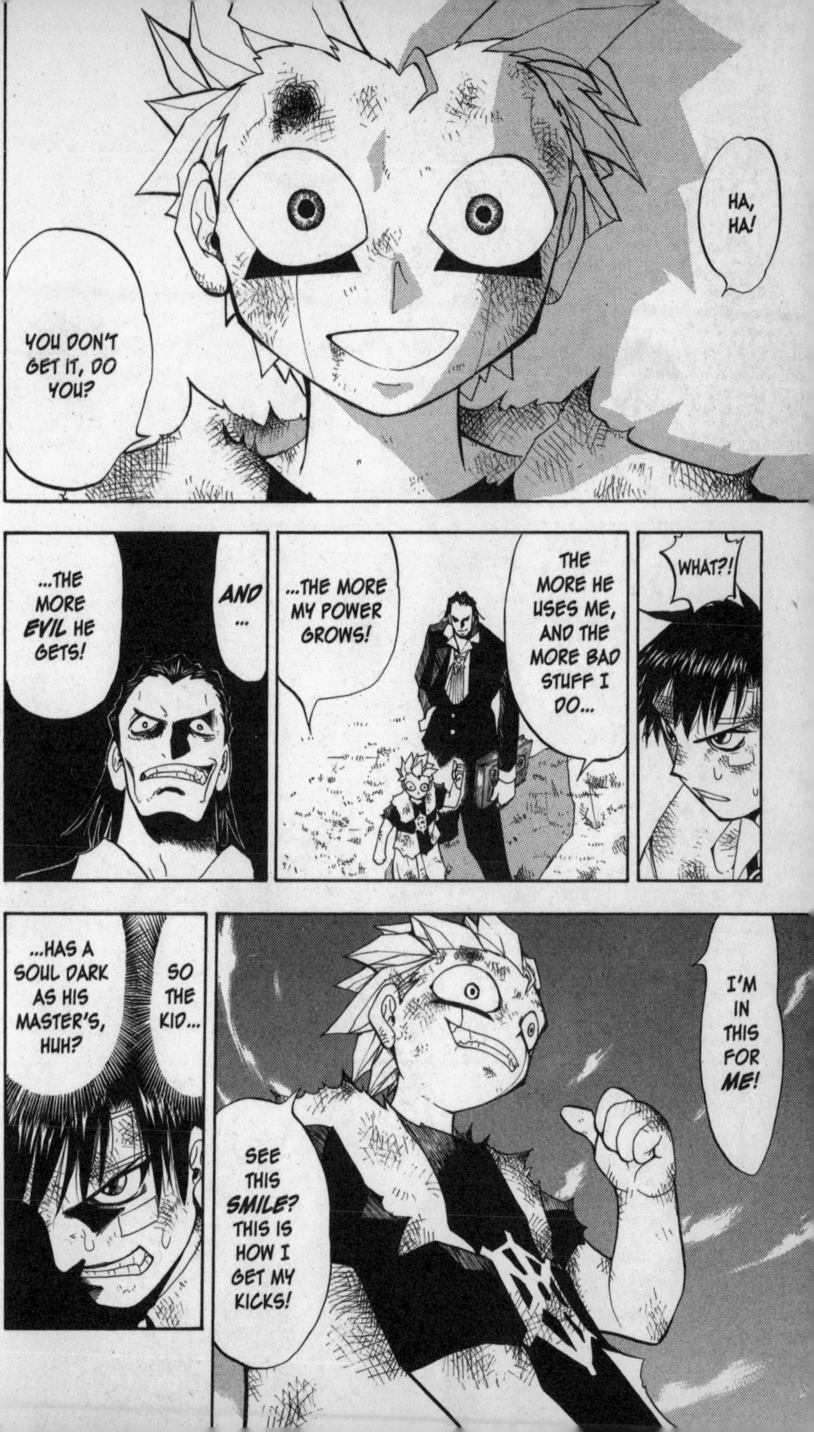
HA, HA!
YOU DON'T GET IT, DO YOU?
WHAT?!
THE MORE HE USES ME, AND THE MORE BAD STUFF I DO...
...THE MORE MY POWER GROWS!
AND...
...THE MORE *EVIL* HE GETS!
I'M IN THIS FOR *ME!*
SEE THIS *SMILE?* THIS IS HOW I GET MY KICKS!
SO THE KID...
...HAS A SOUL DARK AS HIS MASTER'S, HUH?

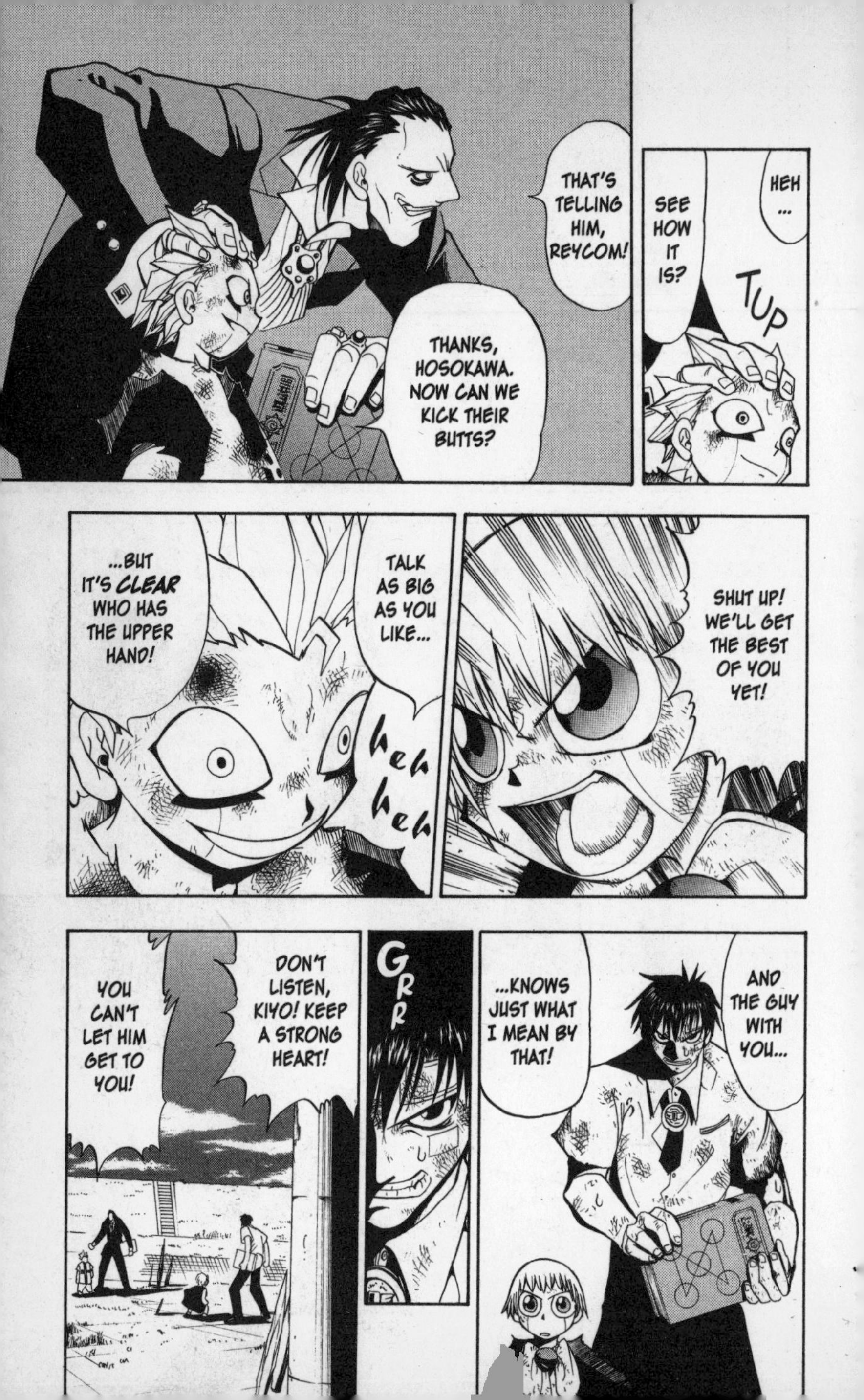
HEH ...
SEE HOW IT IS?
TUP
THAT'S TELLING HIM, REYCOM!
THANKS, HOSOKAWA. NOW CAN WE KICK THEIR BUTTS?
SHUT UP! WE'LL GET THE BEST OF YOU YET!
TALK AS BIG AS YOU LIKE...
heh heh
...BUT IT'S **CLEAR** WHO HAS THE UPPER HAND!
AND THE GUY WITH YOU...
...KNOWS JUST WHAT I MEAN BY THAT!
GRR
DON'T LISTEN, KIYO! KEEP A STRONG HEART!
YOU CAN'T LET HIM GET TO YOU!

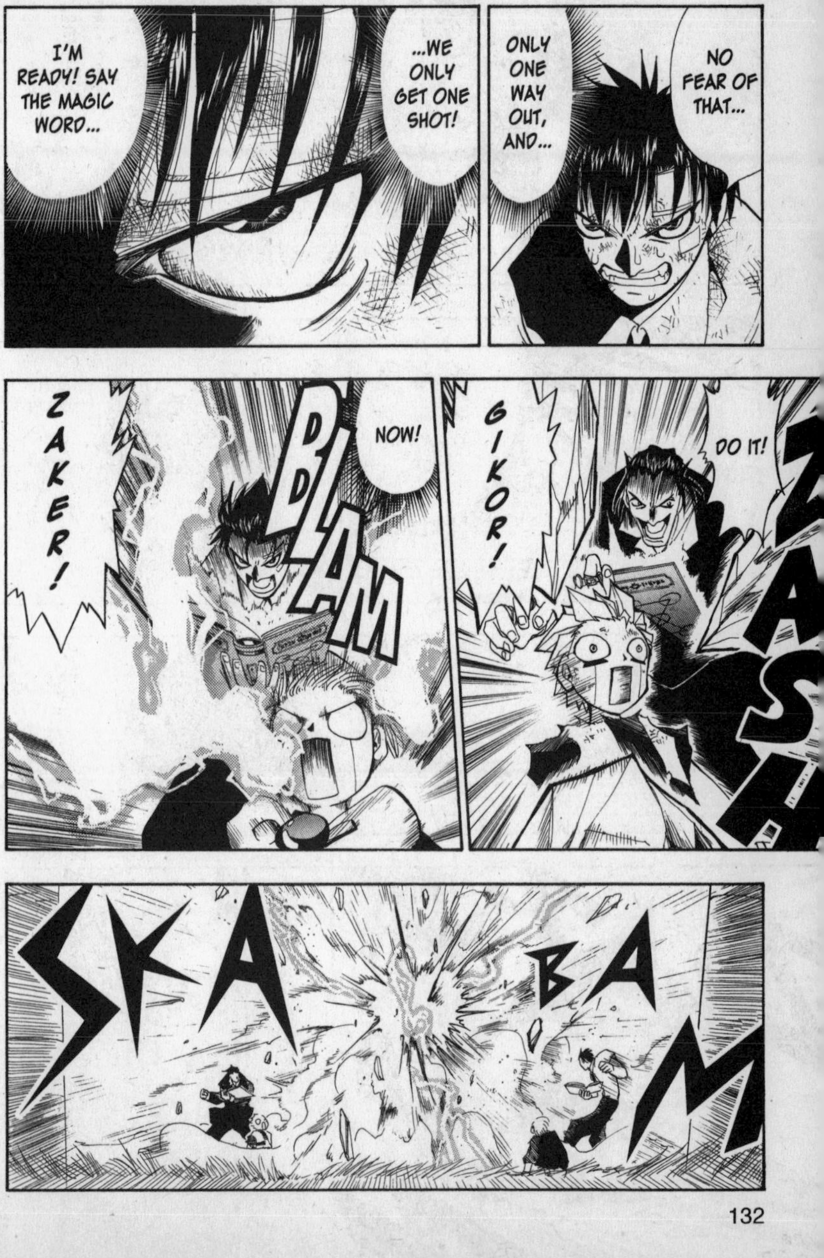
NO FEAR OF THAT...
ONLY ONE WAY OUT, AND...
...WE ONLY GET ONE SHOT!
I'M READY! SAY THE MAGIC WORD...
ZASH!
DO IT!
GIKOR!
NOW!
BLAM
ZAKER!
SKABAM

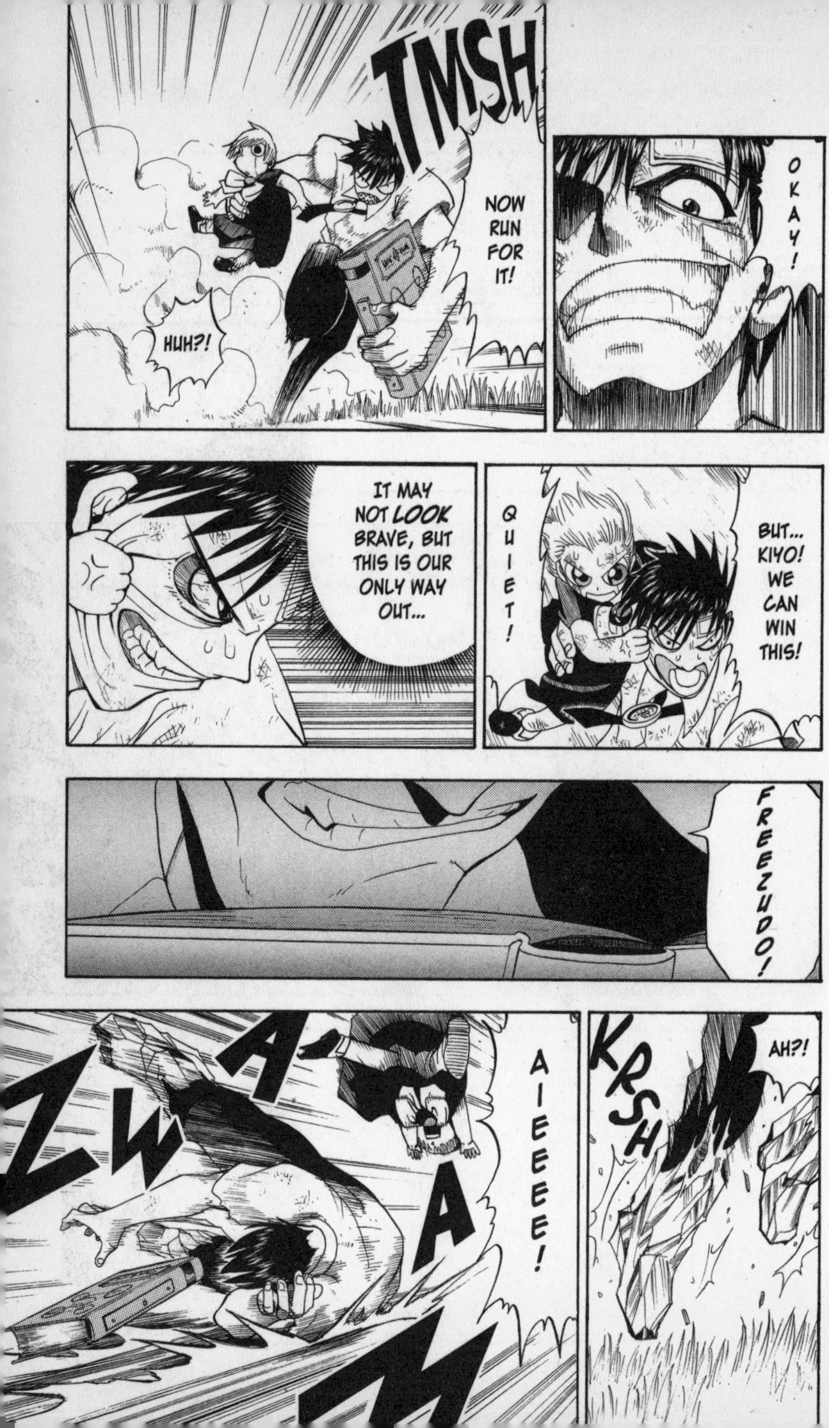
OKAY!
TMSH
NOW RUN FOR IT!
HUH?!
BUT... KIYO! WE CAN WIN THIS!
QUIET!
IT MAY NOT LOOK BRAVE, BUT THIS IS OUR ONLY WAY OUT...
FREEZUDO!
AH?!
KRSH
AIEEEEE!
ZWAAM

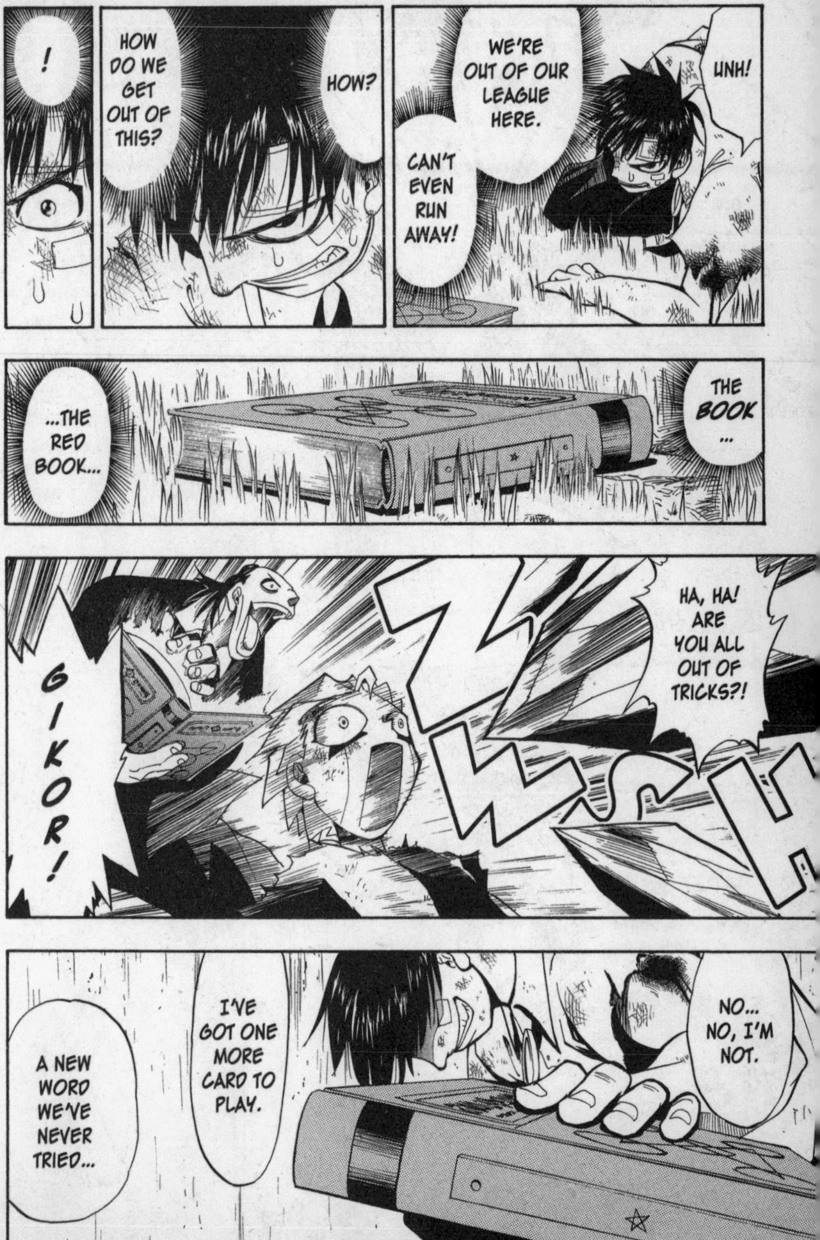
UNH!
WE'RE OUT OF OUR LEAGUE HERE.
CAN'T EVEN RUN AWAY!
HOW?
HOW DO WE GET OUT OF THIS?
!
THE BOOK ...
...THE RED BOOK...
HA, HA! ARE YOU ALL OUT OF TRICKS?!
ZWSH
GIKOR!
NO... NO, I'M NOT.
I'VE GOT ONE MORE CARD TO PLAY.
A NEW WORD WE'VE NEVER TRIED...

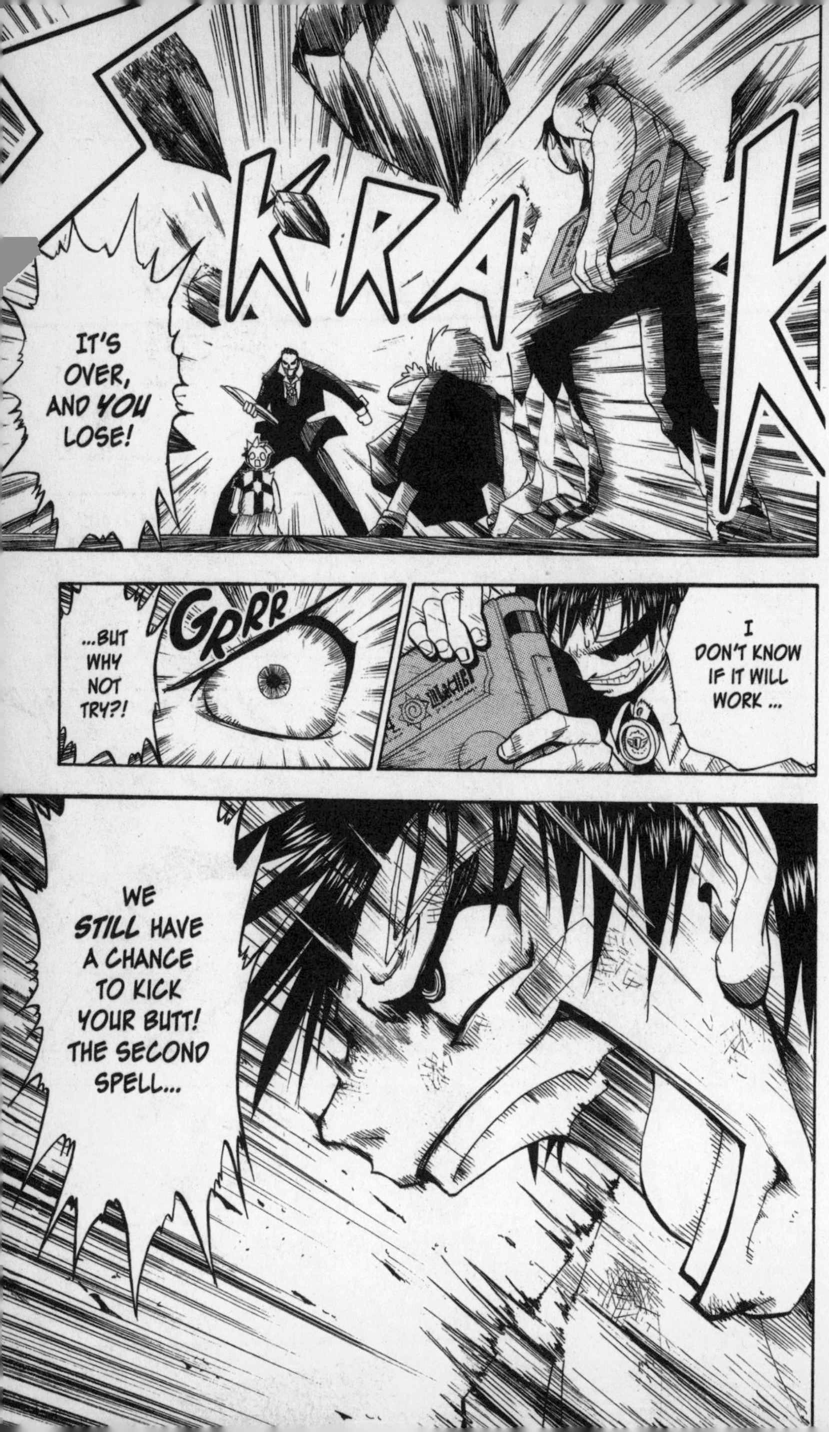
KRA-K
IT'S OVER, AND YOU LOSE!
I DON'T KNOW IF IT WILL WORK ...
GRRR
...BUT WHY NOT TRY?!
WE STILL HAVE A CHANCE TO KICK YOUR BUTT! THE SECOND SPELL...

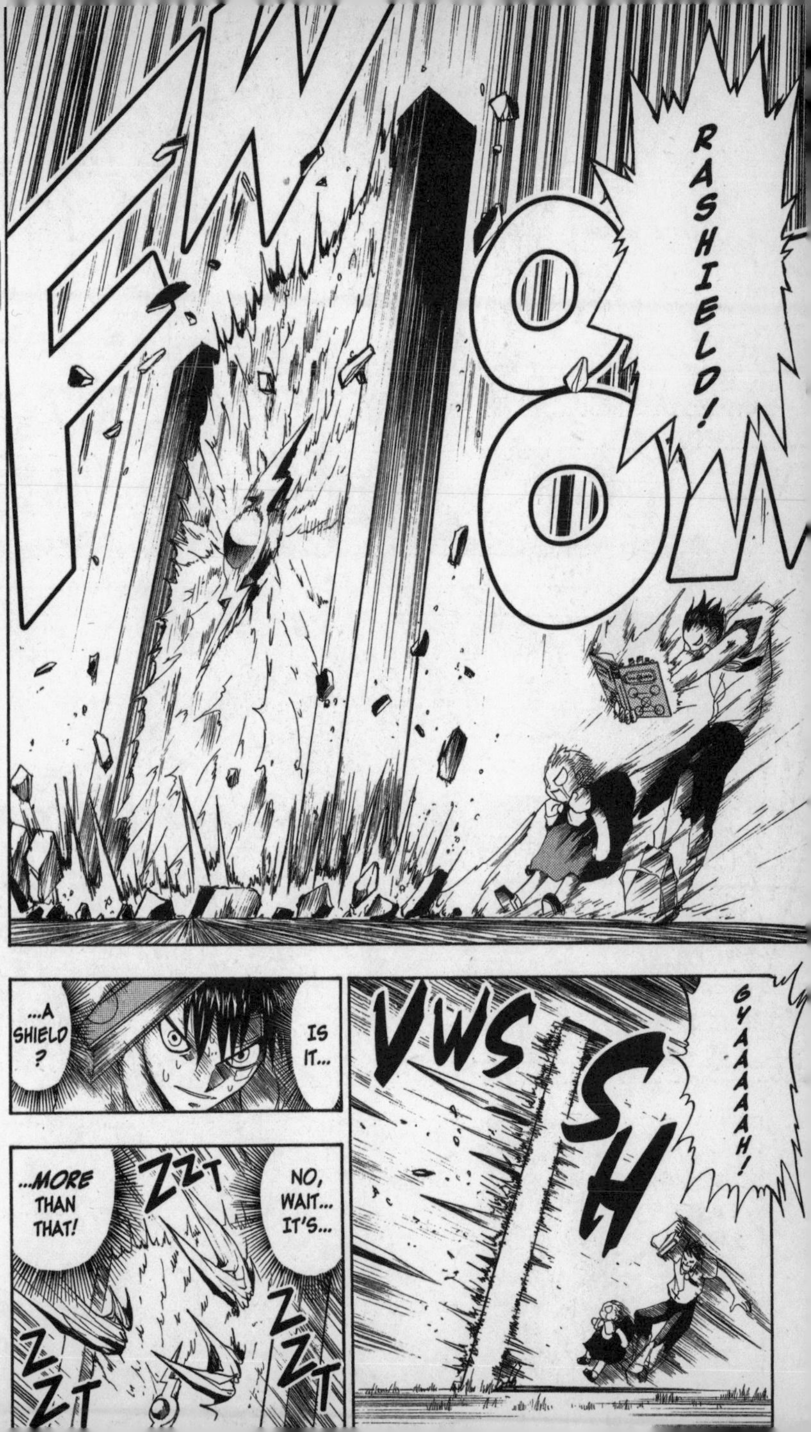
RASHIELD!
GYAAAAAH!
VWS
SH
IS IT...
...A SHIELD?
NO, WAIT... IT'S...
...MORE THAN THAT!
ZZT
ZZT
ZZT

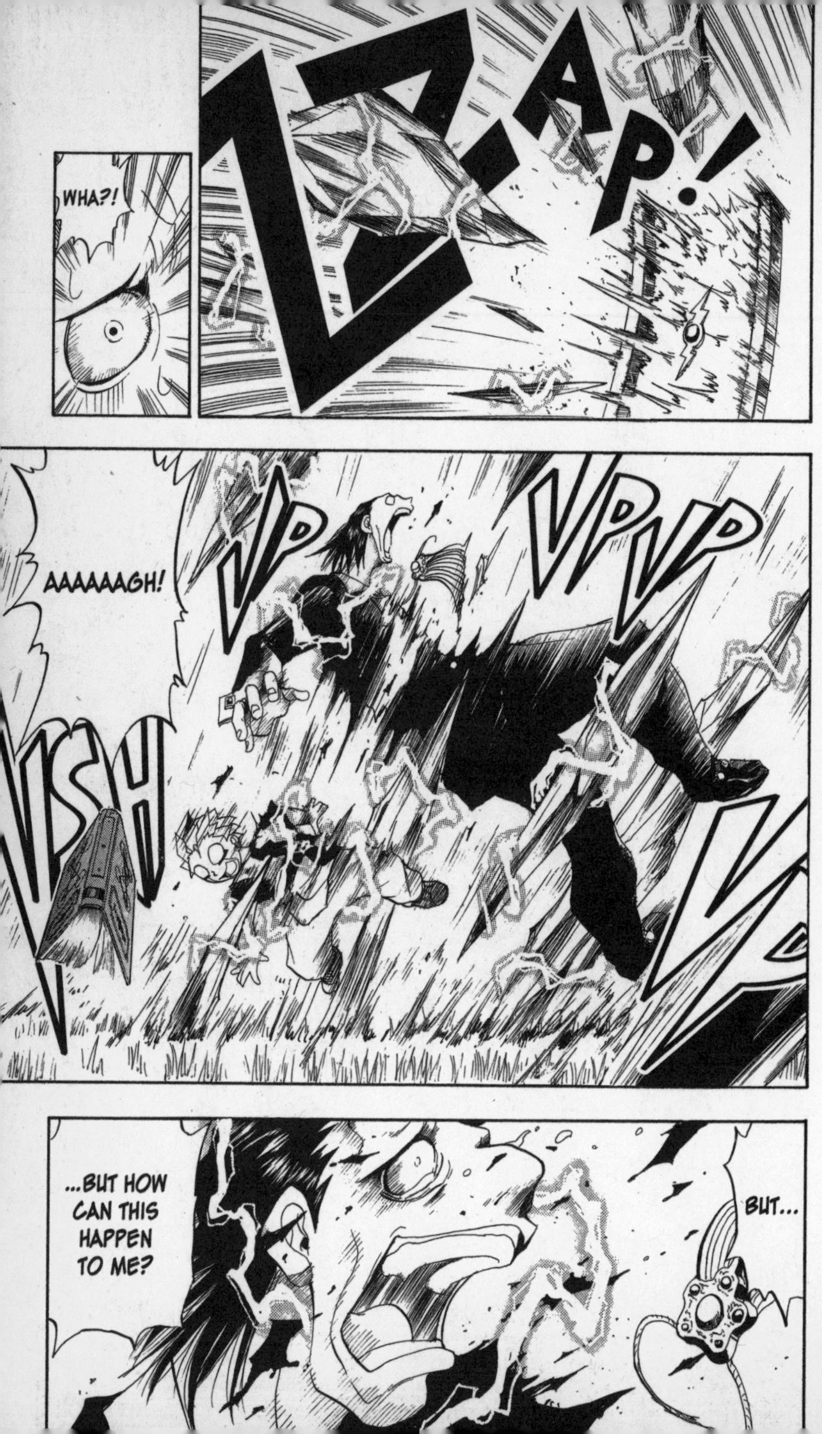
ZAP!
WHA?!
VPVP
VP
AAAAAAGH!
VSH
BUT...
...BUT HOW CAN THIS HAPPEN TO ME?

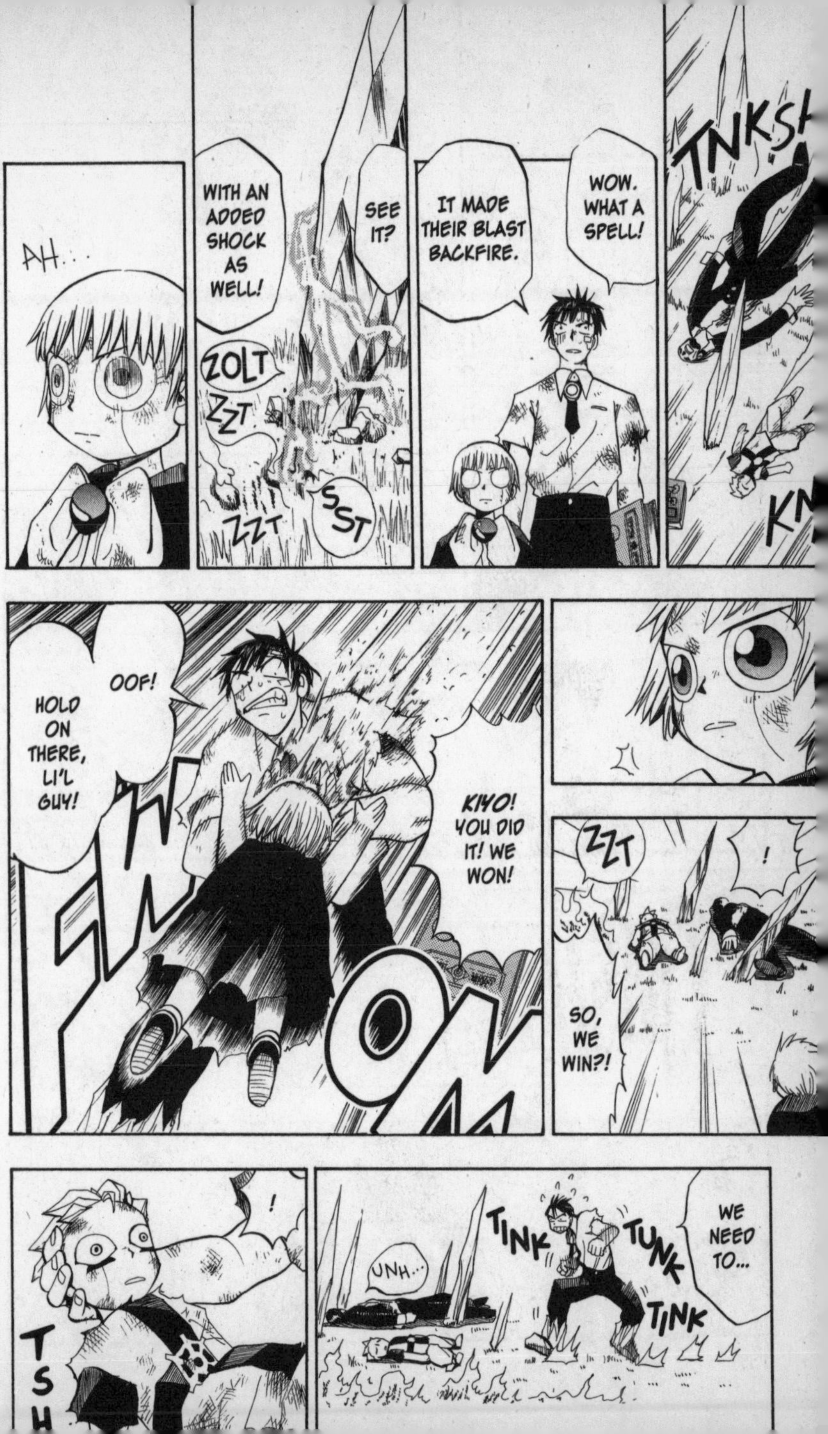
TNKSH
KN
WOW. WHAT A SPELL!
IT MADE THEIR BLAST BACKFIRE.
SEE IT?
WITH AN ADDED SHOCK AS WELL!
ZOLT
ZZT
SST
ZZT
AH...
ZZT
!
SO, WE WIN?!
KIYO! YOU DID IT! WE WON!
OOF!
HOLD ON THERE, LI'L GUY!
WE NEED TO...
TUNK
TINK
TINK
UNH...
!
TSH

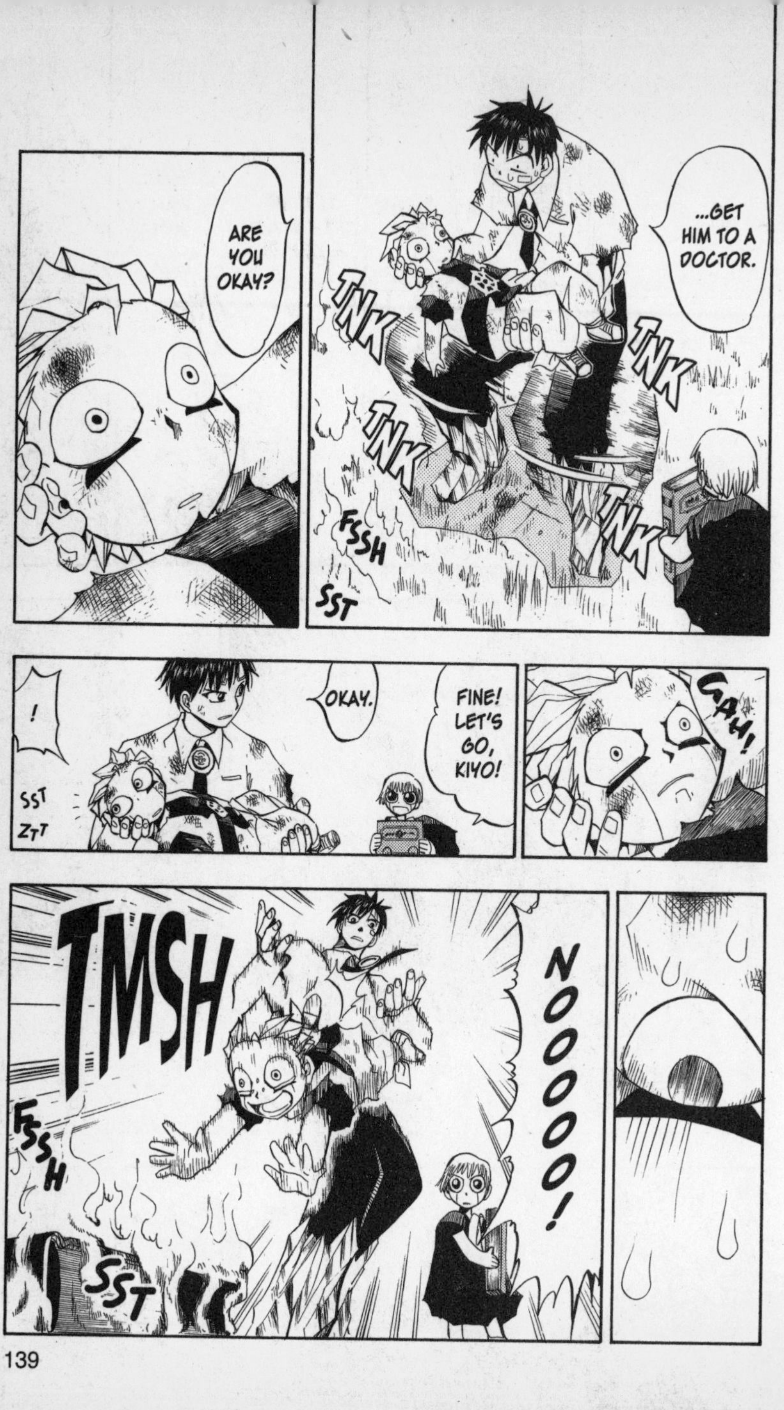

...GET HIM TO A DOCTOR.
TNK
TNK
TNK
TNK
FSSH
SST
ARE YOU OKAY?
GAH!
FINE! LET'S GO, KIYO!
OKAY.
!
SST
ZTT
NOOOOOO!
TMSH
FSSH
SST

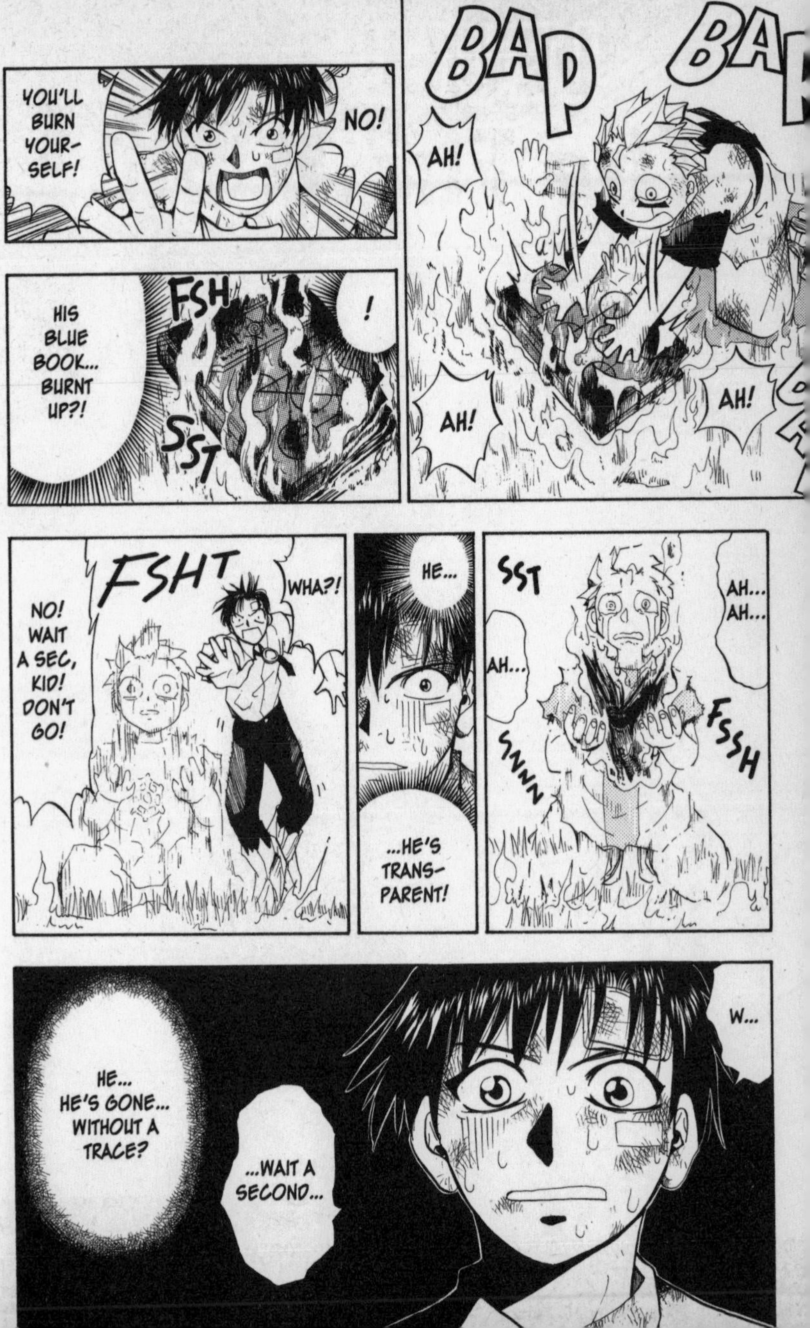
BAP
BA
AH!
AH!
AH!
NO!
YOU'LL BURN YOUR-SELF!
!
FSH
HIS BLUE BOOK... BURNT UP?!
SST
AH... AH...
SST
AH...
FSSH
SNNN
HE...
...HE'S TRANS-PARENT!
WHA?!
FSHT
NO! WAIT A SEC, KID! DON'T GO!
W...
...WAIT A SECOND...
HE... HE'S GONE... WITHOUT A TRACE?

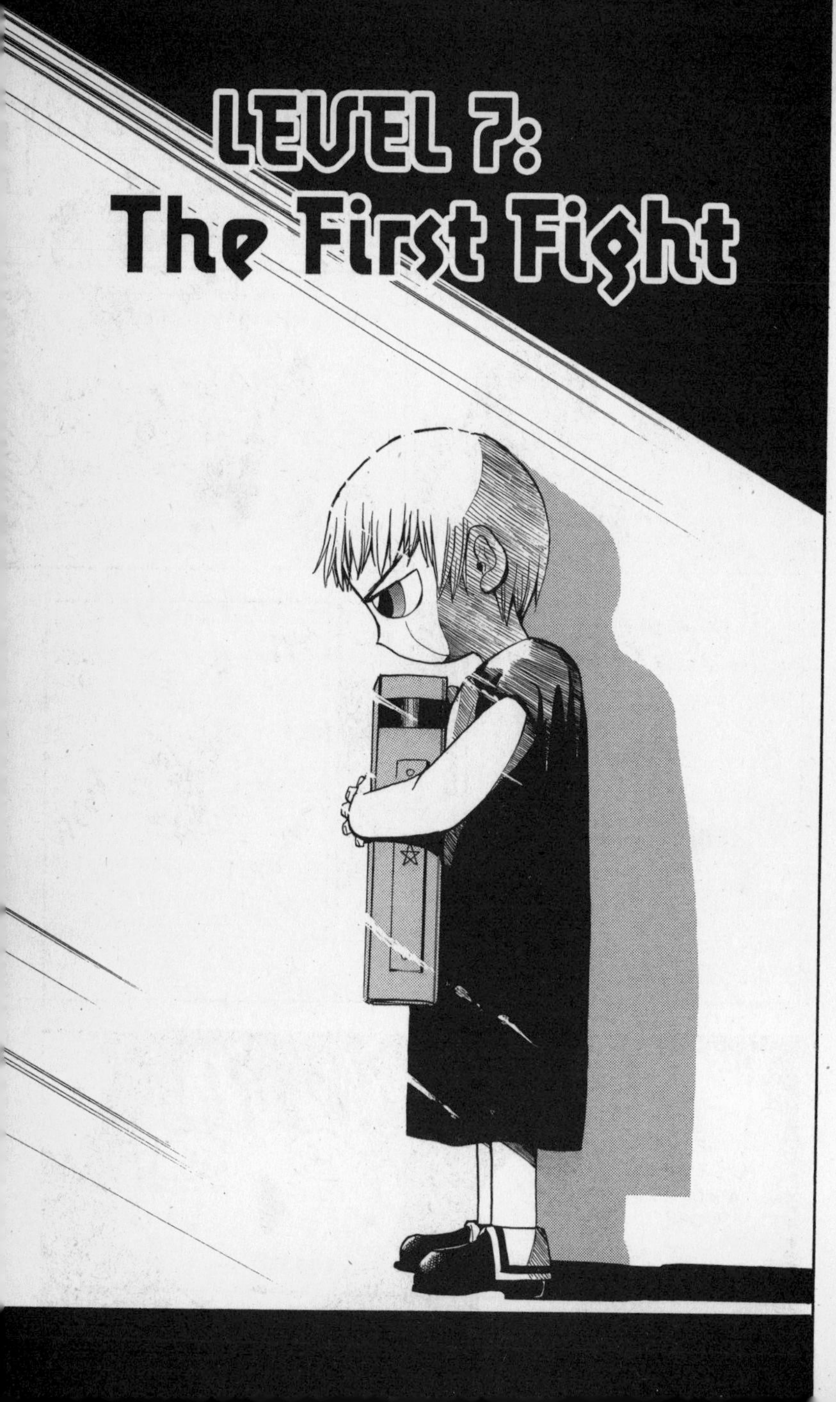
LEVEL 7:
The First Fight

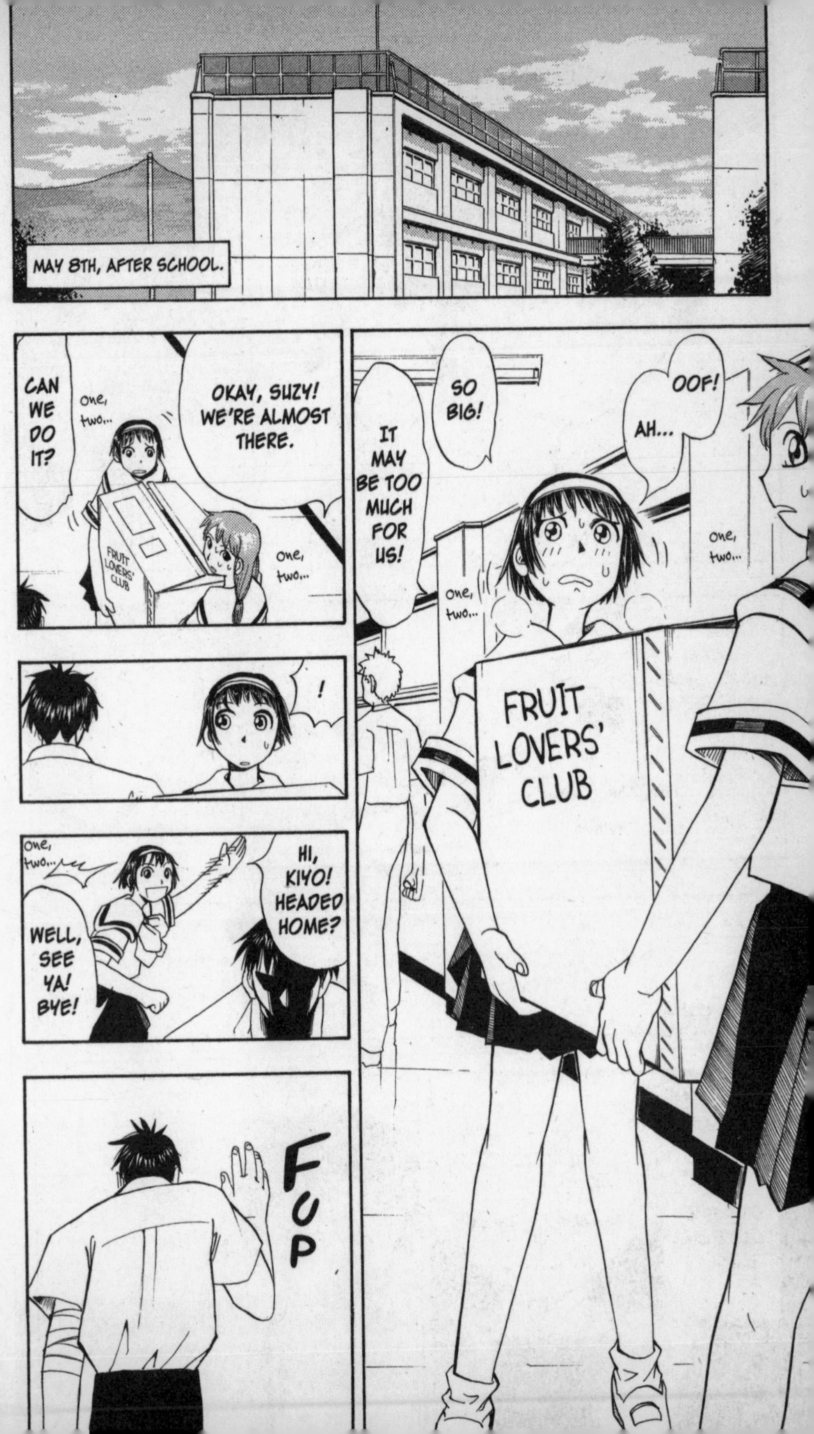
MAY 8TH, AFTER SCHOOL.
OOF!
AH...
SO BIG!
IT MAY BE TOO MUCH FOR US!
One, two...
One, two...
FRUIT LOVERS' CLUB
OKAY, SUZY! WE'RE ALMOST THERE.
One, two...
FRUIT LOVERS' CLUB
CAN WE DO IT?
One, two...
!
HI, KIYO! HEADED HOME?
One, two...
WELL, SEE YA! BYE!
FUP

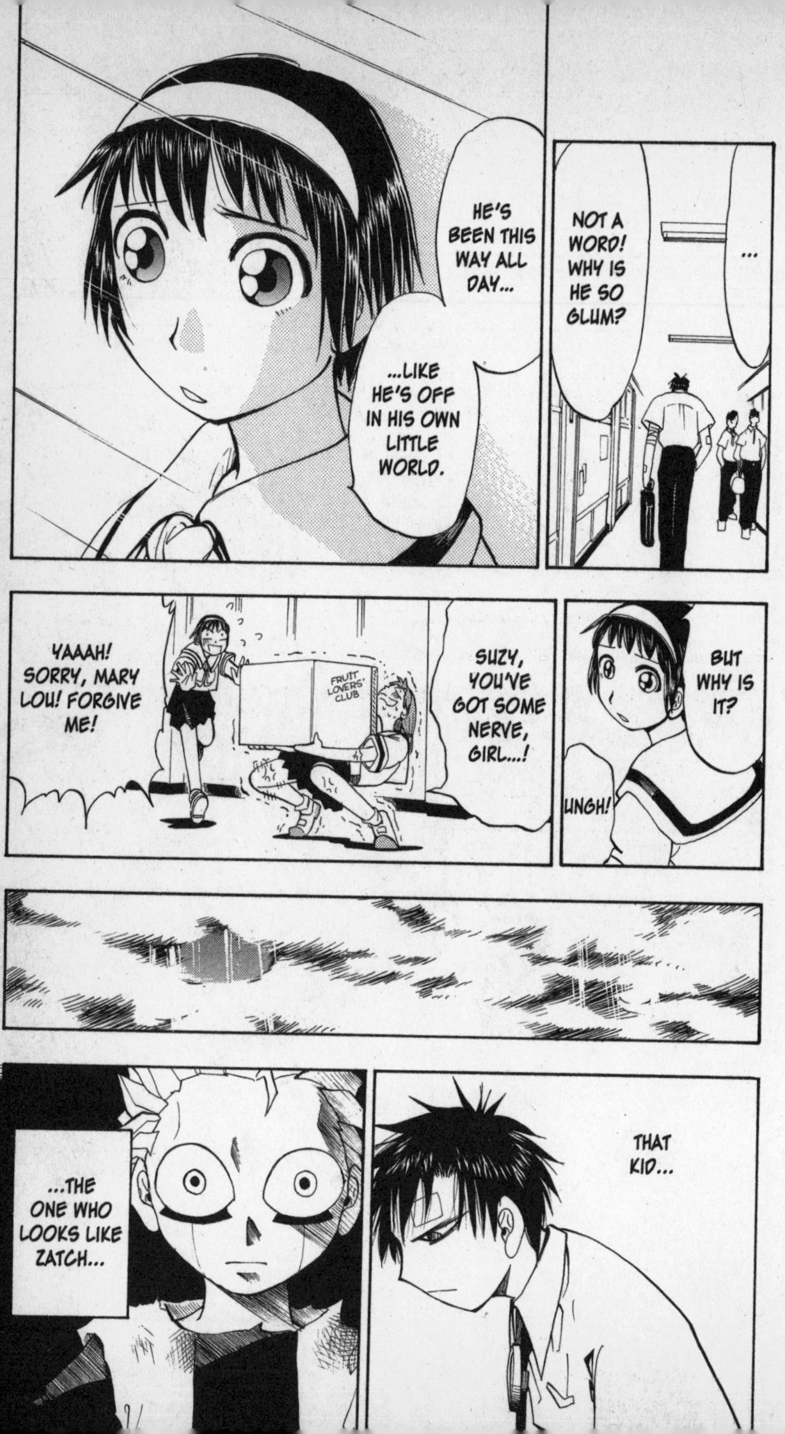
...
NOT A WORD! WHY IS HE SO GLUM?
HE'S BEEN THIS WAY ALL DAY...
...LIKE HE'S OFF IN HIS OWN LITTLE WORLD.
BUT WHY IS IT?
UNGH!
SUZY, YOU'VE GOT SOME NERVE, GIRL...!
FRUIT LOVERS' CLUB
YAAAH! SORRY, MARY LOU! FORGIVE ME!
THAT KID...
...THE ONE WHO LOOKS LIKE ZATCH...

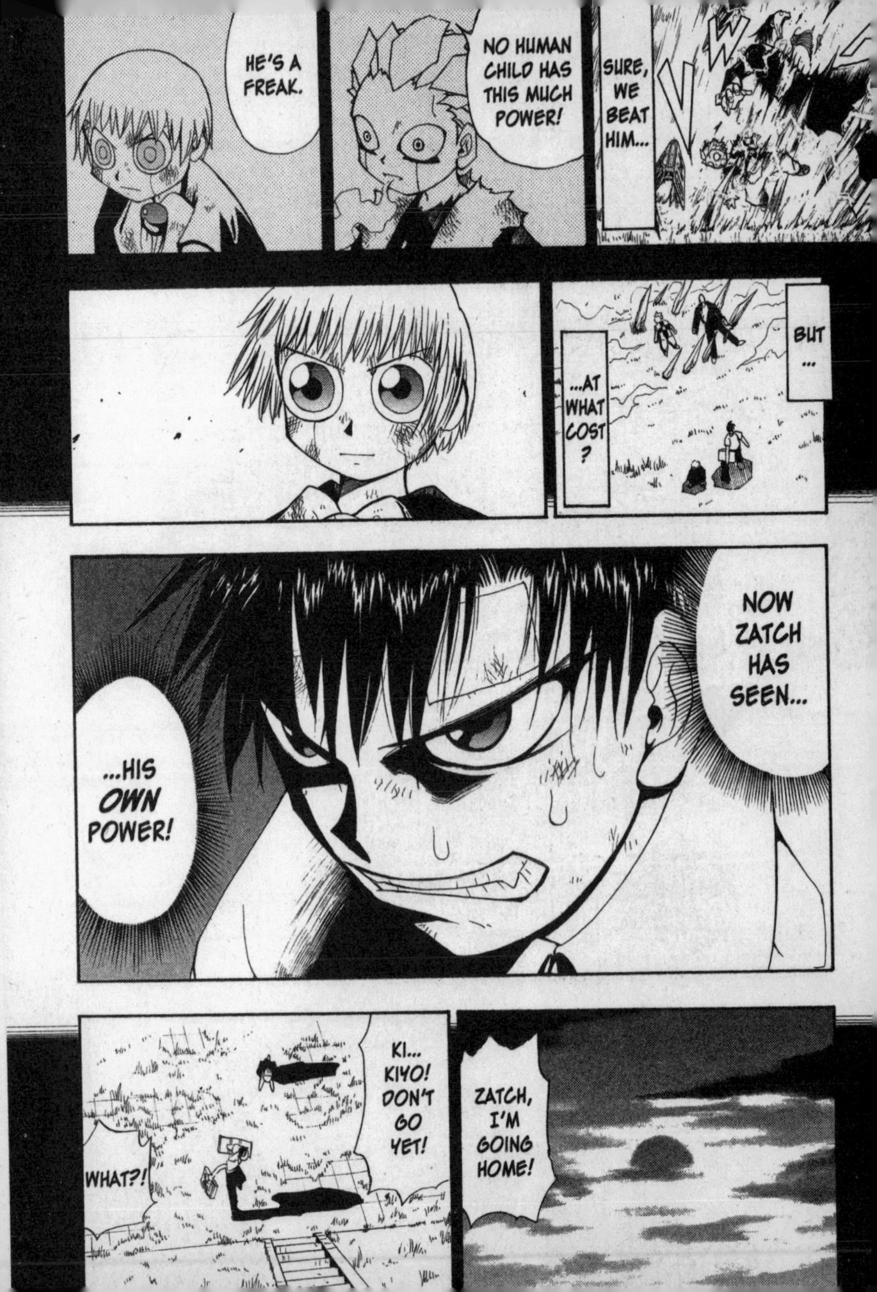
SURE, WE BEAT HIM...
NO HUMAN CHILD HAS THIS MUCH POWER!
HE'S A FREAK.
BUT ...
...AT WHAT COST ?
NOW ZATCH HAS SEEN...
...HIS *OWN* POWER!
ZATCH, I'M GOING HOME!
KI... KIYO! DON'T GO YET!
WHAT?!

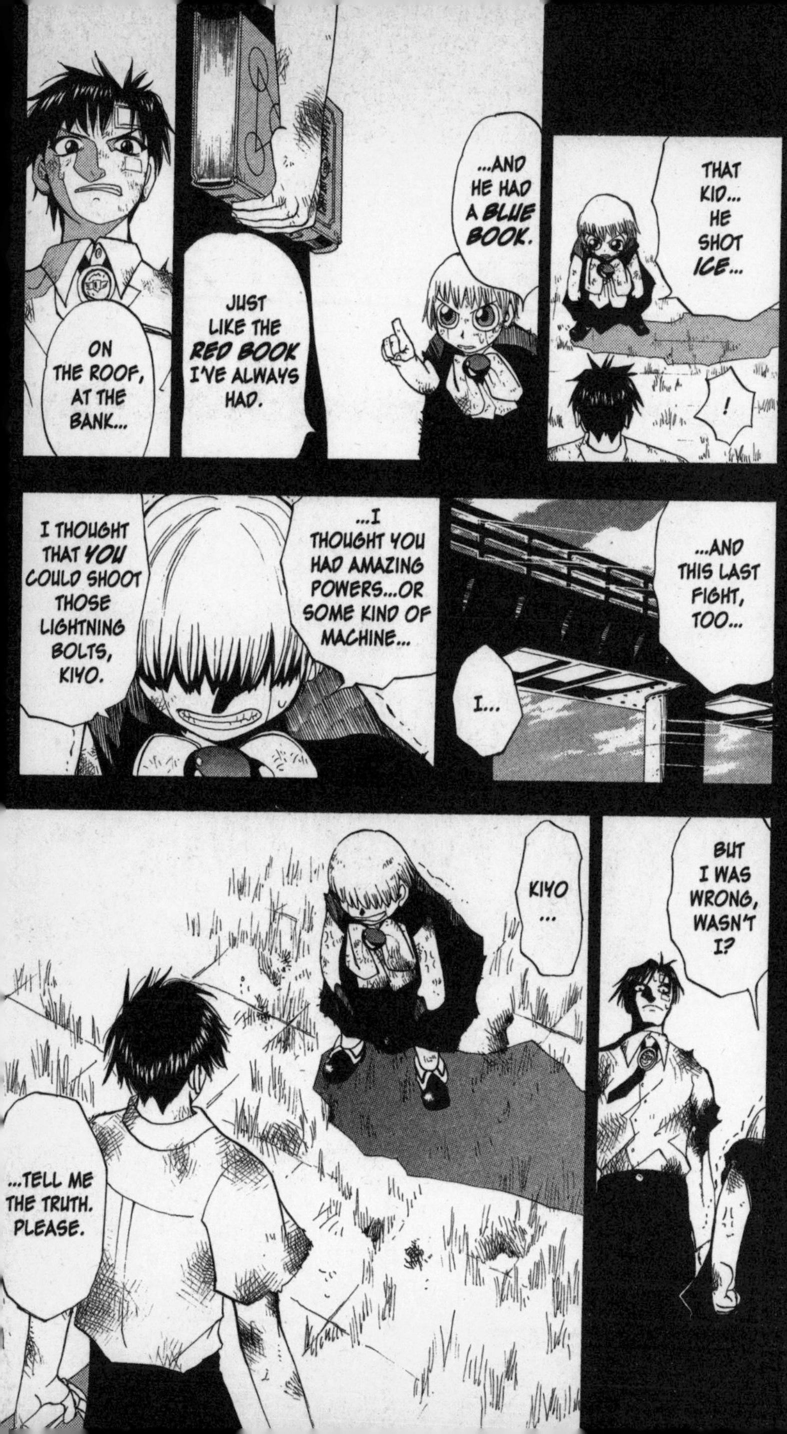
THAT KID... HE SHOT ICE...
!
...AND HE HAD A BLUE BOOK.
JUST LIKE THE RED BOOK I'VE ALWAYS HAD.
ON THE ROOF, AT THE BANK...
...AND THIS LAST FIGHT, TOO...
I...
...I THOUGHT YOU HAD AMAZING POWERS...OR SOME KIND OF MACHINE...
I THOUGHT THAT YOU COULD SHOOT THOSE LIGHTNING BOLTS, KIYO.
BUT I WAS WRONG, WASN'T I?
KIYO...
...TELL ME THE TRUTH. PLEASE.

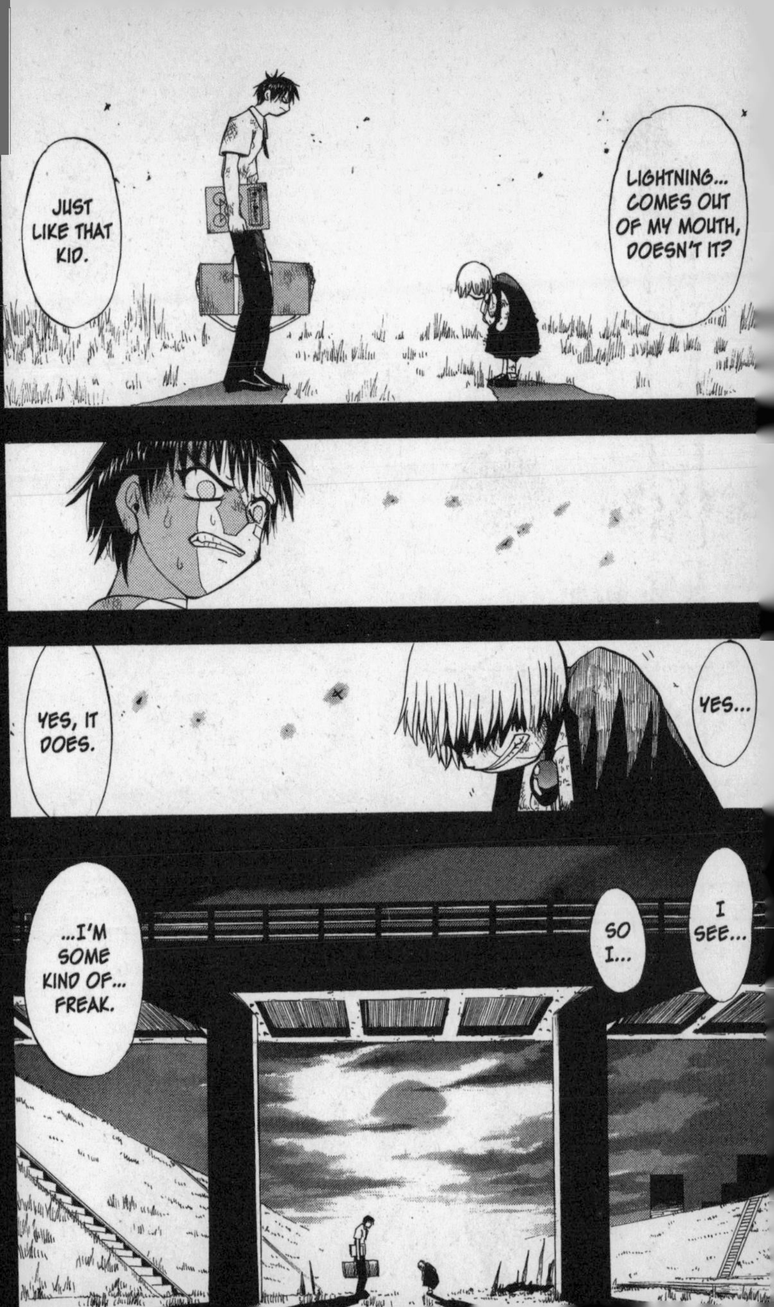
LIGHTNING... COMES OUT OF MY MOUTH, DOESN'T IT?
JUST LIKE THAT KID.
YES...
YES, IT DOES.
I SEE...
SO I...
...I'M SOME KIND OF... FREAK.

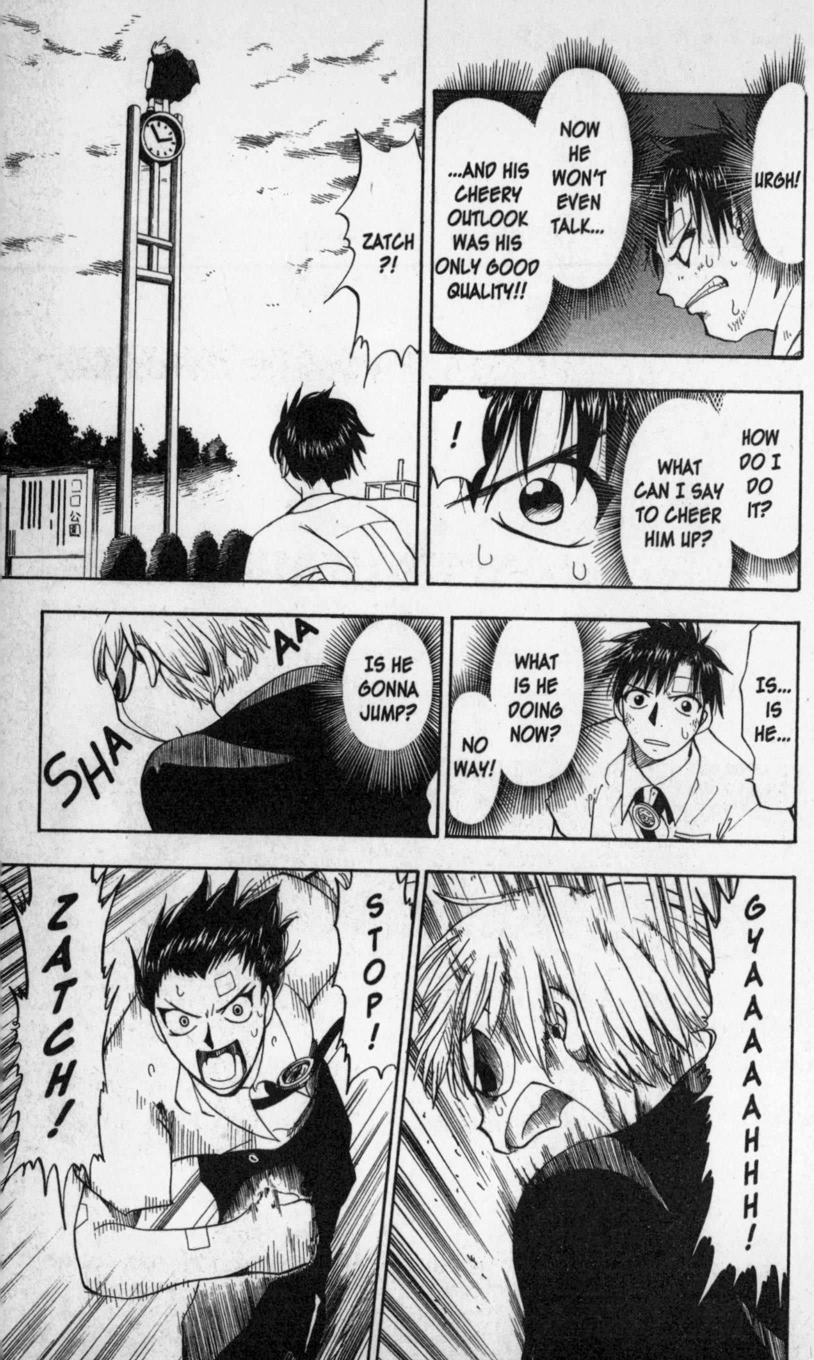
URGH!
NOW HE WON'T EVEN TALK...
...AND HIS CHEERY OUTLOOK WAS HIS ONLY GOOD QUALITY!!
HOW DO I DO IT?
WHAT CAN I SAY TO CHEER HIM UP?
!
ZATCH?!
...
IS... IS HE...
WHAT IS HE DOING NOW?
NO WAY!
IS HE GONNA JUMP?
AA
SHA
GYAAAAAAHHHH!
STOP!
ZATCH!

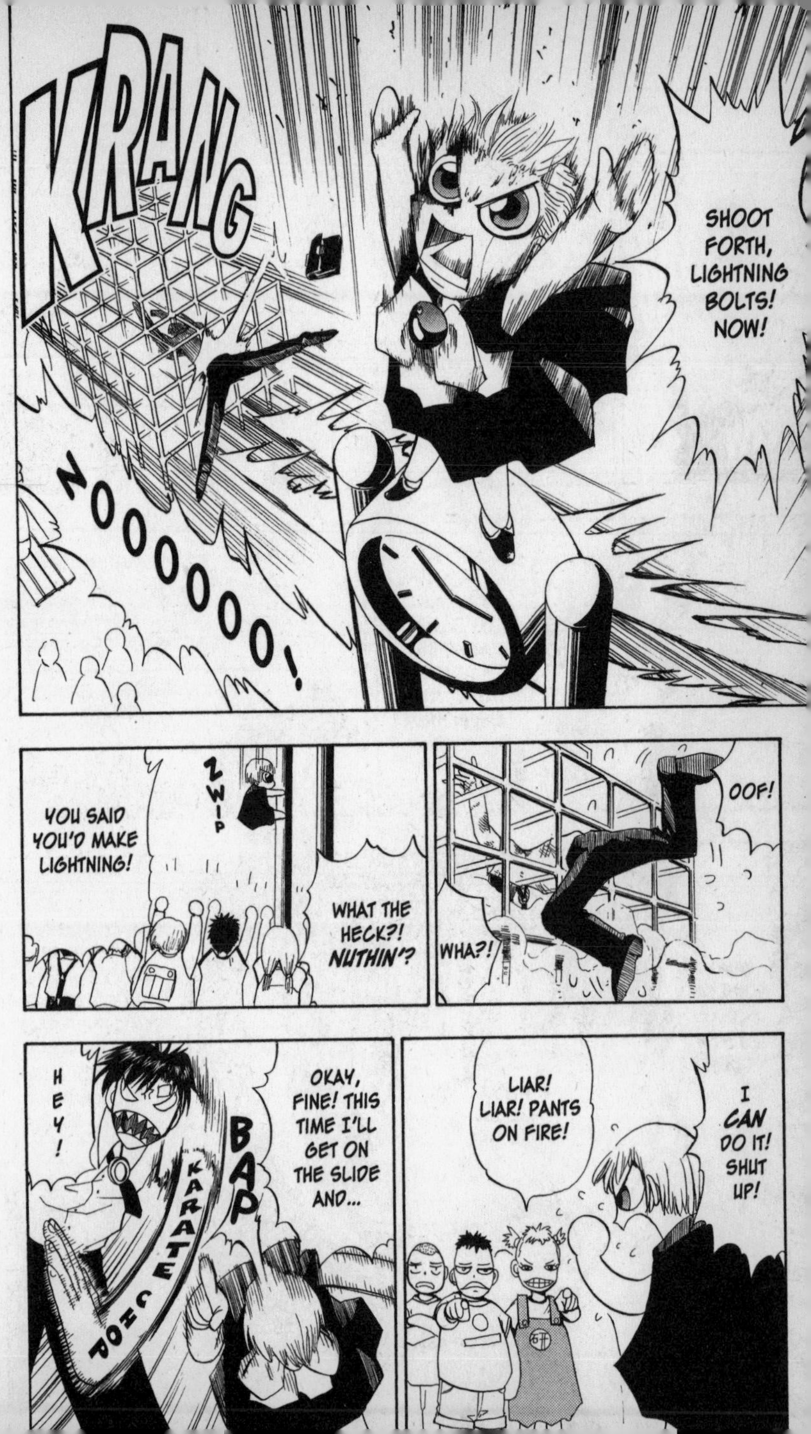
SHOOT FORTH, LIGHTNING BOLTS! NOW!
KRANG
NOOOOOOO!
OOF!
WHA?!
WHAT THE HECK?! NUTHIN'?
ZWIP
YOU SAID YOU'D MAKE LIGHTNING!
I CAN DO IT! SHUT UP!
LIAR! LIAR! PANTS ON FIRE!
OKAY, FINE! THIS TIME I'LL GET ON THE SLIDE AND...
BAP
HEY!
KARATE CHOP

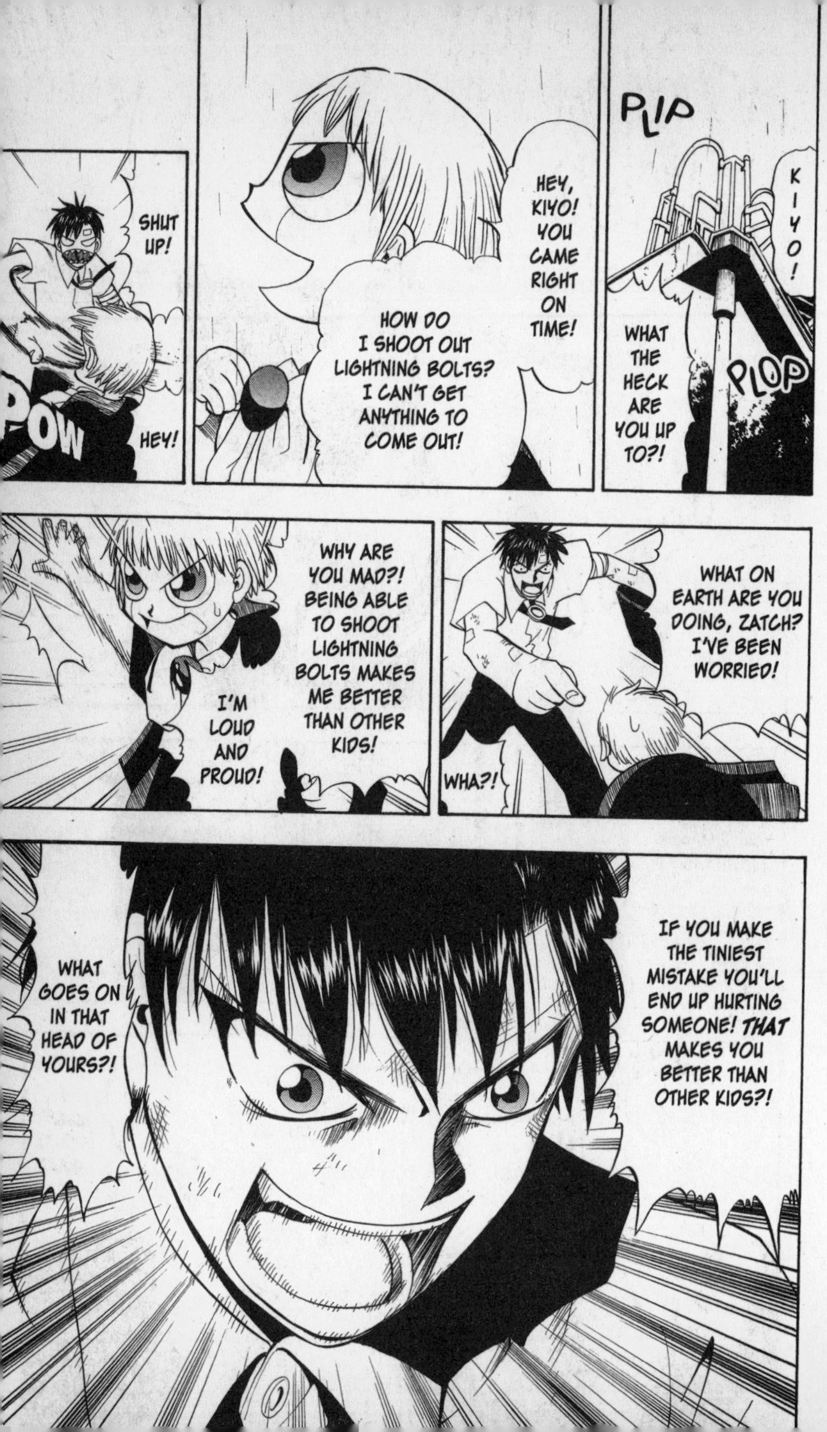
PLIP
KIYO!
WHAT THE HECK ARE YOU UP TO?!
PLOP
HEY, KIYO! YOU CAME RIGHT ON TIME!
HOW DO I SHOOT OUT LIGHTNING BOLTS? I CAN'T GET ANYTHING TO COME OUT!
SHUT UP!
POW
HEY!
WHAT ON EARTH ARE YOU DOING, ZATCH? I'VE BEEN WORRIED!
WHA?!
WHY ARE YOU MAD?! BEING ABLE TO SHOOT LIGHTNING BOLTS MAKES ME BETTER THAN OTHER KIDS!
I'M LOUD AND PROUD!
IF YOU MAKE THE TINIEST MISTAKE YOU'LL END UP HURTING SOMEONE! THAT MAKES YOU BETTER THAN OTHER KIDS?!
WHAT GOES ON IN THAT HEAD OF YOURS?!

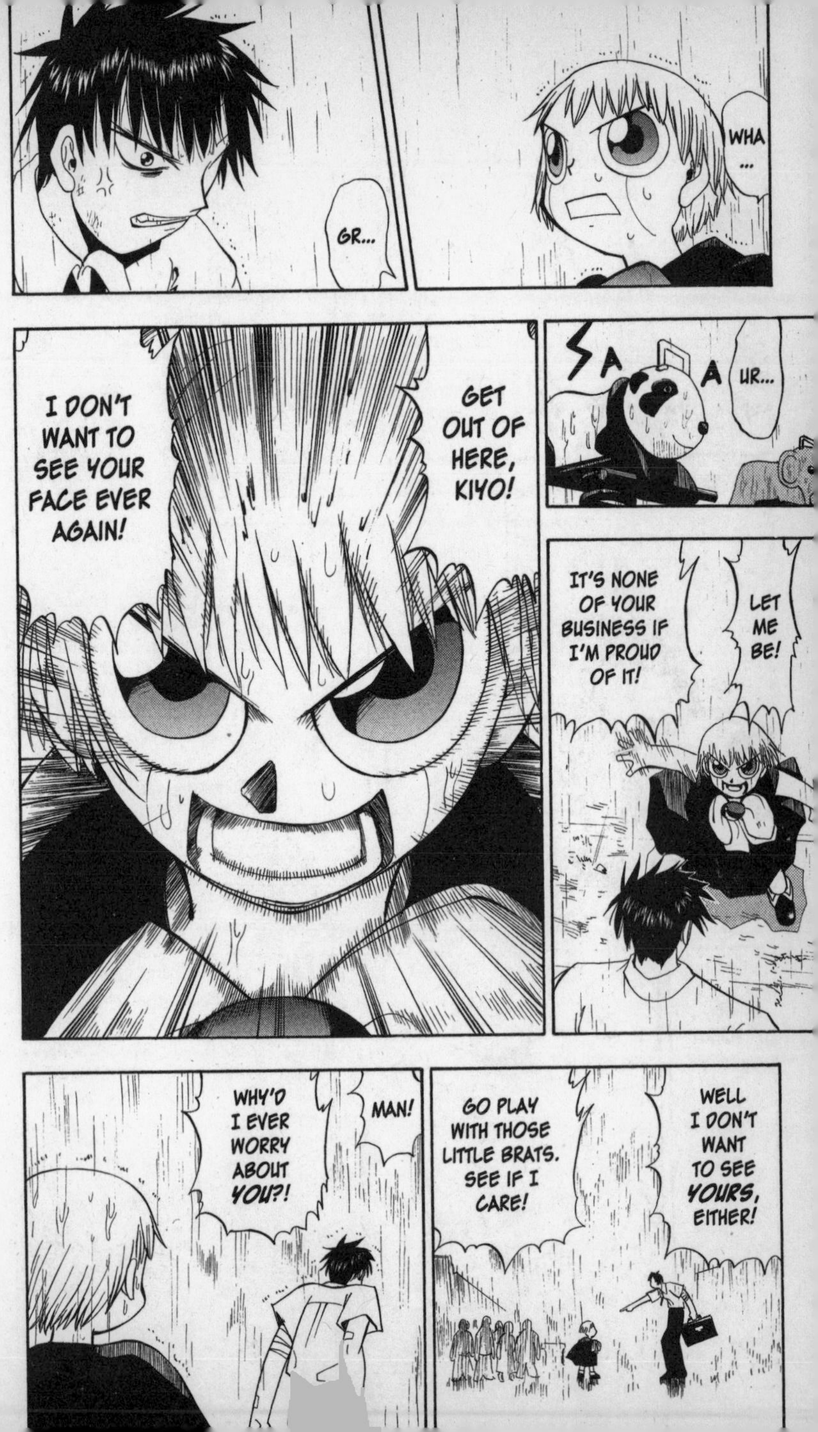
WHA...
GR...
SA A
UR...
LET ME BE!
IT'S NONE OF YOUR BUSINESS IF I'M PROUD OF IT!
GET OUT OF HERE, KIYO!
I DON'T WANT TO SEE YOUR FACE EVER AGAIN!
WELL I DON'T WANT TO SEE YOURS, EITHER!
GO PLAY WITH THOSE LITTLE BRATS. SEE IF I CARE!
MAN!
WHY'D I EVER WORRY ABOUT YOU?!

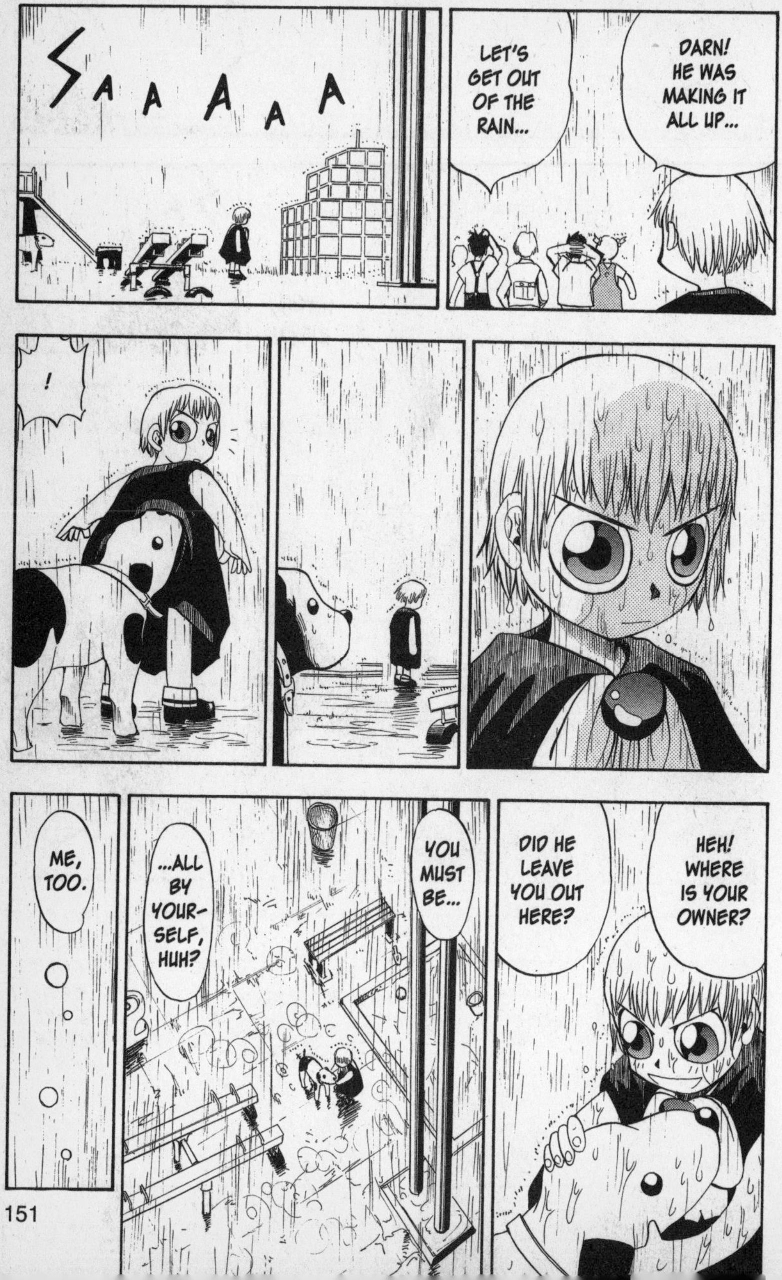
DARN! HE WAS MAKING IT ALL UP...
LET'S GET OUT OF THE RAIN...
SAAAAA
!
HEH! WHERE IS YOUR OWNER?
DID HE LEAVE YOU OUT HERE?
YOU MUST BE...
...ALL BY YOURSELF, HUH?
ME, TOO.

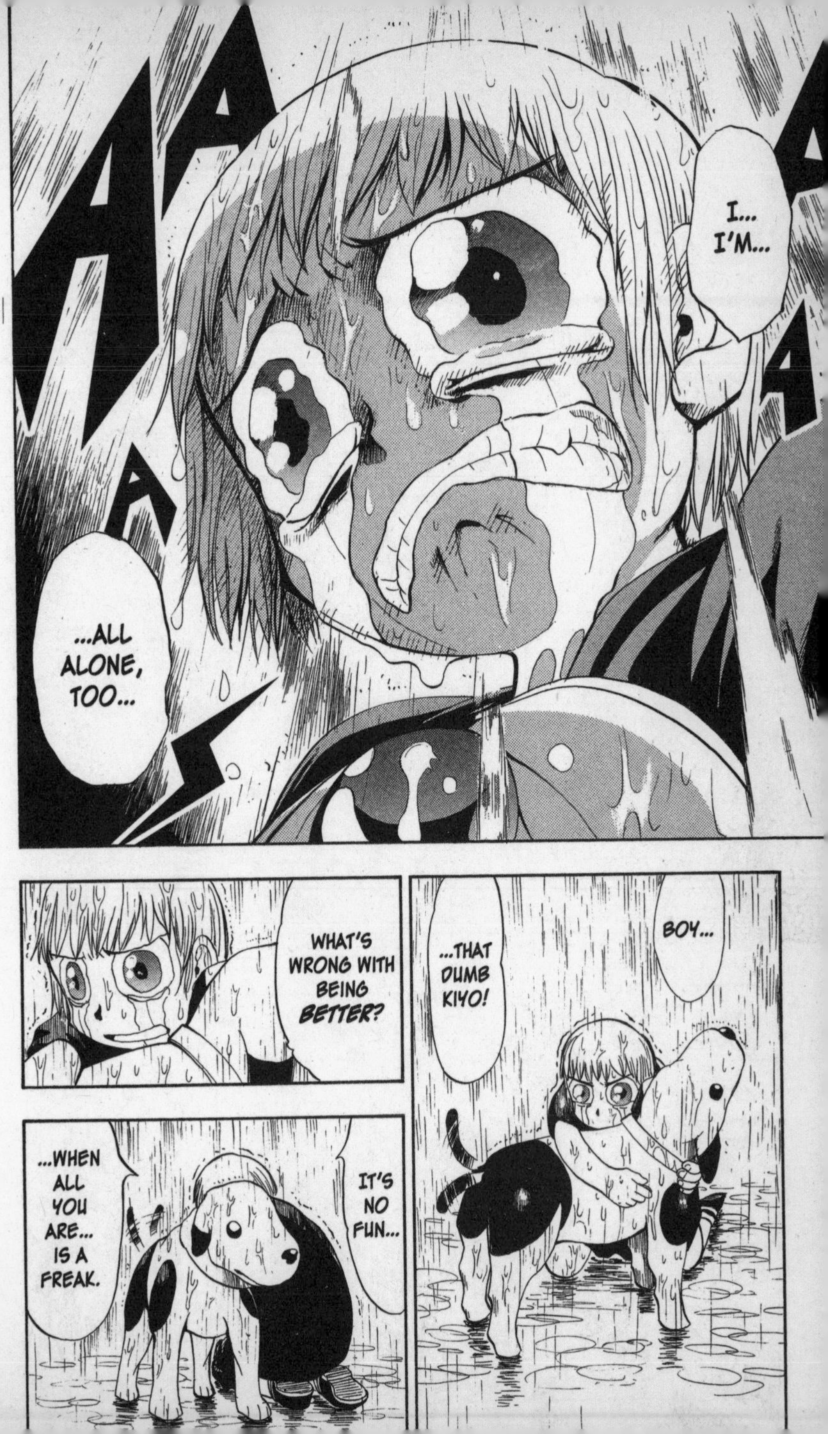
I... I'M...
...ALL ALONE, TOO...
BOY...
...THAT DUMB KIYO!
WHAT'S WRONG WITH BEING *BETTER?*
IT'S NO FUN...
...WHEN ALL YOU ARE... IS A FREAK.

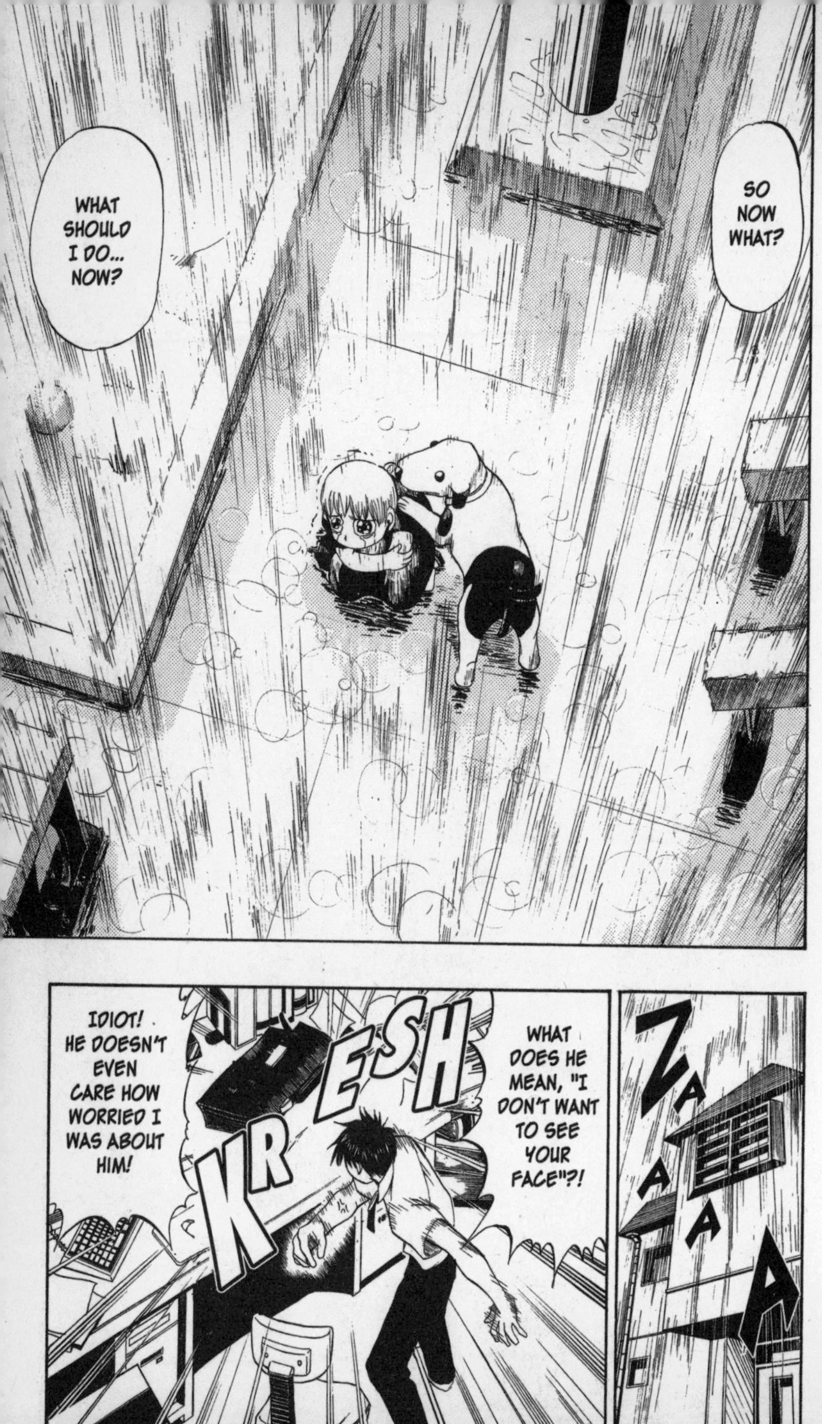
SO NOW WHAT?
WHAT SHOULD I DO... NOW?
ZAAAAA
WHAT DOES HE MEAN, "I DON'T WANT TO SEE YOUR FACE"?!
KRESH
IDIOT! HE DOESN'T EVEN CARE HOW WORRIED I WAS ABOUT HIM!

DING DONG

WHO'S THAT, AT *THIS* HOUR?

DING DONG

!

TMP

TMP

TMP

I HOPE IT'S SOME STUPID SALESMAN! I'LL LET 'IM HAVE IT!

!

KRRK

MY FOLKS AREN'T HERE RIGHT NOW, SO...

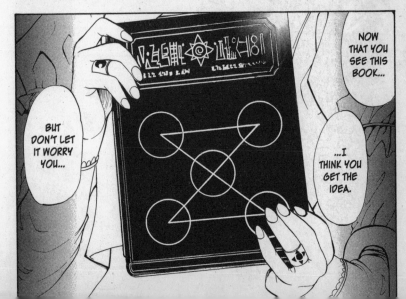

NOW THAT YOU SEE THIS BOOK...

...I THINK YOU GET THE IDEA.

BUT DON'T LET IT WORRY YOU...

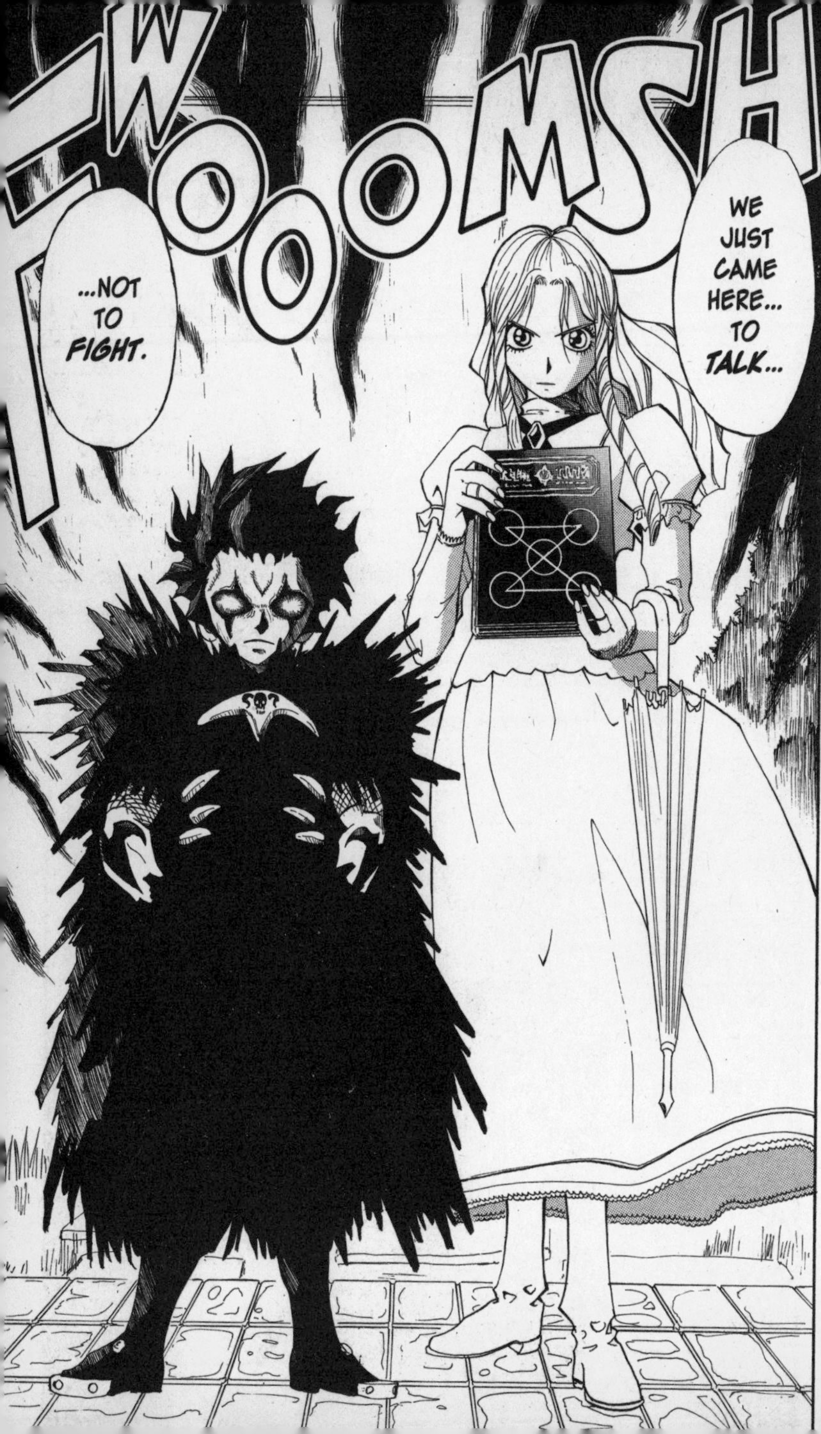
FWOOOMSH
WE JUST CAME HERE... TO TALK...
...NOT TO FIGHT.

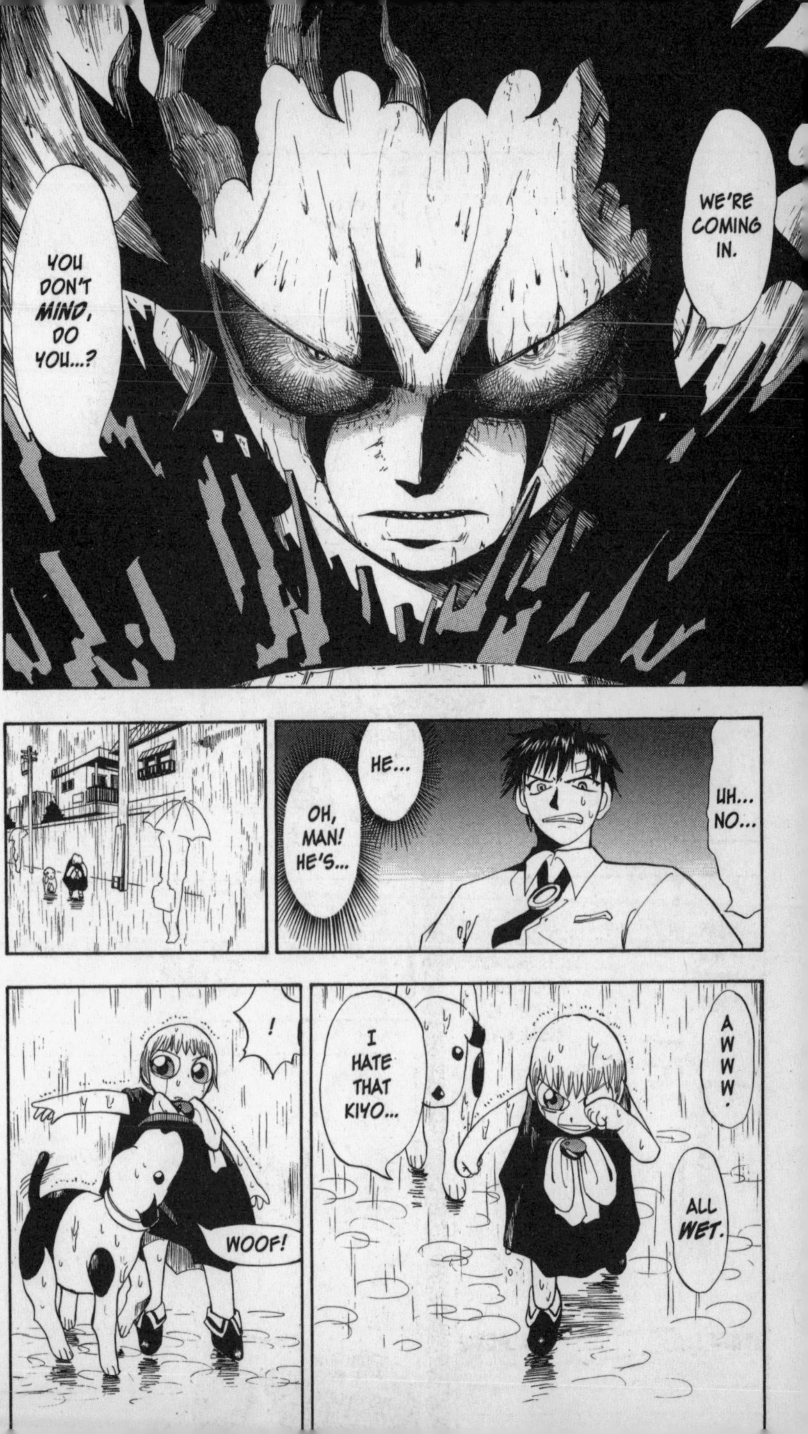
WE'RE COMING IN.
YOU DON'T MIND, DO YOU...?
UH... NO...
HE...
OH, MAN! HE'S...
AWWW.
ALL WET.
I HATE THAT KIYO...
!
WOOF!

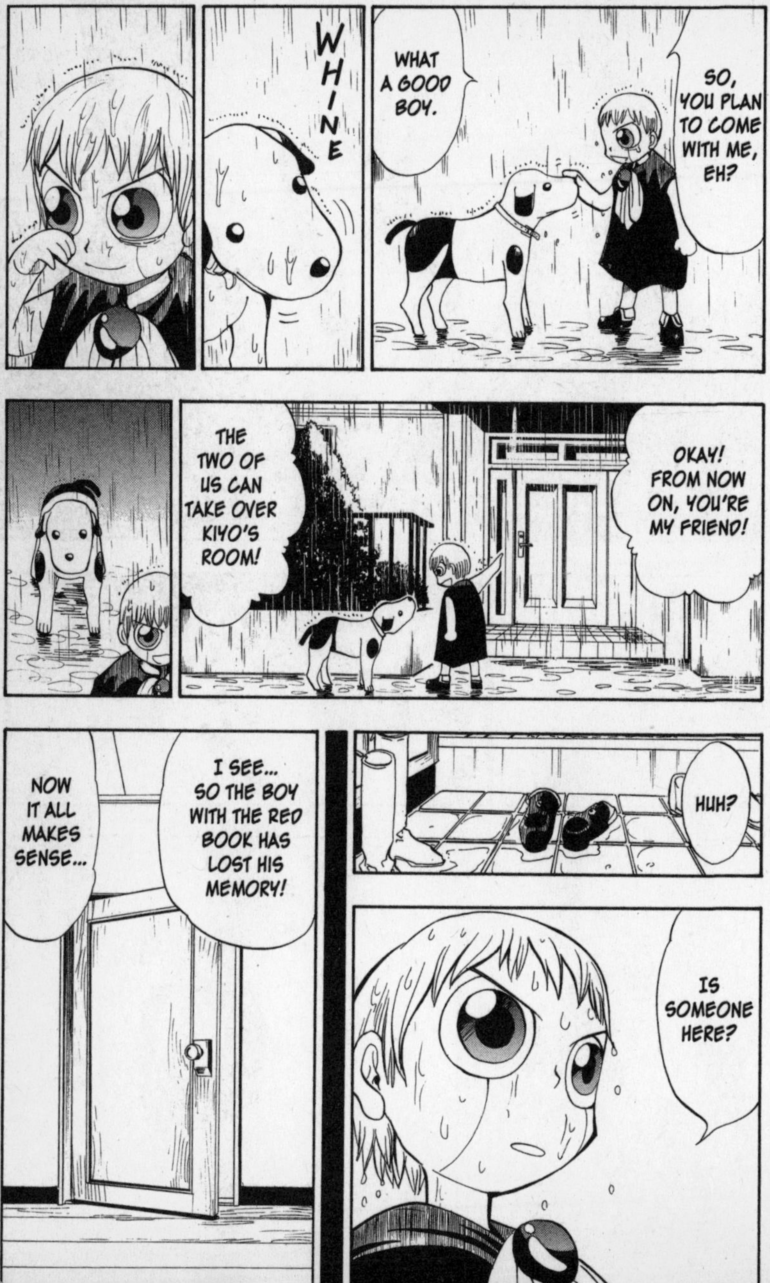
SO, YOU PLAN TO COME WITH ME, EH?
WHAT A GOOD BOY.
WHINE
OKAY! FROM NOW ON, YOU'RE MY FRIEND!
THE TWO OF US CAN TAKE OVER KIYO'S ROOM!
HUH?
IS SOMEONE HERE?
I SEE... SO THE BOY WITH THE RED BOOK HAS LOST HIS MEMORY!
NOW IT ALL MAKES SENSE...

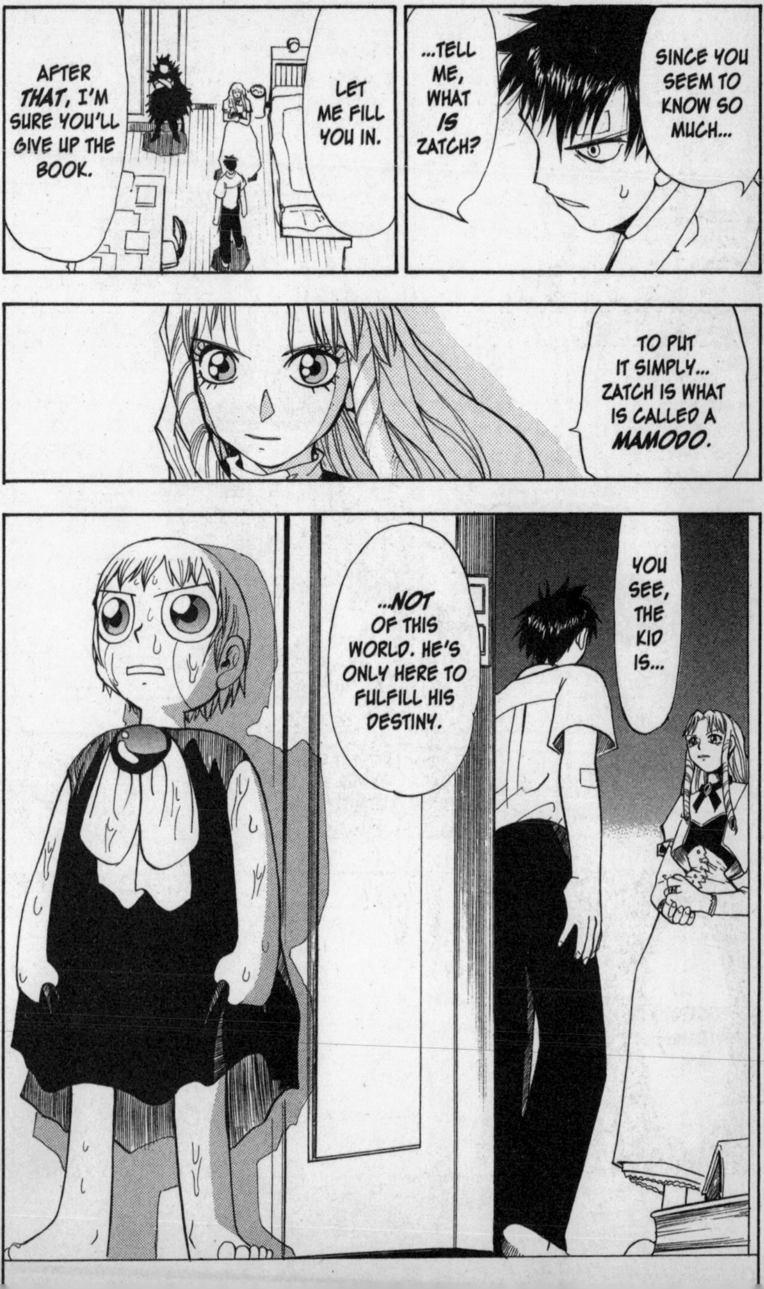
SINCE YOU SEEM TO KNOW SO MUCH...
...TELL ME, WHAT *IS* ZATCH?
LET ME FILL YOU IN.
AFTER *THAT*, I'M SURE YOU'LL GIVE UP THE BOOK.
TO PUT IT SIMPLY... ZATCH IS WHAT IS CALLED A *MAMODO*.
YOU SEE, THE KID IS...
...*NOT* OF THIS WORLD. HE'S ONLY HERE TO FULFILL HIS DESTINY.

LEVEL 8: The Qualifications to Be King

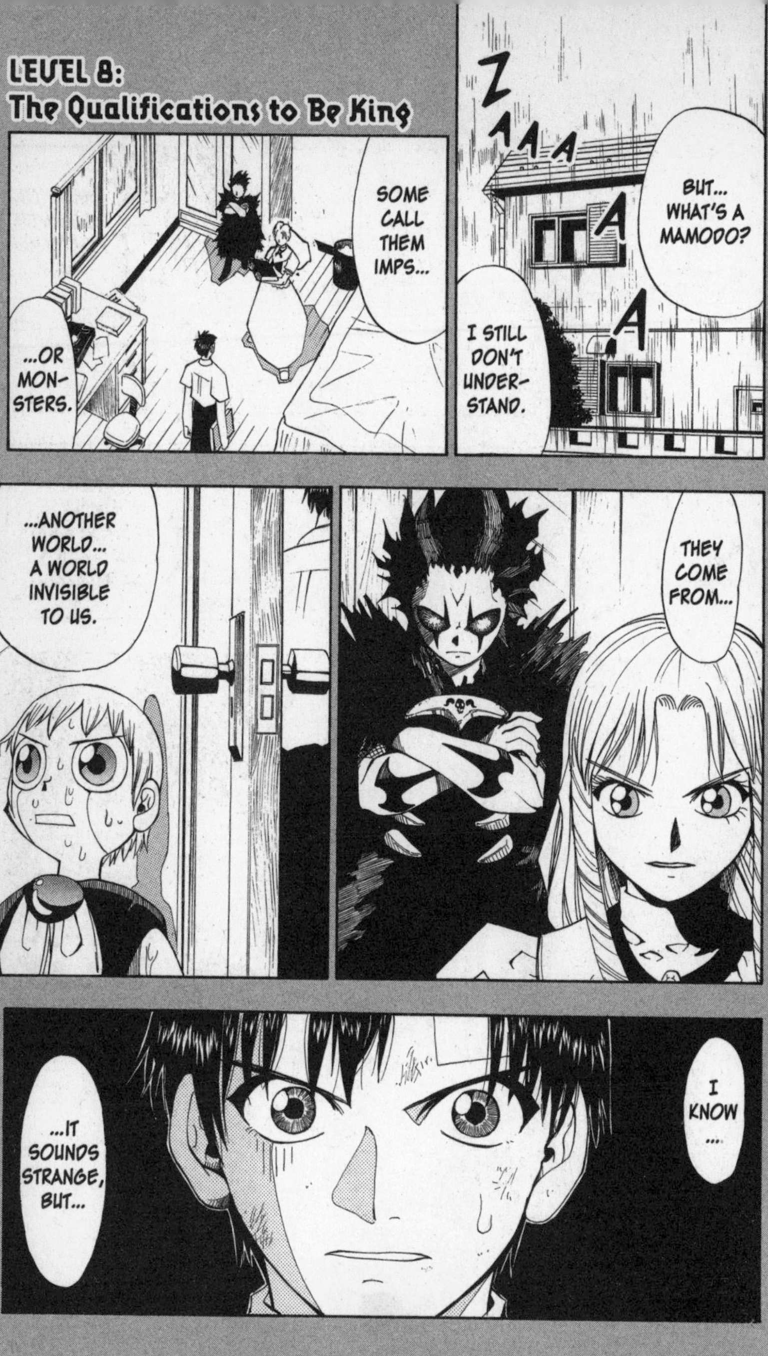
ZAAAAA
BUT... WHAT'S A MAMODO?
I STILL DON'T UNDERSTAND.
SOME CALL THEM IMPS...
...OR MON-STERS.
THEY COME FROM...
...ANOTHER WORLD... A WORLD INVISIBLE TO US.
I KNOW...
...IT SOUNDS STRANGE, BUT...

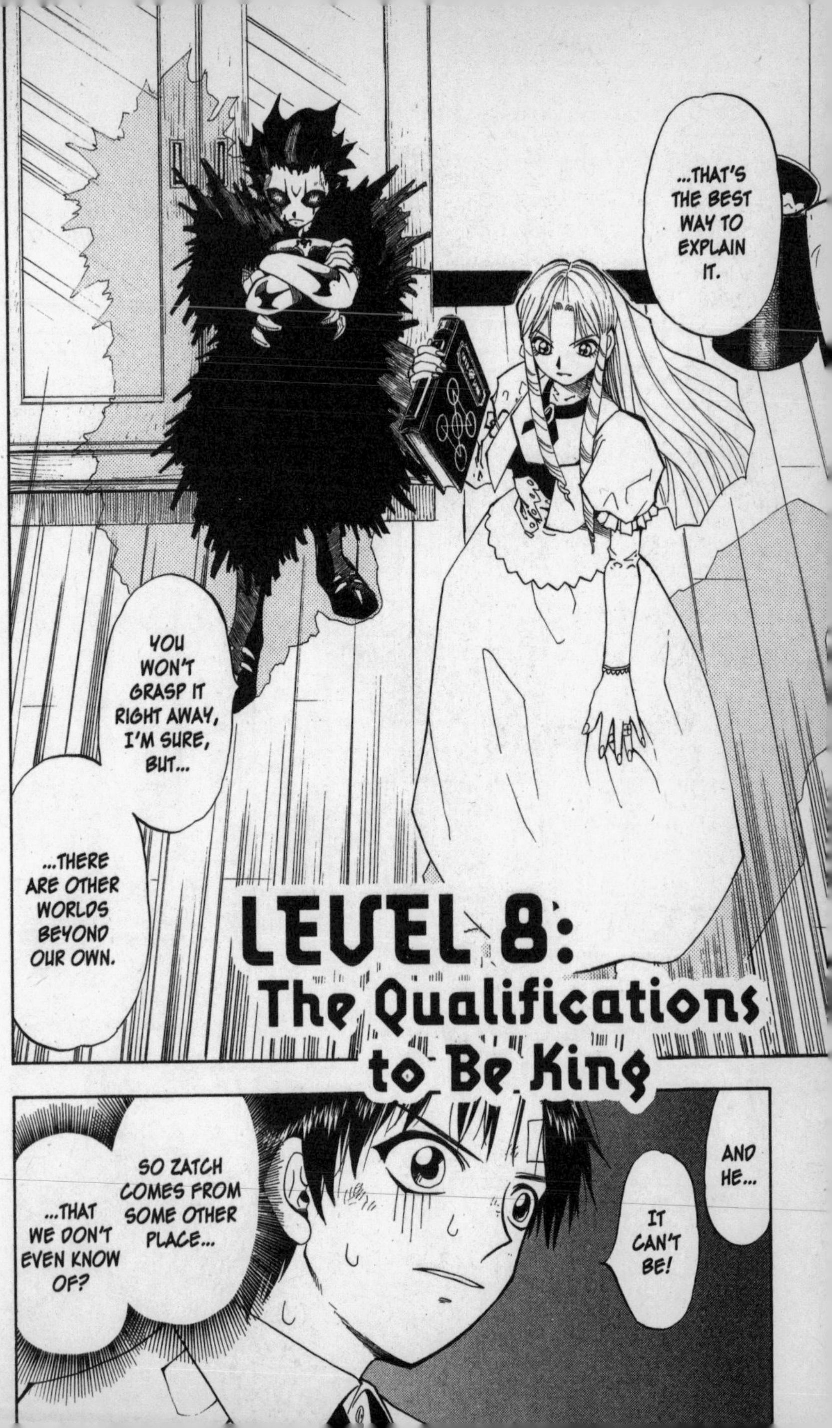
...THAT'S THE BEST WAY TO EXPLAIN IT.
YOU WON'T GRASP IT RIGHT AWAY, I'M SURE, BUT...
...THERE ARE OTHER WORLDS BEYOND OUR OWN.
LEVEL 8:
The Qualifications to Be King
AND HE...
IT CAN'T BE!
SO ZATCH COMES FROM SOME OTHER PLACE...
...THAT WE DON'T EVEN KNOW OF?

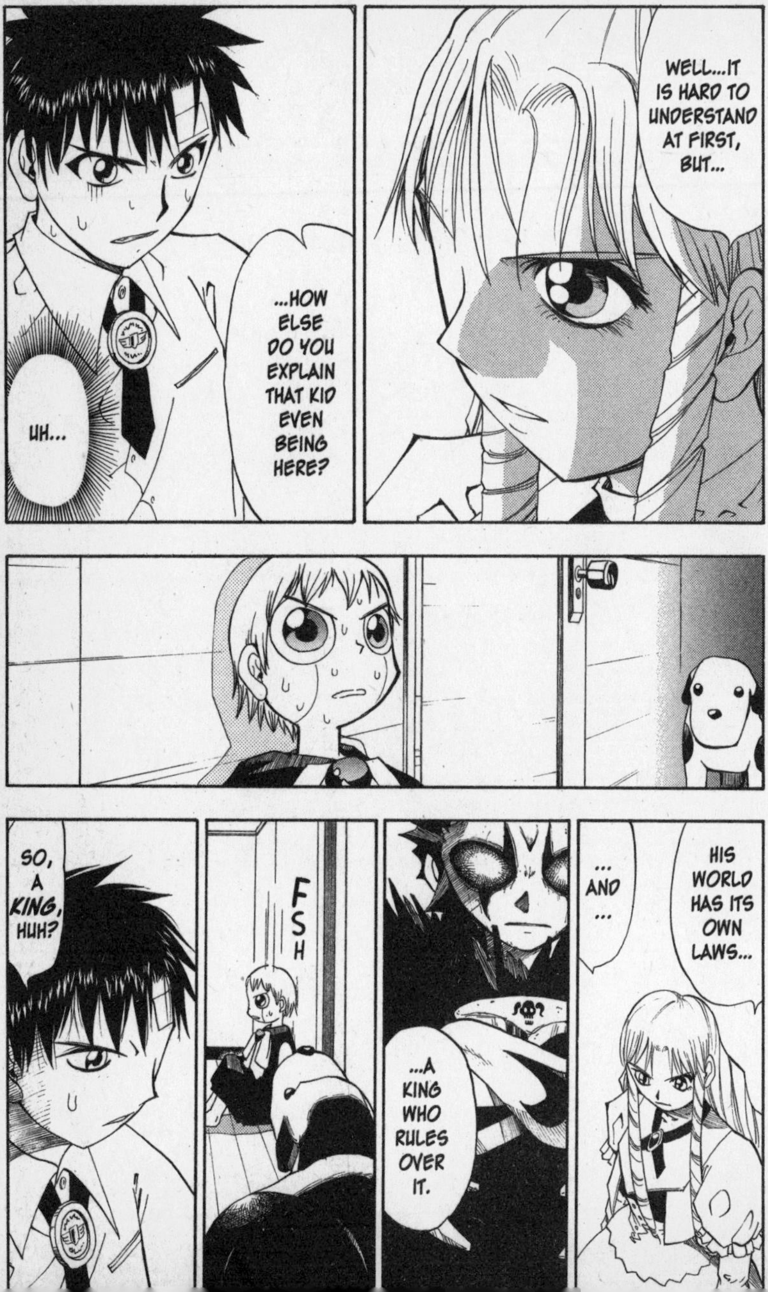
WELL...IT IS HARD TO UNDERSTAND AT FIRST, BUT...
...HOW ELSE DO YOU EXPLAIN THAT KID EVEN BEING HERE?
UH...
HIS WORLD HAS ITS OWN LAWS...
...AND...
...A KING WHO RULES OVER IT.
FSH
SO, A KING, HUH?

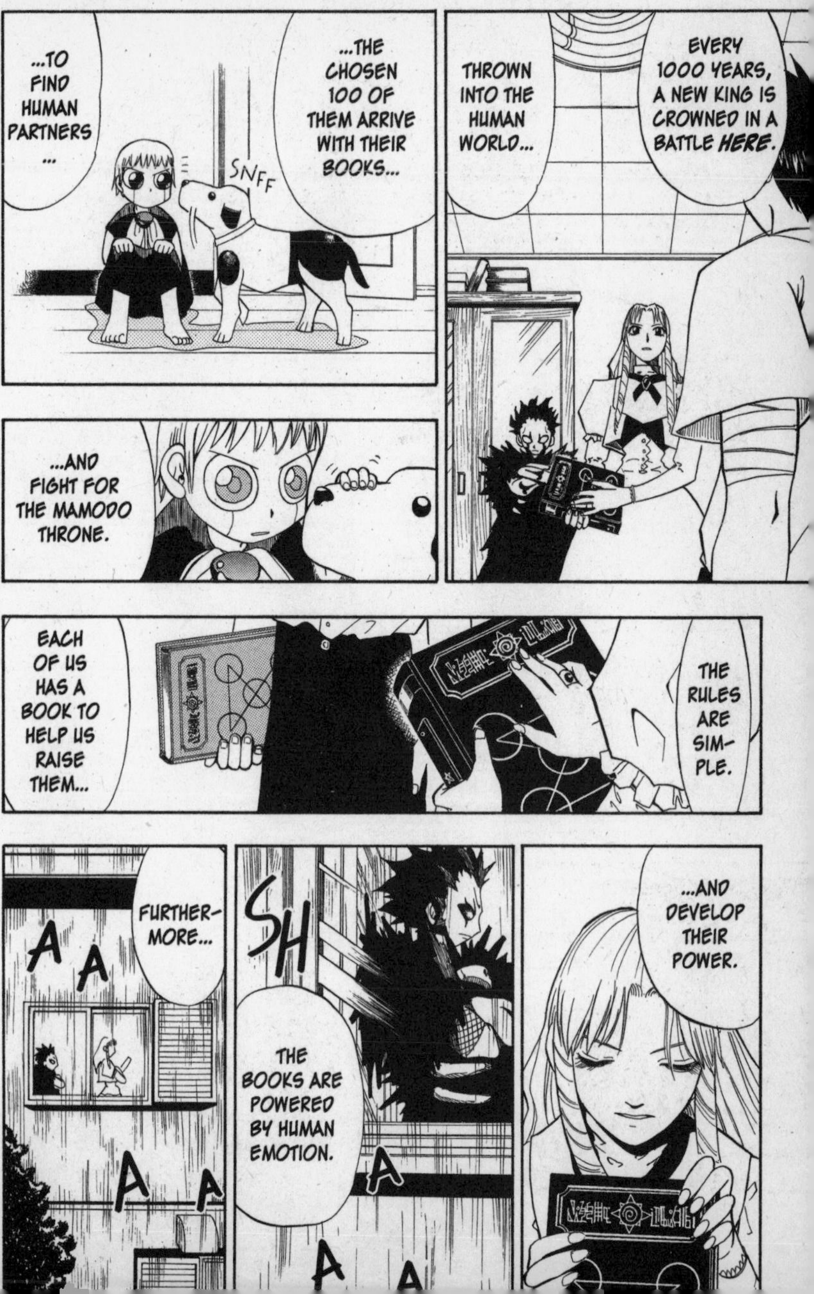
EVERY 1000 YEARS, A NEW KING IS CROWNED IN A BATTLE HERE.
THROWN INTO THE HUMAN WORLD...
...THE CHOSEN 100 OF THEM ARRIVE WITH THEIR BOOKS...
SNFF
...TO FIND HUMAN PARTNERS ...
...AND FIGHT FOR THE MAMODO THRONE.
THE RULES ARE SIMPLE.
EACH OF US HAS A BOOK TO HELP US RAISE THEM...
...AND DEVELOP THEIR POWER.
SH
THE BOOKS ARE POWERED BY HUMAN EMOTION.
A
A
FURTHER-MORE...
A
A
A
A

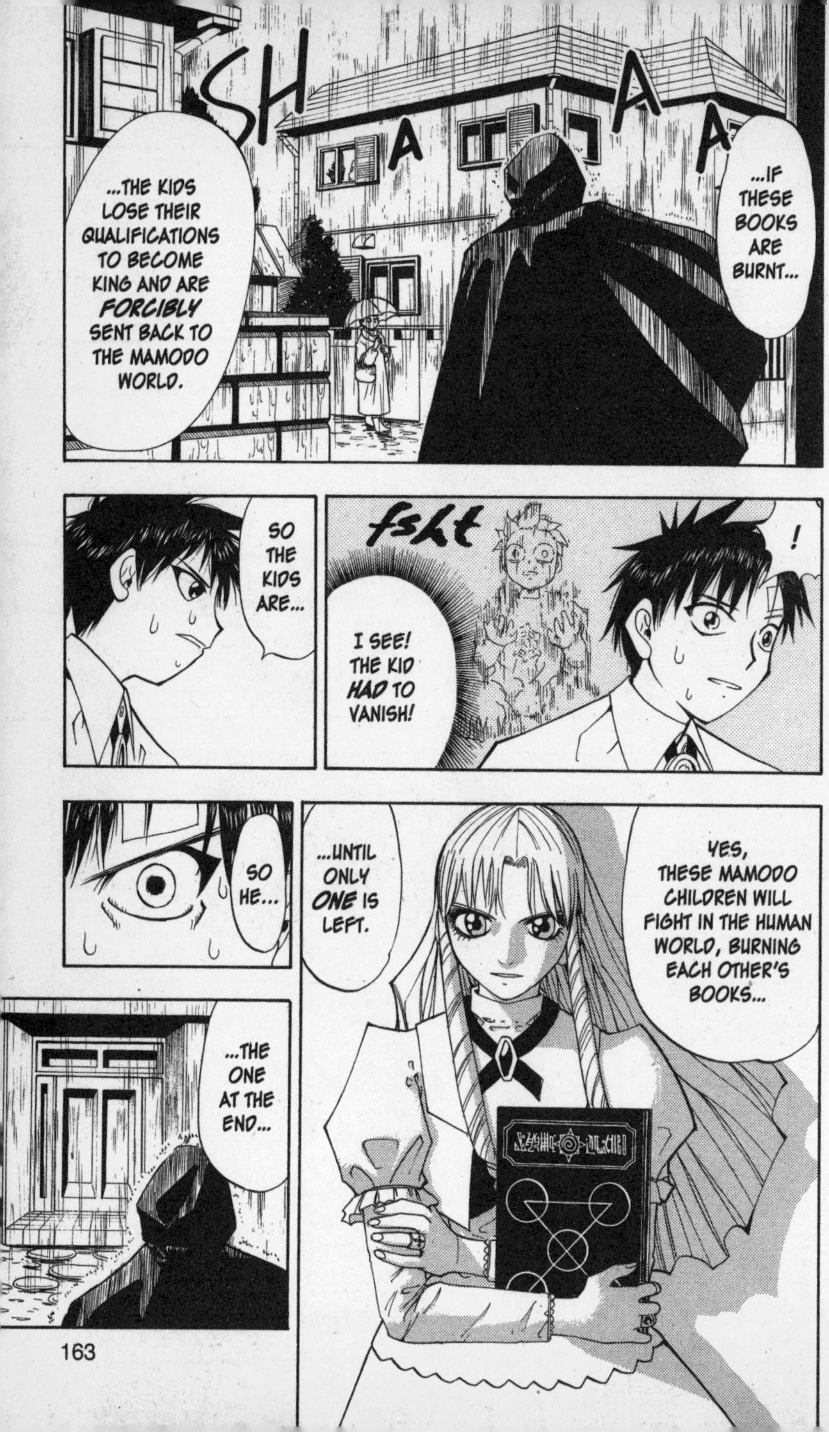
SHAAA
...IF THESE BOOKS ARE BURNT...
...THE KIDS LOSE THEIR QUALIFICATIONS TO BECOME KING AND ARE FORCIBLY SENT BACK TO THE MAMODO WORLD.
!
fsht
I SEE! THE KID HAD TO VANISH!
SO THE KIDS ARE...
YES, THESE MAMODO CHILDREN WILL FIGHT IN THE HUMAN WORLD, BURNING EACH OTHER'S BOOKS...
...UNTIL ONLY ONE IS LEFT.
SO HE...
...THE ONE AT THE END...

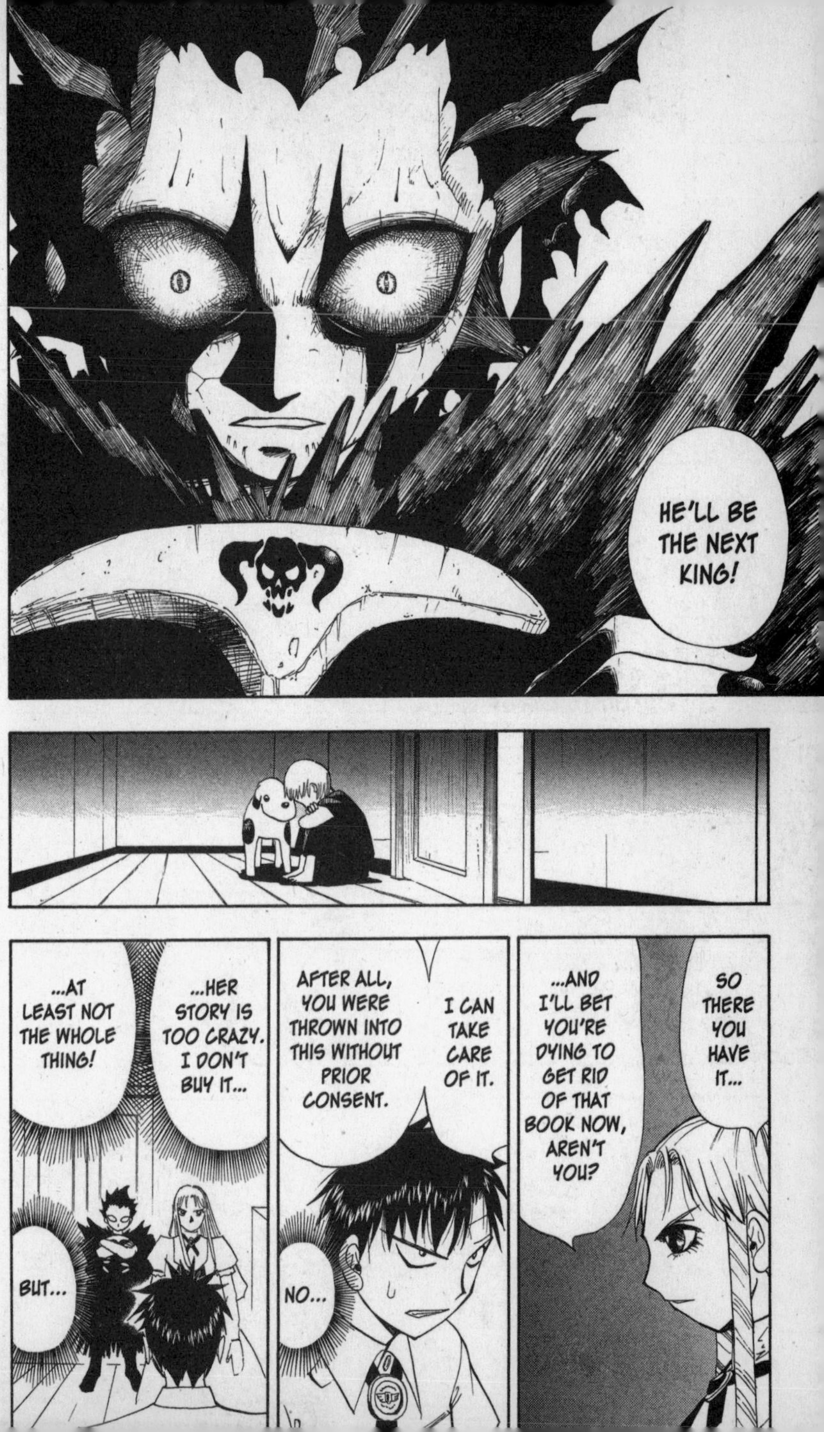
HE'LL BE THE NEXT KING!
SO THERE YOU HAVE IT...
...AND I'LL BET YOU'RE DYING TO GET RID OF THAT BOOK NOW, AREN'T YOU?
I CAN TAKE CARE OF IT.
AFTER ALL, YOU WERE THROWN INTO THIS WITHOUT PRIOR CONSENT.
NO...
...HER STORY IS TOO CRAZY. I DON'T BUY IT...
...AT LEAST NOT THE WHOLE THING!
BUT...

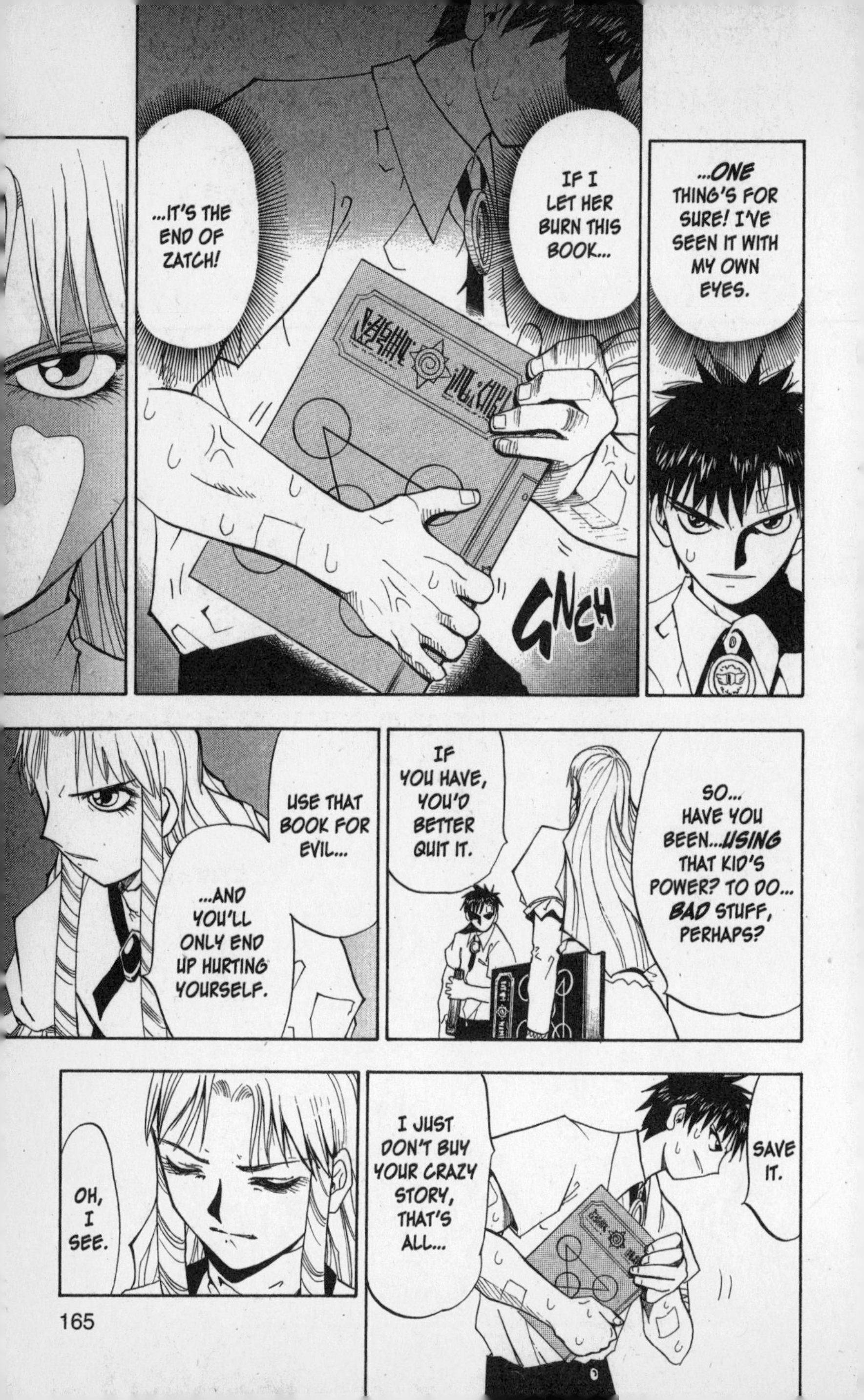
...ONE THING'S FOR SURE! I'VE SEEN IT WITH MY OWN EYES.
IF I LET HER BURN THIS BOOK...
...IT'S THE END OF ZATCH!
GNCH
SO... HAVE YOU BEEN...USING THAT KID'S POWER? TO DO... BAD STUFF, PERHAPS?
IF YOU HAVE, YOU'D BETTER QUIT IT.
USE THAT BOOK FOR EVIL...
...AND YOU'LL ONLY END UP HURTING YOURSELF.
SAVE IT.
I JUST DON'T BUY YOUR CRAZY STORY, THAT'S ALL...
OH, I SEE.

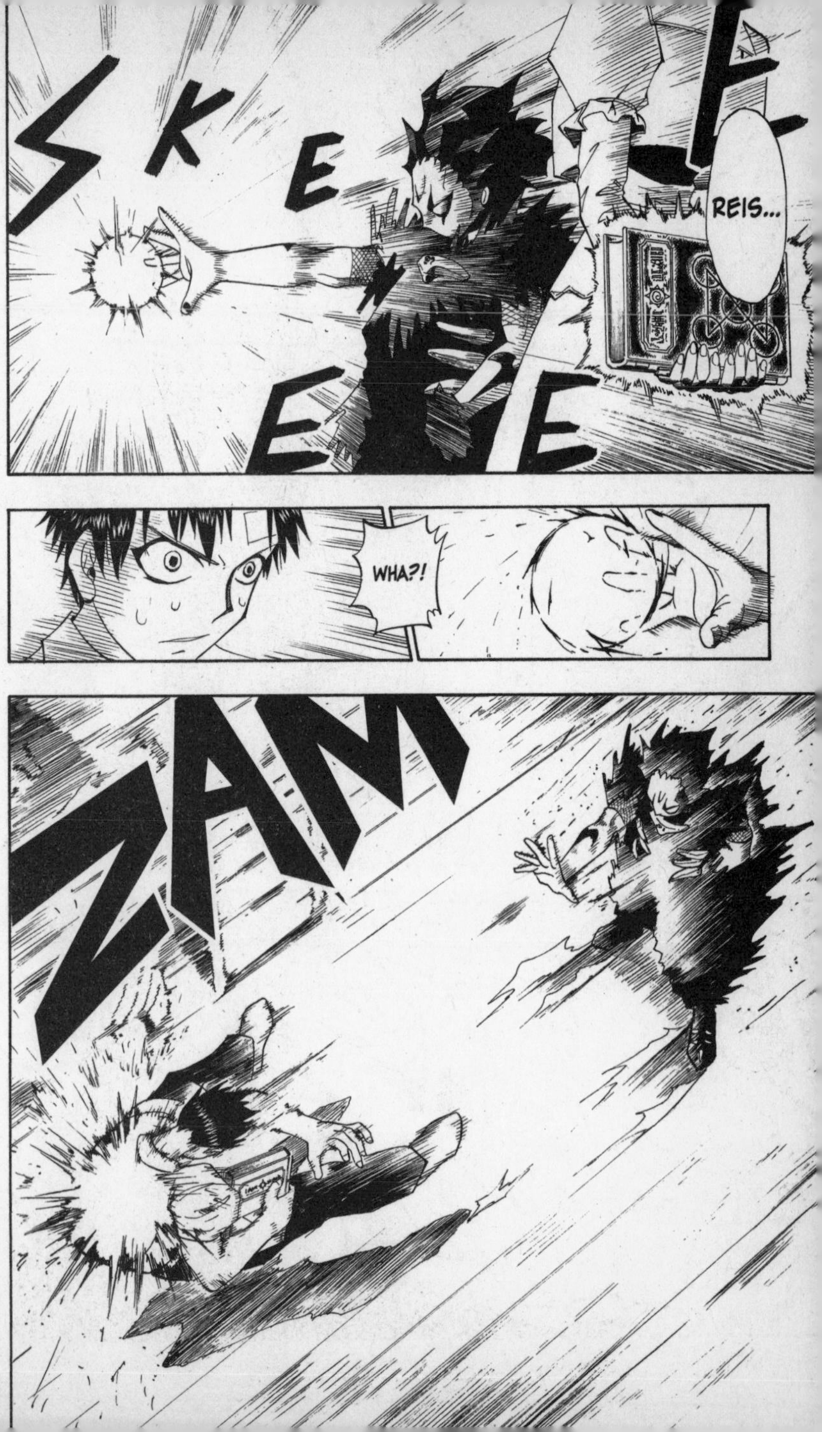
REIS...
SKEEE
WHA?!
ZAM

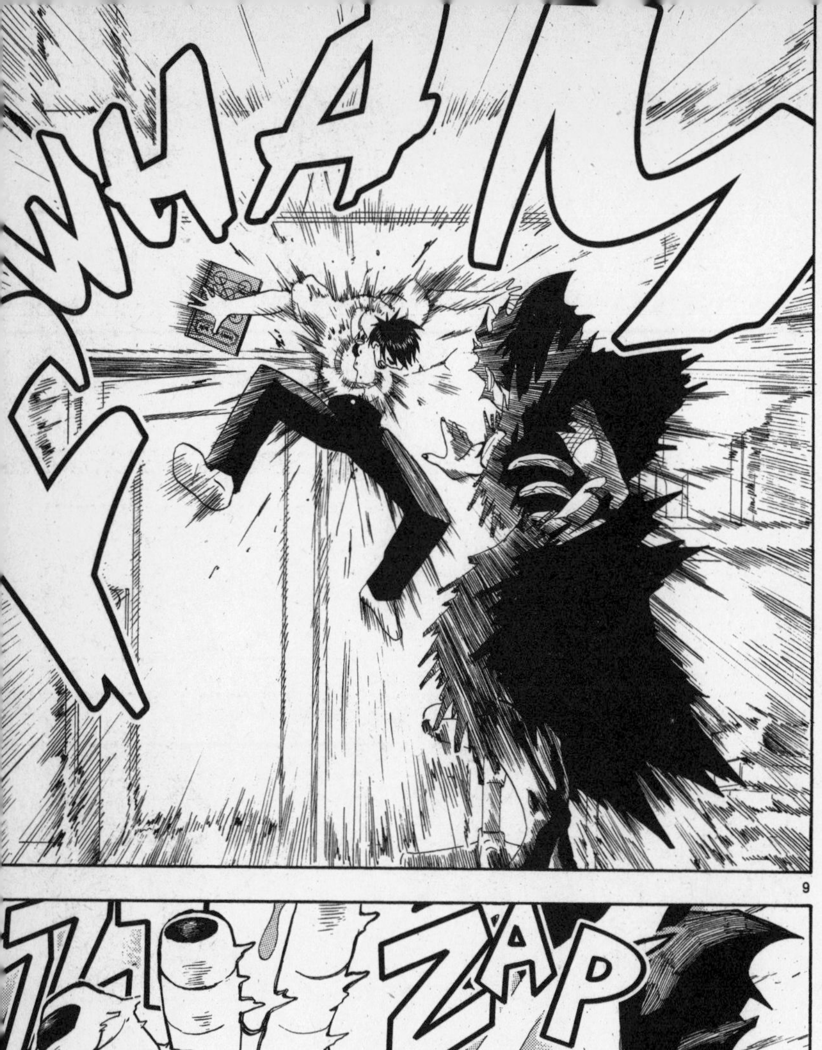
WHAM

9

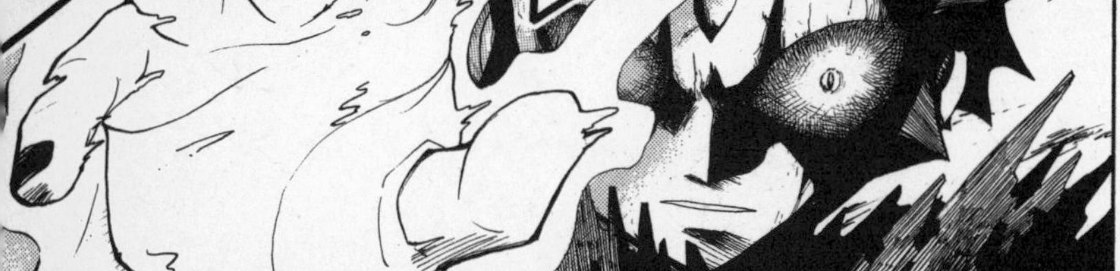
ZAP

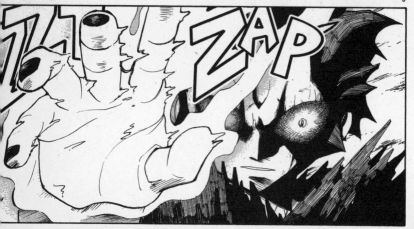

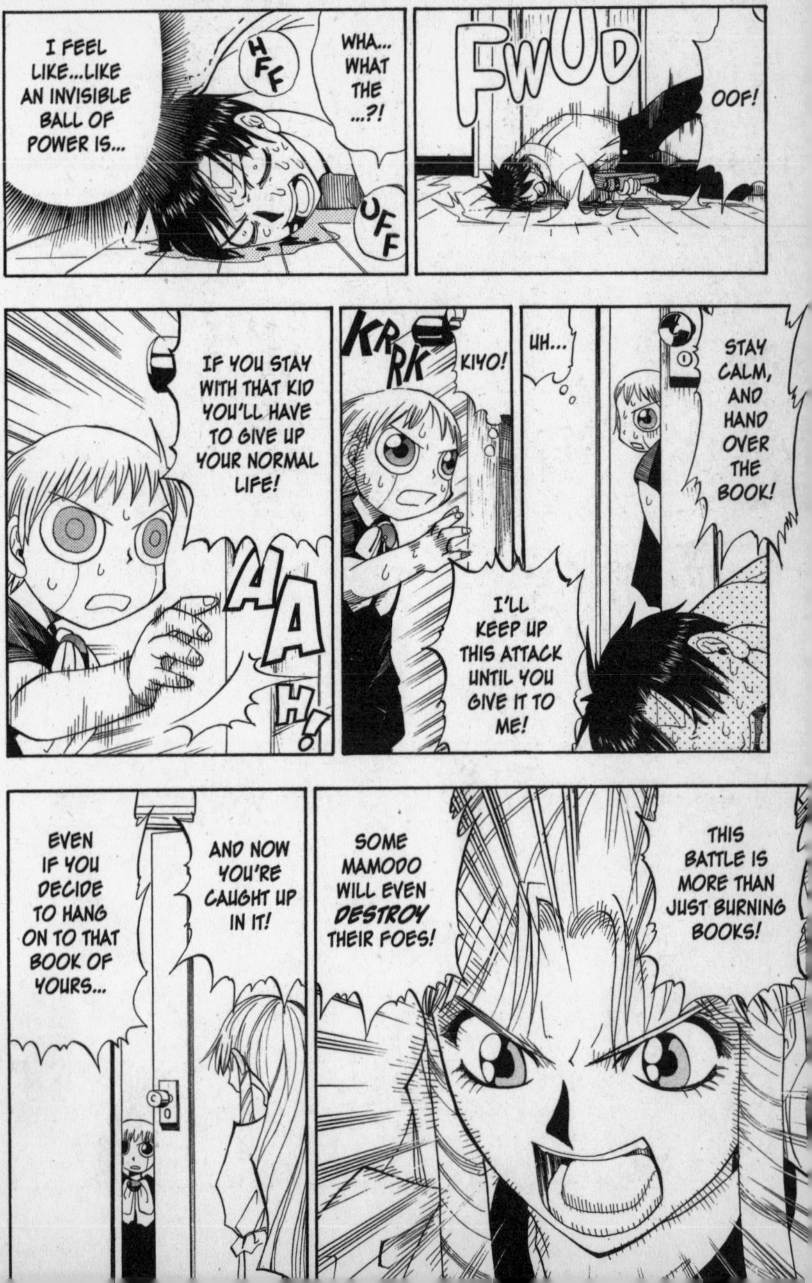
FWUD
OOF!
WHA... WHAT THE ...?!
HFF
OFF
I FEEL LIKE...LIKE AN INVISIBLE BALL OF POWER IS...
STAY CALM, AND HAND OVER THE BOOK!
UH...
I'LL KEEP UP THIS ATTACK UNTIL YOU GIVE IT TO ME!
KRRK
KIYO!
IF YOU STAY WITH THAT KID YOU'LL HAVE TO GIVE UP YOUR NORMAL LIFE!
HAAH!
THIS BATTLE IS MORE THAN JUST BURNING BOOKS!
SOME MAMODO WILL EVEN *DESTROY* THEIR FOES!
AND NOW YOU'RE CAUGHT UP IN IT!
EVEN IF YOU DECIDE TO HANG ON TO THAT BOOK OF YOURS...

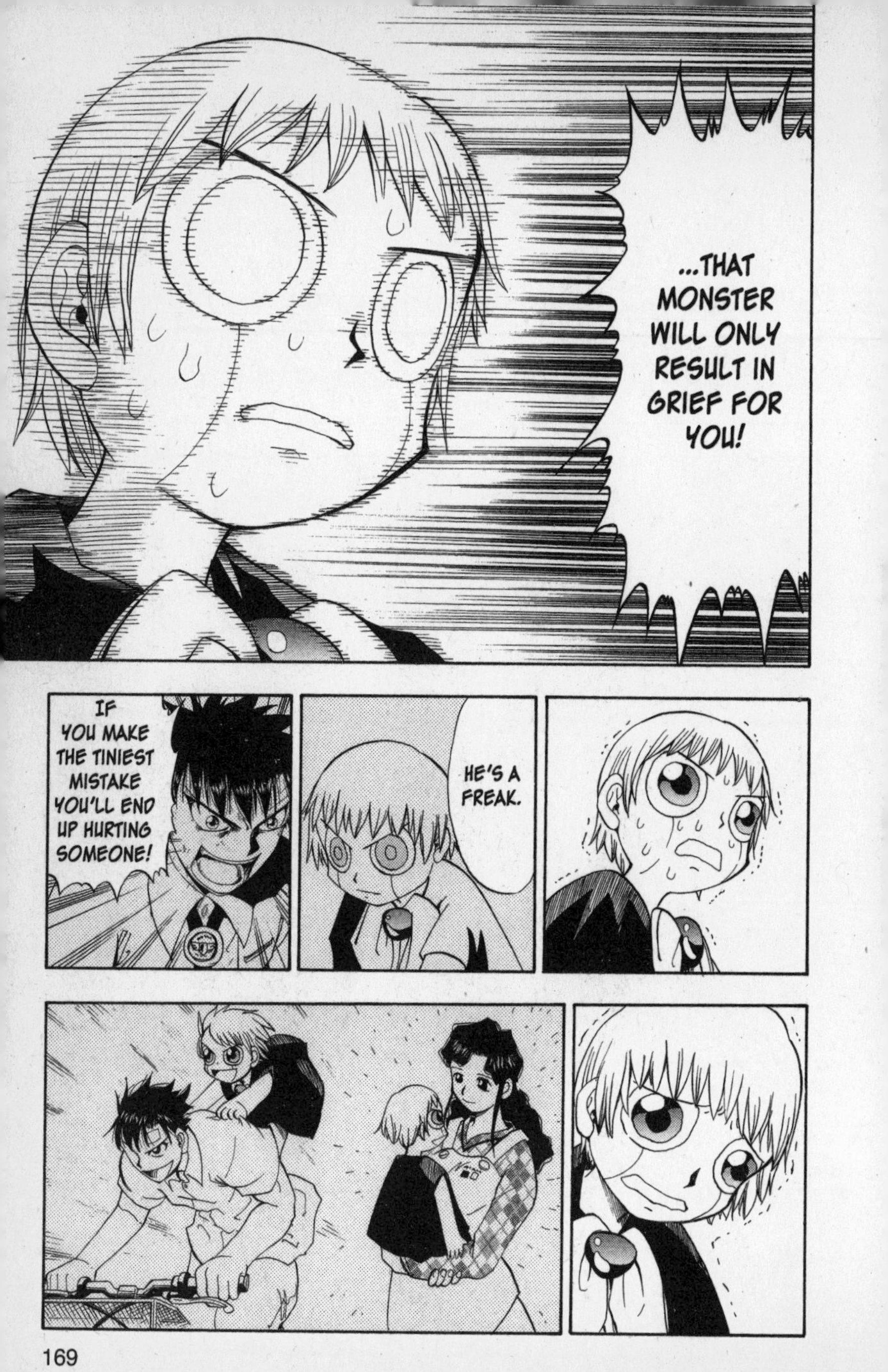
...THAT MONSTER WILL ONLY RESULT IN GRIEF FOR YOU!
HE'S A FREAK.
IF YOU MAKE THE TINIEST MISTAKE YOU'LL END UP HURTING SOMEONE!

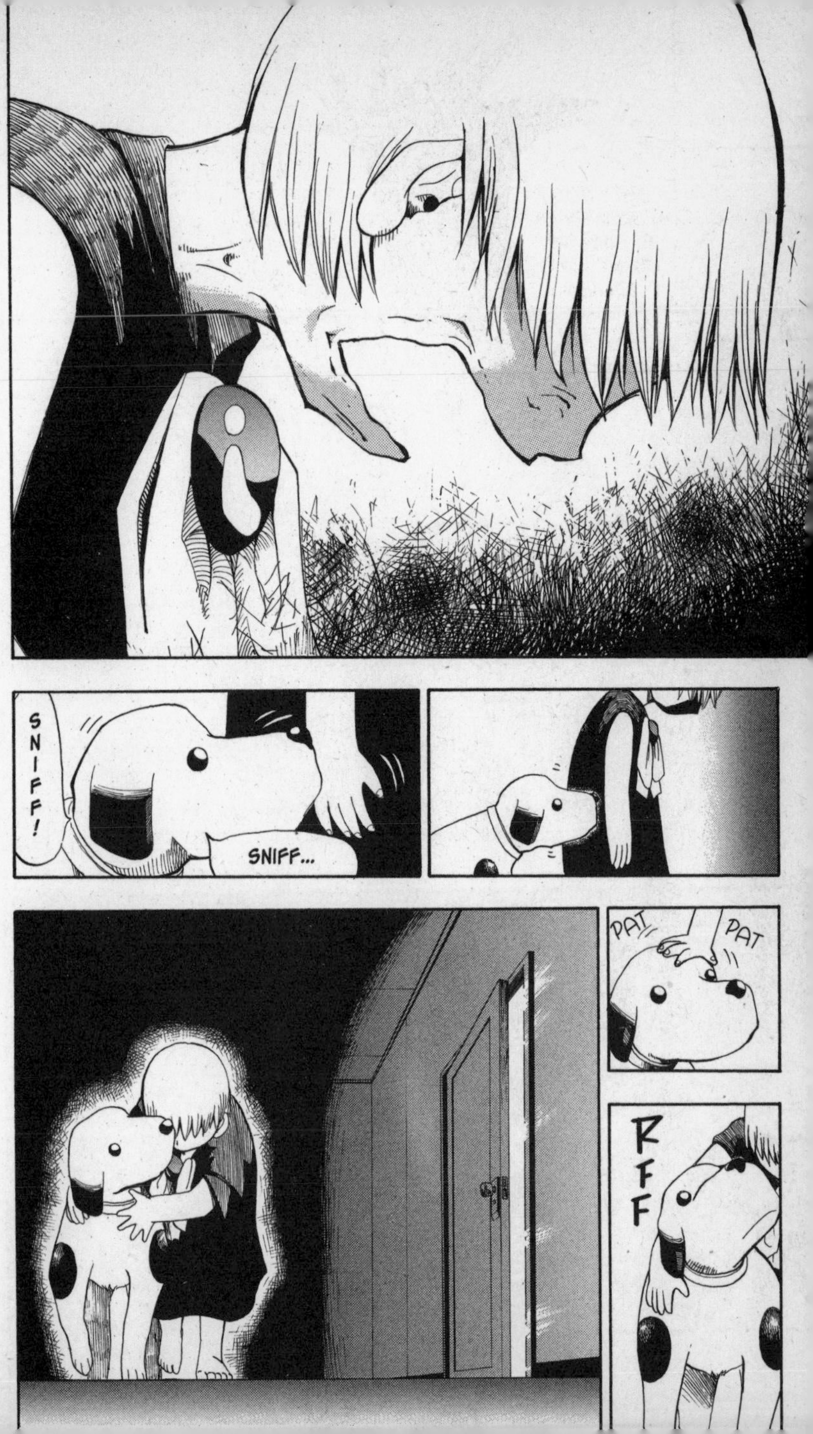
SNIFF!
SNIFF...
PAT PAT
RFF

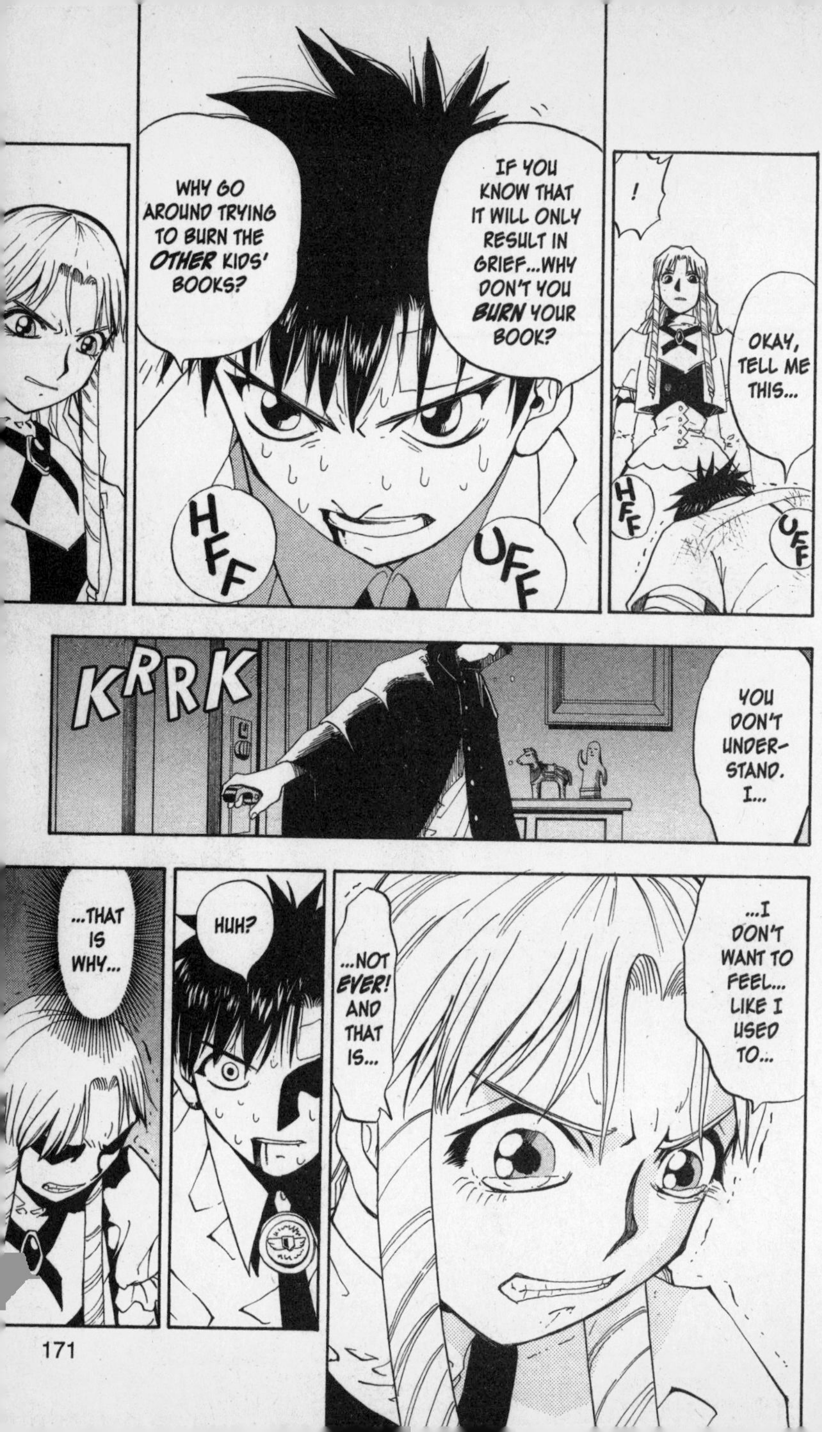
!
OKAY, TELL ME THIS...
HFF
UFF
IF YOU KNOW THAT IT WILL ONLY RESULT IN GRIEF...WHY DON'T YOU *BURN* YOUR BOOK?
WHY GO AROUND TRYING TO BURN THE *OTHER* KIDS' BOOKS?
UFF
HFF
YOU DON'T UNDER-STAND. I...
KRRK
...I DON'T WANT TO FEEL... LIKE I USED TO...
...NOT *EVER!* AND THAT IS...
HUH?
...THAT IS WHY...

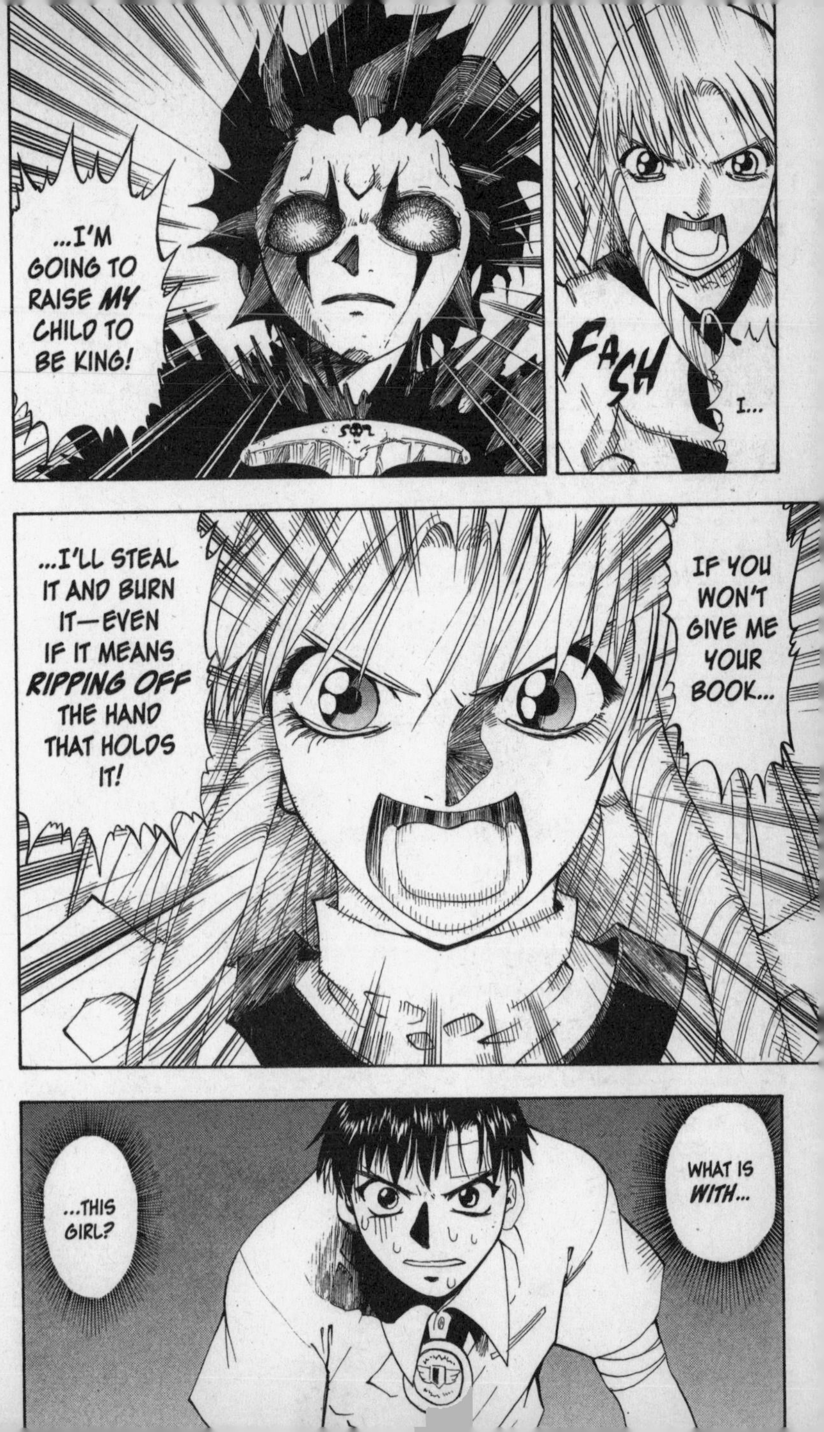
FASH
I...
...I'M GOING TO RAISE MY CHILD TO BE KING!
IF YOU WON'T GIVE ME YOUR BOOK...
...I'LL STEAL IT AND BURN IT—EVEN IF IT MEANS RIPPING OFF THE HAND THAT HOLDS IT!
WHAT IS WITH...
...THIS GIRL?

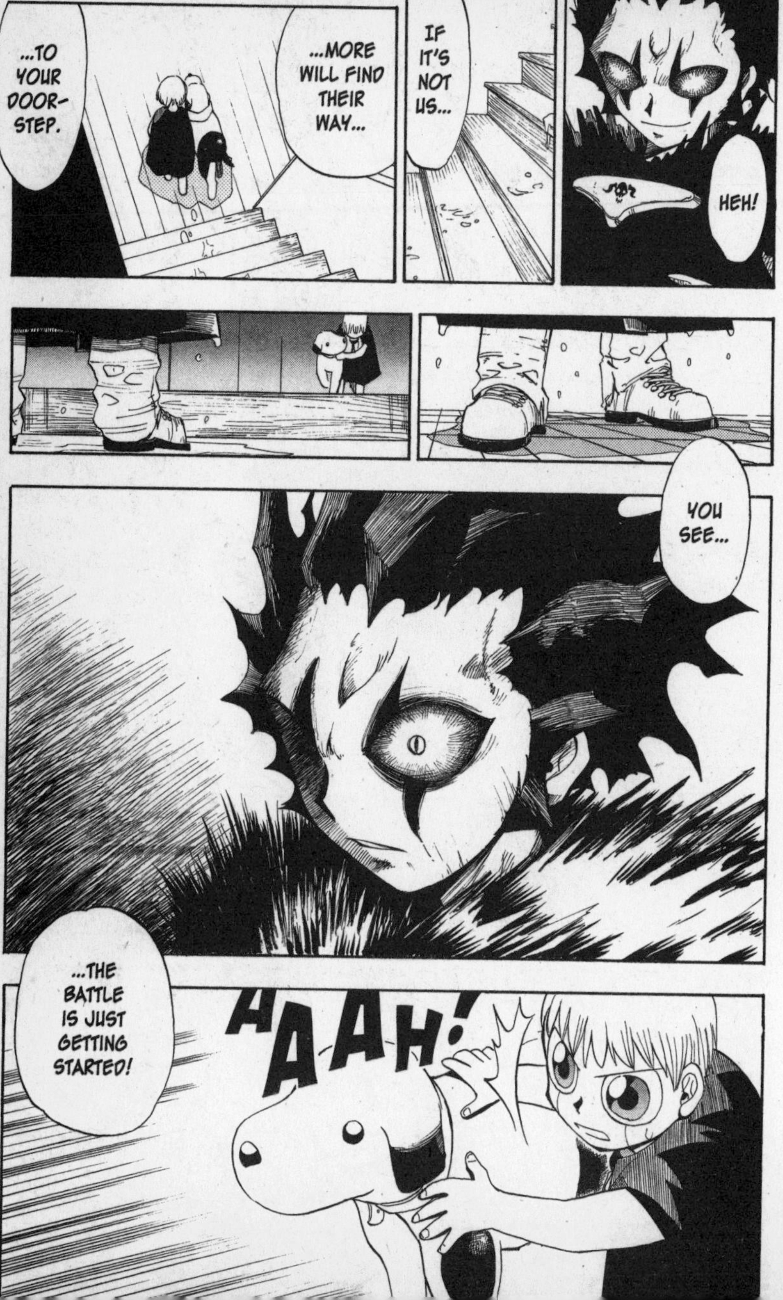
HEH!
IF IT'S NOT US...
...MORE WILL FIND THEIR WAY...
...TO YOUR DOOR-STEP.
YOU SEE...
...THE BATTLE IS JUST GETTING STARTED!
AAAH!

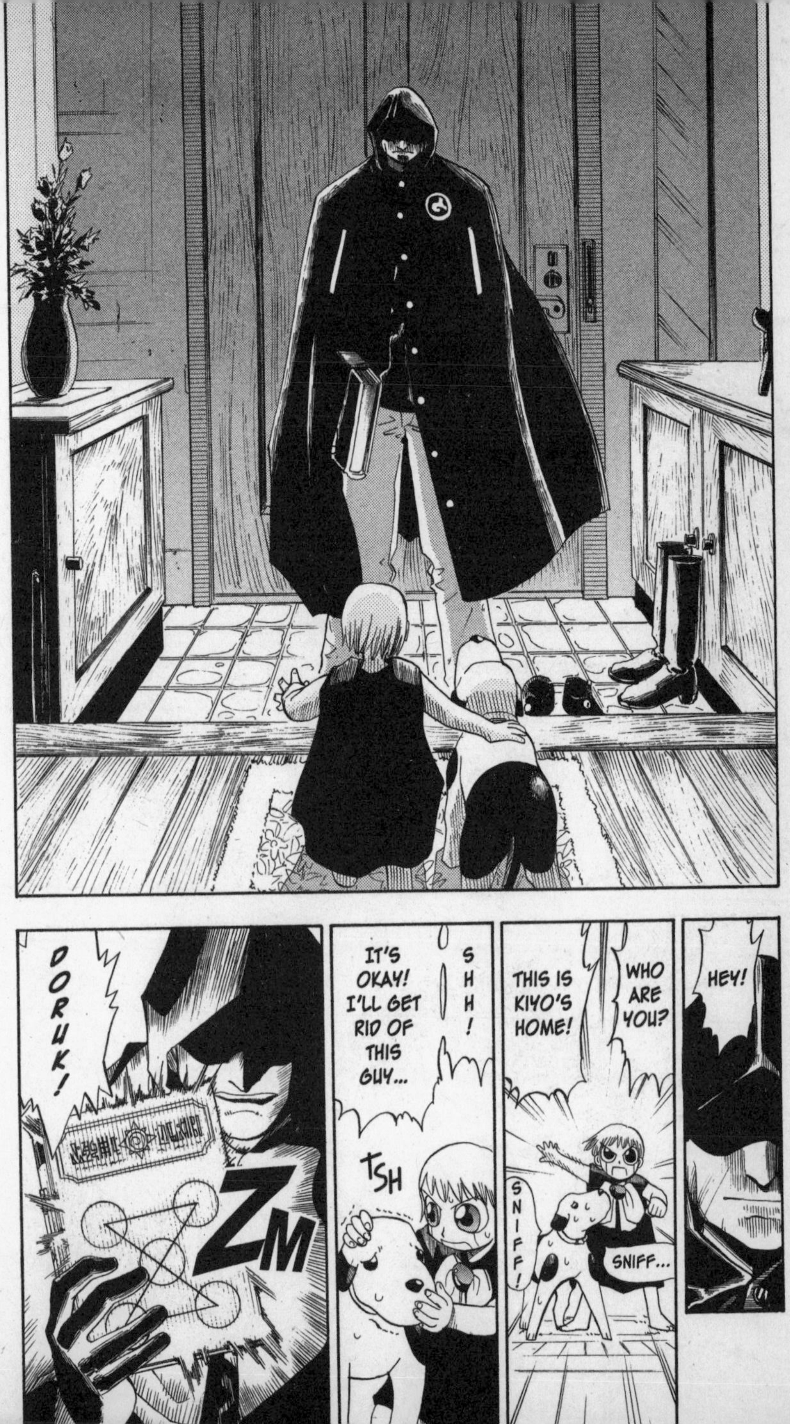
HEY!
WHO ARE YOU?
THIS IS KIYO'S HOME!
SNIFF!
SNIFF...
SHH!
IT'S OKAY! I'LL GET RID OF THIS GUY...
TSH
DORUK!
ZM

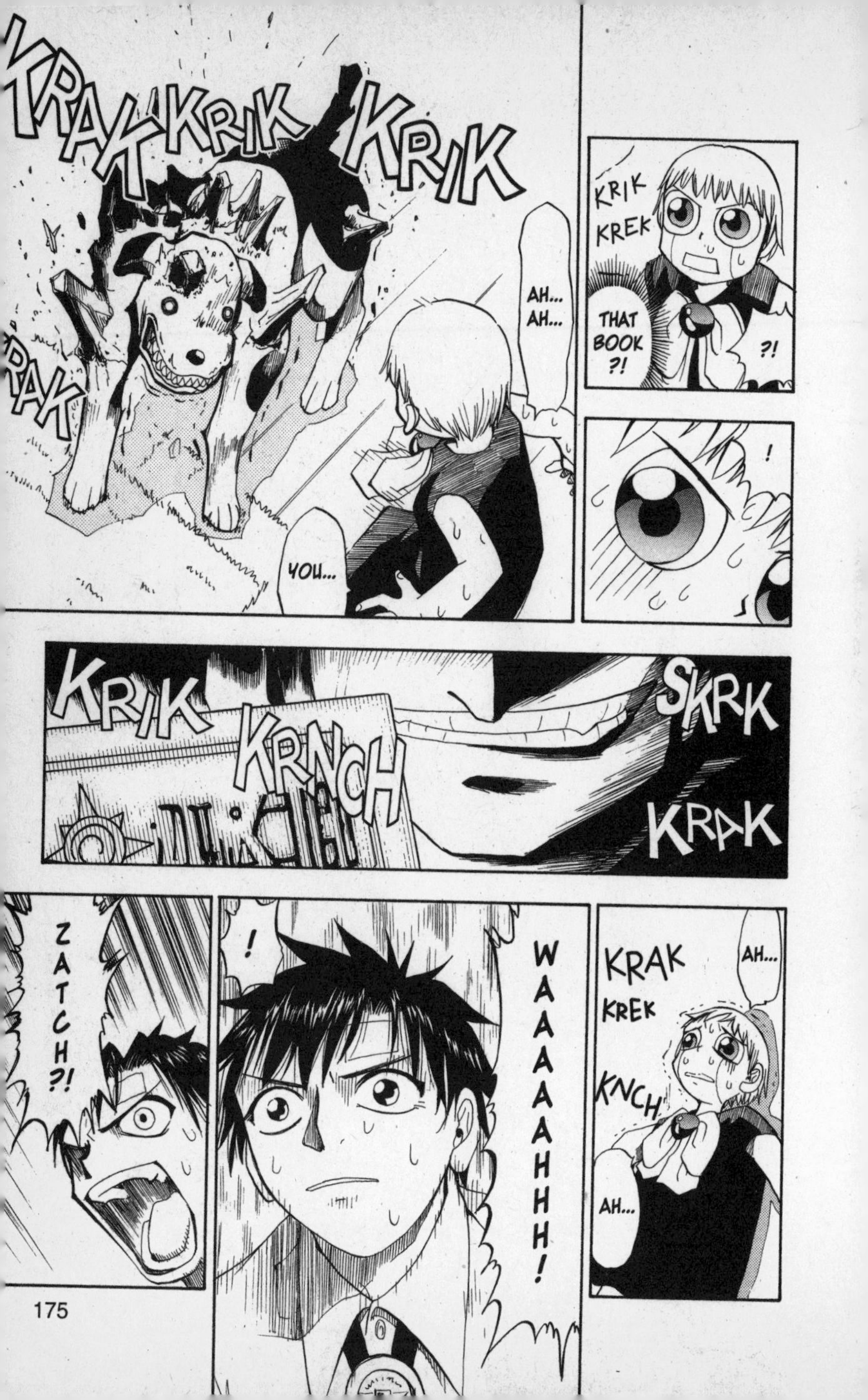
KRIK
KREK
THAT BOOK ?!
?!
!
KRAK KRIK KRIK
RAK
AH... AH...
YOU...
SKRK
KRAK
KRIK
KRNCH
AH...
KRAK
KREK
KNCH
AH...
!
WAAAAAAHHHH!
ZATCH?!

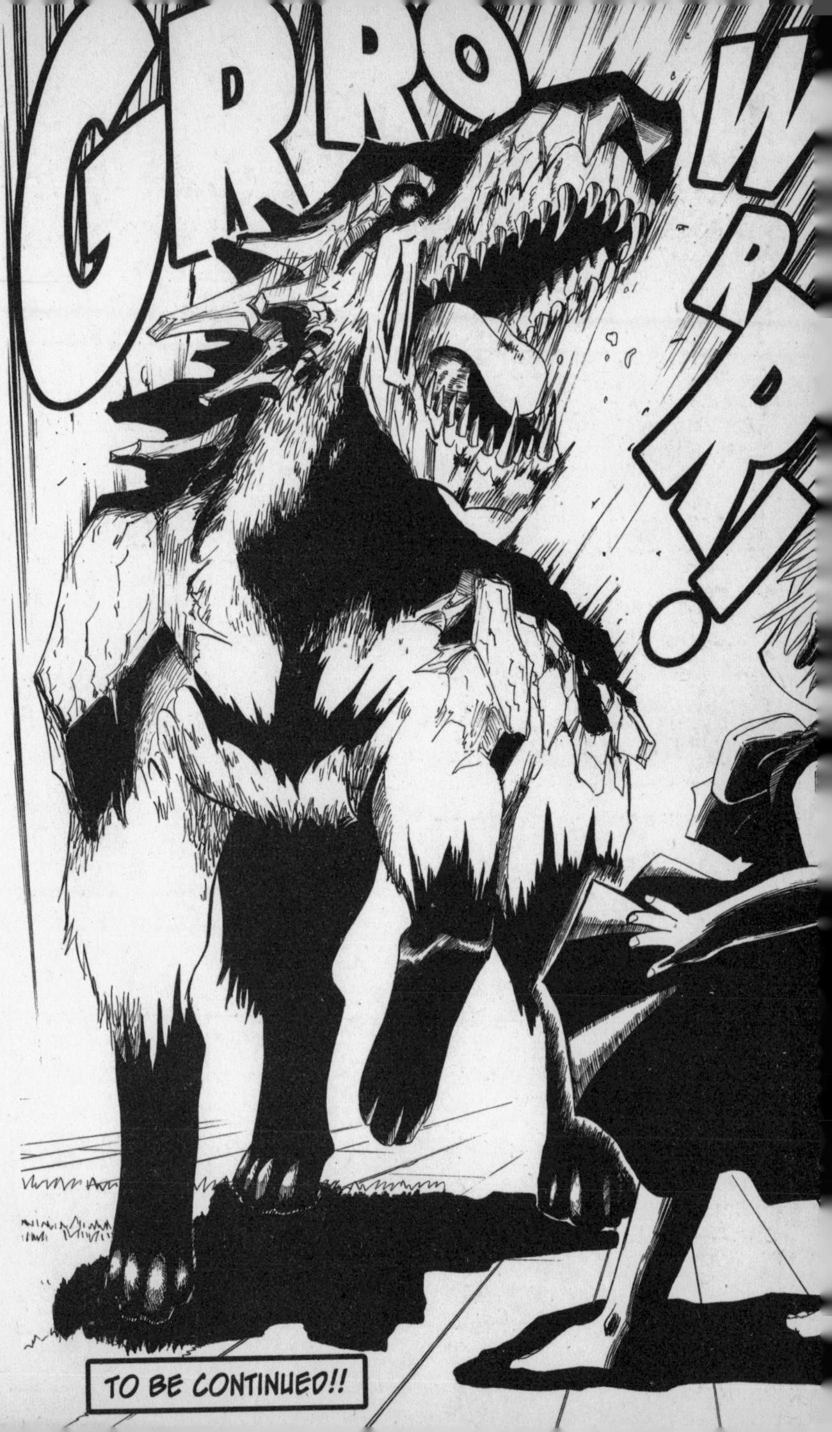
GRROWWRR!!
TO BE CONTINUED!!

BONUS PAGES

BY MAKOTO RAIKU

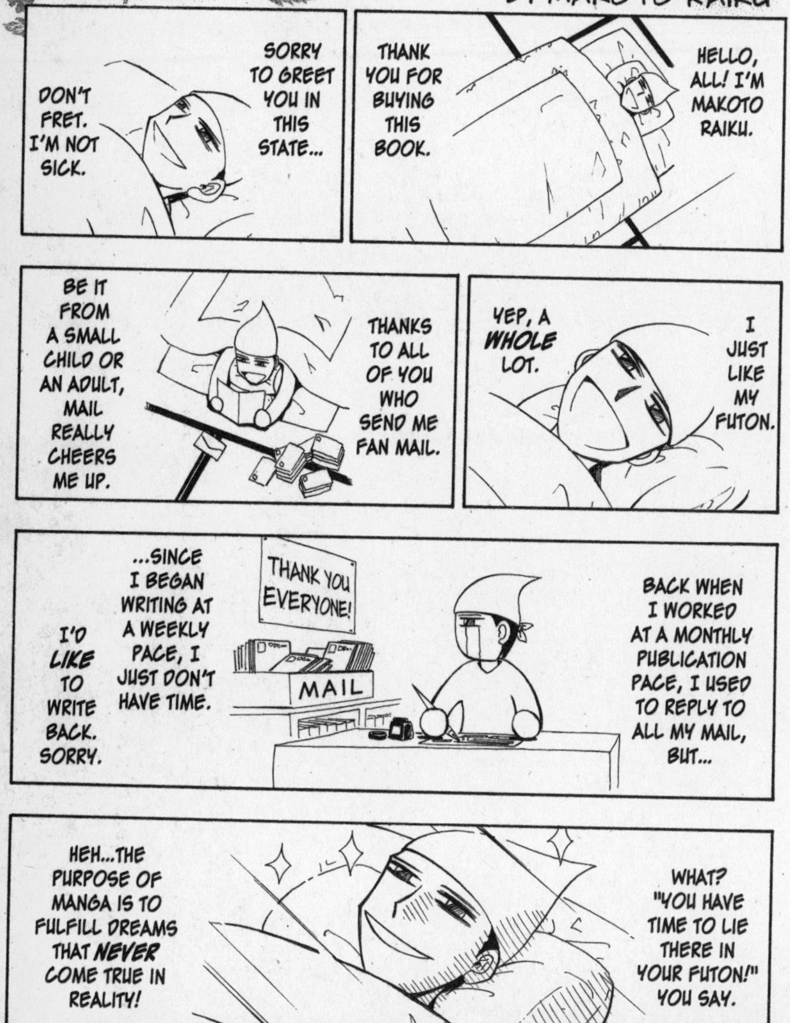
HELLO, ALL! I'M MAKOTO RAIKU.
THANK YOU FOR BUYING THIS BOOK.
SORRY TO GREET YOU IN THIS STATE...
DON'T FRET. I'M NOT SICK.
I JUST LIKE MY FUTON.
YEP, A **WHOLE** LOT.
THANKS TO ALL OF YOU WHO SEND ME FAN MAIL.
BE IT FROM A SMALL CHILD OR AN ADULT, MAIL REALLY CHEERS ME UP.
BACK WHEN I WORKED AT A MONTHLY PUBLICATION PACE, I USED TO REPLY TO ALL MY MAIL, BUT...
THANK YOU EVERYONE!
MAIL
...SINCE I BEGAN WRITING AT A WEEKLY PACE, I JUST DON'T HAVE TIME.
I'D **LIKE** TO WRITE BACK. SORRY.
WHAT? "YOU HAVE TIME TO LIE THERE IN YOUR FUTON!" YOU SAY.
HEH...THE PURPOSE OF MANGA IS TO FULFILL DREAMS THAT **NEVER** COME TRUE IN REALITY!

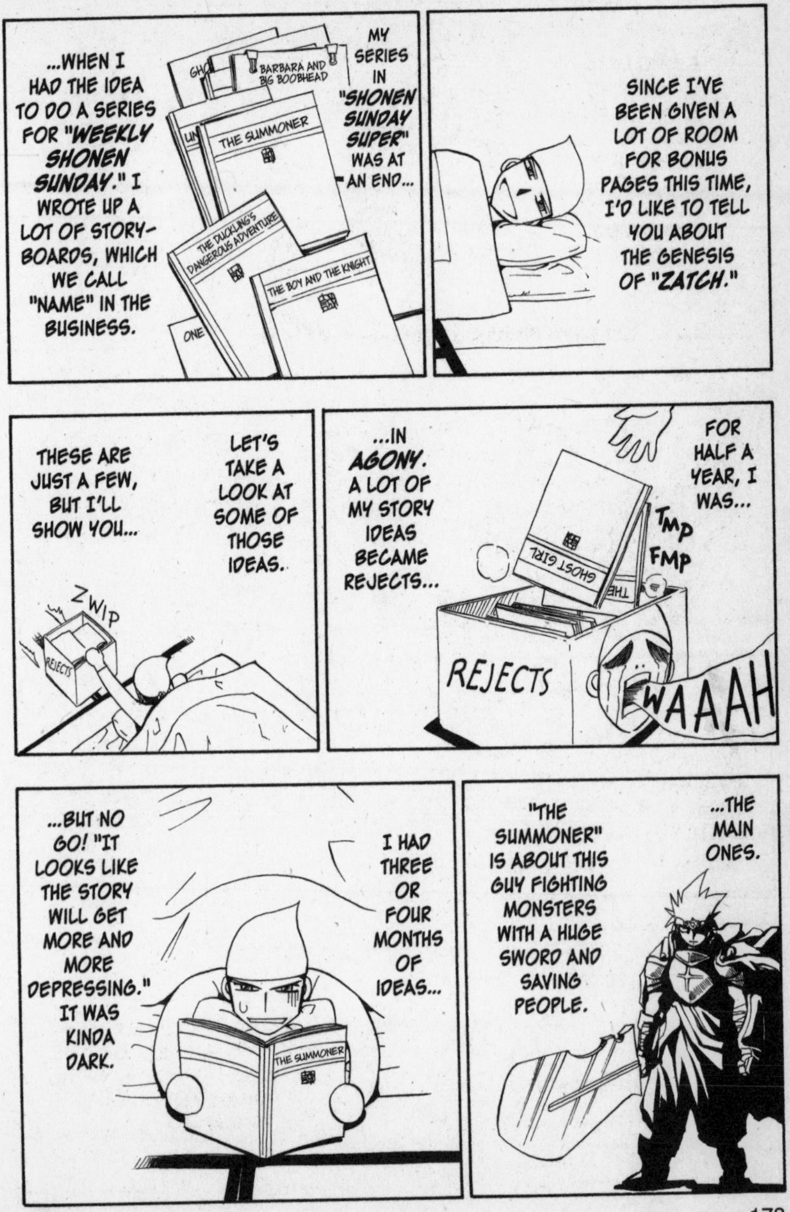
SINCE I'VE BEEN GIVEN A LOT OF ROOM FOR BONUS PAGES THIS TIME, I'D LIKE TO TELL YOU ABOUT THE GENESIS OF "ZATCH."
MY SERIES IN "SHONEN SUNDAY SUPER" WAS AT AN END...
...WHEN I HAD THE IDEA TO DO A SERIES FOR "WEEKLY SHONEN SUNDAY." I WROTE UP A LOT OF STORY-BOARDS, WHICH WE CALL "NAME" IN THE BUSINESS.
BARBARA AND BIG BOOBHEAD
THE SUMMONER
THE DUCKLING'S DANGEROUS ADVENTURE
THE BOY AND THE KNIGHT
ONE
FOR HALF A YEAR, I WAS...
...IN AGONY. A LOT OF MY STORY IDEAS BECAME REJECTS...
TMP
FMP
GHOST GIRL
REJECTS
WAAAH
LET'S TAKE A LOOK AT SOME OF THOSE IDEAS.
THESE ARE JUST A FEW, BUT I'LL SHOW YOU...
ZWIP
REJECTS
...THE MAIN ONES.
"THE SUMMONER" IS ABOUT THIS GUY FIGHTING MONSTERS WITH A HUGE SWORD AND SAVING PEOPLE.
I HAD THREE OR FOUR MONTHS OF IDEAS...
...BUT NO GO! "IT LOOKS LIKE THE STORY WILL GET MORE AND MORE DEPRESSING." IT WAS KINDA DARK.
THE SUMMONER

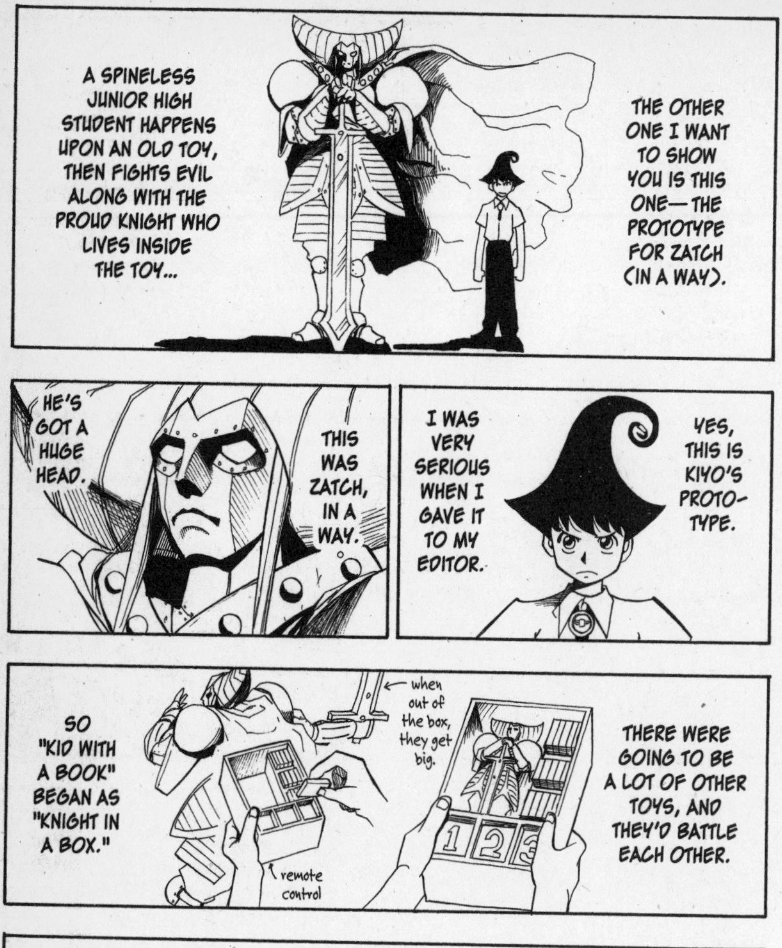
THE OTHER ONE I WANT TO SHOW YOU IS THIS ONE— THE PROTOTYPE FOR ZATCH (IN A WAY).
A SPINELESS JUNIOR HIGH STUDENT HAPPENS UPON AN OLD TOY, THEN FIGHTS EVIL ALONG WITH THE PROUD KNIGHT WHO LIVES INSIDE THE TOY...
YES, THIS IS KIYO'S PROTO-TYPE.
I WAS VERY SERIOUS WHEN I GAVE IT TO MY EDITOR.
THIS WAS ZATCH, IN A WAY.
HE'S GOT A HUGE HEAD.
THERE WERE GOING TO BE A LOT OF OTHER TOYS, AND THEY'D BATTLE EACH OTHER.
1 2 3
when out of the box, they get big.
SO "KID WITH A BOOK" BEGAN AS "KNIGHT IN A BOX."
remote control
THAT'S WHEN MY EDITOR GAVE ME THIS ADVICE: "WHY DON'T YOU MAKE SOME CUTE CHARACTERS FIGHT EACH OTHER?" AND ZATCH WAS BORN.
ED
uh-huh...

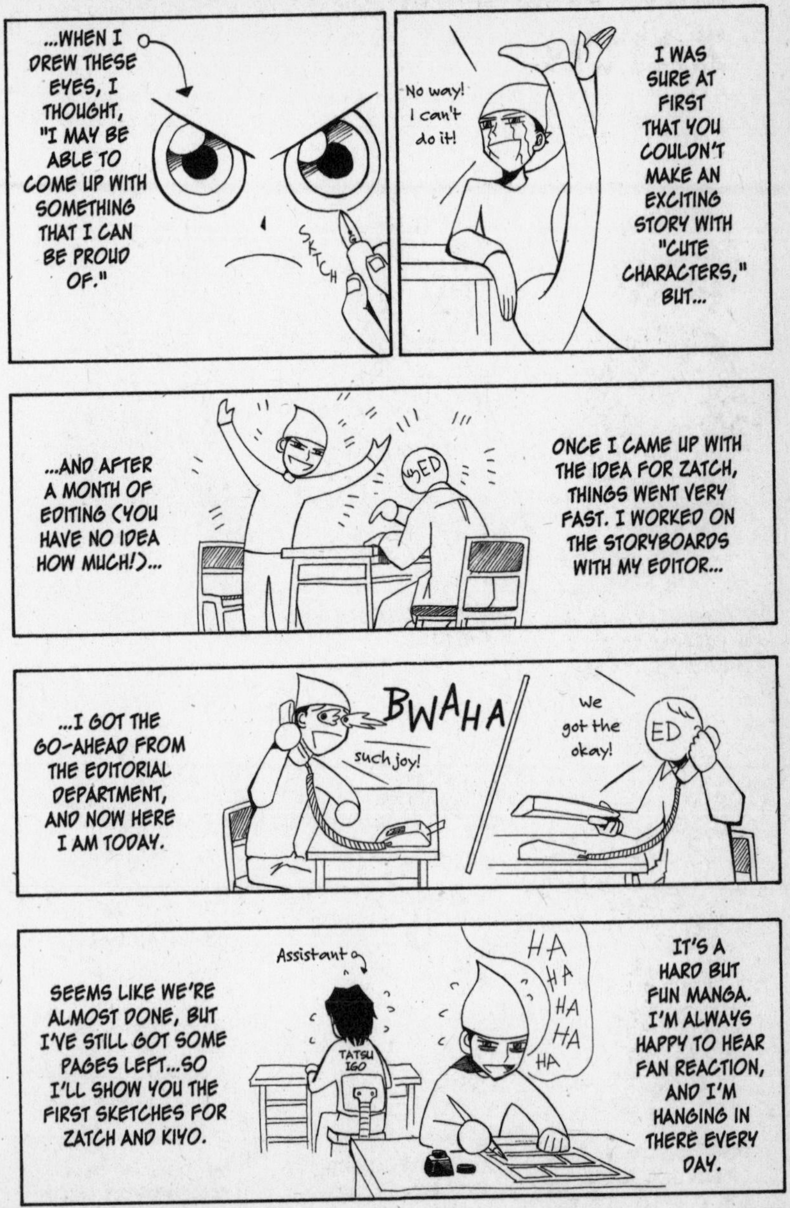
I WAS SURE AT FIRST THAT YOU COULDN'T MAKE AN EXCITING STORY WITH "CUTE CHARACTERS," BUT...
No way! I can't do it!
...WHEN I DREW THESE EYES, I THOUGHT, "I MAY BE ABLE TO COME UP WITH SOMETHING THAT I CAN BE PROUD OF."
SKTCH
ONCE I CAME UP WITH THE IDEA FOR ZATCH, THINGS WENT VERY FAST. I WORKED ON THE STORYBOARDS WITH MY EDITOR...
ED
...AND AFTER A MONTH OF EDITING (YOU HAVE NO IDEA HOW MUCH!)...
We got the okay!
ED
BWAHA
such joy!
...I GOT THE GO-AHEAD FROM THE EDITORIAL DEPARTMENT, AND NOW HERE I AM TODAY.
IT'S A HARD BUT FUN MANGA. I'M ALWAYS HAPPY TO HEAR FAN REACTION, AND I'M HANGING IN THERE EVERY DAY.
HA HA HA HA HA HA
Assistant
TATSU IGO
SEEMS LIKE WE'RE ALMOST DONE, BUT I'VE STILL GOT SOME PAGES LEFT...SO I'LL SHOW YOU THE FIRST SKETCHES FOR ZATCH AND KIYO.

ZATCH BELL! EARLY ROUGH SKETCHES.
ZATCH

OF COURSE THIS IS THE CURRENT ZATCH. I LIKED IT RIGHT AWAY.

A ROUNDER HAIRSTYLE AND FACE.

SHARP POINTY HAIR. YOU CAN TELL HE'S NOT THE MAIN CHARACTER.

VERY WILD. MORE LIKE A MAIN CHARACTER. ONE OF MY FAVORITES.

HAIR LIKE AN ONIGIRI RICE BALL. I WAS JUST PLAYING...

SAME AS THE NEXT ONE, WITHOUT WHITE TIPS ON HIS HAIR.

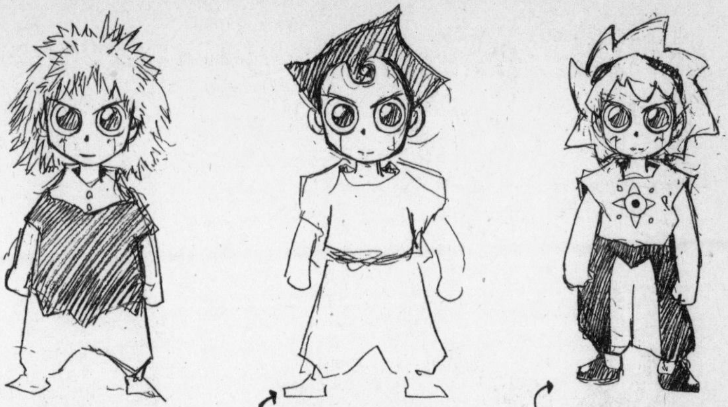

MY EDITOR LIKED THIS DESIGN—HE MUST GO FOR THE WILD LOOK.

I HAVE NO DESIRE TO USE THIS GUY... BUT I DREW HIM ANYWAY.

ANOTHER MAIN CHARACTER TYPE DESIGN. A ZATCH RIVAL?

KIYO TAKAMINE SECTION

TYPICAL HAIRSTYLE FOR SHONEN MANGA HEROES. IF KIYO WEREN'T A GENIUS, I MIGHT'VE GONE WITH THIS...

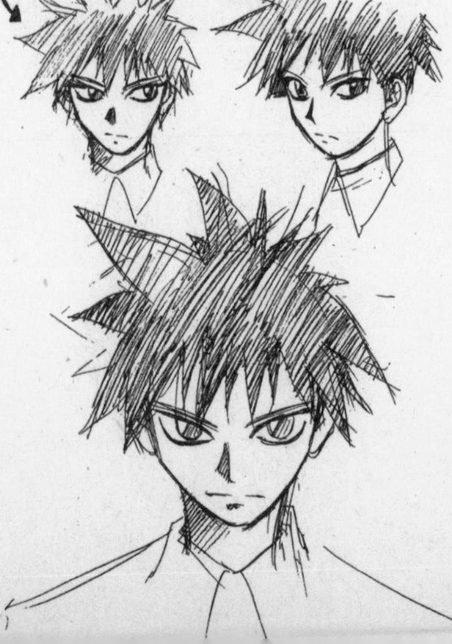

THE CURRENT KIYO IS BASED ON THIS DESIGN, ONLY WITH BLACK HAIR. NEITHER TOO QUIET NOR TOO AGGRESSIVE.

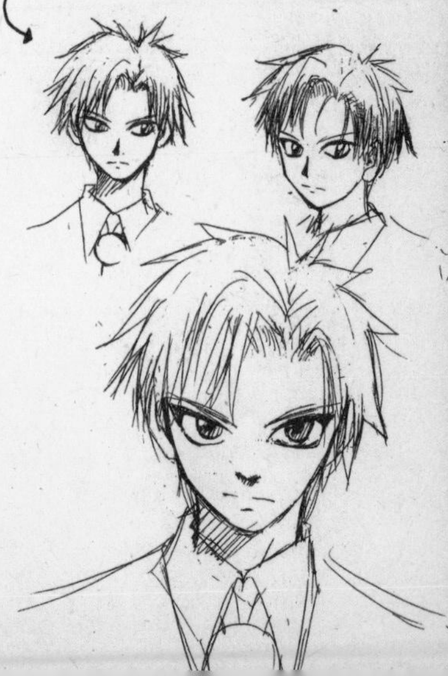

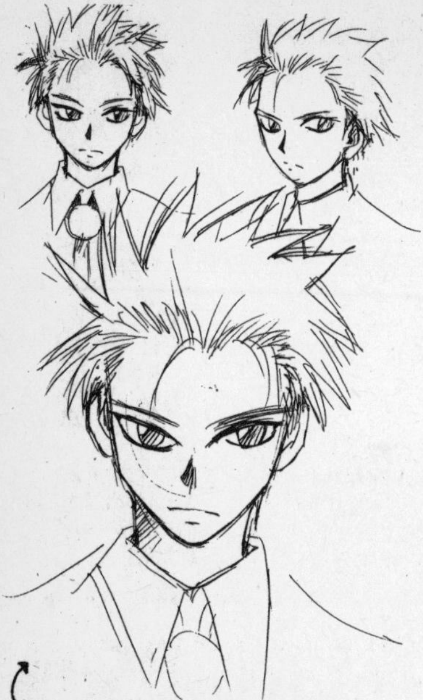

I LIKE THIS ONE, BUT IF KIYO LOOKED LIKE A GOOD FIGHTER, IT WOULD CHANGE HIM TOO MUCH.

THE WEAKEST LOOK FOR KIYO.

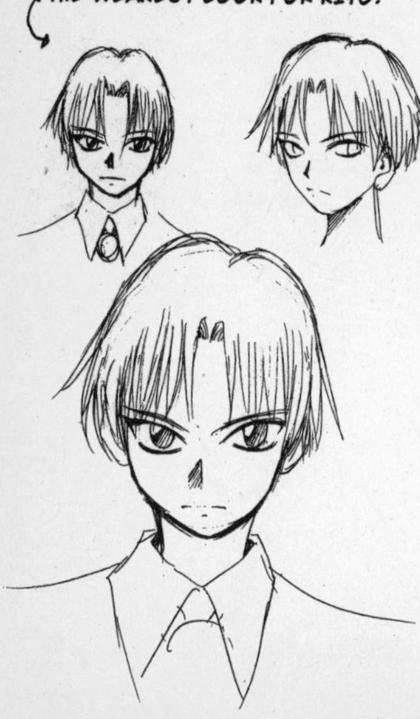

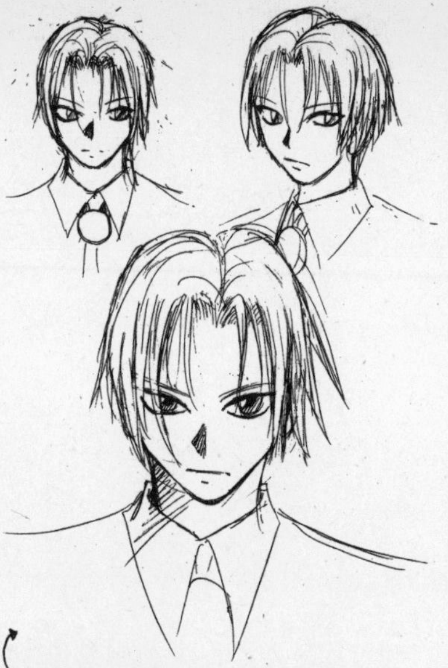

HMM...HE LOOKS VERY ELITE.

I CAN'T DRAW THIS TYPE OF LONG HAIR VERY WELL. I WONDER HOW I COULD HAVE MADE IT LOOK COOL...

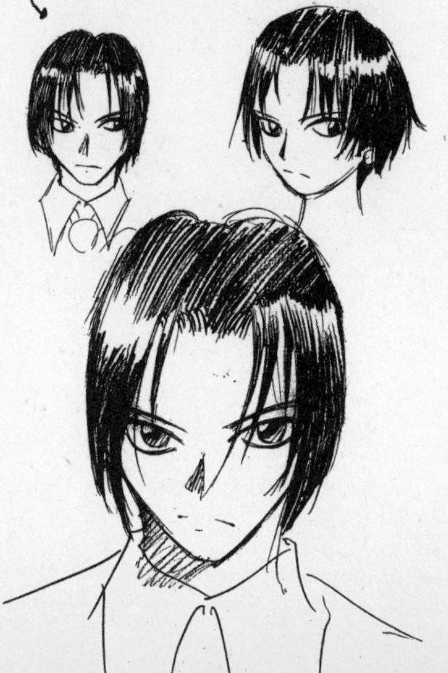

SUZY MIZUNO SECTION

THE CURRENT SUZY. FOR SOME REASON I ALWAYS GO WITH SHORT HAIR FOR HAPPY CHARACTERS.

ANOTHER VERSION OF SUZY. I DIDN'T THINK I'D BE ABLE TO MAKE HER LOOK EXCITED ENOUGH.

WELL, THAT'S IT FOR MY COLLECTION OF ROUGH SKETCHES. WHEN I WAS DECIDING ON THE CHARACTERS, I WOULD DRAW THESE AND THEN MAKE MY CHOICE AFTER DISCUSSING THEM WITH MY EDITOR. FOR THE MOST PART, I ENDED UP USING THE CHARACTERS THE WAY I ENVISIONED THEM, SO I WAS HAPPY. WELL, THIS IS THE END OF THE PAGE, SO GOODBYE.

See you next time!

ZATCH & SUZY

BY MAKOTO RAIKU

ARE YOU AFRAID OF ANYTHING, SUZY?
I DON'T LIKE MEAN DOGS.
YES, THOSE ARE AWFUL.
YEAH, THEY SCARE ME.
GRRRRR
RARRR

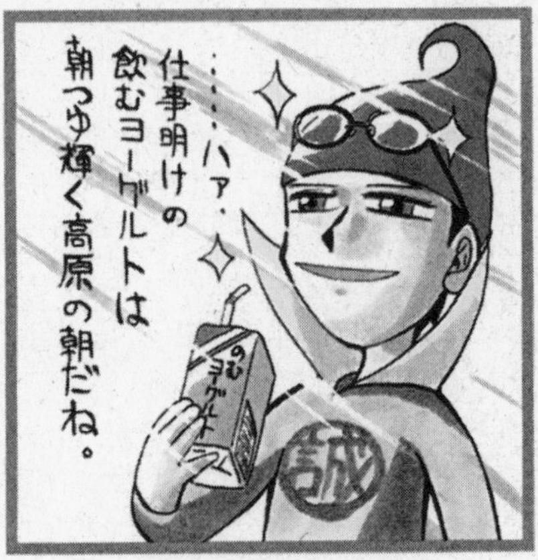
……ハァ…
仕事明けの
飲むヨーグルトは
朝つゆ輝く高原の朝だね。

MAKOTO RAIKU

Ahh! My after-work yogurt drink is like waking up in a grassy field, fresh with morning dew…

Zatch is a tough kid, but he's also a crybaby. He's full of energy, but he's still just a child. That's just the way he is…and this manga is about his life, as it unfolds step by step!

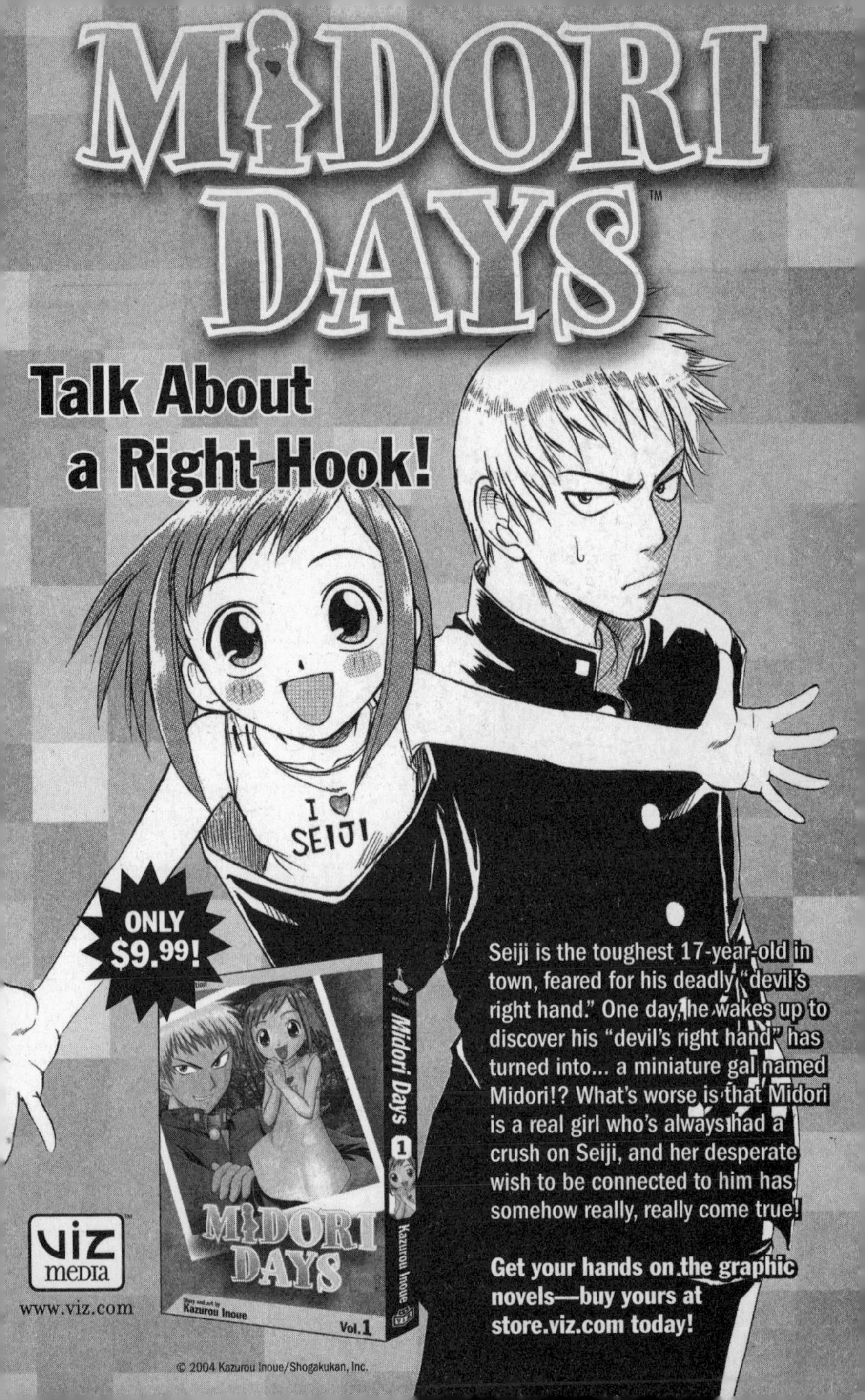
MIDORI DAYS™
Talk About a Right Hook!
I ♥ SEIJI
ONLY $9.99!
Midori Days 1
Kazurou Inoue
MIDORI DAYS
Story and art by Kazurou Inoue
Vol. 1
Seiji is the toughest 17-year-old in town, feared for his deadly "devil's right hand." One day, he wakes up to discover his "devil's right hand" has turned into... a miniature gal named Midori!? What's worse is that Midori is a real girl who's always had a crush on Seiji, and her desperate wish to be connected to him has somehow really, really come true!
Get your hands on the graphic novels—buy yours at store.viz.com today!
VIZ media™
www.viz.com
© 2004 Kazurou Inoue/Shogakukan, Inc.

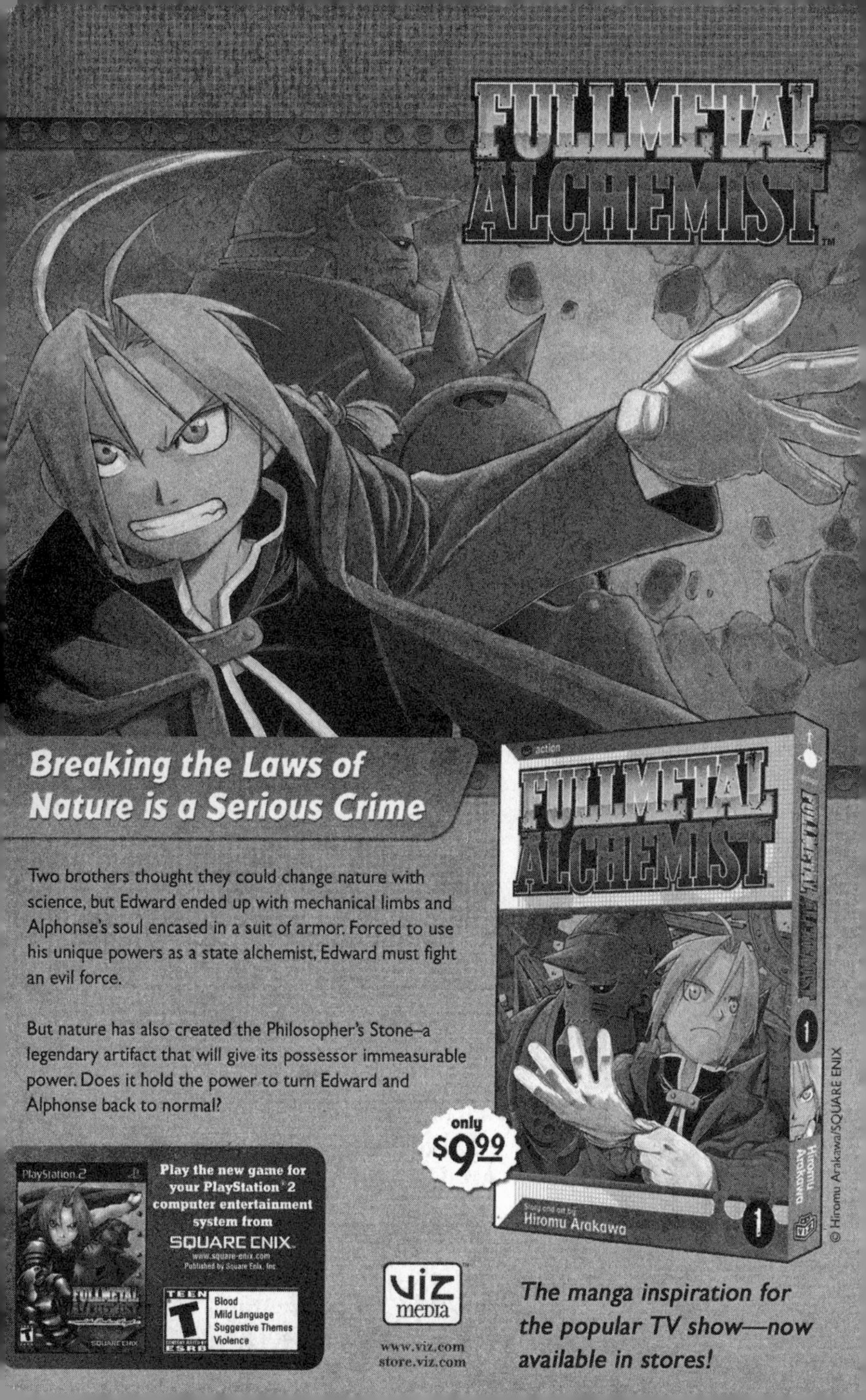

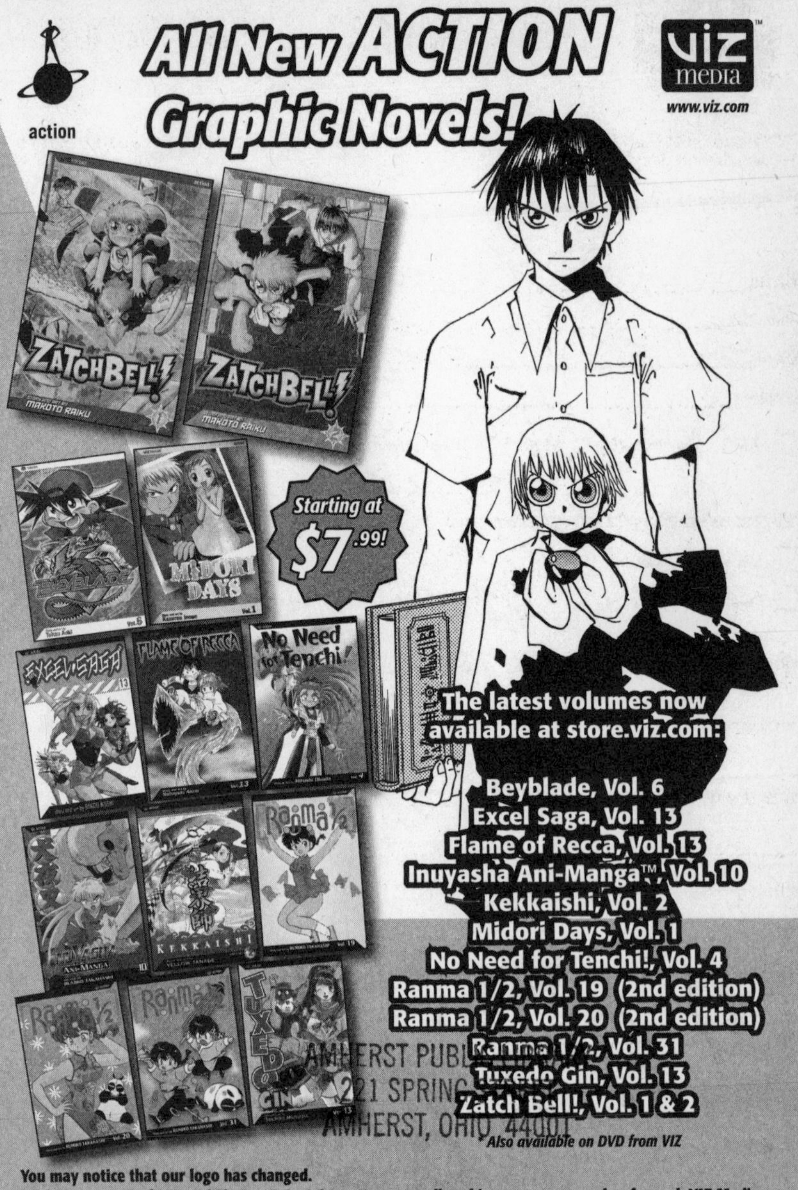
action
All New ACTION Graphic Novels!
VIZ media
www.viz.com
ZATCH BELL! MAKOTO RAIKU
BEYBLADE
MIDORI DAYS
Starting at $7.99!
EXCEL SAGA
FLAME OF RECCA
No Need for Tenchi!
KEKKAISHI
Ranma 1/2
TUXEDO GIN
The latest volumes now available at store.viz.com:
Beyblade, Vol. 6
Excel Saga, Vol. 13
Flame of Recca, Vol. 13
Inuyasha Ani-Manga™*, Vol. 10
Kekkaishi, Vol. 2
Midori Days, Vol. 1
No Need for Tenchi!, Vol. 4
Ranma 1/2, Vol. 19 (2nd edition)
Ranma 1/2, Vol. 20 (2nd edition)
Ranma 1/2, Vol. 31
Tuxedo Gin, Vol. 13
Zatch Bell!, Vol. 1 & 2
* Also available on DVD from VIZ